Tropic of Cancer

Hawaiian Iˢ

Marshall Iˢ

Clipperton I.

P O L Y N E S I A

Equator

Kiribati

Tuvalu

Marquesas Iˢ

Wallis & Futuna

Samoa

Tuamotu

Fiji

Cook Iˢ

Society Iˢ

Tonga

Tropic of Capricorn

Austral Iˢ

Gambier Iˢ

Pitcairn Iˢ

Easter I.

New Zealand

ARTS OF VANUATU

ARTS OF VANUATU

Edited by
Joël Bonnemaison
Christian Kaufmann
Kirk Huffman
Darrell Tryon

CRAWFORD HOUSE PUBLISHING
BATHURST

A CHP Production

Published in Australia by
Crawford House Publishing Pty Ltd
PO Box 1484
Bathurst NSW 2795

Published in France by
Réunion des musées nationaux, 1996 [*Vanuatu Océanie*]

National Library of Australia Cataloguing-in-Publication entry
   Arts of Vanuatu

   Bibliography.
   ISBN 1 86333 142 5.

   1. Anthropology – Vanuatu. 2. Arts – Vanuatu. 3.
   Vanuatu – History. I. Bonnemaison, Joël, 1940- .
   II. Title. Vanuatu Océanie. English.

306.08995

Copyright © 1996 Editions de la Réunion musées nationaux

All rights reserved. No part of this publication may be reproduced, stored in an electronic retrieval system, or transmitted in any form or by any means, electronic, mechanical, photocopying or otherwise, without the prior permission of the publishers.

Printed in Hong Kong by H & Y Printing Limited

10 9 8 7 6 5 4 3 2 1

Contents

8	Preface *José Garanger*
12	The arts of Vanuatu: between traditional imagery and force of expression *Christian Kaufmann*
13	Letter from Ambrym *Roger Boulay*
19	Masks, 'headdresses' and 'ritual hats' in northern Vanuatu *Kirk W. Huffman*
34	The metaphor of the tree and the canoe *Joël Bonnemaison*
53	**CHAPTER I: LANGUAGES AND PEOPLE – AN EARLY HISTORY**
54	The peopling of Oceania: the linguistic evidence *Darrell Tryon*
62	The original colonisation of Vanuatu *Paul Gorecki*
66	Tongoa, Mangaasi and Retoka – history of a prehistory *José Garanger*
74	The archaeology of Vanuatu in a Pacific perspective *Matthew Spriggs*
79	Vanuatu seen from Maré *Marie-Joseph Dubois*
83	Vanuatu rock art *David Roe*
89	**CHAPTER II: MEN'S ART, WOMEN'S ART**
90	An agricultural art: taro irrigation in Vanuatu *Matthew Spriggs*
94	Pottery and potters of Vanuatu *Jean-Christophe Galipaud*
100	The feminine art of mat-weaving on Pentecost *Annie Walter*
110	Dyed designs on Pentecost mats *Alfreda Mabonlala*
112	Tahigogana's sisters: women, mats and landscape on Ambae *Lissant Bolton*
120	Woven female waistbands of northern Vanuatu *Kirk W. Huffman*
123	Arts of language and space, south-east Tanna *Lamont Lindstrom*
129	The 'decorated cloth' from the 'island of good yams': barkcloth in Vanuatu, with special reference to Erromango *Kirk W. Huffman*
141	Haircombs *Kirk W. Huffman*
145	Music in Vanuatu *Peter Russell Crowe*
150	Single bamboo flutes *Kirk W. Huffman*
158	The boars of Bali Ha'i: pigs in paradise *William Rodman*

169	**CHAPTER III: THE ART OF RELATING**
170	Dialect chaining and the use of geographical space *Darrell Tryon*
174	A web of connections *Joël Bonnemaison*
182	Trading, cultural exchange and copyright: important aspects of Vanuatu arts *Kirk W. Huffman*
195	Kiamu, the southern canoe *Michel Aufray*
199	**CHAPTER IV: THE ART OF POWER**
200	Graded societies and societies based on title: forms and rites of traditional political power in Vanuatu *Joël Bonnemaison*
204	Wooden and bamboo food knives from northern Vanuatu *Kirk W. Huffman*
217	Traditional housing and architecture of Vanuatu *Christian Coiffier*
226	Plates and bowls from northern and central Vanuatu *Kirk W. Huffman*
232	Wooden *nalot* pounders *Kirk W. Huffman*
234	Masked faces from the country of the dead *Bernard Vienne*
238	Series of incised bamboo and cane ornaments from the Torres and Banks islands, Ambae and Maewo *Kirk W. Huffman*
247	'*Su tuh netan'monbwei*: we write on the ground': sand-drawings and their associations in northern Vanuatu *Kirk W. Huffman*
254	Mastering the arts: an examination of the context of the production of art in Ambrym *Mary Patterson*
263	**CHAPTER V: TOWARDS A HISTORY OF THE VISUAL RECORD**
264	European perceptions of the arts of Vanuatu: engendering colonial interests *Margaret Jolly*
265	A brief history of Vanuatu collections in France *Sylviane Jacquemin*
278	History of audiovisual documents: earliest 'European' paintings, photographs, films and recordings of Vanuatu *Kirk W. Huffman*
288	Audiovisual documentation of living cultures as a major task for the Vanuatu Cultural Centre *Jacob Sam*
290	The fieldworkers of the Vanuatu Cultural Centre and their contributions to the audiovisual collections *Kirk W. Huffman*
295	**CHAPTER VI: THE PASSING SCENE**
296	Bislama: origins and functions *Jean-Michel Charpentier*
302	From condiminium to republic *Jean-Marc Philibert and Margaret C. Rodman*
305	The Felix Speiser collection *Christian Kaufmann*
307	The *nevimbumbao* of the Picasso Museum *Philippe Peltier*
309	Transforming representations: a sketch of the contemporary-art scene in Vanuatu *Ralph Regenvanu*
318	The demographic past *Jean-Louis Rallu*
320	Vanuatu today *Gilbert David*
323	**BIBLIOGRAPHY**
334	Contributors
336	Photographic credits
337	Object dimensions and museum registration

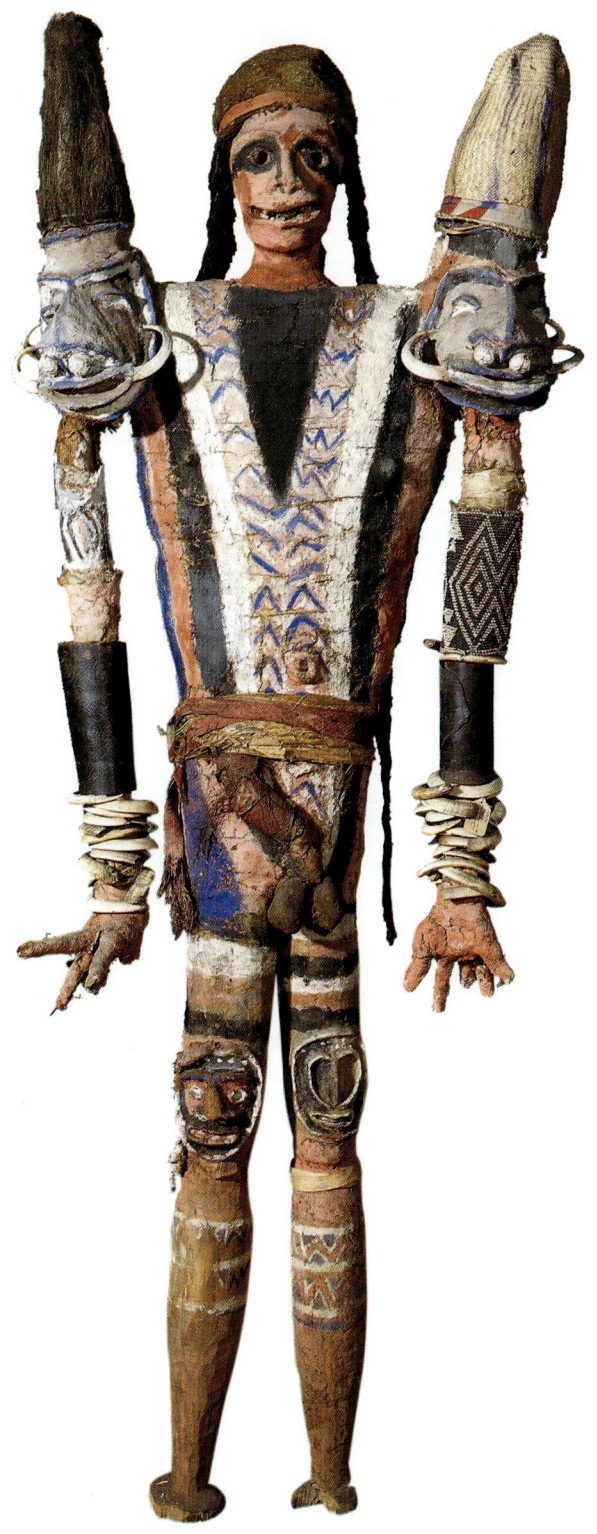

Fig. 1
Funerary effigy, *rambaramp*; plant fibres, wood, pig's tooth, over-modelled skull, pigments. South-west Malakula. Cambridge, University Museum of Archaeology and Anthropology.

Fig. 2
Ritual figure; bark and plant fibres, pigments. Banks Islands. Bordeaux, Musée d'Aquitaine.

Fig. 3
Grade sculpture; black palm fern. Collected by Speiser between 1910 and 1912 (cf. fig. 43). Gaua, Banks Islands. Basel, Museum für Völkerkunde.

Fig. 4
Headgear for *tamate* ceremony. Banks Islands. Leipzig, Museum für Völkerkunde.

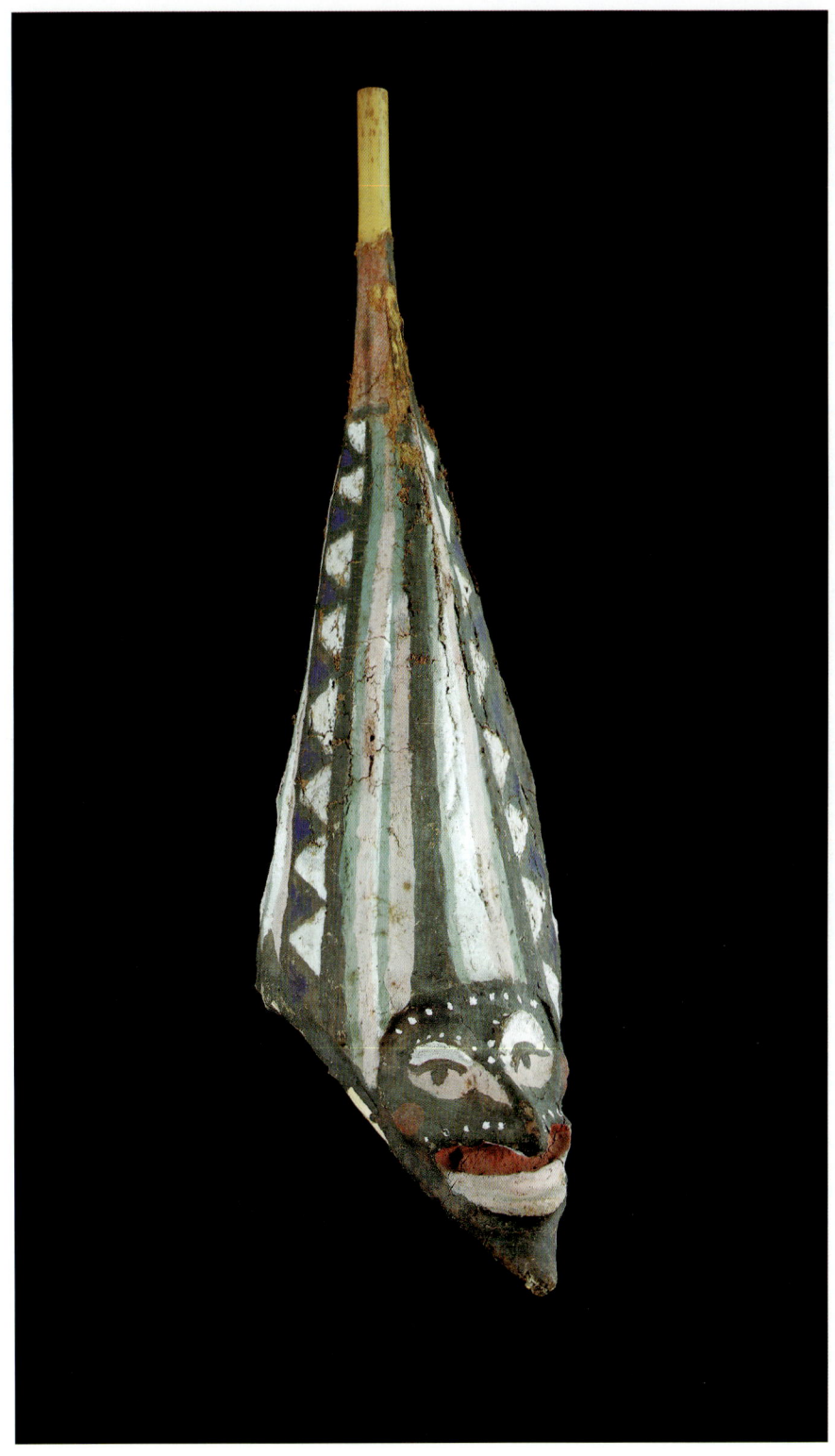

Fig. 5
Mask of *ngulong* type, collected by Speiser between 1910 and 1912. East Malakula. Basel, Museum für Völkerkunde.

Fig. 6
Grade figure; black palm fern. Collected by Speiser between 1910 and 1912.
North Ambrym.
Basel, Museum für Völkerkunde.

Fig. 7
Figure, *luan*; plant material.
Ambrym.
London, Museum of Mankind, British Museum.

Preface

José Garanger

Vanuatu (meaning 'the country that stands up') was the name chosen by the indigenous people for their islands when they became independent in 1980. It replaced the name New Hebrides, bestowed on the islands by Captain Cook in 1774. Six years earlier, de Bougainville had called them the Great Cyclades. The Englishman and the Frenchman obviously had quite a different view of the archipelago, one of them reminded of the dark and misty Hebrides, the other of the luminous, gentle islands of the Aegean.

Cook and de Bougainville, however, were not the first Europeans to visit the archipelago. As early as 1606, the Spanish expedition led by de Quirós had reached the large northern island and named it *La Austrialia del Espiritu Santo*. De Quirós, who later described the island as an earthly paradise, thought he had discovered the fabled southern continent conceived by the Greeks of antiquity and hitherto sought in vain by navigators. The myth of a great continent overflowing with riches was not put to rest until Captain Cook proved that such a land did not exist, when he sighted the frozen shores of the Antarctic.

Nonetheless, because of the beauty of its islands, Vanuatu is one of the most attractive of tropical island groups. It stretches for about 900 kilometres of the central Melanesian chain, and its more than eighty islands and islets form a Y shape running from north to south (see fig. 8). The earliest discoverers of these islands, and the missionaries and settlers who came after them, were surprised by their natural and cultural diversity. These 'islands of ashes and coral', to use the felicitous phrase coined by the geologist Aubert de la Rüe, are made of rocks from the depths of the earth and the ocean; but what geological complexity, and what seismic, tectonic, and volcanic activity there is here, in one of the most active parts of the Pacific ring of fire! The almost continual seismic movement sometimes alters the appearance of the islands in a matter of moments, and several of the numerous volcanoes, both terrestrial (the 'fire-belching islands', as they have been called) and submarine, are still active. Tradition has preserved the memory of devastating cataclysms; one of the most famous, in the 15th century (a date confirmed by archaeology), destroyed the island of Kuwae, of which only the tiny Shepherd Islands remain. Tradition also records that there was once an island, west of Emwae, whose inhabitants specialised in making a colouring powder based on turmeric, 'in the time of my grandfather's grandfather', as Ti Tongoa Mata, the chief of the village of Mangarisu on Tongoa, told me, and he offered me a sample. All that remains of

Fig. 8

Figs 9, 10, 11, 12: Drawings done in 1879 by N.N. von Mikloucho-Maclay (1950-1954, vol. 5).

Fig. 9
Views of Tanna.

that island now is the underwater shoal known as Cook's Reef. Again according to tradition, a small island off the coast of Ambae is said to have disappeared about three centuries ago. Who knows how many others there may have been? And then there are the violent tropical cyclones and tidal waves (tsunamis or storm surges). What enormous consequences for human behaviour and social organisation for people faced with such a permanently tumultuous natural world! Differences in soils, altitude (nearly 2000 metres on Espiritu Santo), latitude, and windward or leeward situations also bring many contrasts in climate and landscape.

Human diversity is just as great, and to call all the people Melanesians seems an oversimplification, so different in appearance are they from one island to another, within the same island, and even within the same village. The multiplicity of languages echoes that diversity, and although some have died out, more than a hundred still survive. They all belong to the large Austronesian family of languages found throughout island Oceania, in South-East Asia and as far away as Madagascar. Despite their linguistic kinship, the various groups do not understand one another from one end of the archipelago to the other, and communicate via intervening neighbours. This intelligibility of neighbours forms what the specialists call a series of linguistic chains, which also correspond to inter-island exchange networks described by ethnologists and archaeologists (pp. 66, 74, this volume). De Bougainville and Cook had already noticed these differences, physical and linguistic, and when Cook called at Tanna (fig. 9), the naturalist John Forster noted that a man from 'Erro-Mango' who happened to be there was ignorant of the language of Tanna, but that the Tannese understood him; also that they sang songs musically very different from his. This multiplicity of languages, of facial appearances and cultures of implies very complex settlement patterns.

Archaeological research began in the Fiji Islands in 1947, in New Caledonia in 1952, and in the New Hebrides ten years later, and more and more is being done throughout the whole 'Melanesian' region, and in Samoa and Tonga in Polynesia. This research is gradually casting light on Western Pacific prehistory (and consequently on the prehistory of other parts of Oceania), and is revealing the extreme complexity of its processes of settlement, a large number of the factors of which remain very obscure. This is particularly the case in Vanuatu, the crossroads of settlement routes and of the inter-island networks of relations and exchange characteristic of pre-European Pacific societies.

Several of these problems are dealt with in the following chapters. I will simply mention the main ones. We know that, like all Pacific Islanders, the very remote ancestors of the ni-Vanuatu came originally from South-East Asia, but how long ago did they leave, and how long did it take them? Australia, and New Guinea with its neighbouring small islands, were colonised by *Homo sapiens sapiens* as early as the late Pleistocene, some 50 000 years ago. These people, however, were not the Austronesian-speakers who arrived much later in the Pacific, and there is no evidence yet that they reached other Melanesian islands such as Vanuatu. Opinions, as we shall see, are divided on this point. The oldest evidence of human presence in Vanuatu and New Caledonia, Fiji and eastern Polynesia, are sherds of pottery from 1500 BC (a little earlier in the north, a little later in the south and east). The first pottery tradition found is known as 'Lapita', and it is still posing problems to prehistorians. It was first thought to be the work of Austronesians, the ancestors of the people we call Polynesians (which has yet to be demonstrated), but other peoples practising animal husbandry and horticulture, though not

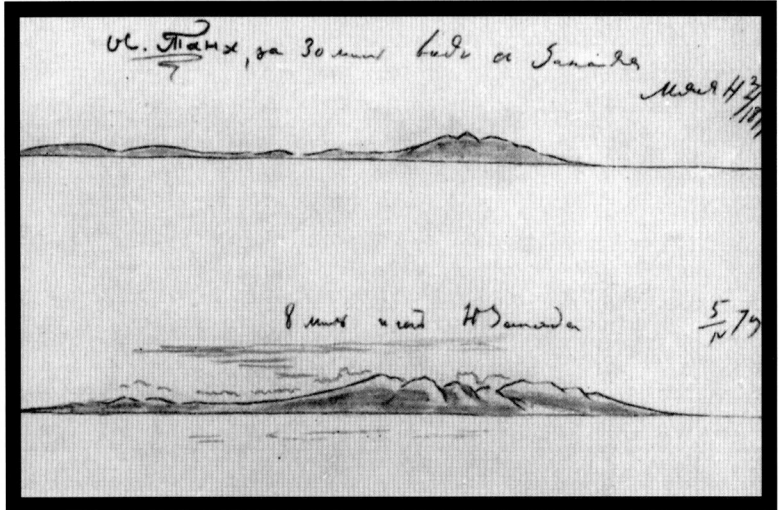

  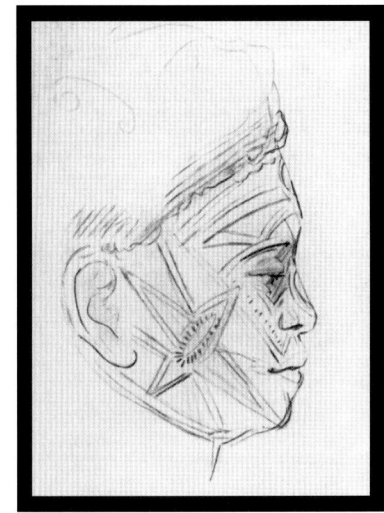

pottery makers, may have preceded them into the islands. This seems now to have been proved in the case of some northern Melanesian islands, but not yet elsewhere. Less Lapita pottery is found in Vanuatu than in other south-west Pacific islands – at least as far as research to date can tell us. In the central islands of the group, we find more abundant evidence of another, later, pottery tradition than of the Lapita, the so-called Mangaasi tradition (from the eponymous site on the coast of Efate, dating from the 6th century BC), which will also be dealt with in this volume. Its geographical extension is now known to be greater, and may indicate the continuity of systems of inter-island relations, already revealed by the Lapita tradition and still to be seen at the beginning of the 20th century. The existence in Vanuatu of Polynesian language isolates, and changes in material culture in the 13th century AD, are further evidence of the complexity of these islands' prehistory. Land of exchanges, land of encounters, Vanuatu has played a determining role in the settlement of the Pacific and occupies a very special place in Oceania as a whole. These islands are characterised by both unity and diversity. A philosopher once wrote that this was the nature of anything truly beautiful. We shall see in this book that the art of Vanuatu is no exception to that rule.

From another, much more general point of view, preserving this tradition of diversity and unity that makes the natural and cultural harmony of these islands so singular is, for its inhabitants, an overriding necessity in the world of today, a world which, in its rush towards technological progress, is growing closer together but at the same time becoming dehumanised and demoralised. We hope that this publication may help to make known and to safeguard the unique cultural identity of Vanuatu.

Fig. 10
A men's house of a rare type on Malo.

Fig. 11
A man of Leleppa, north-west Efate.

Fig. 12
Face tattoo of a woman. Vanua Lava, Banks Islands.

The Arts of Vanuatu: Between Traditional Imagery and Force of Expression

Christian Kaufmann

1. As figure 8 shows, the islands of Vanuatu lie between the 13° and 21°S and 166° and 170°E, and stretch for approximately 900 km in a generally north-south-south-east direction, and approximately 250 km from east to west.

The numerous artistic works from Vanuatu (figs 1-7) bear witness to an extraordinary creativity, even compared with the great diversity of other Melanesian countries. This is all the more true when we consider that this abundance is created by a small population scattered over the more than eighty small and medium-sized islands in southern Melanesia that make up what were known as the New Hebrides (from Aneityum in the south to Espiritu Santo and Maewo in the north), the Banks Islands, and the Torres Islands.[1]

What does an international exhibition of Vanuatu art mean today? There are three answers to that question. The first concerns the quality of the individual works, which have come to us from collections dating from about 1890 onwards; that quality is quite remarkable. It is obvious and can be appreciated even by those who are not familiar with Vanuatu's cultural traditions. Technical mastery characterises all forms of artistic expression, from sculpture to painting, and from drawing to body decoration and dance. The illustrations in this volume are an attempt to do justice to the high quality of these artistic manifestations.

The second answer is that this cultural heritage is of exemplary importance to the history of the people and the country of Vanuatu, as well as of Melanesia. The real knowledge that, within local societies themselves, connects the material expression with the very heart of their lives and their traditions has been the subject of numerous ethnographical studies and basic research on it is still going on in Vanuatu. Those responsible for the Cultural Centre, and their local collaborators, the men and women who make up two very effective networks, are working with great energy to grasp, learn, understand and assimilate better the rich sources of their artistic and linguistic traditions. Some of the contributions to this catalogue, particularly those of Darrell Tryon (p. 172, this volume), Jacob Sam and Kirk Huffman (pp. 290, 292, this volume), give us a more precise idea of the scope of this unique material, compiled by the people of Vanuatu themselves.

The third answer concerns art history. When, in 1974, Jean Guiart (cf. also his *Nouvelles Hébrides*, 1965) installed the first permanent exhibition of Vanuatu artworks at the Musée des Arts africains et océaniens in Paris (now called the Musée National des Arts d'Afrique et d'Océanie), it came as the fulfilment of a wish expressed by many artists since the beginning of this century, including Max Ernst and Alberto Giacometti, and the desire of men of vision such as André Malraux. It was a question of deepening and strengthening appreciation of the cultural

Fig. 13
Staging a *toka* dance in a *nekowiar* ceremony. The arrival of a *kweriya* feather pole at night. Dancing ground at Ipaï, Tanna, in August 1995.

Letter from Ambrym
Roger Boulay, Fantan, August 1995

Dear reader, dear visitor,
You have only to travel around Ambrym, Malakula and Tanna to appreciate the strength of tradition in Vanuatu. Seen from the distance of Paris, tradition may look like a mere survival from the past, an obstacle to development, an impediment to the growth of national identity, but, from here on the spot, it seems much more like a rich endowment, the ground on which the new nation is rising, and the framework which has supported it throughout its rich history.

When you leave Vila for the outer islands, you find *kastom* – traditional culture – everywhere, not simply hidden away in isolated valleys as tourist brochures would have it. The importance of tradition obviously has a great influence on present-day art. In Vila you can meet a dozen artists. They seem to be struggling with a tangle of different dictates on creativity and their timid desire to 'do something different'. Ralph Regenvanu, Emmanuel Watt and Sero Kuautonga talk passionately about these difficulties.

But – *kastom* oblige – how beautiful and moving the gardens of Ambrym are! Everywhere they reveal a deep talent, expressed in the arrangement of the landscape, in the way works of art are placed in the spaces that you find here: the green banyans, the black earth swept every day and carefully packed down, the sparkling silver sand, men carved from tree ferns standing in rows, with cordilynes and crotons in between, then the big slit-gongs. Artists are everywhere, in the Banks Islands, at South West Bay (Malakula), on Ambrym, on Maewo, and so on. People know their names. They carve, they weave (the women particularly), they paint, they put things together every day. You only have to tour the *nasaras* of north Ambrym to dismiss the myth of a vanished art, of art bastardised by the effects of producing potboilers for tourists, dealers and big hotels. A walk around Fantan (Ambrym) will reveal many carvings already standing, many others being made. Few countries in the world can provide a spectacle in which the front yard of every man of influence – and there are many of these today – contains monumental sculptures.

Seeing the art objects by themselves in an exhibition is, of course, frustrating for those who have seen them where they were originally presented; and I really am talking simply about presentation, or demonstration, without going into a dissection of the whole society, simply to put on record everything which helps show the work to the full: the space that has been shaped, the choreography. The Malakula headdresses without their wearers, the art objects without the 'art gallery', without the 'opening' they are entitled to, the Ambrym slit-gongs without their dancing ground, the Tannese feather sculptures without the 500 dancers who show them off, the Ambae women's mats without the accumulation and display … I must admit that I find it even more frustrating when I try to describe to artists here what the exhibition of their ancestor's and their own works will look like in our country – smooth pedestals for objects to stand on, pretty lighting, no natural shadows, muted sounds, the squeak of footsteps on waxed parquet floors …

We must not forget that these artists are also masters of 'crowd aesthetics', not only in dancing, but in moving space, progressions, entrances and exits from the dancing ground, actions staged between day and night. There is a refined art of sequencing, dramatisation and change of pace in the way the ceremony unfolds. The *nekiowar* of August 1995 on Tanna (figs 13, 14) was an amazing display of all these qualities: amazing for the 3000 local spectators and, even more so, for the thirty wandering tourists, duly furnished with their access cards and relieved of their entry fees. The only plastic work displayed in two days and a night of festivities was the simple, superb column of

Fig. 14 *Nekowiar* ceremony: *toka* dance with *kweriya* at dawn. Dancing ground at Ipaï, Tanna, August 1995.

feathers, the *kweria*, worn by the dancers; but what a work of art it was, when seen amid the dance, in this space, this scenario, this staging, these sounds … And then there are the sand-drawings, all the ephemeral arts to be seen for the brief moment of a ceremony, or until the next wave sweeps over the black sand.

How astonishingly vital this contemporary art is. At Meltmes, a ceremonial ground and *nakamal* have been cleared and restored, so the people inaugurate it with a hundred works of art; a small airport is opened on Ambrym – again, artifacts are made; the Malakula mission is celebrating its 100th anniversary – same thing again; a new cultural centre is to be set up – people are already planning a year ahead a whole set of carved objects to be cradled in the men's arms and danced around the dancing ground in front of the crowd. It's like a travelling art gallery. On every occasion, ni-Vanuatu not only perform a dance, which is easy to take from place to place, but they also always make masks, headdresses, statuettes, sculpted poles, and mats.

And, when they make art, it's unstintingly. What is sought is the effect of numbers, the effect of reduplication, not economy; never one single great piece, never the miserly production we seem to take as a sign of the true artist. Each piece shows off its neighbour, every piece reflects the whole. There is no argument to justify a selection or a choice; it's all or nothing. The coherence of the whole mass of objects produces an aesthetic effect; I am thinking here of the great objects from southern Malakula. At a deeper level, from whichever angle you look at the motives and reasons, success is owing only to the power of the spirits of the ancients: they are there, always there, underpinning the transmission of forms from one generation to another.

Their great-great-grandchildren are there too. Apprenticeship is taken seriously; the tradition is handed on. You are struck, everywhere in the islands, by the sight of children, babies, dancing, declaiming, gravely carrying artifacts. Their shrill voices are the counterpoint to those of their fathers, who are keeping an eye on them; they stand next to the dancers and imitate them studiously. They are encouraged, teased, but they are included in the world of men.

They are just as attentive to the sculptor's son who last month put up his first slit-gong, near Olal, on Ambrym. You should have seen the pride of his father, who is passing on his skill and is himself preparing to acquire new rights to ancient motifs. If it had not been for his desire to do so, those motifs would probably have been forgotten. The *bisnis* of purchasing the rights to certain forms occupies him as much as his carving does. *Bisnis* in Bislama is synonymous with worry, difficult business, complex obligations. He will soon be able to carve a fourth, and then a fifth head at the top of his gongs. It is a matter that preoccupies everyone, this work of his; people talk about it, comment on how he is progressing with the carving, wait for the new design to appear … and then thirty stalwarts arrive to carry the carving down to the little inter-island trading vessel at Craig Cove.

The latest novelties appear on artifacts. In the Banks, people are dancing with the helicopter from the Club Med cruise ship on their heads. In Tanna, a dance stick is incised with the emblems of the two local societies: a pig and a camera. They do the craziest things for their cameras, these whites, these *mastas*: it seems to be a part of them. At the *toka*, they were prepared, though they did protest, to pay 3000 French francs to be allowed to use a video camera. People must wonder what they can possibly do with all those pictures. In fact, two groups of image-makers are curiously observing each other. One group pays a high price in pigs to reveal the images, the other seems just as anxious to make big sacrifices to use up film. My neighbour at the *nekiowar* was asked by a smiling young dancer, 'Did you get a good picture?' Strange – my neighbour must have been the only one without a camera. It was a matter of checking that we were doing our job, just as seriously as they were doing theirs. Making pictures and taking pictures.

Obviously, extending *bisnis* to include images and ceremonies is not without its problems; selling the right to take photographs or film encourages people to put on a show, just as the demand for 'exotic' artifacts stimulates the supply. What strikes an observer is the seriousness with which all this is negotiated in terms of *kastom*. They don't do just anything, nor sell just any image; those who break the rules are punished (some well-meaning colleagues learnt this lesson here, not long ago), the proper channels are followed to obtain permission.

The acquisition of an Ambrym slit-gong, for us, costs far more when we want some sense to attach to the object, its making, its presentation. It is always possible to get out your chequebook; that works. But in that case, the product carries no guarantee (culturally correct!). Some amateurs with a yen for the exotic get what they want this way. Sometimes, when they are lucky, the desire for money overcomes the desire to preserve heritage and tradition; quite a responsibility. Then the image is dead, has been destroyed, and its disappearance (whether object or film) somewhere far away becomes a source of trouble, remorse and regret, sometimes a sorrow that lasts for years. People have fallen ill for less. Something with meaning can neither be exchanged nor exported without some precautions being taken, because these things have an effect. Kirk Huffman and Joël Bonnemaison have talked a great deal about this … Making art on Ambrym, or elsewhere, is paid for in many different ways. It is serious work.

I have been fortunate to see the gravity which, in this place, fills the act of creating an image even today. If only we can convey a sense of it in our exhibitions.

2. For an overall view of the history of collections outside Vanuatu, see Sylviane Jacquemin (p. 267, this volume) on French collections, and my note on the Speiser collection (p. 307, this volume). In the special issue of the journal *Cahiers d'art* devoted to the art of the South Pacific and edited by Christian Zervos in 1929, Speiser wrote about Ambrym, Malakula and Banks Islands sculptures.

heritage of the South Pacific. Thanks to this initiative and others in Europe, the artistic traditions of Vanuatu have acquired an exemplary value in Western thinking on the role of art in human society. We must now pursue that thinking on Vanuatu's societies and traditions, at a more general and, at the same time, a more personal level.

Finally, the arts of Vanuatu show amazing vitality, as Roger Boulay describes in his 'dispatch from the field' (p. 13, this volume).

Melanesian art in European eyes

European artists of the Modern period – that is, the first half of the 20th century – as well as anthropologists and museologists, have all paid tribute to the intrinsic values of Melanesian cultures. This makes the documents (figs 16, 17), collections, exhibitions and publications, into something of the nature of a two-way mirror reflecting both Western and Vanuatu history.[2]

These documents enable us to retrace the long road covered by Western society on its way to encounter its distant, almost inaccessible cousins. The trail that began with the first 'voyages of discovery' is described by Margaret Jolly (p. 266, this volume), while Kirk Huffman gives us a detailed history of the visual documents (p. 280, this volume).

Misunderstandings and even disdain undoubtedly affected the appreciation of these arts, taken at the time to be evidence of what the arts of our distant ancestors had been, and thus too easily described as 'primitive'. It is noteworthy that there was at times a fierce debate, particularly during the 1920s and 1930s, which not only enables us to trace the development of 'modern' thinking, but also to see a revival of neocolonialist thought, with its disinclination even to attempt to understand the mental world of the subjects of empire it was exploiting. This emphasises the important role played by the emergence of a new awareness and a new ethnological discourse, founded on a better knowledge of local societies and their histories, as is shown, for example, by Codrington (1891:24-27) and (1942). This discourse focused on the role of the individual's personality in his – not so much her – society, and so began the reconstruction of an inner vision, a gaze from within. Confronted with art created by another society, we are faced, in an immediate fashion, with this gaze from within as it is directed at the way of life, thought and expression. This confrontation takes shape first of all not through texts, but by visual means, such as gesture, dance, ceremony, and the panoply of ephemeral works such as headdresses and masks. Then the impact of sculpture in 'hard' materials, wood or stone, is perhaps even more pregnant with significance; these forms of expression are, of course, often accompanied by words, spoken in the form of songs, magical formulas, commentaries, legends or even myths. When we go back to the source of the gaze and can appreciate it, even minimally – that is to say, from the outside – it becomes an external gaze on man, the projection of universalist thought, and on ourselves and modern society, saturated by the total commercialisation of all values. This situation is today still more accentuated by contemporary developments in art in Melanesia (as Ralph Regenvanu writes (p. 311, this volume), and as is mentioned by Roger Boulay). It will only evolve significantly when there is an exchange of views and a dialogue on the different gazes of the artists themselves. As Jean-Hubert Martin (1993:32-36) has reminded us, this dialogue between individuals belonging to different societies is a long-term matter, subject to the typical time lapses which arise between the articulation, then the sending of a message by one artistic group and its first decoding at a basic level by another group, and again between the articulation of the response and its later reception in the original society.

Arts and history

Despite those who once affirmed that the non-European world had no history, systematic analysis of the forms of artistic expression and data on their significance has made it possible to establish basic thinking about the history of Melanesia and the Melanesians before the arrival of Europeans. This approach was developed by such as Alfred C. Haddon (1894, 1895) and Felix Speiser. To the latter we owe the first synoptic attempts at a reconstruction of Melanesian history based on the evolution and diffusion of artistic styles (Speiser 1936, 1966). Haddon and Speiser treated art as a very material form of Melanesian civilisation, which was capable of transforming in an original way even those inspirations it may have received from outside. The greater part of these diffusions apparently were directly related to the history of the Austronesian-speaking peoples of Oceania and did not therefore depend on a single close (as seen from Europe), Near Eastern cradle of civilisation, as W.H. Rivers still thought when he wrote his history of Melanesian society in 1914.

With the arrival of the first archaeological fieldworkers in the 1960s, historical hypotheses could develop further. The data uncovered by archaeology, especially by José Garanger and his colleagues and successors, now shows that it is highly probable that the Vanuatu region went through its own particular historical development. Periods marked by indigenous growth alternated with periods of transformation, set off either by exchanges with the outside, or by the arrival of new immigrants. According to Garanger (p. 66, this volume) and Galipaud (p. 96, this volume), the Vanuatu region went through such a period of very marked transformation between the 11th and the 16th centuries. The disappearance, after the Mangaasi period, of local styled pottery, and the change in the types of tools used – shell blades replacing stones as adze heads – are evidence of this. This archaeological example, and David Roe's data on cave art (p. 83, this volume), demonstrate that any cultural style owes its definition, and thus its existence, to the fact that it can change in due course. Because we are not in a position to know the various causes of these changes, simply noting stylistic variations is not enough for us to reconstruct history, but it does at least allow us better to judge the complexity of the traditions which produced those variations. In a country like Vanuatu, about which pseudo-scientific myths have perpetuated the idea of societies immobilised by the weight of their traditions, innate cultural dynamism remains an important propagator of development in all Melanesian civilisations.

Artistic styles and typology

The basic attraction of Melanesian art lies in the tension between, on one hand, innovative elements – creations that feed change – and, on the other, those elements deeply rooted in tradition and respect for

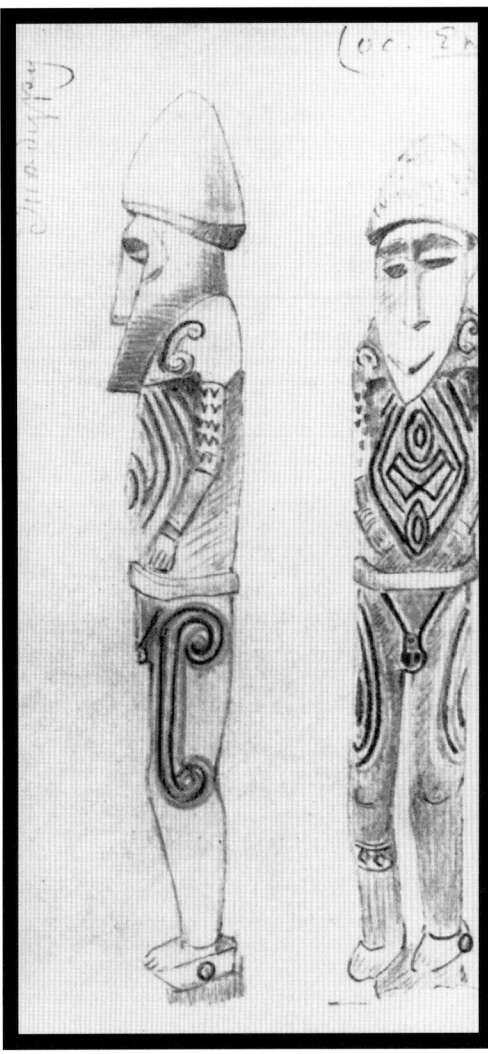

Fig. 15
Wooden figure. Drawing by Mikloucho-Maclay in 1879 on Epi Island.

Fig. 16
Two masked dancers, before 1891, Maewo. After Codrington 1891.

Fig. 17
Old mat of a style as yet undocumented. Said to be acquired on Efate Island in the 1880s, but exact origin unknown. Paris, Musée national des Arts d'Afrique et d'Océanie.

the work accomplished by the ancestors – factors promoting stability. The former is easy to discern in the stylised forms which we find in different objects of the same kind – see, for example, the masks (figs 27-31). The second, the deep-rootedness, is quite often translated by the adoption (or its opposite, the rejection) of certain kinds of objects.

If we group the works strictly according to their geographic origins, we find first of all a concentration of certain kinds in certain areas, such as, for example, slit-gongs between Efate and Maewo (Crowe, p. 147, this volume), and an almost total absence of sculpture in the south of the country, except for the rare Futuna *marae* statues, an exception to which I will return. On the other hand, the mats decorated with woven and, especially, coloured patterns, produced by a reserve technique, proliferate in the eastern central area, on Pentecost, Ambae, also long ago on Malakula and even Efate (fig. 17), and on Ambrym and Epi. The contributions of Annie Walter, Alfreda Mabonlala and Lissant Bolton on the feminine art of plaiting and mat-decoration, and their social implications, are an outstanding feature of this volume (pp. 102, 112, 114, this volume).

Another approach might be an ethnographic and then an ethnological study of the social and religious context of typical works as it can now be reconstructed by their original societies. Mary Patterson sketches out such an approach to the sculptures of northern and western Ambrym (p. 256, this volume). Even with detailed documentation, we are still far from being able to describe systematically the sociocultural context, as Bernard Vienne shows in the case of the Banks Islands *tamate* masks (p. 236, this volume), and as John Layard pointed out long ago in 1942, in particular for Atchin Island off eastern Malakula.

So, though we cannot for the moment draw up a synthetic inventory of the types of objects in use in local societies, we can, taking an almost completely opposite approach, study the expressive qualities of these very diverse, often composite, and for that reason artistically complex forms. Through these multiple variations a fundamental transformation of motifs is sometimes revealed. Their qualities are based as much on the sculptural or other materials used as on the ideas represented. Many of these

Fig. 18 Ambrym

Masks, 'headdresses' and 'ritual hats' in northern Vanuatu

Kirk W. Huffman

Trying to outline the distribution, manufacture, form and function of masks, headdresses and ritual headgear in northern Vanuatu in a short note is about as easy as trying to write the history of the world on the head of a pin. From northern Epi through many of the northern-central islands and to the Banks and Torres, there existed such an astonishing array of various types of these ritual materials that it is almost impossible to comprehend the variety, and hundreds, if not thousands of these different forms exist or could be produced, in the present day. Ni-Vanuatu in these areas today will have varying depths of knowledge relating to such material belonging to their own, and neighbouring cultural areas, depending upon their immersion in the traditional system, and a fascination for viewing the (public) ritual displays of them from areas unknown to them, an opportunity now provided in the relatively regular National and Island Arts Festivals held in Vanuatu since December 1979. The latter are not organised for purposes of tourism and there is little danger of a 'generic' spread of a particular type of mask or headdress type, because such an occurrence is impossible to conceive of in the area 'controlled' by ancient and strict forms of ritual traditional copyright.

The outside world may be aware of aspects of the spread, stylistic variations and functions of many of these objects through the excellent fieldwork or collections, or both, of R.H. Codrington, E.G. McAfee, F. Speiser, A.B. Lewis, J.W. Layard, A.B. Deacon, Jean Guiart, Bernard Vienne, Jean-Michel Charpentier and Mary Patterson. It is absolutely essential though, to repeatedly emphasise to the 'uninitiated European reader/viewer' that the meaning

Fig. 19
Ambrym.

20 ▼ INTRODUCTION

Fig. 20
North-east Malakula.

and feelings of beauty, admiration, fear, excitement and respect that these numerous art forms engender among niVanuatu can only be glimpsed by seeing them in use in their proper cultural context, and not necessarily on display somewhere in a glass cabinet. Ni-Vanuatu are grateful that certain overseas institutions have carefully preserved old and rare masks and objects from the country, but as these cannot be 'used' overseas, some are often slightly puzzled to the reasons for the collections, the European way of looking at them being so different from the traditional way.

Most of such objects are extremely fragile and, except for those carved in wood, are often, as is sometimes the case in Ambrym, central and northern Pentecost, north-eastern Malakula, Maewo and the Banks and Torres, destroyed after ritual and/or public use. This can be done sometimes, for example, to certain Banks Islands *tamate* headdresses, certain Ambrym *rom* (of both the horizontal 'mask' and the vertical 'headdress' types; figs 18, 19), or to the numerous large and fragile styles of north-eastern Malakula (fig. 20) that can, at least on Atchin, be classed of the *botmolmoli* ('round head') type, used there in *umanen* dances that close the graded ritual cycles. Other head-dresses, such as those of stronger materials over-modelled with vegetable-fibre paste from southern Malakula (as the *temes napal*, 'bald-headed' spirit variety; figs 21, 22) from the numerous *nalawan* or other ritual cycles, may some-times be stored in the men's house (or elsewhere) after use and (if not disintegrated) eventually repaired and re-painted if used again. Some such Malakulan figures (for

Fig. 21

Fig. 23

Fig. 21
South Malakula.

Fig. 22
South Malakula.

Fig. 23
South Malakula.

Fig. 24
South Pentecost.

Fig. 25
Ambrym.

Fig. 26
Ambrym.

Fig. 22

Fig. 24

Fig. 25

Fig. 26

example, *temes malau,* the 'megapode bird spirit', fig. 23) on a heavy tree-fern base and large enough to cover the whole upper body of the wearer, can be reused (if repaired) many times. Face masks of the particular rare type, vegetable-fibre paste on a spider-web base and collected by Speiser in east-south-eastern Malakula (fig. 24), are at the origin of the dreaded Ambrym *temar ne are* type, and were usually kept well-stored, being for special (and 'rather tabu') occasions. Ambrym *tamake* (figs 25, 26), more playful and less 'culturally heavy' can often be reused or just discarded after use although earlier black hardwood *tamake* were dangerous, deadly and tabu.

The use of heavier wooden masks (fig. 27) has now disappeared from northern Ambrym, but masks of similar nature existed in southern Pentecost (fig. 28), whereas those in the latter area of the *juban/chubwan* style (of which there were many variations; for example, figs 29, 30, 31) served important functions in aspects of rituals relating to the sacred relationship between men and yams. Some of the latter link up stylistically with the numerous types of wooden face-held masks used in tragicomedy mime sketches interspersing stages in the extensive grade rituals

Fig. 27 North Ambrym.

Fig. 28 South Pentecost.

Fig. 29 South Pentecost.

on the 'Small Islands' off north-east Malakula. On Vao these masks are of a general type known as *narut* (fig. 32 is an example of the general north-east Malakulan style).

On Maewo, numerous fragile headdresses of the type associated with the men's *n'kwat* societies are still periodically made, and can sometimes obviously be stored, or 'sleep', but are able to reawaken quickly – the author was terrified by one appearing suddenly out of the bush near Umlongo in central Maewo in 1983 (see Codrington 1891 illustration, fig. 16, in Kaufmann, p. 17, this volume). Masks do not appear to have existed on Santo, but when one moves further north into the Banks Islands, into the area of the *tamate* societies, one encounters a bewildering array of men's headdresses, dealt with in Bernard Vienne's article (p. 236) in this volume. The number and variety of these secret societies' accoutrements has to be seen to be believed, each society having numerous variations. Compared to the minuscule Torres Islands, the Banks Islands are large and with a much larger population – particularly in the old days – and it should be borne in mind that, before missionisation, there were around 100 men's secret societies in the Torres alone, each with their array of headdresses (generally smaller and more fragile than those in the Banks).

Unfortunately, in this short note, I have dealt with northern Vanuatu masks in a rather 'European' style, not really the way to do it. I should point out that all the above deals specifically with male materials – certain areas within northern Vanuatu have important female ritual headgear traditions. None of these can really be appreciated without the ritual dance, music, complete costume, feathers, cloaks (if used for that particular type), and other aspects that complete the various forms of these often spiritual experiences. The effect on ni-Vanuatu spectators is often electrifying. One should not, however, forget the possible effect upon the wearers of certain of these masks, if the wearers

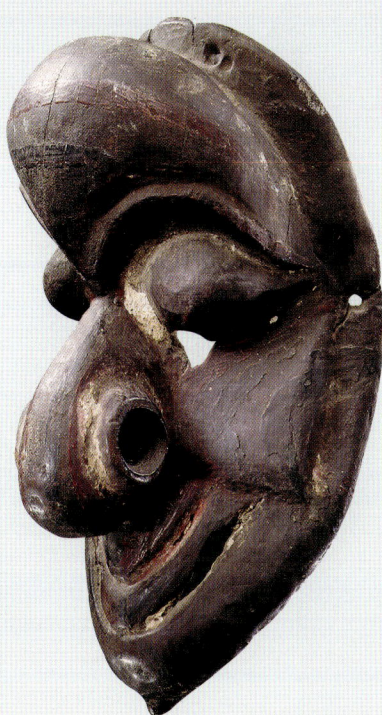

Fig. 30 South Pentecost.

Fig. 31 South Pentecost.

Fig. 32 North-east Malakula.

are human (some are thought not to be, some are or become spirits): some of the rarer, more powerful ritual masks can be dangerous to wear. This aspect was often brought home to the author viewing aspects of a powerful type of spiritual mask use in the interior of southern Malakula in the 1970s and 1980s. These particular types of masks (which I will leave unnamed), for non-dancing aspects of funerary rituals, have to be worn with great care: no body cloak or covering is worn and one could see the wearer's heart beating in trepidation as he performed the spirit's obligations.

There are internal as well as external aspects to mask-use in Vanuatu, as there are levels of naming of most of the types of masks. I have used only general local language terms as befits a brief survey of this nature.

Fig. 33
Male figure. Wood. Collected by Speiser between 1910 and 1912.
Atchin, north-east Malakula.
Basel, Museum für Völkerkunde.

Fig. 34
Male figure. Wood, pigments. Collected by the *Korrigane* expedition.
Savakas village, Malo.
Paris, Musée de l'Homme.

Fig. 35
Grade figure. Black palm fern. Collected by Higginson in 1890.
Banks Islands.
Paris, Musée de l'Homme.

works thus make use of forms which one could analyse according to their structure and composition; for example, the presentation of perfectly symmetrical, frontal, standing human figures (figs 33 and 34), the way of reducing arms and legs to essentials by lengthening and attenuating them in solid representations, thus emphasising the hard element, the bones, as against the soft parts, the flesh and the fluids (fig. 35). Even if we do take such an approach, we should take care to avoid systematisation, this being too formal a process and one which seems to reveal, yet again, a very Western way of thinking.

The distribution of forms of artistic expression

From the formal point of view, Vanuatu seems to be divided into at least three parts. First the south, Tafea province – Tanna, Aneityum, Futuna, Erromango and Aniwa – where there are no, or almost no images in permanent materials. The second broad area, in itself not very homogeneous, groups all the northern and north-central islands, from the Banks to Malakula, the Maskelynes, Paama and northern Epi. This region is the richest in forms. Tree-fern or wooden statues, platters, pestles and pig-killing clubs, ceremonial houses (*nakamal*), sometimes decorated with carvings, a large number of types of masks and other objects of ceremonial use, pregnant with imagery – all these are found in large numbers.

The third area is a transitional zone in the centre of the country, connecting Efate and the Shepherd Islands with Erromango – if we base it on the painted barkcloth described by Huffman (p. 131, this volume) – or the centre with Malakula, Paama, Ambrym, and even Santo and the Banks Islands, if we use as our criterion the symbolic use of objects of value (traditional shell money, chiefly insignia, and so on), or again, architectural forms, as Christian Coiffier describes them (p. 219, this volume).

Depending on which of these elements we look at, the dividing line between the central and northern zones shifts. The northern zone could even be subdivided into several sub-zones, each gravitating around a regional artistic centre, in particular the Banks Islands around Gaua and Ureparapara (small incised bamboos, tree-fern carvings, *tamate* masks), Malakula and Ambrym (masks, wood and tree-fern carvings), and Ambae, central and northern Pentecost, and Maewo (mats). Mats dyed with red designs are at present only made in a few areas on Ambae and Pentecost, where they serve to maintain exchange relations, mats being the most important items of exchange after pigs, as Huffman shows (p. 184, this volume, with map). It remains probable, however, that red-patterned mats used also to be produced on Ambrym, Malakula and even down into the central islands. The existence in the Banks Islands of a tradition of making belts dyed red using the reserve technique leads us to suppose that there were ancient links throughout the northern zone. This underlying unity also appears to be confirmed by the distribution of carved tree-ferns through Malakula, Paama, and Ambrym, right up to the Banks, even though tree ferns are not documented on Ambae, Pentecost, Maewo, Santo or Malo. On the other hand, slit-gongs rule out the idea of a common network in the north both by their forms – carved out of wood or cut from bamboo – and by their typology – placed upright or horizontally. They appear not to have existed in the Banks, though they were well-represented in the centre as far south as Efate.

It may be of interest to note the existence of other sequences of forms, particularly wooden knives and the pestles used to prepare *laplap* for cooking in hot stone ovens (pp. 206 and 234, this volume), combs, and ear ornaments with incised decoration (pp. 143 and 240, this volume). While the knives and engraved ear ornaments are found mainly in the Banks Islands, the combs are found throughout a larger network.

The masks and headdresses which are found in great variety on Malakula, Ambrym, south Pentecost and the Banks, and are sporadically documented on Epi and Maewo, refer us to networks of more regional significance. It is these networks of social cohesion, organised in the northern zone as men's (and also women's) graded societies and classic chiefdoms (with the exception of that of the Big Nambas, in which the eldest son succeeds his father directly), that often explain the continuities as well as the discontinuities of ritual works of art.

At first sight, one might say that a large number, if not the majority, of the figurative forms that are so abundant in the north are related to the standing human figure or part of the human figure. This does

Fig. 36
Portable effigy. Triton shell, overmodelled fibres, pigments, pig's teeth, feathers. Collected by Speiser between 1910 and 1912.
South Malakula.
Basel, Museum für Völkerkunde.

not imply that each one of the works in question necessarily alludes directly to images of human beings or near-human beings.

References to the ancestral world often come in complex forms (fig. 36). We must not forget that they are often presented in a combination of several media – dance, song, instrumental music, gesture – in which each plays a specific and determining role. Thus, though a few sculptures do represent venerated individual ancestors, most seem to be more truly associated with particular aspects of the ancestral world. This world can take on a different appearance according to place and prevailing beliefs in the local society.

In the intermediate zone, on Efate, in the Shepherd Islands and southern Epi, slit-gongs are the only form of carving, sometimes ornamented by figures which are individualised in relation to the others set up in the same place (fig. 37). On the other hand, in places where carving is less important, mats, especially decorated mats, predominate. It would be tempting to explain this distribution solely in terms of matrilineal values in the case of decorated mats, or patrilineal values in that of carvings. Things are more complicated than this, however, as the southern islands demonstrate. There, in spite of the prevalence of patrilineal systems, sculpture is practically nonexistent.

This reminds us once again that our knowledge is still too limited. Radical demographic change – between 1830 and 1920 the population is said to have fallen by between 50 and 90 per cent, depending on local conditions, according to estimates based on both eyewitness and indirect testimony (reports by the earliest missionaries, archaeological evaluation on Aneityum) (Speiser 1922, 1991; Spriggs 1981; see also Rallu, p. 320, this volume) – as well as conversion to Christianity, in many places threw the social context into complete disarray. On Futuna, for example, there was still, in the mid-19th century, a tradition of use, if not of production, of carving in coral (figs 38 and 39), a tradition which is reported to have been stamped out by the missionaries. We possess only some five statues, which a ship's captain named Wolsch left with the Australian Museum in Sydney in 1884. All other images of gods were taken from sacred places such as the *marae*, the 'temple' (*nakamal*), and other secret places, and buried or burnt in pits (Gunn 1914:52, 103), or taken out to sea and thrown overboard, as John Paton, on neighbouring Aniwa, described (Jolly, p. 266, this volume). These statues must have had great importance in the eyes of the islanders. Presbyterian missionaries, excepting John Paton, did think of rescuing some of them for posterity (Inglis 1887:35-36). This story seems to echo the sadly

Fig. 37
A group of slit-gongs, photographed by Lucas in 1895.
Mele, Efate.

Figs 38, 39
Seated figure and double-headed figure. Coral stone. Collected by Captain Wolsch in 1884.
Futuna Island, Tafea Province.
Sydney, Australian Museum.

similar experiences of the Cook Islanders and Austral Islanders with their English and French missionaries respectively. In both cases, these same missionaries who were converting them to the Christian faith felt themselves compelled 'to save ... the effigies of the traditional gods and take them to a safe place in London' – or in Paris (Jacquemin 1992:28-29).

The carvings from a *marae* on Futuna – where a Polynesian language is still spoken – are particularly interesting because they more closely resemble works from the central or southern Solomon Islands than those of western or central Polynesia. Perhaps there was a link between these carvings and the idea of the sacred canoe represented by the stone platform, *marae* – an idea evoked elsewhere by the tabu places of Tanna (Bonnemaison, p. 202, this volume) and Aneityum (Aufray, p. 197, this volume). This brings us to the representation of ideas peculiar to a community; that is, the existence of cultural images.

The significance of forms

Most of what we in the West call the material forms of artistic expression have, in Vanuatu, a traditional place defined in *kastom*; that is, within the local traditional values and ceremonial performances in which they take their place. Permanent, durable works of art, as well as ephemeral or deliberately transitory productions, are revelatory signs of a deep and often hidden layer of meaning (fig. 40). Instead of reading individual works as simple signs, we can attempt to consider them as the visual transcription of images more deeply rooted – rejecting the oversimplistic interpretation that would take them for primitive imitations of something real and natural. Their authors would then no longer be confined in an isolated corner by our European artistic code, which relegates non-European artists to the role of mere imitative artisan. These guardians of the images, whose task is to reveal what they judge to be right to reveal, would then at last gain their own determining place in a global vision of the arts. In many cases, the non-figurative character of the works relegates any meaning to a secondary level, a process which is well-illustrated by the decorated mats of the north-central parts of the country, and their ornaments (Mabonlala, p. 112, this volume).

30 ▼ INTRODUCTION

Fig. 40
Ceremonial ground for a chief's funeral, with a black palm fern sculpture. Probably in the area of Port Sandwich, east Malakula. Photographed by F. Gaillard in 1887. South-east Malakula.

One might compare their codes to the relation between audible form and the rules of musical knowledge that Crowe describes (p. 147, this volume). In other cases, the figurative forms allow us to make an initial approach with which we will deal now.

Images

When Codrington rejected the idea that each 'image of native workmanship' should be considered an 'idol', which it habitually was during the colonial period, he denied that such images were representations of the sacred. According to him (and relative to the areas where he tried to gather as much information as possible, particularly the Banks Islands), the name 'idol' was only applicable to stones and arrangements of stones (Codrington 1891:171-175, 181-186). The images, for the Anglican missionary that he was, thus became figurative things of no great importance. As we have already realised, however, we should take it that every traditional image is precisely the contrary, a reference to a deep layer of signification. As material images do not, deliberately, imitate natural forms or events – what photographs do technically – their function would, rather, be to reveal some aspects, while leaving a large part in the dark. The latter belongs to a more important entity, but not necessarily a sacred one. The visible image thus only represents a partial view, a glimpse, and so opens a window onto a real world. In fact, the expressive strength of these forms that we can register visually is the only evidence that the deeper layer underpinning the social life of people exists.

When analysing the figurative sculptures, we arrive at a number of culturally coded expressions. The fact that they appear in several places and on specific occasions suggests they may be tools of cultural memory. Cultural memory is even more complex than individual memory, and serves to

Fig. 41
A shelter for a pig of high grade, photographed in a state of abandonment by Speiser between 1910 and 1912.
Vao.

organise that of individuals in relation to the experiences of social coherence. The three most typical representations of traditional images in Vanuatu are, without a doubt, the bird with outstretched wings, the pig with circle tusks and the entirely or partly human standing figure. This last seems also to contain a reference to the image of the tree, metaphor of rootedness. If we add the canoe that we find in the south to symbolise movement, our list is complete, although, apart from the case of the sacred canoe of Futuna, references to a representa-

Fig. 42
Two main elements of a grade monument. Wood, pigments. Gift of Father O'Reilly. Peterhul, Vao, northeast Malakula.
Paris, Musée national des Arts d'Afrique et d'Océanie.

tive and directly accessible depiction remain rare. On Tanna, chiefs used to use a *kava* cup called 'the canoe' in their sacred ritual. Joël Bonnemaison offers us a lucid view of the fundamental importance of two opposing metaphors, the tree and the canoe, to social discourse in Melanesia.

The bird with outstretched wings

The flying bird, either a kind of hawk found inland or a falcon, provides a complex image used in a

Fig. 43
Ceremonial house, *gamal*, for a person of high rank, with sculpture and paintings. Photographed by Speiser between 1910 and 1912.
Gaua, Banks Islands.

theatrical context in which a dancer plays the part of the bird, as on Tanna or in the northern part of the group among the Big Nambas of Malakula, and also in the form of a carved image in central and northern Vanuatu.⁹ Often the carvings are part of a ceremonial house, *nakamal*, as on Nguna, in the Shepherd Islands, or, even more often, part of a grade monument, as on Vao (figs 41, 42), Ambrym, and Gaua in the Banks Islands (fig. 43). The same type of representation, although absent in southern Vanuatu or in New Caledonia, is found from central Melanesia north as far as Papua New Guinea. Its rapid interpretation as a symbol of male aggressiveness and the spiritual forces of the chiefs in warrior societies deserves more study in relation to the special character of the societies in question and the metaphors they use. Taking into account other images of birds with extended wings, however, as well as the role of substitute or helper that may be played by certain birds and animals (figs 48, 49 and 50; Layard 1942:682, fig. 82), it would be premature to accept too generalised an explanation.

The 'men of the sky' (*iremëra*) are the lords of Tanna, the hawk (*kweriya*) their symbol. The *toka* feast is held in their honour. The bird with outstretched wings reigns on the *nakamal* rooftops of Tongoa, also symbolising the great power and the spirit of the canoes. In this wider context, one may wonder if the canoe prows (*naho*) of north-eastern Malakula (Vao, Atchin) refer to the image of the frigatebird, a bird of the open sea which steals the fish caught by other birds (fig. 51).

Pigs with tusks

W. Rodman gives us an excellent introduction to the importance of the image of the pig with curved tusks (p. 160, this volume). Pigs and pig-killing ceremonies (figs 52, 53, 54 and 55) have become extremely important throughout almost all of Vanuatu (with a few exceptions still in the south). It should be pointed out that raising pigs with curved

Fig. 44
Banks Islands.

The metaphor of the tree and the canoe[1]

Joël Bonnemaison

Islands are always fragments torn, the ends of the route, the shores of anxiety; the harmony of the world dissolves in their confined spaces, as do certainties of the soul with the breaching of borders. Once one has landed, the boat or the canoe has departed, one's tie with the inexorability of time is broken. Islands are placed without time. 'What sets an island apart from a garden is time. An island is suspended in a kind of intemporality,' writes Michel Tournier (1979:14). All that remains is a space, a restrained space, bounded by surging seas, a rare space and, as from within, an infinitely precious space, the only constant.

The canoe-people who discovered the islands of Vanuatu became the dividers of their spaces. In these broken lands, without ties, without time, they formed their simple truth: in such enclosing horizons they sank a destiny of rootedness; then in the places where they had landed and from their first forays they drew their founding signs and the primal marks of their identity.

Michel Serres (1983: 28-29), in a fabulous passage where he explores the Chinese countryside ('Chine Lise'), described himself as a peasant from the plain of La Garonne (south-west France), but by doing so, also became a sort of sailor. The sky, he said, the sky is the only way out from the plains: 'Up there, by going up. All streams upwards, like us, from the plains ... to soar vertically is the only possible direction.'

People of the Melanesian islands don't look up to the sky; they plunge their view into the ground. They are not of the plain, but from the island; not of space, but of place. Their attention digs into the ground all the more that they seek not to soar in the skies. They are the trees, those trees with deep roots piercing downwards, towards the magical bed of the world. The truth, the beliefs of these people are fastened there, not in the infinite expanse of the sky, but in the dizzying depths of place and in communion with the entrails of the earth, a belly in which they are its blood.

Melanesian places are thus not of expanse, but of depth. The tree is the metaphor of the man; he does not launch himself towards the limitless sky because his roots lead into the profundity of the earth. He who holds himself upright in his place also plunges with it into the sacred bed of the depths. Even if a tree grows vertically upwards, it is not for it to win the expanses, but to enroot itself. The expanses, it follows, have an inconsequent, almost ungraspable value; the only thing that counts is that which is vertical, and depth is greater than expanse.

As the land is punctuated with trees, so the space is sown with people-places. Implantation is without doubt the first among all Melanesian values. But if places make people, it is roads which make places. The island peoples have conserved the memories of their origins; they are as much people of voyage as of roots, people of place as much as peoples of roads.

The Melanesian metaphor expresses this duality of origin. Man is a tree, but the local group is a canoe. Man's identity is given by his place, but his canoe draws him along the roads. The canoe only exists thanks to the strength of the wood of the tree whence it is hollowed-out – it thus rested on the roots of the tree – but its destiny is to follow a route leading from place to place, from island to island. It thus possesses a mobile value, a 'wandering territory', which weaves links between implanted local groups.

From each place there are roads fanning out like rays of a star, designating collective itineraries: if man himself must remain bound to his place, he has with his group to explore the routes of his canoe. External alliances are the

Fig. 45 *Niel* ritual on Tanna. Garlands made from bananas are hung in the banyans of the *yimwayin* (*nakamal*) as offerings. Further to the bananas, pigs are given. Engraving or lithograph after A. Hagen, 1893.

cost of this, most often alliances of marriage. Neither can there be a place without roads, than can there be man without canoe. Man-tree only lives through the group-canoe, which gives him the alliances necessary to his survival and his reproduction. Each area of *kastom* (custom) is thus a segment of the route, the nexus of places, a system of trees and of canoes. Insular spaces are perceived as the sea; the aim is not to win it, but to assure the means of crossing it. The places themselves are clusters picked from islands along the routes the canoes follow. Each territory is an archipelago of places surrounded by a moving expanse

Fig. 46 Canoe race in Havannah Bay, north Efate, photographed by J.W. Lindt in 1891.

of land or sea that the canoe routes traverse as far as other island-places that are on the horizons of alliance.

The image of insular space – an island surrounded by water, which one reaches by canoe – is reproduced in the metaphors of mental organisation of space. By the force of this vision, the torn space of the archipelago is reunified: man and canoe can indeed live on an island, as if it were of no moment, as if no rupture of the connections had ever taken place, as if (to go back again to the words of Tournier) 'the pre-established harmony' were recovered. In effect, the lack of extension of a territory is compensated by its depth of place, and man can forget the finite nature of his space thanks to the infinite nature of his routes.

Melanesian society affirms itself as much as a society enrooted as of voyage: its trees are its canoes and its canoes are its trees. Melanesian territories are networks of places which are equal yet independent, but connected to pathways of alliance.

If he had not kept this initial ambiguity in the depths of his identity, man-of-the-islands might perhaps have lost his mind. These islands are in effect segments cut from a founding trajectory; should the trajectory perish, each island would revert to the absolute solitude of its original, splintered state. Melanesian society has constantly sought to keep open those links which permitted the trajectory; it has sought to alleviate the confinements of space by diversifying its territory, by enriching it with as many signs and symbols of place as was possible to invent; it has also sought to escape physical isolation by making each of its places a junction, a crossroads.

Archipelago societies are thus network-societies constructed by spaces bearing relationships, in fluid structures. They attempt to replace by culture those connections that nature does not provide, and to recreate a space of harmony and continuity in a physically ruptured universe. Perhaps the [ultimate] paradigm of an Oceanic society consists in this searching for a cultural binding of that which unites and yet separates nature; perhaps this is the only way, from within, for culture to respond to this face-to face confrontation with nature. Melanesian islands, therefore, should never be thought of merely as islands; they should be thought of as they always have been since their discovery – that is to say, as canoes.

The network-society and reticulated space

The metaphor of the tree and the canoe (figs 46, 47) is part of a wave of ideas redefining conceptions of space, which in itself has implications for conceptions of what makes society. In the traditional view of space, made up of interlacing routes, of enrootment in places which interconnect from one to another, the territories are the nexus, while space itself is a reticulated system,[2] whose links (whether more or less frail or more or less solid) are not meant to delimit the areas, but to run between them.

The reticulated space of [ni-Vanuatu] traditional society is organised on the basis of linkings of places which are as much 'paths of alliance' (Bensa and Rivierre 1982) as they are territories that succeed one another along an itinerary. This model may be seen in the 'weft of nexus' of Melanesian linguistic spaces: the 100 or 120 tongues of the archipelago do not correspond with separate [physical] linguistic areas, but to segments which cross over in chains, thus creating crisscross pathways of mutual intelligibility (Tryon 1976). Local Melanesian groups are of the same order: they are not groups enclosed by some 'frontier', but networks of little local societies in relatively constant communication one with the other, according to their proximity.

Space in traditional Melanesian society is not perceived by its divisions, nor by its limits, but by relations along the route: some routes are friendly, others are hostile. A place retains its integrity not because it is static, but from its position along the route. One understands from that just why a local group, as on Tanna, defines itself by the metaphor of the canoe, for it is the route as followed which is the definitive basis of group identity. The actual space of the canoe itself is merged with its trajectory, with the succession of end-to-end segments, making up the paths of alliance. For each segment there is a territory; that is, a nodule, a link (be it more or less stable, be it more or less weighty), but which only exists through the structural relationships maintained with the other links in the network.

Here, there is no such thing as a central place. The organisation of space, whether according to concentration of population or by 'deprived' peripheries, is a new kind of effect coming from the imposition of colonialist controls, as well as the impact of modern distributive networks of commerce and produce. Inversely, indeed, customary space axiomatically proposes that each succeeding place along the routes be the equal of all others. So that such relationships may persist, the continuity of each segment of the route remains indispensable. If one of the links snaps, should one of the places perish, the route is damaged. Every place is thus an essential complement of any other, and, therefore, its equal. A network-society can only (fully) function through the multiple connections that each of its elements maintains in successive order with the others.

If this reticulated space is a structure knit in a fluid system, or 'weft of nexus', it cannot possess a centre. By contrast, it knows its 'foundations', which are the only places representing, perhaps, in this flowing universe, some truly stabilised realities. Melanesian routes converge toward junctions where they knit with others, but they also continue on those foundation-places which have been theirs from the

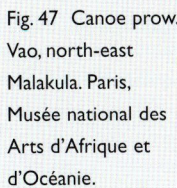

Fig. 47 Canoe prow. Vao, north-east Malakula. Paris, Musée national des Arts d'Afrique et d'Océanie.

▶ ▶ ▶ ▶

THE METAPHOR OF THE TREE AND THE CANOE ▼ 37

beginning. These departure points hold, in themselves, the fundamental principles of origin. Differing from a *central-place* (which would cause the rest of a structure to converge towards it), a *foundation-place* by contrast launches outwards, toward the exterior, those forces which have welled-up within it. Far from creating peripheries, it creates more places further away, which are all 'the same', which enchain and possess their own powers, or a portion of the founding powers. The original or 'primordial' place, as Elaide (1952) calls it, endows [new] spaces from within itself, and quickens all that entire [and networked] space with its [fundamental] animation.

The Melanesian route of alliances proceeds from the nearby to the nearby. The Melanesian canoe's destiny is to extend its alliance-relationships to the infinite, along the routes its territories indicate. This horizon does not buckle back upon itself: the links implied are literally without end.

Such a perception of space, understood as [potential] routes, engenders the network-society. This kind of society comes into being only because it depends upon, and is in harmony with, a reticulated space. Seizing that space does not give, here, a 'product': on the contrary, it represents that which had founded society and had let it reproduce itself. In other words, as Paul-Levy and Segaud write (1983: 19), 'The spatial configurations are not merely the products, but also the producers of social systems; or, let us say, they occupy not only the position of effect, but also that of cause.'

Melanesian social systems draw their coherence from a fertile harmonisation with their spatial systems In this model, forms of social and spatial organisation are in constant interaction.

This reticulated space, tied to a network geography, corresponds well with territorial societies organised on linkage principles, as described elsewhere by Claude Raffestin in his *Géographie du pouvoir* (1980). Here, the territory is a place where social unity is based on particular links with space, connected with others by a proximity principle.

Doubtless the Melanesian network-model may be applied to other insular societies, but to go beyond that, it is not without universal dimensions. The world of the 'new modernity', that of [instant] communication networks, may give rise to new societies in our own Western world, being articulated by fluid relations of proximity, which will burst the compact [physical] frontiers inherited from the 19th century. The renewal of interest in notions of territory – which seems today to be found among architects, anthropologists (Paul-Levy and Segaud 1983) and geographers (Raffestin 1980, Ferrier 1982, Maurel 1984) – indicates the presence of some front-runners. There can be no doubt that here is another way of thinking about space, and following from that, about models of society.

'We are the beginning of the world …' (Tanna)

Tanna was the last island where I worked, but when I arrived there the *kastom* men told me, pretty much in these words: 'You're not at the end. You're only starting, because Tanna is the island of commencements (*stamba*, 'the seat'), it is the beginning of all *kastom* routes.'

The people of the island would not agree that they were at the centre of the world, but only at its debut. Doubtless Tanna *kastom* is not the paradigmatic last-word on the other cultures, but on this island the model of the geographic network-society has crystallised in a very pure manner. That led me to think my work would be incomplete were it not followed-up by a plunge into one of the most significant local societies.

The 'cultural wars' that have raged on this island for more than a century have, as well, made this society especially emblematic. The conflict of *Kastom* and Modernity, of a Christian god and the gods of the traditional pantheon, of Protestant pastors in face of the John Frum movement, of the revival of customary ways – all this concentrated on a grand scale, and in a compact space, the cultural clashes that had come as a shock to those societies which made up Oceania.

---

1. These are the final pages (pp. 518-523) of book 1 of *Les fondements d'une indentité: territoire, histoire et société dans l'archipel de Vanuatu (Mélanésie)*. For more details, see Bonnemaison 1986b in the bibliography. The work was translated by Peter Crowe, and published in *Pacific Arts* 9 & 10, July 1994, pp. 21-24.

2. The term 'reticulated space' was first used by the logician-philosopher, G. Simondon, in a book which came out in 1969, *Du mode d'existence des objets techniques*. Gilles Sautier drew my attention to it.

Fig. 48

tusks is a specialty of central and northern Vanuatu; it does not exist in the south. There, the turtle appears to have played a similar ceremonial and symbolic role. In fact, raising pigs whose lower tusks form a circle is considered an art form in itself – a transformation of biological life. When the tusks complete their first circle – that is, when the tip penetrates the jaw – the pig takes a significant step up in the hierarchy of symbolic values, for pigs too go through grades. The breeders try to ensure that their pigs, which are fed on premasticated food, produce a pair of tusks, each of which completes up to two full circles (fig. 56). In West Santo the tradition is taken even further; they obtain two

Fig. 48
Nombuav'kor, chiefly forehead band. Carving of woven pandanus, cut pigs' canine teeth, tortoiseshell. May represent the cardinal honeyeater (*Myzomela cardinalis*). Erromango.
Nouméa, Musée territorial de Nouvelle-Calédonie.

Fig. 49
Flying fox made from overmodelled fibres, collected by Kal Muller, 1970, from the interior of southern Malakula. Paris, Musée national des Arts d'Afrique et d'Océanie.

Fig. 50
Bird made from overmodelled fibres, collected around 1930. South Malakula. Paris, Musée national des Arts d'Afrique et d'Océanie.

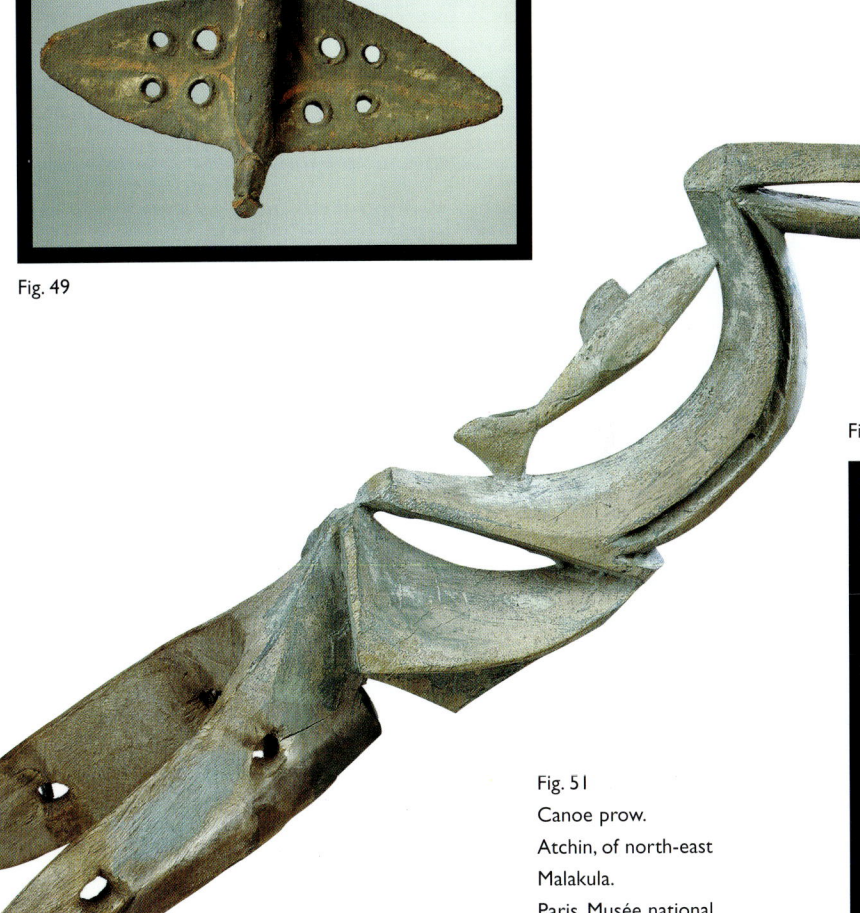

Fig. 49

Fig. 50

Fig. 51
Canoe prow.
Atchin, of north-east Malakula.
Paris, Musée national des Arts d'Afrique et d'Océanie.

THE ARTS OF VANUATU ▼ 39

Fig. 52
Club for pig-killing ceremonies.
Ambrym Island?
Zürich, Museum Rietberg.

parallel pairs of curved tusks, one pair on the left side and the other on the right side of the lower jaw.

Effigies of circle-tusked pigs are fairly rare and found principally on kava bowls reserved for the ceremonies of chiefs and *kastom* specialists in northeast Malakula and west Ambae. On the other hand, there are numerous representations of jaws with curved teeth, especially if we include drawings of them. It is an easy step from tusks entering the jaw to the design of an open double arch, if there is a pair of them, and this was confirmed by local specialists in 1994 in the case of designs on pottery belonging to a Santo chief (figs 57, 58). We can also confirm Speiser's interpretation of a characteristic shape on Banks Islands grade monuments (fig. 59). Furthermore, real pig's jaws and teeth can be incorporated into a work, either simply in the form of a row or pile of jawbones or teeth, or in the hands of a *rambaramp* (figs 1, 60, 66), or inserted into a mask (fig. 61) or a modelled skull (fig. 62), or even, in a more direct fashion, as an ornament worn by a human being or a sculpture. As a general rule, they indicate the social status of each individual – the work's sponsor or the person represented by it – and show off the number of pigs presented or killed at the corresponding ceremonies.

The turtle

Our knowledge is very imprecise about the ceremonial role formerly played by sacred turtles in the chiefdoms of the southern islands, though we do know it was important. We do not know yet if they were there represented in material form, except for sand-drawings on Tanna. Turtle shell seems to have had a similar role, as ornament, to pig's tusks in the north. On Tanna, the turtle preceded the fat, hairless pig as the most important symbol in the alliance system. The turtle would also be shared on Tanna into five pieces; four would be sent off along paths of alliance, the shell remaining in the place where the turtle was cooked. The chiefs ate the head. There was a turtle-skull cult (Bonnemaison 1979) reminiscent of the cult of the circle-tusked pig.

The shark

From a certain point of view, the shark (fig. 63) occupies in Vanuatu the metaphorical position that

Fig. 53
Pig-killing club, collected by Speiser between 1910 and 1912.
South Malakula.
Basel, Museum für Völkerkunde.

Figs 54, 55
Pig-killing club, collected by Speiser between 1910 and 1912.
Ambrym.
Basel, Museum für Völkerkunde.

Fig. 57
Pottery with chiefly ornament, collected by Speiser between 1910 and 1912.
Pespia, west Santo.
Basel, Museum für Völkerkunde.

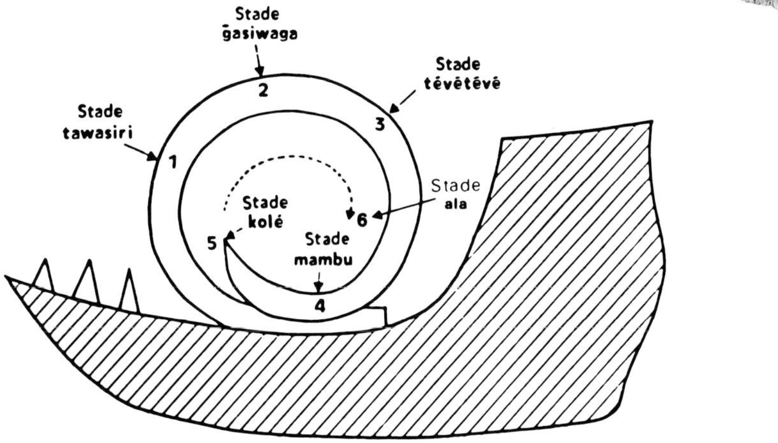

Fig. 56 A ceremonial pig's curved tooth, and the successive growth stages associated with it. North-east Ambae). After Bonnemaison, 1986b:300.

1 *Tawasiri*: beginning of pig tusk growth curve.
2 *Gasiwaga*: tusks begin to pierce the cheek.
3 *Tévétévé*: tusks inside the mouth approach the lower jaw.
4 *Mambu*: tusks slide onto the lower jaw.
5 *Kolé*: tusks begin a second circle inside the first one.
6 *Ala*: tusks complete, or almost complete, the second circle.

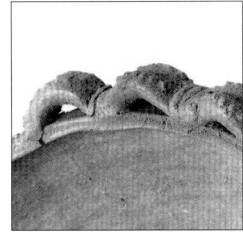

Fig. 58
Detail of figure 57.

THE ARTS OF VANUATU ▼ 41

Fig. 59
Grade sculptures representing the pigs' jaws offered at ceremonies, photographed by Speiser between 1910 and 1912. Vanua Lava, Banks Islands.

Fig. 60
Rare *rambaramp* with two overmodelled skulls. South Malakula. La Rochelle, Musées d'Histoire naturelle et d'Ethnographie.

belongs to the crocodile from the Solomon Islands to Papua New Guinea. Its aggressiveness marks it as a ferocious aquatic animal. It is also the messenger of the ancestral underworld and thus, by extension, of the undersea world. The shark can function in this context as a sort of bridge between the two modes of existence; it lacks, however, the crocodile's ability to live both on land and in the water, though

Fig. 61
Headpiece of mask-helmet with pig's tusks, representing Nevimbumbao and her son Sasndaliep, who is hiding behind the ear.
South West Bay, south Malakula.
Paris, Musée national des Arts d'Afrique et d'Océanie.

Fig. 62
Overmodelled skull, collected by Speiser between 1910 and 1912.
South Malakula.
Basel, Museum für Völkerkunde.

THE ARTS OF VANUATU ▼ 43

Fig. 63
Animal mask, collected by Speiser between 1910 and 1912.
Malakula.
Basel, Museum für Völkerkunde.

it is said to be linked to certain pigs in some instances.

The lizard

Land reptiles play a considerable part throughout Melanesia. They seem predestined by their natural shape and their rapid movements to serve as a second skin for ancestral beings, as a costume for them when they wish to visit living men. But there are not many such direct depictions of them in Vanuatu (fig. 64).

Plant motifs

While true yams (*Dioscorea alata*) play a fundamental role in many ceremonies, they are rarely represented in carvings. We should, however, at least mention their importance in sand-drawings.

We can only speculate on the role that the pandanus family, and especially its edible fruits, may have played before the arrival of the Europeans and the subsequent destabilisation of the traditional economic system. The use of breadfruit reportedly declined. Judging by a simply formal analogy, a fairly well-known figurative element may perhaps have alluded to the use of these plants (cf. Huffman, pp. 228 and 234, this volume). Many plants were used for ceremonial purposes, including the cordylines (*nangaria* in Bislama) and the *Cycas* (cycad) palms (*namwele*), the latter often associated with death. Local informants have long insisted on the importance of a whole range of more or less colourful plants, but unfortunately little systematic research has been carried out. A whole symbolic language remains to be discovered through the co-ordination of linguistics, botany, cultural geography, and the anthropology of knowledge and aesthetics.

The human figure

Let us come back to the human figure. If we look at the works in detail, our list certainly needs some refining. Standing figures, for example, cover a vast range, from the Banks Islands grade monuments (fig. 65) to the fascinating memorial figures, the *rambaramp*, of south and central Malakula (figs 60, 66). According to Layard (1928:207), referring to information gathered in 1915, these are a direct representation of the body of the dead man, at the first mourning ceremonies, personalised by placing on it the modelled head of the dead man. This image, with its rather public purpose, would have been brought ritually to the ceremonial house after a period in which the body was kept in the dead man's house. Alongside the standing figures, carved out of wood, with their static frontality, there is a series of sculptures which are more dynamic, either

Fig. 64
Mask of *ngulong* type, with lizard, collected by Speiser between 1910 and 1912.
Ambrym.
Basel, Museum für Völkerkunde.

Fig. 65
Female grade sculpture.
Fern tree.
Banks Islands.
Paris, Musée de l'Homme.

because the figure is modelled and thus less stark (figs 67-70), or because it transports us into another domain. The standing slit-gong of Ambrym takes on life as a figure through the sound it can emit. It may, according to M. Patterson, embody the symbolic being of the dead grandfather, the ancestor of the lineage. The Ambrym slit-gong has today become a sort of typical image of Vanuatu, like the Pentecost Jump – clichés known almost around the globe as a result of tourist advertising.

The squatting human figure is the last very complex subject (fig. 71). It is well-known from Malakula sand-drawings (Deacon 1934b; Layard 1942: 669-677), as well as from drawings from the Banks and Maewo. It is hard to assess its importance. Layard demonstrates relations, on the formal level, with forms of flying foxes, and in the case of Malakula he suggests a link between this type of representation and the image of the great guardian spirit of the world of the dead. Furthermore, Rivers (1914:96-129) places the Banks Islands drawings, especially those of Mere, in the context of the *tamate liwoa* society.

Finally, the list of essential images should certainly include the figures of spirit beings (fig. 72). Here we venture into the ritual and social context. According to the concept ni-Vanuatu have of *kastom* matters, such details can only be seriously discussed by the holders of 'copyright' in such matters. Otherwise, there is the risk of infringing the rights of a third party and finding that one has broken the rules. The control of rights over traditional knowledge is a serious matter, which must be meticulously observed when written records are being made, or photographs taken.

For these same reasons, we will not comment on some of the most accomplished examples of expressive forms, the carved stones supposedly used in pig magic (and formerly turtle magic). Stones can facilitate exchanges, but also 'eat up the pigs', according to the special characteristics of the stone and its master's knowledge. There are links here between several fundamental aspects: between society and its living symbol of patrimonial goods and, vice versa, between control of the capital necessary for any ceremony and the perpetuation of society.

Where knowledge of origins, of how to produce and perform, is concerned, it is clear that tradition

Fig. 66
Funerary effigy, *rambaramp*. Gift from François (after 1893). South Malakula. Paris, Musée de l'Homme.

Fig. 67
Overmodelled and painted figurine, formerly from the collection of James Hooper. South Malakula. Paris, Musée national des Arts d'Afrique et d'Océanie

Fig. 68
Carved post with human figure.
Ambrym.
Bordeaux, Musée d'Aquitaine

Fig. 69
Headpiece with modelled seated figure.
Fern tree.
South Malakula.
Paris, Musée national des Arts d'Afrique et d'Océanie.

Fig. 70
Seated human figure, perhaps representing Temes-Sump-Sump.
South Malakula.
Paris, Musée national des Arts d'Afrique et d'Océanie.

Fig. 69

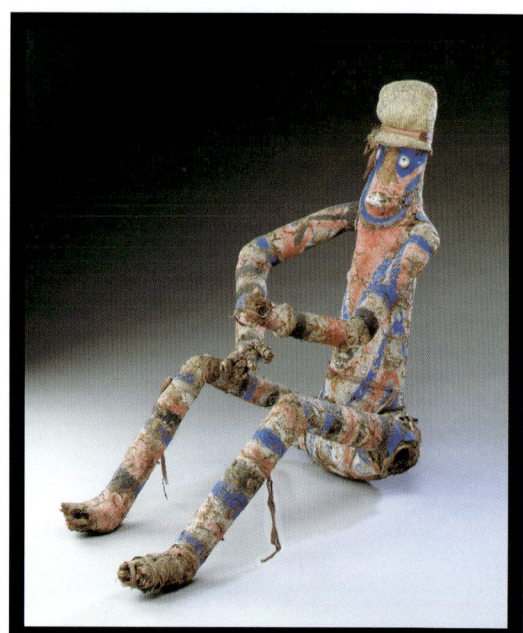

Fig. 70

Fig. 71
Painted grade board.
Gaua, Banks Islands.
Basel, Museum für Völkerkunde.

is much more vital today than the hurried visitor is able to see. This certainly applies to knowledge of the great traditional images. On the other hand, for the 'minor arts' that help transmit important signs, such as body ornaments and tattoos (fig. 46), there is an increasing danger that they will be lost. For this reason, the exhibition organisers have chosen preferably small but fine and delicate objects: witness the series of dishes, ear ornaments, women's belts, combs, pestles, knives and flutes (cf. pp. 122, 143, 152, 206, 234, and 240, this volume).

From canonical form to stylisation

We have already seen that Melanesians have a highly developed taste for formalised expression, whether in dance or the spoken word, in drawing or sculpture. What are stylised by individuals, always in the context of their audience (that is, their local

Fig. 72
Face mask, *n'dem nabwikai*.
South-central Malakula.
Nouméa, Musée territorial de Nouvelle-Calédonie.

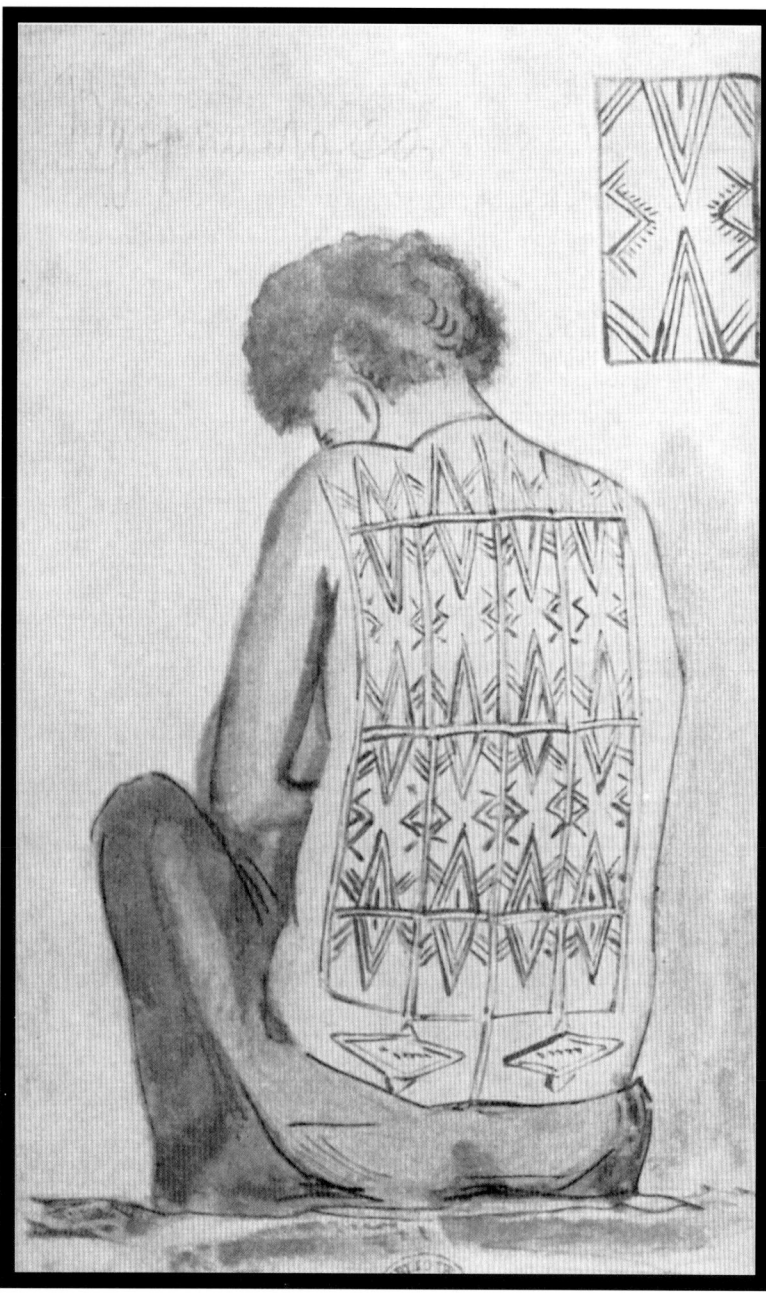

Fig. 73
Woman with tattooed back. Drawing (done in 1879) from Mikloucho-Maclay 1950-1954, vol. 5. Vanua Lava, Banks Islands.

society), are forms made canonical by virtue of their ritual role (or, more broadly, their ceremonial role in the case of works of a public nature orchestrated by the grade societies). Apart from the geographical distribution of the principal types of secondary objects and images, we can attempt, on the basis of the form given to typical works, to define purely stylistic areas; this is, in particular, valid for Malakula, with its offshore islands to the north, north-east and south, and Ambrym, south Pentecost, Ambae and Malo, as well as the Banks Islands.

It is fairly easy to see that these areas correspond roughly to certain areas of a social network or linguistic network type. We are particularly concerned here with the different styles of sculpture in the south-west, north-east and south-east of Malakula, and in the west or north of Ambrym, not forgetting to compare them with the style of south-east Ambrym, as is clear from Huffman's description of ceremonial exchanges of objects and copyright (p. 184, this volume). The study of relations between languages may provide us with key elements for a better grasp of the origin of stylistic differentiations. In choosing linguistic data as our point of departure, we merely acknowledge that the links between the visual means of expression and those of language and words are very strong, but also that they can transcend them.

Stylistic chains and linguistic chains

Having said this, we will take care not to affiliate plastic works and the texts of oral tradition too readily. I have deliberately chosen the widely used term 'affiliation' to label what we want to avoid, because we really must strike a perfect balance between the material form of visual image and the metaphor evoked by the oral text. The sculpture no more depends on its text than any text remembering a ritual depends on the works largely used in the same context.

Furthermore, the linguists use the very simple image of the chain to explain why any model based on maps that use the far too rigid notion, at least in Melanesia, of cultural borderlines (Tryon 1976, and this volume, p. 172; Bonnemaison 1986b:151-156), can never do justice to the social reality. This metaphor has the attractive advantage of simplicity (the links as basic elements appear clearly drawn and complete in themselves) and complexity (each link overlaps on both sides a partial field or space which is also enclosed by the next link). As Tryon explains (p. 172, this volume), linguistic chains do not always find their direct equivalent in the actualised systems of exchange – this can easily be verified on the maps provided by Tryon (fig. 172) and Huffman (fig. 213). These systems are the results of a lived and active reality in the present, rooted in a historic tradition whose beginning and duration we often do not know exactly. As for linguistic relations, they reflect a different reality, whether it is anterior, frozen as a result of the inherent conservatism of every language in the course of preceding generations, or whether it has only been partially documented, because in their analyses linguists prefer the spoken language and everyday vocabulary to the words of the ceremonial or ritual language. It is quite possible that the two elements are cumulated. The fact that exchange networks and linguistic chains often differ considerably, at least in central Vanuatu, suggests such a model.

This rapid overview will, I hope, enable readers to take better advantage of what the assembled texts have to offer. Many thanks to the authors, on behalf of the editorial team. By explaining and illustrating many points for us with real and fascinating detail, they have contributed to this first collective awakening to the arts of Vanuatu.

Fig. 74
Figure made from coral tuff.
Perhaps Epi.
Nouméa, Musée territorial de Nouvelle-Calédonie.

Chapter 1
Languages and people – an early history

The Peopling of Oceania: the Linguistic Evidence

Darrell Tryon

Within the region known as Oceania, that area of the Pacific to the east of and including the great island of New Guinea, there are some 1800 different languages spoken today. This represents more than 25 per cent of all of the world's languages.

Oceania is divided into three main areas, thus:
1. Melanesia: Papua New Guinea, the Solomon Islands, Vanuatu, New Caledonia and Fiji.
2. Polynesia: Tonga, Wallis, Futuna, Samoa, Tuvalu, Cook Islands, French Polynesia, Hawai'i and New Zealand.
3. Micronesia: Guam and the Marianas, Yap, Belau, the Caroline Islands (Federated States of Micronesia), the Marshall Islands and Kiribati.

All of the languages of Oceania belong to two great language families, the Austronesian and the Papuan. On the margin of this area, the languages of Australia, some 200 to 300, are members of yet another family, the Australian. (It has not been conclusively established, however, that the Aboriginal languages of Tasmania, extinct since 1877, are genetically related to the Australian languages).

The Papuan languages occupy nearly all of the great island of New Guinea, except for some coastal areas. Papuan languages are also spoken in northern Halmahera, and in Eastern Indonesia on Alor and Pantar and parts of Timor. On the eastern side of the great island of New Guinea, Papuan languages are spoken in parts of New Britain, New Ireland, Bougainville, and scattered parts of the Solomon Islands as far south-east as the Santa Cruz group. According to Wurm (1982:13), there are 741 known Papuan languages. The Papuan languages are unrelated to any other language family, and it is not even certain that they are all genetically related to each other, although it appears that many of them are members of a single language subgroup, known to many as the Trans-New Guinea Phylum (Wurm 1982, Foley 1986).

The Austronesian family of languages, of which the languages of Vanuatu are members, is arguably the largest language family in the world, second only to the Indo-European family in geographical extent. It is estimated (Tryon 1995:6) that there are roughly 1200 Austronesian languages today, spoken by a total of around 270 million people. All but about 2 million of these people live west of a line north-south at about 130°E longitude, extending from just west of the Caroline Islands to just east of the Bird's Head on the island of New Guinea (see fig. 76). On either side of the north-south line just described there are more than 500 languages spoken.

The Austronesian languages extend from Madagascar in the west (actually, the furthest point west is Mayotte in the Comoros) to Easter Island in the eastern Pacific, a distance of some 15 000 kilometres. Austronesian languages are spoken not only in Madagascar, but also in most of Malaysia, Singapore and Indonesia (with the exception of most parts of Irian Jaya, North Halmahera, Alor and Pantar and East Timor, where many Papuan languages are spoken). They are spoken in parts of southern Vietnam and Cambodia, in Taiwan, and throughout the Philippines. Further to the east they are spoken in the coastal areas of Papua New Guinea (but not generally the interior), in New Britain and New Ireland, and right down the Melanesian chain through the Solomons and Vanuatu, as far as New Caledonia and Fiji. From there they extend eastwards to include all of the languages of Polynesia and northwards to take in all of the languages of Micronesia. Austronesian languages are also reported in the Mergui Archipelago of the coast of Myanmar (Burma), in the Andaman Islands, and on Hainan Island in southern China.

Language distribution

The higher-order subgrouping of the Austronesian languages remains controversial. The grouping in the box below is based on the work of Robert Blust (1977, 1978, 1982).

The original homeland of the Austronesians is widely considered to be the island of Taiwan (Formosa). This island was formerly inhabited solely by Austronesian speakers. As a consequence of continued Chinese settlement from mainland China since the 17th century, however, the Austronesian languages of Taiwan today are largely confined to the mountainous interior of the island. The Formosan languages are internally diverse, considered by most scholars to fall into three highest-order subgroups, Atayalic, Tsouic and Paiwanic. These three subgroups enjoy coordinate status with a single other highest-order subgroup, Malayo-Polynesian, which includes all of the Austronesian languages spoken outside Taiwan.

The Western subgroup (WMP) is not well-established. At present it consists of all of the languages of the Philippines, as well as the Indonesian islands of Sumatra, Java, Madura, Bali, Lombok and, to their north-west, Kalimantan (Borneo). Also included are the Malay Peninsula (with the exception of a few Mon-Khmer languages in the interior of Malaysia), and the Chamic languages of Vietnam and Cambodia. Added to these are the language of Madagascar and two languages of Oceania, Chamorro (Mariana Islands) and Palau (Western

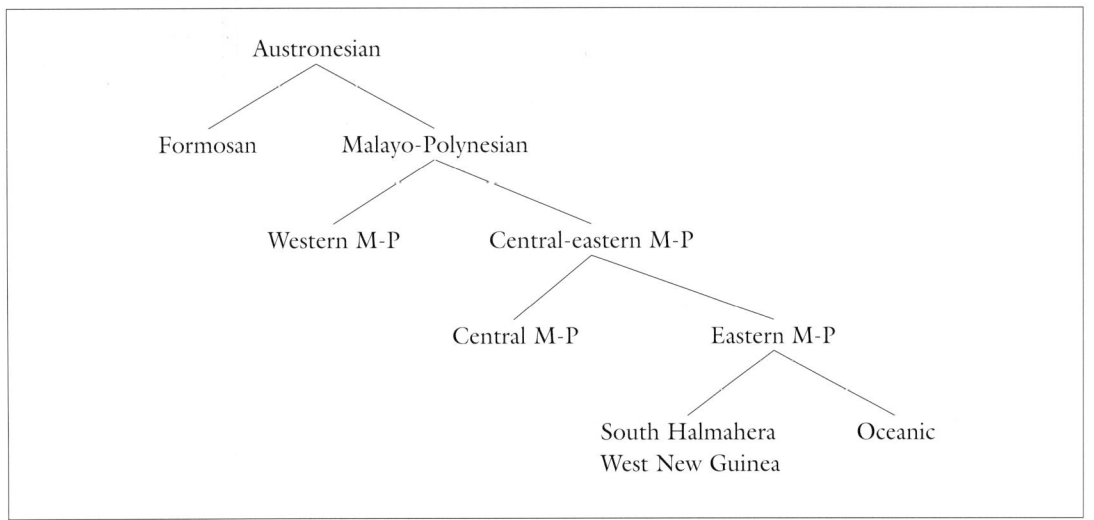

Fig. 75 Austronesian languages.

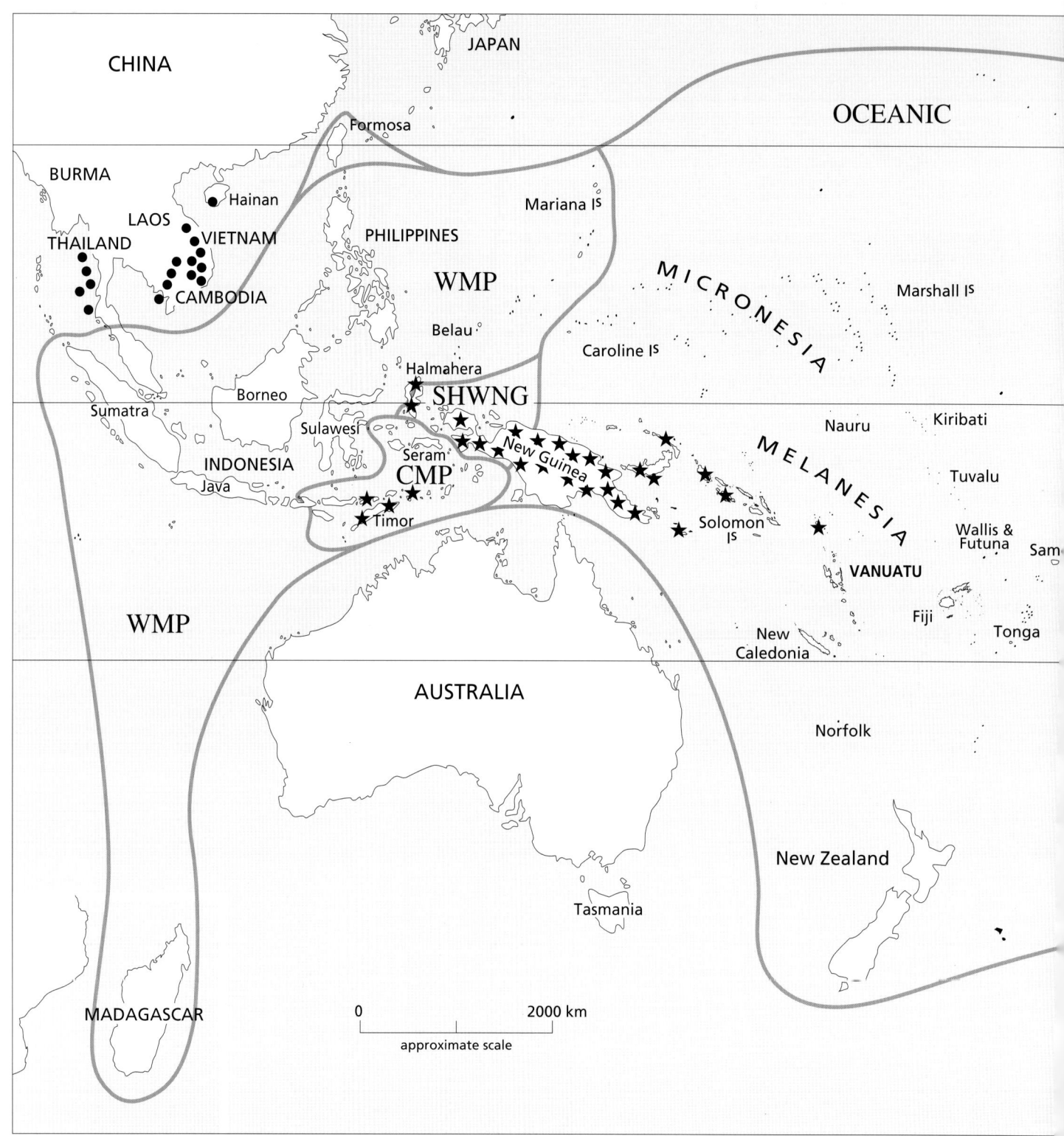

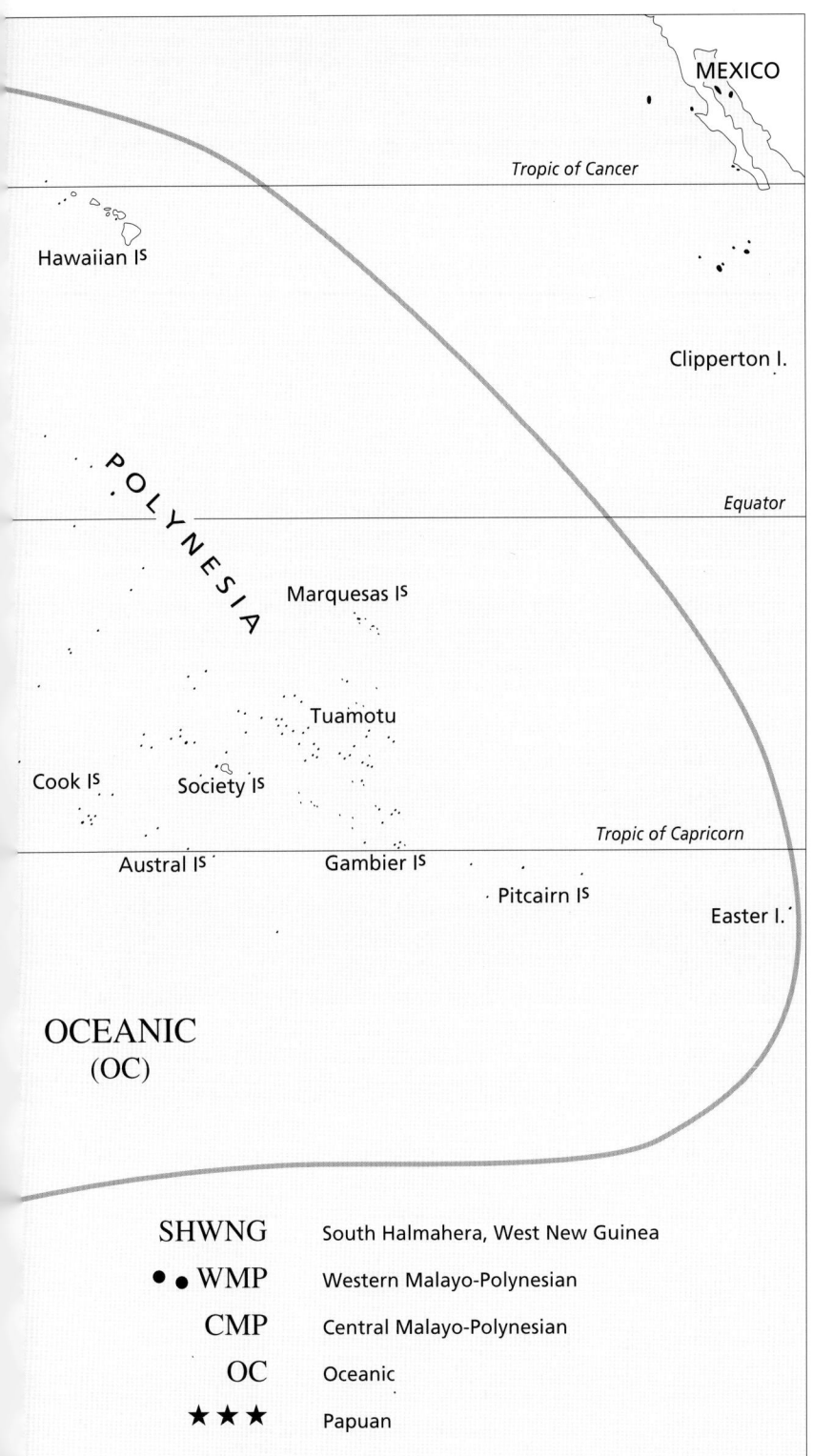

Fig. 76 Map of Austronesian languages from Easter Island to Madagascar.

Carolines), believed to have originated in the Philippines-Indonesia area.

The Central-Eastern subgroup of Austronesian (CEMP; see fig. 75) consists of the languages of Eastern Indonesia, namely the Lesser Sunda Islands (Nusa Tenggura), the Moluccas, and the coastal regions of Irian Jaya, as well as the Oceanic subgroup discussed in more detail below. The Austronesian languages of Eastern Indonesia are extremely diverse and even today their inter-relationships are not well-established. Evidence has been adduced, however, which would separate the Austronesian languages of South Halmahera and West New Guinea (SHWNG) from the other languages of Eastern Indonesia.

The huge Oceanic subgroup of the Austronesian languages (OC) lies to the east of a north-south line drawn about 130°E longitude (see fig. 76). It begins on the great island of New Guinea and extends eastwards right across Oceania. The Oceanic languages are rather different from their western relatives, for while they number more than 500, they have no more than 2 million speakers. Melanesia exhibits one of the highest linguistic densities in the world, in terms of number of languages relative to total population, with an average of a little more than 3000 speakers per language. Indeed, in Vanuatu this ratio is even higher, with a ratio of one language per 1500 persons.

The higher-order classification of the Oceanic languages can still only be regarded as tentative, especially with regard to those of Melanesia. Some scholars distinguish three higher-level subgroups:

1. A large Western Oceanic subgroup, consisting of all the Austronesian languages of Papua New Guinea, including New Ireland, New Britain and Bougainville, plus the Austronesian languages of the Western Solomons as far south-east as Bughotu on the island of Santa Isabel.
2. An Admiralties group, consisting of the languages of the Admiralty Islands to the north of the island of New Guinea.
3. A Central-Eastern Oceanic subgroup, consisting of the remaining Austronesian languages of Melanesia, together with those of Polynesia and Micronesia.

In Papua New Guinea, there are an estimated 220 distinct Austronesian languages. As with Irian Jaya, the Austronesian languages are basically limited to coastal areas, the interior of the island being occupied by Papuan speakers. Austronesian languages extend in patches along the north coast and also along the south-east coast of Papua as far west as Cape Possession, about 150 kilometres west of Port Moresby. They are also found in the north-east, in the Sepik, Morobe and Madang areas, and on the offshore islands. They are also spoken in parts of New Britain, New Ireland and Bougainville. The Admiralty Islands to the north of Papua New Guinea also host a large number of Austronesian languages.

In the Solomon islands, south-east of Papua New Guinea, there are sixty-two languages spoken, fifty-seven of which are Austronesian, the remainder Papuan. A number of Polynesian languages (also known as Polynesian Outliers) are spoken in the Solomons, namely Luangiua (Ontong Java), Sikaiana, Rennell-Bellona, Pileni, Tikopian and Anutan. These languages, the result of back migrations from Polynesia in the last 600 to 800 years, are spoken over a wide area of island Melanesia, from Papua New Guinea to New Caledonia. At the same time, there are a number of Papuan languages spoken in the Solomons, dotted along the chain from Vella Lavella in the north-west to the Santa Cruz group in the south-east. The Santa Cruz group marks to easternmost limit of the Papuan languages.

Further to the south-east lies Vanuatu, where more than 100 Austronesian languages are spoken by a population of approximately 150 000. All of the languages of the northern and central islands are members of a single subgroup. The languages of Erromango, Tanna and Aneityum also form a single subgroup, whose closest relatives are found in northern and central Vanuatu. There are three Polynesian languages spoken in Vanuatu: Emae, Mele-Fila and Futuna-Aniwa.

In New Caledonia, at the end of the Melanesian chain, there are some twenty-five languages spoken by an indigenous population of approximately 45 000. The languages of New Caledonia and the Loyalty Islands form a single subgroup, even though they are internally rather diverse. There is one Polynesian language, West Uvean, spoken in New Caledonia, on Ouvea in the Loyalty Islands.

Fig. 77
For peopling Oceania, canoes of different types were used. This single-outrigger canoe was photographed by Speiser between 1910 and 1912. Ureparapara, Banks Islands.

In island Melanesia the ratio of languages to numbers of speakers is spectacularly high, while in Fiji, Polynesia and Micronesia, languages often extend over a number of neighbouring islands, making for relatively large speech communities. The Fijian dialects, considered by many to constitute two distinct languages, have more than 200 000 speakers.

Polynesia covers a vast area in the central and eastern Pacific. The Polynesian Triangle, as it is commonly known, is bounded by Hawai'i, Easter Island and New Zealand. The sixteen languages of Triangle Polynesia belong to a well-defined subgroup, which also contains the Outliers referred to above. The Polynesian languages have their nearest relatives in south-eastern Melanesia, and almost certainly developed their distinctive characteristics during a period of isolation in the Fiji-Tonga area. The Polynesian languages fall into two major subgroups, Tongic (Tongan and Niuean) and Nuclear Polynesian (the remaining Polynesian languages).

The languages of Micronesia are spoken on a multitude of tiny islands in an area which lies to the north of Melanesia, between the Philippines and Triangle Polynesia. There are some twelve to fifteen Micronesian languages, depending on the distinguishing criteria used. The Micronesian languages, with the exception of Chamorro (Guam) and

Palauan (Belau), discussed above, are members of the Oceanic subgroup.

Settlement and migrations

The first Austronesians are thought to have originated in the South China area. Some of their number moved off the Asian mainland about 5000 to 6000 years ago and settled on the island of Taiwan, where they remained relatively undisturbed until Chinese migrations there during the 17th century. As discussed above, the aboriginal languages of Taiwan constitute three of the four first-order subgroups of Austronesian. The linguistic evidence has made them prime candidates for Austronesian homeland status, based on the principle that the centre of greatest linguistic diversity is likely to be the major dispersal point. It should be added that an earlier Austronesian presence in China is indicated by evidence from material culture, and that no linguistic traces of the Austronesians in China remain today.

The Austronesian languages outside Taiwan are considered to be members of a single first-order subgroup called Malayo-Polynesian. Members of this subgroup moved south from Taiwan to the Philippines and eventually spread right through that archipelago. From the Philippines, one group apparently moved south-west, through Borneo, and subsequently Sumatra and Java, with branches penetrating the Malay Peninsula and eastern parts of Indochina, Vietnam and Cambodia. A second migration from the Philippines carried the Austronesians south, first probably to northern Sulawesi. From there they are believed to have followed two paths. One would have moved south through Sulawesi and into the Ceram-Ambon area and Timor. The other was directed towards southern Halmahera and Irian Jaya, and along the north coast of the great island of New Guinea. It is believed that the Austronesians reached Irian Jaya about 2500 BC.

Apart from the migrations discussed above, there were evidently numerous and more-or-less continuous smaller-scale migrations crisscrossing the Austronesian-speaking area to the west of the island of New Guinea, especially in the Philippines and western Indonesia. In this context, it is noteworthy that the large island of Madagascar, off the east coast of Africa, was settled by an Austronesian migration from south-eastern Borneo, via Sumatra, probably about 1300 years ago.

Speakers of what were to become the Oceanic languages probably moved from the Halmahera-Irian Jaya area, passing along the northern coast of Papua New Guinea before settling in the New Britain-New Ireland area around 2000 BC.

Migrations subsequently radiated from the New Britain-New Ireland area into the Pacific. Austronesian speakers moved relatively quickly south-east, making their way right through the Melanesian chain, the Solomon Islands, Vanuatu and New Caledonia, reaching Fiji about 1000 BC. Incidentally, the earliest settlement in Vanuatu, with sites attested on Malo and Efate, is reckoned to have taken place about 1200 BC, or more than 3000 years ago.

A number of additional migrations are attested a little later, the major one being the gradual spread of the languages of the Western Oceanic subgroup of Austronesian (see above) across much of Papua New Guinea and as far south-east as the island of Santa Isabel in the Solomon Islands. This spread also included later moves westwards to the north and north-east coast of the mainland of Papua New Guinea, and moves south to various parts of the coast of the main island, right around to the Papuan Gulf on the south coast. Another set of migrations is believed to have originated in northern-central Vanuatu. One moved north, spreading the Austronesian languages throughout Micronesia, where there is evidence of an east to west spread. Another moved south-east to the Fiji group. From that area, after a period of consolidation, the Polynesian languages evolved, moving east from the Tonga-Niue area sometime after 1000 BC.

The migration history of the Polynesians has been fairly unequivocally established over the past thirty years. From the Tonga area, the Polynesians spread first to the Samoas and the Tokelau group (Spriggs and Anderson 1993). From Samoa, the Polynesian languages moved eastwards, to the Marquesas (AD 300 to 600), the Society Islands and the Tuamotu Archipelago (AD 750), Mangareva (AD 800) and Easter Island (AD 700 to 800?). Hawai'i (AD 650) was settled from the Marquesas, while from the Society Islands the Polynesian languages found their way to the Cook Islands (AD 900) and finally to far-off New Zealand (AD 1000 to 1400). Rapanui, the language of Easter Island, is still regarded as problematic, for while it is widely recognised as the first to break away from the languages east of Samoa, details of its development are still uncertain.

One further remark concerns the Polynesian Outliers. These are Polynesian languages that originated from movements from Polynesia and that have drifted westwards into parts of Melanesia and Micronesia during the past thousand years or so (AD 1000 to 1400).

The Initial Colonisation of Vanuatu

Paul Gorecki

Archaeological evidence found from sites throughout the Pacific Islands clearly indicates that the ultimate origin of the island societies lies somewhere in South-East Asia (Bellwood 1978, 1985). It is from there that people first moved eastward across open seas to what is now the island of New Guinea, and then, over many millennia, gradually colonised the rest of what is now Melanesia and Polynesia.

After thirty years of archaeological investigation in most Melanesian archipelagos, including Vanuatu, we are now in a better position to understand not only some of the mechanisms involved in that colonisation, but also some of the major difficulties that will always hinder this understanding.

Melanesia could be seen as a region of natural catastrophes designed to upset the archaeologist. Being on the collision course between two major continental plates, the region is subject to tectonic uplift and subsidence, to volcanic eruptions, earthquakes, tidal waves and landslides. And Vanuatu has not escaped these events (for example, Eissen et al. 1994). To cap all this, the end of the last glaciation some 10 000 years ago caused the sea to rise, permanently submerging a substantial landmass that had been occupied by humans for milleniums.

All these events result in constant landscape change, still dynamic and not at all conducive to the preservation of ancient archaeological sites (see Enright and Gosden 1991). This is particularly serious along coastal belts, precisely where we think most of the early sites indicating initial colonisation would be located. Therefore, current coasts are young and not necessary reflective of topographic conditions at the time of first settlement. Exceptions to this general pattern are areas where, because of tectonic activity, ancient coastlines are uplifted and preserved.

It is precisely in this type of landscape that is found the earliest evidence of human colonisation of Melanesia. Along the uplifting northern coast of the island of New Guinea, near the Irian Jaya border, a rock shelter excavated by me was first occupied some 35 000 years ago. Further east, on the Huon Peninsula, an open site was occupied about 40 000 years ago (Groube et al. 1986). In New Ireland, a number of coastal rock shelters were first used around 33 000 years ago (Allen and Gosden 1991), while on Buka island, at the northern end of the Solomon Island chain, another shelter was visited by people some 28 000 years ago (Wickler and Spriggs 1988).

Although we still know little about the behaviour and material culture of these first Melanesians, a number of important points emerge from this early material. They were the first true sailors of the world, crossing open seas on a number of occasions. This is a skill that must have been developed in their homeland, presumably one dominated by a coastal and island environment backed by rainforest.

One can speculate that it could be a combination of population pressure and loss of land caused by the last sea-level rise that induced these maritime-oriented people to seek new horizons. Based on current archaeological evidence, it is likely that the first crossings into Melanesia occurred not long before 40 000 years ago (Allen 1989; Thiel 1987).

From an economic viewpoint, it is clear from the remains found at the sites mentioned above that the essential resources exploited were from reef and mangrove environments, with additions derived from the inland forests (for example, Gosden and Robertson 1991). Two-way voyages were probably maintained between these newly colonised islands (Irwin 1992) leading to the foundation of an inter-island exchange 'network' by 20 000 years ago.

Other important developments occurred on the island of New Guinea. The major ecological zones, including the high valleys, were occupied by 25 000 years ago (for example, Gorecki 1986), and land degradation caused by people was early and severe (Swadling and Hope 1991). Economies seemed to be closely linked to forest products, including a large range of plants (Yen 1990), particularly nuts, leaves and fruits.

This emphasis on trees may involve a manipulation of natural tree distributions, or arboriculture (Groube 1989; cf. Yen 1974), leading to proper plant cultivation, or horticulture, perhaps by 9 000 years ago in the high valleys of central New Guinea (Golson 1990). This fundamental economic change led rapidly to the development of complex social systems (Golson and Gardner 1990). The possibility that this early horticultural knowledge was shared with or introduced to the communities of New Ireland and Buka should not be discounted.

Fig. 78
Lapita pottery representing a mask. Excavation by Daniel Frimigacci. New Caledonia.

It is likely that by 6000 years ago, when horticulture in the New Guinea highlands intensified dramatically, the islands found in the Bismarck and Solomon seas were effervescent with activities. It is still unclear if these activities remained restricted to this region or if they spread into new lands such as Vanuatu. The problem for regions such as the Solomons, Vanuatu and New Caledonia is that not only has little archaeological investigation been carried out, but the areas investigated tend overwhelmingly to concentrate along current (and therefore young) coastal strips.

We know that the northern tip of the Solomons was settled by 28 000 years ago, at a time of low sea level that resulted in fewer but much larger islands in the chain. It is likely that this would have allowed people to rapidly explore and settle along the whole chain (by land and by sea). The break-up of these large islands into smaller ones following the last sea-level rise would have further entrenched people on these islands, including Makira (San Cristobal) at the southern tip of the Solomon Islands. What lies beyond Makira are the islands of Vanuatu.

By the time people settled on the shores of southern Makira and contemplated the horizon towards Vanuatu, they already had the skills, developed over the preceding 20 000 years, to navigate between islands sometimes 200 kilometres apart, they had inter-island contacts through which they could exchange goods and ideas, and they understood how to promote plant resources through arboriculture and horticulture. In other words, by 6000 years ago these early Melanesians had a profound knowledge of the sea, of the land, and of each other. For the larger islands, there could be a clear division and specialisation between inland and coastal communities (Bonnemaison 1986a, 1986b).

At about the same time, some 6000 years ago, another great human adventure, which would have a profound impact on the Pacific Islands, started in Asia: the Austronesian expansion, out of which the all important and complex Lapita culture (see fig. 78, and Spriggs, this volume) eventually emerged some 3500 years ago (Allen and Gosden 1991; Galipaud 1992; Spriggs 1990a; Kirch 1986; Green 1979b). New archaeological evidence from northern New Guinea indicates that by about 5500 years ago, important additions, perhaps of Austronesian origin, had been integrated with the local material culture and economies. These include bows and arrows, pigs, and pottery (Gorecki et al. 1991; Swadling et al. 1989).

To better explain the successful and very rapid Lapita expansion in Vanuatu, one has to seriously consider the possibility that there was already another population in place on which the Lapita people could have added their own identity (Gorecki 1992). Some evidence for this may already exist, such as the possible links between the Mangaasi (fig. 79) and Sepik (New Guinea) pottery traditions (Garanger 1972a), and the bush (pre-Lapita?)-beach (post-Lapita?) cultures found on large islands such as Santo, Malakula and Tanna.

Answers to these questions can only be provided by archaeological investigations in Vanuatu. One of

Fig. 79
Mangaasi pottery.
Eponymous site. About 600 BC.
North-west Efate.

Fig. 80
Rare whole pottery, 19th and 20th centuries, collected by the trader Ewen McAfee, based on Malakula, donated in 1920.
North-west Santo, probably from the Olpoï region.
Cambridge University, Museum of Archaeology and Anthropology.

these would be to examine archaeological collections from Museums to reassess possible links with the Solomons and New Guinea. Pottery would undoubtedly be a key material in this (Galipaud 1990). Most importantly, there is a need to undertake excavations of stable environments that have the potential to yield ancient cultural deposits: a high priority should be given on large islands to sites such as rock shelters found inland from current coastlines, and to areas which are known to be tectonically uplifting. Such investigations may reveal that Melanesian roots in Vanuatu are much older and more complex than presently thought.

Tongoa, Mangaasi and Retoka: History of a Prehistory

José Garanger

Tongoa, Mangaasi and Retoka, in central Vanuatu, are without apparent cultural relationships or geographical importance. Retoka is a tiny coral islet a short distance off the main island of Efate. It is uninhabited, like Mangaasi on the north-west coast of Efate. Mangaasi is regularly visited by canoes from Leleppa island. Because of the semiarid soils on Leleppa, its inhabitants maintain gardens at Mangaasi and other coastal flats nearby, which are uninhabited because they can only be accessed by sea. The young women of Leleppa used to sail to Mangaasi to do the family washing in the crystal waters of Pwanmwou creek. In contrast, the small Shepherd archipelago, lying much further north, is relatively highly populated, the island of Tongoa in particular, but economically poor because of the predominance of young and therefore infertile volcanic soils. For this reason it has not been affected by European colonisation; it is a kind of haven for indigenous people and their oral traditions.

Tongoa and Kuwae

In the 1880s, the first missionary in Tongoa, the Reverend Oscar Michelson, heard of a legend stating that the Shepherd islands were all that remained of a large island called Kuwae which had been destroyed by a cataclysmic event. Using the genealogy of the chiefs of Tongoa, he dated the event to about AD 1540.

Other Europeans who visited the archipelago later also recorded this 'legend' and proposed various dates for the event. Some of them even placed it in the 19th century (they had obviously not read the writings of Cook, who had seen the Shepherds in July 1774 and named them in honour of one of his friends). The fullest and most precise details of this oral tradition were collected in 1958 by the French anthropologist Jean Guiart. He gave me a copy of his manuscript notes in 1963, at the time of my departure for Oceania. This account guided my research. It was later published (Guiart 1973).

In Makura, Tongoa and Tongariki, Guiart was told about the Kuwae cataclysm. The descriptions vary somewhat depending on the informant, but the whole is coherent and can be summarised thus:

Tombuk (in Tongoa, Tobaka in Tongariki), a man from Lopevi island was tricked by people from Kurumwambe who, as a joke, made him unknowingly sleep with his mother, a woman of loose morals. He recognised her too late and, in despair at his incestuous act, decided to die and to bring about the deaths of the men who were responsible for his misdeed. He

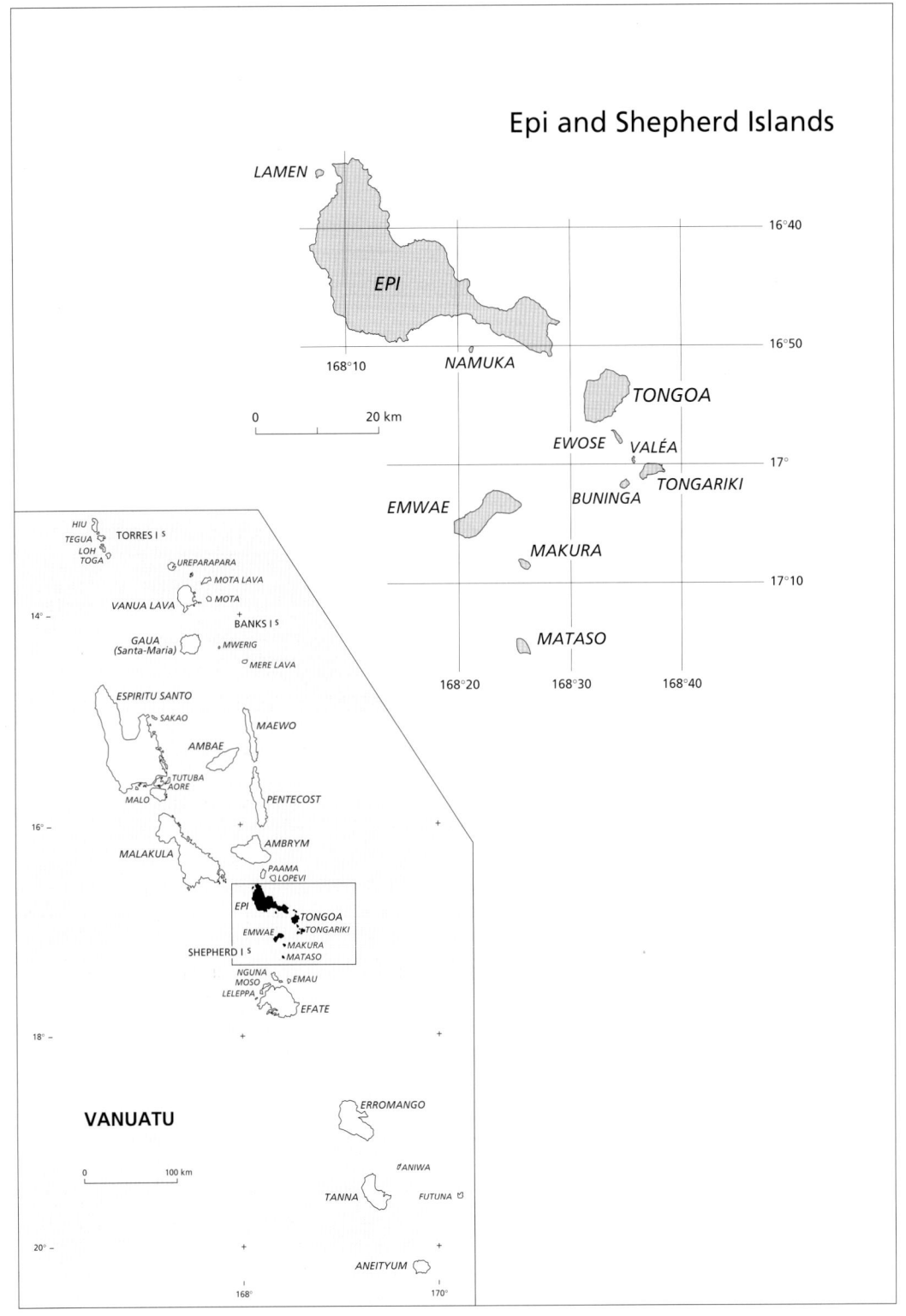

TONGOA, MANGAASI AND RETOKA ▼ 67

1. I had thought that this chronological inversion was due to contamination by volcanic materials. This was later confirmed, and for other areas, by physicists from Pullman University (Washington State, USA).

2. Researchers from the TOA Department of ORSTOM have recently restudied the vulcanism of Kuwae and dated its explosion ('... one of the seven most important in the in the earth's history during the last 10,000 years ...') to about AD 1420 to 1430, plus or minus several decades. This confirms the three radiocarbon dates obtained in 1964 and 1966 (cf. supra Eissen et al. 1994:1200-1202).

3. 'This exception to the general rule of maintaining ancient hierarchies ... is explained by the halo of supremacy which today surrounds the name of Roy Mata ... nobody would dare to admit to having the ambition to aspire to such a title, as if it was kept in reserve for the day when ... the long awaited reversal of the respective positions of white and black men will take place' (Guiart 1973:287). This also explains a certain reserve among his informants when speaking of this

Fig. 82 Mangaasi pottery, partly restored from scattered sherds from the lower level of the site.

went to Lopevi island where his uncle gave him the means of his revenge in the form of a lizard, the bearer of the volcano's power. He organised a feast which lasted six days. Each day, he killed a pig and hung the inflated bladder in an ironwood tree. He had hidden the lizard, concealed in a bamboo, under this tree. One after the other he burst the first four bladders, causing the earth to tremble more and more. Kuwae tilted and broke into pieces as the fifth bladder exploded. When Tombuk burst the sixth bladder, a volcano erupted from the earth where the oak tree and the lizard stood. All those present were killed.

Asingmet, a boy from Mangarisu (some say he was the son of Taripua Mata) had escaped the cataclysm because he was busy hunting birds on the land bridge which used to link Tongoa and Tongariki. He fled to Tongariki along the coast of Kuwae and hid inside a slit drum, where he was later discovered by a young lady named Tarifegit who had also escaped the disaster. Both of them were given a home by people of Makura island. Asingmet (or Semet) became Matanauretong and later Ti Tongoa Liseiriki. Six years later, he returned to one of the islands remaining from old Kuwae, which since then has been called Tongoa. This name comes from a thorny plant, *worotongoa*, which first recolonised the new island. Ti Tongoa Liseiriki planted a tree and erected a memorial stone where the old meeting house used to stand. Later, some chiefs who had escaped to Efate at the beginning of the cataclysm came back little by little to settle on Tongoa. (Garanger 1972a)

The Reverend Michelsen had noted the occurrence of pottery fragments and bones in the layers covered by the volcanic deposits that were visible along the cliff of Mangarisu. Bernard Hébert, Administrateur de la France d'Outre-Mer in the New Hebrides visited this site and collected two undecorated sherds (Hébert 1963-1965c:91). The aims of the research I undertook in 1964 and 1966 were to study the pre- and post-volcanic levels and to try to verify details of the tradition about old Kuwae.

These investigations have already been published elsewhere (Garanger 1972a) and only the main results will be described here.

Archaeological levels containing stone tools and many sherds of pottery belonging to the Mangaasi tradition were discovered under a thick pumice layer at Mangarisu and Euta. The oldest levels are dated to about 500 BC. Could this be the date of the earliest settlement of Kuwae? New research in the Shepherd islands could confirm this or not. In the last occupation level below the volcanic deposits, as well as in post-volcanic occupation levels, pottery is completely absent. Radiocarbon dates from this aceramic level below the volcanic deposits are aberrant: nearly 2000 years older than the dates of the deepest levels.[1] At Makura, in an identical stratigraphic context (first aceramic level), a date of about AD 1000 to 1200 seems acceptable. On this island, too, pottery completely disappears about 20 centimetres below a thin pumice layer from the Kuwae eruption and, as in Tongoa and other islands, stone tools are replaced by shell tools of Micronesian type. It was at the request of the chiefs of Mangarisu and Panita that the burial of Ti Tongoa Liseiriki was excavated at Panita. Both chiefs were in agreement about the location and internal arrangement of this structure (apart from a detail indicating which of them had precedence over the other, given in connection with their hierarchical proximity to Ti Tongoa Liseiriki; this was subsequently resolved). The location and internal arrangement were in accordance with the oral tradition. A radiocarbon analysis of bone collagen gave a date of AD 1475 ±85. A piece of burnt wood collected from the pyroclastic layers in the Mweriu cliff was dated to AD 1320 ±80; a second piece collected from the same context by the geologist J.J. Espirat (pers. comm. 1966) gave a result of AD 1460 ±37. These three dates are in agreement, when their standard deviation is taken into account. The archaeological study confirmed the account given by the oral tradition about the development of the seismic, tectonic and volcanic cataclysm (the successive explosion of the six pigs' bladders: see Garanger 1972a:98); the cataclysmic cycle has also been described by J.J. Espirat (in Guiart 1973:40) and, much more recently, by a team from ORSTOM.[2]

Mangaasi

At Leleppa, Guiart was told that Roy Mata 'had been the paramount chief of Retoka and that the last holder of the title to which no one could aspire any more[3] was buried there ... his *farea*[4] was at Mangaasi'. When a day's work on the excavation is over and dusk falls, it is time for conversation in the village, dialogue between the researcher and his hosts, a very precious time for learning, understanding and evaluating. So it was that one evening at Natapao (Leleppa island), I inquired where Mangaasi and the *farea* Serelapa were, wondering to myself whether this place had ever really existed.[5] It was right in front of us, on the coast of Efate. We planned to visit the site by canoe the following Sunday, which we did. The site was promising: some sherds of pottery on the surface, fallen but still visible stone walls which used to surround the living space, *farea* (including the *farea* Serelapa), and dancing grounds, one of which, named Mwalafaoom, belonged to Roy Mata, who is said to have planted the huge tree growing there today.[6] We returned in 1967, after finishing the last work at Leleppa, for site survey, map and excavations of the *farea* Serelapa. A first group of individual burials, dated to AD 1720 ±85, was exposed in the uppermost level. In the underlying levels, some sherds of pottery of simple form, decorated with incisions and applied relief, appeared. These belonged to the same pottery tradition as sherds already found elsewhere around Efate, and on Makura, Tongoa, and so on. They were so numerous at Mangaasi that this name was chosen to represent this tradition (fig. 82). The lowest level is dated to the 6th century BC. There is a progressive but slight evolution of decorative motifs from bottom to top of the site. The end of the ceramic sequence seems to be later here than elsewhere, and particularly than in the sites of Makura and Tongoa, namely around AD 1200. The

'hero' or about other traditions he collected. The excavation of his burial gave rise to a desire to speak more about it: several specialists, keepers of traditions, discussed the matter at Port Vila, on the excavation in Retoka and in Tongoa. This was another sign of the eagerness to maintain the memory of this prestigious title and the things it validates.

4. *Farea* 'indicates a residential group: at once the group, the name, the political territory and the house which represents this group' (Guiart 1973:49).

5. I was in the early stages of my research in Vanuatu and had already suffered several setbacks, excavating on request and without success some 'mythical' sites. The discovery of the burial of Ti Tonga Liseiriki (I was doubtful of its reality) made me less sceptical from then on.

6. The successive chiefs of Leleppa, owners of the place, always refused to sell it to timber merchants who coveted it.

 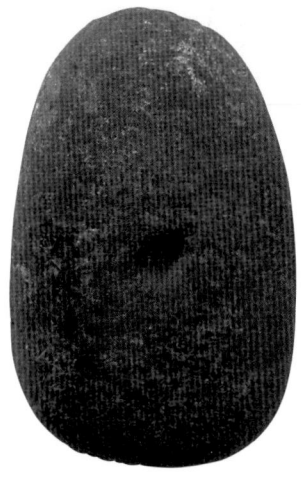 

Fig. 83
Adze and stone tools.
Mangaasi, north-east Efate.

Fig. 84
Coral and shell tools.
Mangaasi, north-east Efate.

loss of pottery, as we have seen, corresponds with the loss of stone adzes (fig. 83), which are replaced by shell adzes of Micronesian type (fig. 84). The date of about AD 1700, originally proposed for the last use of pottery at Mangaasi, was later challenged (notably by the Australian archaeologist Graeme K. Ward, 1974). I agree with him today. The site's stratigraphy is too complex in the later levels for us to be certain of their chronology. It is most likely that the loss of pottery was much earlier here, as it was elsewhere in the central part of the archipelago. New excavations on a site close to Mangaasi but less disturbed should be able to confirm this.

Nevertheless, it is thanks to Roy Mata that Mangaasi, where we sought traces of him, is known to Oceanic prehistorians. 'Mangaasi' or related pottery has now been unearthed, like Lapita pottery, in many parts of the south-west Pacific. The end of the latter is contemporary with the beginning of the former. Their exact relationships remain to be defined, along with their use in day-to-day life, their role in inter-island communication, and the reasons for their disappearance.

Retoka

Roy Mata, as we know, was a paramount chief in the ancient society of central Vanuatu. We could even speak of him as a 'cultural' or 'civilising' hero, if those terms did not have too mythological a connotation, for he represents an historical reality. It is not possible to review here all the details of his cultural and civilising exploits, handed down in oral tradition and already published (Garanger 1972a; Guiart 1973). Among these details, it is said that Roy Mata had arrived on the south-east coast of Efate at Maniura long before the Kuwae cataclysm. Moreover, it was there, on the shore of 'lake Etas' (according to the IGN map, the correct name for this lake is Lukutau and its central islet is called Otaat), that titles were bestowed on the secondary chiefs charged with spreading the influence of the hero throughout Efate and as far as Kuwae and Epi. Some of their successors were able to escape to Efate at the beginning of the Kuwae cataclysm, because of the inter-island hierarchical network previously set up by Roy Mata.

At the end of his life, very ill, Roy Mata was

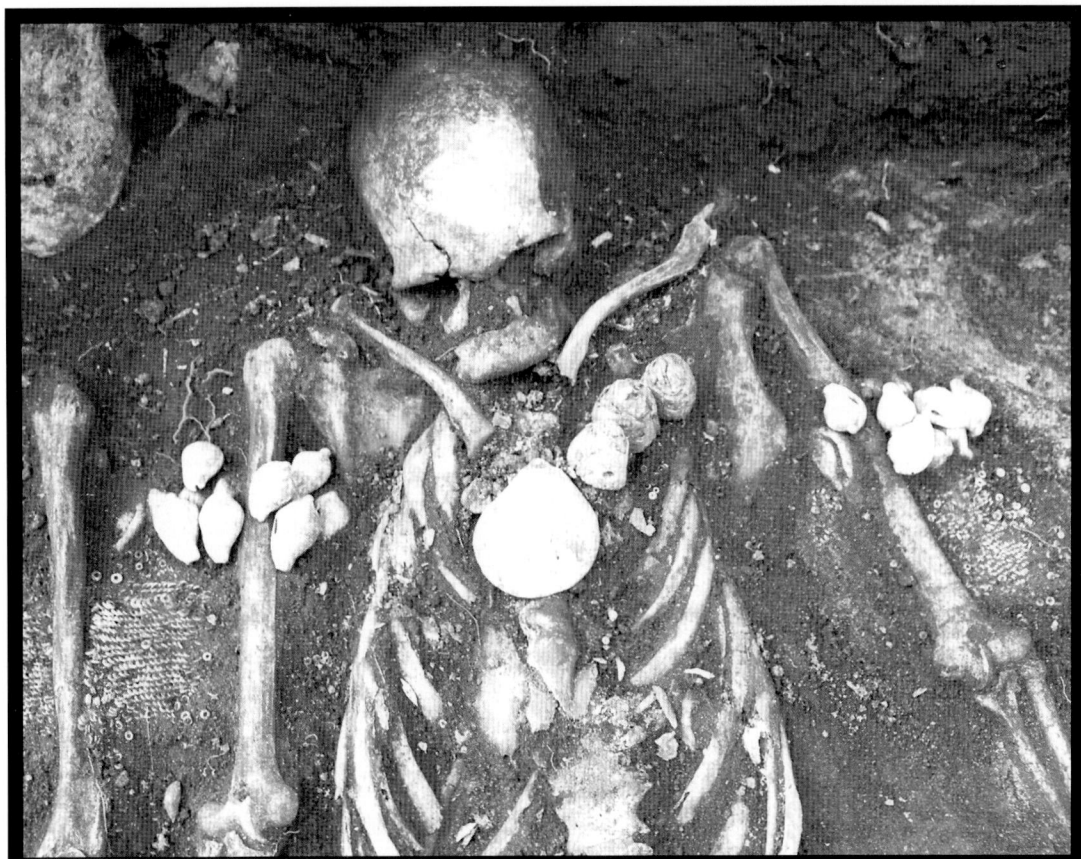

Fig. 85
Detail of the collective Roy Mata burial site, with chiefly insignia. The breast ornament was still in use on Efate at the beginning of the 20th century; cf. fig. 355, p. 284.
Eretoka.

carried to the Feles cave (at Leleppa Island) where he breathed his last (this very large cave contains many rock drawings and carvings). His body was later carried around Efate, through all the villages where the chiefs had owed him allegiance, and finally to Retoka, where he was buried. Ernest Reid, owner of the islet, not only gave me permission to excavate, but showed me the probable site of the burial, information he had obtained from the inhabitants of Leleppa. These people, like all inhabitants of Efate, would never stay at Retoka, which had been declared *fenua tapu* after Roy Mata's burial ceremony. It would have meant death for those who did not comply. Nevertheless, my companions from Leleppa agreed to come and work there with me (taking some special precautions, of course).

The results of the work in Tongoa had already shown them the historic reality of the content of their oral traditions, which was very important to them. On one hand, they were able to validate their own social structures, both to themselves and in the eyes of Europeans. On the other hand, they were able to show Europeans that they had their own 'history', unrelated to Joan of Arc or Waterloo, which were taught in the French or English schools (the New Hebrides were a condominium at that time).

Let us skip the details of the excavation and its results, all of which have already been published. The point to remember is that they confirmed all the information known from the oral traditions (even to those aspects of the funerals which could be reconstructed). The number of people buried simultaneously in this cemetery, and the richness and hierarchical significance of the grave goods (fig. 85), bear witness to the exceptional significance of the

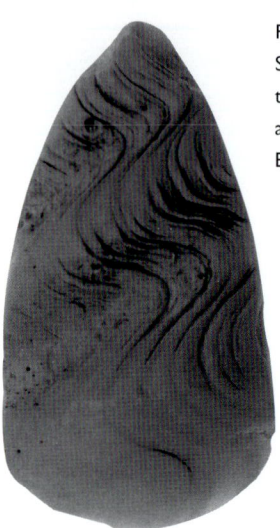

Fig. 87
Shell adzes, collective Roy Mata burial site. Eretoka.

Fig 86
Necklace indicating social rank; shell and whale's tooth; found in the collective Roy Mata burial site. Eretoka.

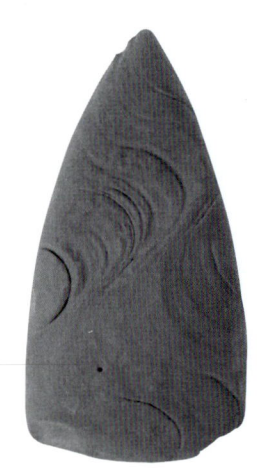

first 'Roy Mata' (fig. 86). In fact, it is very probably him: this burial was dated to AD 1265 ±140 (bone collagen). This date could be estimated more precisely today; physiochemical techniques of absolute dating have advanced a lot in the last thirty years. Nevertheless, we can say that Roy Mata flourished 'a long time before the cataclysm of Kuwae'; and note that this is also the period when pottery disappeared and shell artifacts of Micronesian type appeared (fig. 87). Linguistic studies have found evidence of relationships between some languages of Vanuatu and Micronesia (not forgetting the isolated Polynesian-speaking areas in Vanuatu, related to East Futunan or early Samoan). Could Roy Mata and his people possibly have a Micronesian origin or, earlier still, could their Micronesian forefathers have come from western Polynesia? We must be cautious; the process of colonisation of Oceania seems to have been much too complex for these deductions to be considered anything other than simple working hypotheses … for work that must go on.

Conclusion

Incomplete as these first results may appear, their scientific interest is certain. On the methodological side, they show the utility of a combined approach by the anthropologist and the archaeologist. On the other hand, the continuity of oral traditions (for nearly seven centuries) is explained not only by the impact of a destructive cataclysm or the importance of an exceptional leader. In these societies without writing, this continuity is explained mainly by the role of traditions in upholding the rules of social and individual life. These rules are encoded in myths whose intricate details prohibit any deviation. These archaeological results provide anthropologists with a diachronic dimension to institutions they can observe only in the present. Here, social systems (hierarchy, kinship, land tenure, and so on) are different from those observed in the north and south of Vanuatu, and probably correspond to the area of influence of Roy Mata (the Roy Matas) and his (their) people.

I have adopted an unusually personal tone in this article; I wanted the reader to find himself engaged in discussion in the late afternoon in one or other of these villages where I spent a long time, and where I discovered an unsuspected and exceptional human value, a deeply shared friendship. This modest mutual understanding is by far the most important result of this scientific quest for the past.

The Archaeology of Vanuatu in a Pacific Perspective

Matthew Spriggs

'Near' and 'Remote' Oceania

There is a major ecological boundary at the end of the main Solomons chain of islands at the southern tip of San Cristobal (Makira) (Green 1991). Beyond this boundary lie the eastern outer islands of the Solomons (including Santa Cruz and Tikopia), Vanuatu, New Caledonia, Fiji and Polynesia, forming 'Remote Oceania'. Beyond the main Solomons, there are no land mammals that were not carried there by humans (except bats), thirty genera of land birds and 162 genera of seed plants find their eastern limits, and major disjunctions occur in the natural distribution of other plants and animals.

At present this boundary also represents the limit of Pleistocene (meaning earlier than 10 000 years ago) settlement, and beyond it we have as yet no evidence for human exploration before 3200 years ago. The sea gap from San Cristobal to Santa Cruz is a substantial one, in excess of 300 kilometres, and to reach Vanuatu is even further. Voyaging technology, however, was probably not the problem. Rather, it would seem to be the lack of naturally occurring foodstuffs to sustain life in the absence of an imported agricultural base. In the Solomons, there are wild varieties of many of the crops that were important in later Melanesian agricultural systems: taros, yams, bananas, and so on. In addition, there are several endemic species of large rats and a great variety of other forest foods. In Vanuatu, however, many of these do not occur.

The environmental effects and implications of the levels of vegetation clearance seen in the islands of Melanesia in the period starting around 3000 years ago imply a totally different attitude to the environment and the place of humans in it than that evident before in the region, and a scale of settlement previously unknown. Lowland forest areas were suddenly subject to major clearance by fire, and the hillsides and the valleys below them show the effects of greatly-increased erosion. In some cases, this initial human assault left some areas uninhabitable for hundreds of years, and one can imagine a pioneer pattern of settlement with large areas quickly cleared and planted, and just as quickly abandoned as degradation set in (Spriggs in press a).

The Lapita culture

This sudden change in attitude to the forest and the world begins at the time that the Lapita culture spreads from an early centre in the Bismarck Archipelago through the Solomons and into Vanuatu and beyond. Discussed by Galipaud in this volume in terms of its highly distinctive decorated pottery, it is more than a pottery style. Also included are the first appearance in the island Pacific of the three domestic animals – the pig, the dog and the chicken – new varieties of stone adzes, a distinctive range of shell ornaments (which in the recent past have formed a major component of traditional valuables, or 'money', used in bride-price and blood-feud compensation payments), the first evidence for large villages (including stilt-house construction), a major extension in exchange networks, and the first major new expansion in human settlement since the Pleistocene, as the Remote Oceania barrier was broken and Fiji and western Polynesia were reached (Spriggs 1991, in press b). As well as the pollen and geomorphological evidence already mentioned, we also have the first direct evidence for the full range of agricultural plants in use at European contact.

An argument has arisen among archaeologists as to whether the Lapita culture developed from the cultures already present in the Bismarcks or represents an intrusive culture, a migration from island South-East Asia. While allowing for some local input, both cultural and genetic, I see Lapita as basically an extension of the island South-East Asian Neolithic expansion, representing the intrusion into the region of new settlers from the west. The ultimate origins of this culture might be in what is now southern China some 7000 years ago, but is more certainly traceable in Taiwan just before 5000 years ago. From there its expansion can be tracked through the Philippines and eastern Indonesia, and across to the Bismarcks. This fits closely the linguistic evidence which places all Vanuatu languages within the Austronesian language family whose origins can be traced back to Taiwan in the period before Chinese settlement there (Spriggs 1989). It is ironic that the only aspect of Lapita that appears to

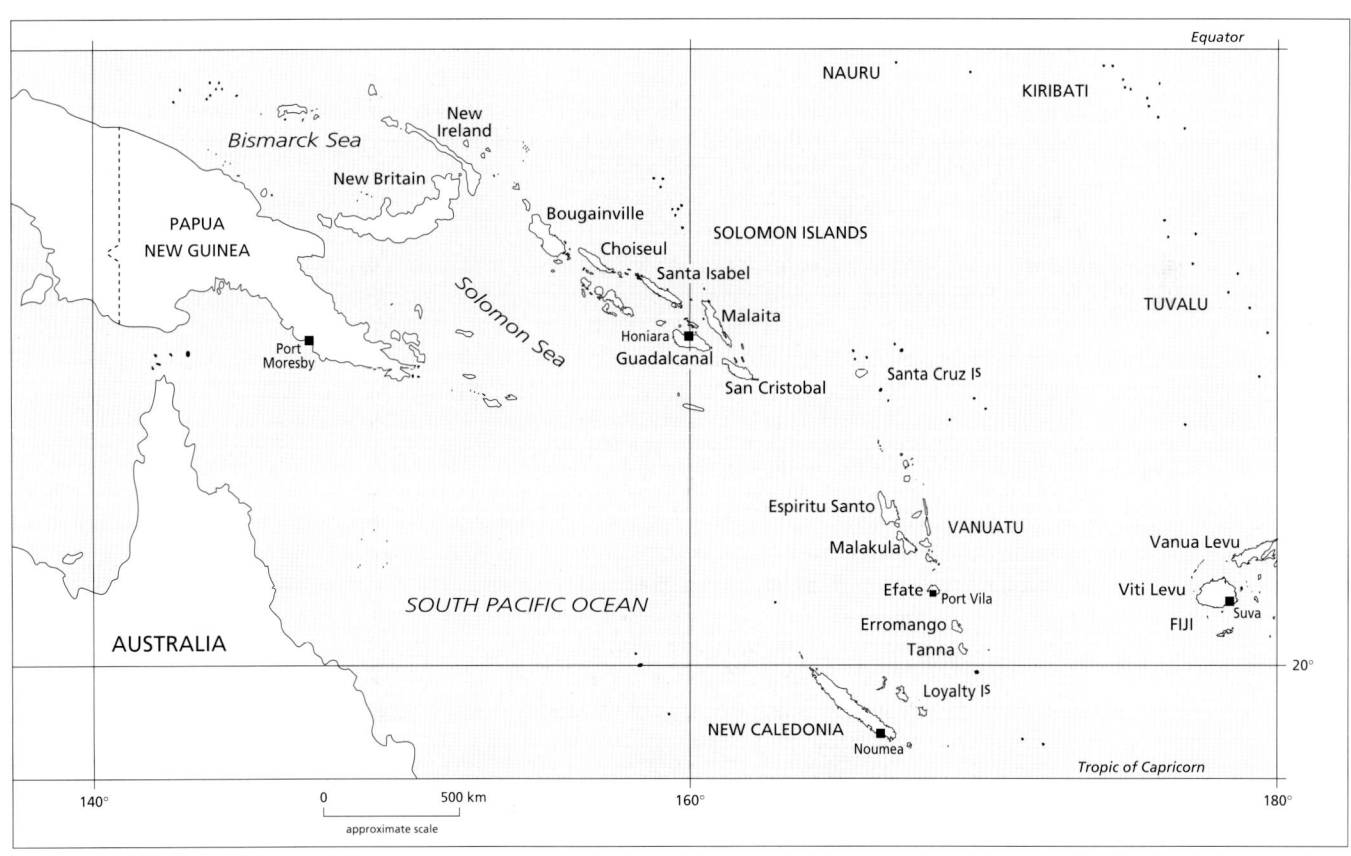

Fig. 88
The Melanesian archipelago.

Fig. 89
Lapita pottery, excavated by Hedrick. North Malo.

be found earlier in the Bismarcks is the design system on the pots themselves. Similar decoration is found on South-East Asian pottery, but, in all cases where it has proved possible to date, it appears to be later than the beginning of Lapita in the Bismarcks. Perhaps it was an art form that developed in Melanesia and spread back to South-East Asia along routes of exchange or with return migrants. Alternatively, the design system may have existed on other media such as barkcloth and tattoos that have not survived, and was first transferred to pots in the Bismarcks (Green 1979a).

The earliest sites known in Vanuatu are of the Lapita culture, and represent settlement by pioneer agriculturists about 3200 years ago. The Lapita pottery decoration from sites on Malo Island (fig. 89) is quite close to that from Fiji, while showing more complex designs. This suggests that settlement of Fiji, a few hundred years later, was launched from somewhere in northern Vanuatu. And from Fiji, Polynesia was settled almost immediately. Humans also colonised New Caledonia at this time, by way of the Lapita expansion through Vanuatu. It should be noted that the independent evidence of linguistics presented by Tryon in this volume is in broad agreement with the archaeology on these points.

It seems a reasonable supposition that Lapita society was hierarchically structured, given the demands of voyaging and colonisation of the far-flung islands of Remote Oceania. Linguistic reconstructions also suggest the presence of chiefs. The details of Lapita social structure cannot at this stage be established on archaeological grounds. We are even further away from understanding the transformations of that society over time, within the Lapita period and between Lapita and the succeeding cultures (fig. 90).

The end of Lapita

While Lapita was at first a remarkably homogeneous culture, the very distances it spread across from the Bismarcks to Samoa meant that regular communications could not be maintained and regional variations soon appeared. Some archaeologists would see the Mangaasi pottery style of Vanuatu, and the Podtanean of New Caledonia, discussed in this volume by Galipaud, as examples of this regionalisation. Other archaeologists have seen the development of the Mangaasi style and related styles elsewhere either as a separate wave of migrants, or as evidence for pre-Lapita settlement from New Guinea. The problem remains unresolved.

The end of Lapita does mark an important contraction in regional exchange systems, and from about 2000 years ago the processes of diversification seem stronger than those maintaining a degree of cultural unity. The ethnographic diversity of Vanuatu and the other archipelagos of Island Melanesia may well turn out to be a product of his immediately post-Lapita era. With a few notable exceptions, especially Garanger's major 1960s project in central Vanuatu (Garanger 1972a), we know much less about this post-Lapita period than we do about those immediately before and after it. It does not have the glamour and beautifully decorated pottery of the preceding Lapita period, nor the accessibility given by oral history and links to the ethnography of the last few hundred years.

We do know that the art of pottery-making ceased entirely in many areas, such as that between the western Solomons and the Banks Islands, and in southern Vanuatu. The post-Lapita pottery of Mangaasi style from Tikopia and Vanikoro in the eastern Solomons was imported from Vanuatu and was possibly made on Santo. Pottery has been found in the Banks Islands, but how long that tradition continued is a matter of dispute between archaeologists (Kirch and Yen 1982; Ward 1979). Pottery was manufactured in parts of northern Vanuatu until the recent past, as discussed by Galipaud, but no archaeological sequence has been established for that area, and so the histories of the various traditions represented is as yet unknown. Even in comparatively well-researched central Vanuatu there is some dispute over how long pottery continued in use, but it is almost certainly the case that pottery went out of use in the area by about 700 years ago.

In southern Vanuatu, pottery has only been excavated from sites on Erromango. There it dates to 2700 years ago and has affiliations to Lapita and to Mangaasi. The scarcity of pottery finds in the south suggests that pottery-making ceased there by about 2000 years ago.

Many sites probably occupied in the period between Lapita and about 700 years ago have been recorded in Vanuatu, but in most cases little has been established about them except the fact of occupation. One kind of evidence that is available is that for the continued environmental impact of agricultural practices. This is best demonstrated for Aneityum, where the long-term impact of hill-slope erosion caused by burning for garden clearance was surprisingly not entirely negative. The soil that washed off the hills filled in the swampy valley floors, creating prime sites for the development of intensive irrigated agriculture (see my paper on taro irrigation, p. 92, this volume) within the last 1000 years. The archaeological investigation of such systems has barely begun, although they were clearly important parts of the economic and political systems in several parts of Vanuatu.

Polynesian influences?

In some areas of the Pacific, the artifacts and the pattern of settlement of the period immediately prior to 750 years ago seem broadly similar to those observed by early European visitors. In parts of the Solomons and in Vanuatu, however, major cultural changes occur at about this time that mark it off from what came before. A series of oral traditions from central Vanuatu, recorded by the anthropologist Jean Guiart (Espirat et al. 1973), have been linked to a series of archaeological sites dated to the last 750 years by Garanger. He excavated a grave said by tradition to be that of Roy Mata, an important chief who came from 'the south', set up the modern system of Efate chiefly titles, and was buried with attendant human sacrifices and 'voluntary' immolation by representatives of the many clans under his control. The grave when excavated was just as the traditions had described (Garanger 1972a; 1972b). Garanger interprets Roy Mata as a Polynesian immigrant. His burial is indeed reminiscent of chiefly burials found on Uvea (Wallis) in western Polynesia. Changes occur in material culture at this time, with a greater reliance on shell tools and the probable end of pottery manufacture. Further collaboration between archaeologists and oral historians is likely to be fruitful in elucidating details of the processes that led to the varied societies of Vanuatu today.

Where chiefs are found in Melanesia, their presence has often been interpreted as a cultural borrowing under Polynesian influence, and the

Fig. 90
Detail of a fragment of the Lapita pottery illustrated in fig. 89.

presence of Polynesian-speaking islands along the eastern fringe of island Melanesia, the so-called Polynesian Outliers, has been invoked as the source. Some areas do indeed show evidence of significant Polynesian influence, and in the main these are areas that also have chiefly systems. But this would seem to contradict models for Lapita society, also suggested as hierarchical. Do the chiefdoms represent recent innovations in social and political organisation under Polynesian influence or intrusion, or are they continuities from Lapita, perhaps with superficial Polynesian trappings?

The grave and the possible Polynesian origin of Roy Mata have already been mentioned. Two chiefly graves on Aneityum display a very similar assemblage of ornaments to the Roy Mata burial, and fit in with oral traditions of chiefly burial rites on the island.

One of these burials, some 300 to 400 years old, was examined by physical anthropologists, and the very tall stature and some other features suggested to them a Polynesian affiliation. There are several other cemetery sites of this period known from Efate, and from Polynesian Outliers in Vanuatu and the Solomons with a very similar material culture.

The existence of Polynesian-speaking peoples on the Outliers, Polynesian words in New Caledonian and Vanuatu languages, local myths involving Polynesian culture heroes such as Mauitikitiki and Tangaroa (possibly the same figure as Tagaro in northern Vanuatu), and oral traditions of 'Tongan' contact, all point to a period of important Polynesian influence in the last 700 years. The nature of the contact and its effects clearly varied from place to place, but whether there is a strong Polynesian influence on the substance rather than merely the outward form of political organisation is not at all clear (Spriggs 1986).

Conclusion

Pushing history back in time from an ethnohistoric or ethnographic baseline, using evidence from oral traditions and continuities in lifestyle in the archaeological record, will be an increasingly valuable technique in island Melanesia, and one that could lead to a particularly rich description of the last 700 years or so. This should help to show us that this region is certainly not 'cold', in Lévi-Strauss's perhaps infelicitous term, unchanging and without history over long periods of time, but presents a dynamic interplay of external and internal cause and effect.

Compared to some other parts of the Pacific, very little archaeological research has yet been undertaken in Vanuatu. This makes it all too easy for us as researchers to interpret the meagre evidence in ways that fit our own preconceived theories. The early history of a region or a nation is never a finished work. It is subject to endless reinterpretation because of new evidence or simply the fashion of the age. Trying to write it is, however, particularly exciting at an early stage of research, when a single new find might entirely rewrite the history books. Today, Vanuatu has a history of about 3200 years, but a single discovery could make it a 32 000-year history.

Vanuatu Seen from Maré

Marie-Joseph Dubois

Vanuatu is mentioned as the place of origin of some human groups in New Caledonia. Various evidence remains of these ancient migrations, and more generally of the exchanges which linked the two island groups.

On Tanna, for example, one finds New Caledonian 'serpentine' stones pierced with a hole and worn as pendants (figs 91, 92). These stones are comparable to those used by the Kanaks to make their axes, and it is possible that they found an outlet in Vanuatu for scraps from axes broken in the making, in the guise of 'jewellery'.

In the other direction, in pre-European times, Vanuatu 'exported' to New Caledonia a number of objects to which a precise meaning or value was attached. This is the case with large specimens of the *Tonna galea L.*, or giant tun, shell, which used to be an object of value. On Maré, in the Loyalty Islands, the giant tun was a chiefly ornament; with four holes pierced in it, it was worn at the top of the forehead and held in place by fastenings of woven flying-fox hair.

There is nothing particularly surprising about the movement of objects between southern Vanuatu and the Loyalties, because Aneityum and Tanna are, after all, only 150 and 200 kilometres from Maré. The Maré people say they can sometimes see the glow of the Yasur volcano, on Tanna, when there is an unusually violent eruption.

Apart from these objects, Maré tradition includes reminders of relations with, and migrations from, southern Vanuatu. On Maré's east coast, there is a small village called Tyèm, which is in fact the name of the southernmost island of Vanuatu: newcomers gave the place where they settled the name of the land of their origins. The prefix *ana-* corresponds to an article, giving Anatyèm, which Europeans later transformed into Anatom and Aneityum.

In the Maré language, Tyèm became Kiamu, which is today's name for Aneityum. The si Gurewabao, who were among the earliest people to settle on Maré, are said to have used 'rafts' fitted with tillers and capable, if they allowed themselves to be carried by the wind, of taking them as far as Kiamu. A part of the population who arrived later say they originate from there: 'We are coconuts who came floating from Kiamu.'

According to oral tradition, migration from Kiamu-Aneityum came in two waves:

Some of the people of Kiamu came ashore at Dranin (eastern Maré). They arrived first after the si Gurewabao. Kiamu is east of Tanna. But the real Kiamu is

1. *Wa*: prefix of respect; *shongo*: growl; *-ne*: suffix indicating respect, from *nene*, itself a transformation of the word *mana*.

very far away, not near Tanna at all, but right away to the east.

The people of Kiamu who arrived last came ashore at Cerethi (more exactly at Watheo, in the south-west of the island) … The Kiamu people are Ma people.

Ma was a 'true' country, very distant, a country of red earth situated to the east; it is said to have disappeared.

The island of Tanna was also known in Maré. The words to a women's dance in an old family in the east-south-east of Maré, *si Thunu serei dradrac*, begin by calling on a divine being, Wa-shongo-shongo-ne,[1] whose belly is 'heated by fire'; to the question: 'Where do you come from?' the divine being replies: 'I come from Kiamu.' The last words of the dance refer to Yasur, Tanna's volcano. The migrants may have been fleeing a cataclysmic eruption.

Kiamu is also mentioned as the place of origin of several important foodstuffs. On the Isle of Pines, Aneityum, under the name Kiamu or Kiamô, or more rarely Tyèm, is the land of the mythological woman Watrepetrua, who landed on the peninsula of Nôgâ, on the east coast of the Isle of Pines, bringing new vegetables and fruits. She allied herself with the first settlers, who were delighted with the abundance she brought with her.

On Maré, the second wave of migration from Kiamu brought 'true' yams (in other words, yams of high quality), three banana trees and a rooster. On Tanna, Jean Guiart (1963b:289) noted a similar tradition in reverse: some of the yams are said to have left on a canoe for the west. The name Kiamu might also, therefore, refer to the island of Tanna.

The 'true' yams which arrived on south-western Maré were accompanied by three banana trees. The most appreciated of them produced the Kiamu banana, *wa-Kiamu*, with pink flesh and yellow skin, which is very soft when ripe. The banana trees went with the yams on their tour of discovery of the

Fig. 91
'Greenstone' pendants.
Tanna.
Basel, Museum für Völkerkunde.

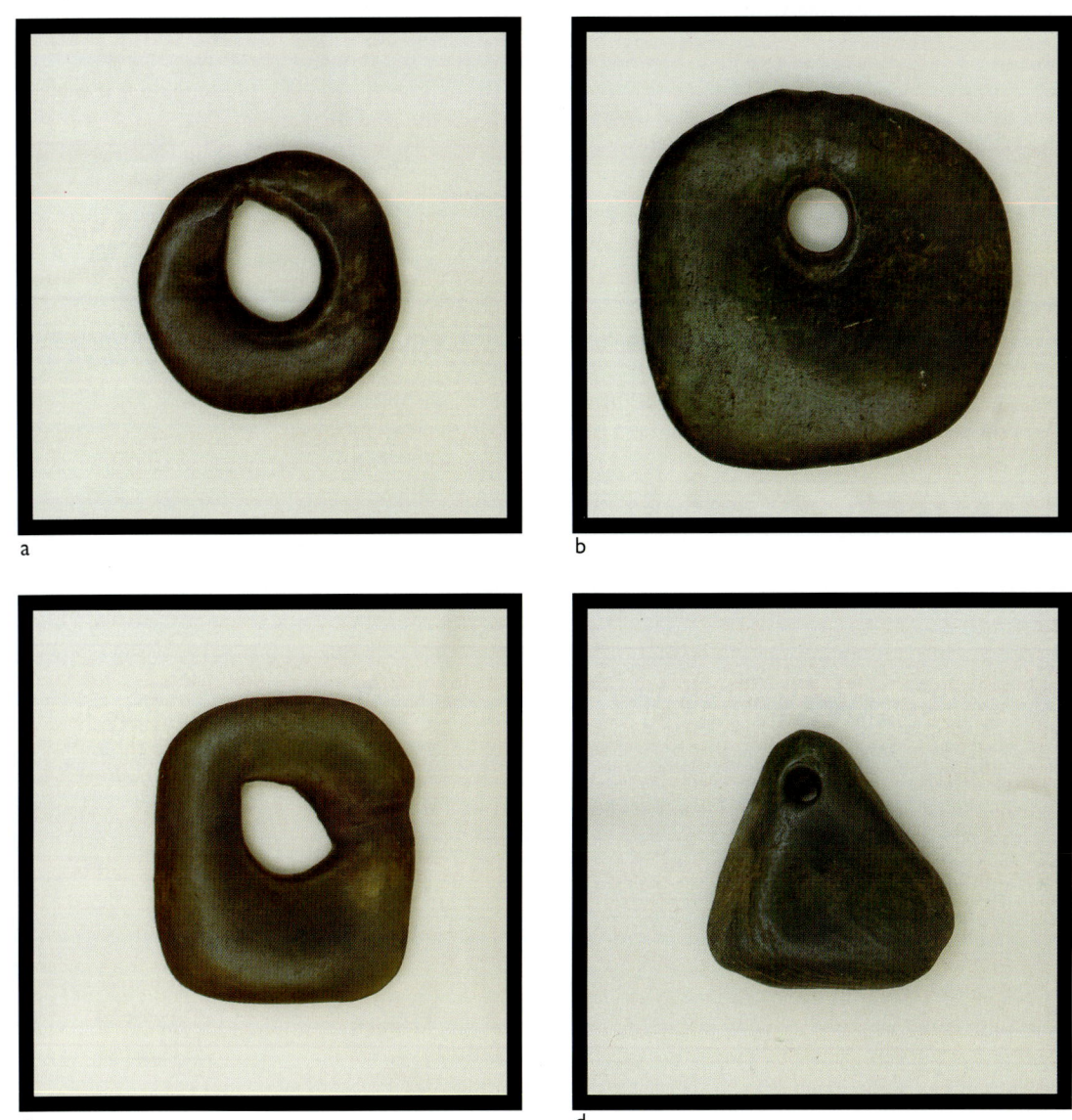

Figs 92a, b, c, d
'Greenstone' pendants.
Tanna.
Basel, Museum für Völkerkunde.

island. They stopped in what is today the southern part of Penelo village, at a place called *Hna waethe kawe*, which means 'place of the light bananas', while the yams went a little further to sit down on a tiny circular atoll to take counsel for the last time and divide Maré up between them.

The migration from Ma or Kiamu brought myths along with it. One of them concerns Nederumele, who lived at Dranin beach and who is the grandmother of Waica i Dranin, the little boy of Dranin. In all the variants of this myth, the little boy is born from Nederumele's blood. They lived in a cove north of the beach at Mele; Mele is the Maré form[2] of Mwele, which is a place near Port Vila, on Efate in Vanuatu. In front of their house grew a *kiamu* banana tree. The grandmother forbade her grandson to eat any of its bananas, or else he would become a wanderer, a vagabond who would die far from home. Her grandson, however, was tempted by the forbidden fruit and disobeyed: seized by an irresistible desire to travel, he parted abruptly from his grandmother. After many adventures, he was killed on Lifou.

Another Maré clan, the si Obu, provides a relationship, not with southern Vanuatu at this time, but with its far north. The clan practises a ritual which can be found in identical form on the island of Loh, in the Torres group in Vanuatu, and of which an account is given by W.J. Durrad (1940). The si Obu lived in a village at Nongoel, whose name comes from *nongon*, meaning 'make rain magic', 'ask for rain'. To do this, the si Obu first came to an agreement with a clan whose task it was to bring the 'big sun', and then those who were to work the magic went down into a hollow in the ground; one of them kept watch, because the procedure was secret. The opening of the hole was surrounded by stones placed on banana leaves. The officiants ate yams grilled in their skins, something which brings on extreme thirst. They could neither drink nor wash until rain came. They called on the rain and the clouds, slowly at first, then faster and faster. Spurred on by impatience and thirst, they challenged the guard: '*Ilo?*' ('Well?'). When the rain came at last, the guard would answer, '*Ci kulu hada ki re el*'[3] ('It's coming from the east, the rain').

Relations with the place of origin do not seem to have been kept up between Maré and northern Vanuatu. Those between Maré and Kiamu-Aneityum, on the other hand, must have continued until fairly recent times, and we may estimate their frequency at about one voyage every generation. One last mythical account refers to their final interruption.

According to tradition, the old path from Peorawa to the beautiful beach at Dranin on Maré was cut by two children: the Little Boy of Rue-Ezi[4] and the Little Boy of Kayec.[5] As they reached Dranin, they saw that the beach had a master, the giant Waene.[6] Waene came out of the sea, saw the land laid waste by the two children, and the *wa-Kiamu* banana skins from his plantations lying about on the ground. He saw the two small boys and tore up some pine trees, which he threw at them like spears. The two boys countered this by peppering him with their toy spears. After a while, the Kayec boy grew weary and gave up the fight, leaving the Rue-Ezi boy to carry on the battle alone. In the end, the giant Waene weakened and flung himself into the sea to flee far away. He shouted to the children, 'I leave you my country.' The little Rue-Ezi boy bounded to the very edge of the sheer cliff, picked up a sharp stone, and threw it so that it skipped over the surface of the sea and cut off Waene's head.

The the Rue-Ezi boy cut six stems from an ipomea vine at the edge of the sea. Holding them by one end, he threw one and caught the Isle of Pines.[7] He pulled, and drew it closer to Maré. He threw another piece of vine and caught the mainland of New Caledonia, pulled and brought it close to Maré. Then he threw two other pieces, which caught Lifou and Ouvea, pulled again and brought them close to Maré. Then he threw one to the north. This one caught nothing. There was no land in that direction. Finally, the little boy threw one last vine in the direction of Kiamu. He pulled and it broke. This is how relations between Maré and Kiamu were broken off.

---

2. *Mele* is a component of many locative or temporal particles; *me* is the indicator of apposition in the Maré language.

3. Hence the woman's name Kuluada concerns the breaking off of these links.

4. Waica i Rue Ezi, who represents the ancient chiefdom of the si Rue-Ezi, which dominated the central grassland.

5. Waica i Kayec, who represents the ancient clan of the si Keyec, which eventually established itself near Wakone.

6. *Wa-* is a prefix denoting respect, which can here be translated as 'old'; *-ne* is an inflection indicating respect. The root of the word is the particle *E*, which designates the 'inward being' ('him').

7. Called *Uzeri*. Note that this is a metathesis of Rue-Ezi, which shows the close relationship between the people of Maré and those of the Isle of Pines.

Vanuatu Rock Art

David Roe

Although widespread in distribution and probably a more common site type than is apparent from the literature, the Vanuatu region's rock art has been paid little more than cursory attention by many archaeologists working in Melanesia. It presents several problems of interpretation, foremost of which are the almost universal lack of ethnographic information about it and, more importantly for the archaeologist, the extreme difficulty of establishing its age and thus of incorporating it into any chronological framework. It remains, therefore, a rather poorly documented and little-understood part of Vanuatu's prehistory.

For this brief review, 'rock art' as a category is taken to include designs executed on rock surfaces where these are not part of other structures or those which might best be described as statuary. It thus excludes, for example, the cupule-marked dolmens of south Malakula (Capitan 1901; Speiser 1913a), the elaborately carved stone kava bowls of northeast Malakula (Regenvanu and Roe 1992) and Ambae (Bühler 1946-49), and stone statues and monoliths (for example, Hébert 1963-1965b).

The study of Vanuatu's rock art began in the late 19th century, when a number of Presbyterian missionaries published descriptions of engravings and paintings at sites on Aneityum and Lelepa (for example, Gunn 1906a, 1906b, 1909, 1914; Inglis 1887; Lawrie 1892; MacDonald 1913; Patterson 1882; for a review of this early literature see Spriggs and Mumford 1992). Many of these early works were concerned with either the ultimate derivation of the motifs – MacDonald in particular seemed anxious to ascertain a link with Phoenicia and Babylonia (1913) – and/or their putative religious associations. Felix Speiser, in his monumental ethnography (Speiser 1923, 1991), gives brief details of a site on Ambrym, but considered the engravings there as 'merely chance products of an idle hour and without significance', and, because of their explicit form, dismissed them as prehistoric pornography. In addition to those from Aneityum, Lelepa and Ambrym, further examples of rock art were recorded from Erromango (Humphreys 1926; Skinner 1923; Woodburn 1944), Emau (Somerville 1894; Hébert 1963-1965b) and Efate (Hébert 1963-1965c). In his major review of Melanesian rock art, Specht (1979) was able to list only nine sites from five islands of Vanuatu in his regional catalogue. Following Specht's review, more intensive archaeological surveys, and in particular Spriggs' research in southern Vanuatu (Spriggs and Mumford 1992), and Vanuatu Cultural and Historic Sites Survey work in Aneityum, Erromango, Efate, Malakula,

Maewo and Pentecost, have increased the total of known sites to fifty. The table (fig. 93) summarises the distribution and main features of these sites.

Despite the increasingly large database of information relating to Vanuatu's rock art, a great deal of additional field survey is required before any proper analysis of its internal and external relationships can be undertaken. It is already clear, however, that a regional rock-art style exists which links the Vanuatu design corpus to sites in New Guinea, the Bismarck Archipelago – such as the Likding site on New Hanover (Lampert 1967) – the Solomons (Roe n.d.), the enviably well-documented sites of New Caledonia to the south (Frimigacci and Monnin 1980), and to some extent also to those of Fiji (Palmer and Clunie 1970). It is also becoming accepted that this broad tradition of rock art, in which some regional 'sub-styles' are apparent, is linked to a much larger design or symbol system that extends into other media such as tattooing,

Fig 93 Rock-art sites of Vanuatu: styles, types and locations

Island	Number of sites	Style			Type				Location			
		E	P	S	B	Cl	C	O	Co	Ri	RS	RT
Torres Islands	3	–	–	3	–	–	3	–	–	–	3?	–
Banks Islands	1	1	–	–	–	1	–	–	1	–	–	–
Santo	–	–	–	–	–	–	–	–	–	–	–	–
Ambae	–	–	–	–	–	–	–	–	–	–	–	–
Maewo	5	5	1	–	2	1	2	–	3	–	2	–
Pentecôte	1	?	1	–	–	–	1	–	1	–	–	–
Ambrym	2	2	–	–	1	1	–	–	2?	–	–	–
Malakula	5	3	3	2	?	?	4	?	3	?	1?	?
Paama/Lopevi	–	–	–	–	–	–	–	–	–	–	–	–
Epi	–	–	–	–	–	–	–	–	–	–	–	–
Shepherd Islands	3	3	–	–	2	–	–	1[a]	–	–	3	–
Efate[b]	5	5	2	2	–	–	5	–	3	–	1	1
Erromango	12	8	4	4	–	5	7	–	10	–	2	–
Tanna	1	1	–	–	1	–	–	–	1	–	–	–
Futuna/Aniwa	–	–	–	–	–	–	–	–	–	–	–	–
Aneityum	12	12	–	–	10	2	–	–	1	2	9	–
All	50	40	11	11	16	10	22	1	25	2	21	1

Notes

[a] Broken stone slab discovered during airport construction.
[b] Including offshore islands.

Style
E   Engravings
P   Paintings
S   Stencils

Type
B   Boulder
Cl   Cliff or outcrop
C   Cave or rock shelter
O   Other (footnotes specify)

Emplacement
Co   Coastal (littoral fringe and coastal plains)
Ri   River course or valley bottom
RS   Ridge slope
RT   Ridge top

barkcloth and the plastic arts (cf. Green 1979a; Gunn 1986).

Distribution

Although rock-art sites have been recorded from the Torres Islands (Langdon 1967; Titus Joel, pers. comm.) to Aneityum, the current geographical distribution of rock-art sites in Vanuatu is almost certainly a reflection of the state of archaeological research. The table, fig. 93, gives basic data for the fifty known sites in the archipelago, but the lacunae this indicates for Santo and Ambae in particular are almost certainly the result of insufficient survey coverage on those islands. Similarly, the apparent predominance of sites at or near the coast probably results from a lack of intensive survey in inland locations. Given recent experience on Maewo, Aneityum and Erromango, where rock-art sites were specifically targeted during surveys, site numbers elsewhere are likely to increase dramatically with further work.

Styles and designs

Rock-art designs in Vanuatu may be divided into three main categories by the techniques employed in their accomplishment: engravings (usually executed by percussive techniques but with some instances of abrading), paintings (applications of pigments to form positive images, including line figures) and stencils (pigments applied to form negative images). Sites with engraved designs are more numerous than those with paintings in the currently known sample, and are found in the greatest variety of locations – caves, rock shelters, exposed cliffs, boulders and beach-rock exposures. Because paintings are known only from caves, it might be assumed that weathering has removed any such designs in open locations; painted sites on exposed cliffs, however, are known elsewhere (Ballard 1988, 1992).

Engraved figurative designs include anthropomorphic figures and heads (especially in the north-west Malakula cave sites; fig. 94; Leaney 1965; Roe in prep.), fish (fig. 95), turtles (on Aneityum), and footprints. The non-figurative elements include

Fig. 94
Engraved anthropomorphic head design from the Abeialau cave site, north-west Malakula. The design is approximately 55 cm in height.

complex geometrical designs (especially on Maewo), enveloped crosses of simple and complex forms (fig. 96), chevrons, rayed concentric circles, bisected ovals, zigzags and, at most sites, lines of cupules. The most impressive examples of the latter are found on the beach-rock exposures of east Erromango (fig. 97), where some groups extend to several hundred metres in length (Spriggs and Mumford 1992; Spriggs and Roe 1989; Roe 1992b).

Painted designs exhibit a similar diversity of form. This is especially marked in the large galleries of art in the north-west Malakula sites, where the motif catalogue includes anthropomorphic figures of two very different forms (fig. 98), birds, fish, dog, and a variety of geometrical designs, including several that are paralleled in the sand-drawings of the same area (Deacon 1934a). Similar designs are found in the

1. BP: before present

other major painted sites, which includes the well-known Feles Cave motif suite recorded by Garanger (1972a, 1982).

Stencilled designs are less diverse in form. The commonest design is the human hand, with or without the forearm; in Malakula, 'double-ended' hand stencils have also been recorded (fig. 99). In many cases, hand stencils are placed high on cave walls (Skinner 1923; Roe in prep.) and could only have been executed from a ladder or scaffolding. Other stencilled forms include zigzags and rows of triangles, possibly executed using leaf or bark stencils similar to those used in the manufacture of dyed mats on Pentecost (Mescam 1989).

Pigment colours are restricted, with black and blue-black predominating, and less frequent occurrences of red and white. Multicoloured designs have been recorded from Erromango (J. Taki, pers. comm.) and Pentecost (Walter, pers. comm.). There is little data on the pigments themselves: red ochre is reported from the Torres Islands (Langdon 1967), charcoal dust from Erromango (Skinner 1923), and *Canarium* almond sap from Wala Island (F. Yoringmal, pers. comm.). The use of *Canarium* sap as a dye for tattoos in Erromango (Humphreys 1926) may also suggest its use as a pigment for rock-art designs there.

A full catalogue of designs is beyond the scope of this brief review and must await further work and better recording methods than generally have been employed in the past.

Dating

There is currently little information on the antiquity of rock art in Vanuatu. In the majority of cases where specific enquiry has been made, local informants profess little knowledge either of the context in which the art was produced, or by whom it was executed. Until recently the only archaeological evidence for the age of rock art in the archipelago came from Garanger's work at the Feles Cave (Garanger 1972a, 1982). Excavations at the site recovered part of a frieze of cupules, fallen from the wall above, and lying above a deposit dated to about 1000 BP.[1] Because the art lies in a secondary position, however, it could have been executed before the age indicated by the radiocarbon date.

Research in New Guinea (Ballard 1992) has indicated a link between the location of a suite of distinctive painted art sites and areas where Austronesian languages are spoken. The inference that may be drawn from this distribution is that the art is associated with, or postdates, the expansion of Austronesian-speaking peoples out of South-East Asia at about 4000 BP (cf. Gorecki, this volume). In the Solomons, engraved designs have been dated at one site to about 3000 BP (Roe 1992a). This further strengthens the postulated link between rock art and Austronesian speakers, as does the presence of rock-art motifs in other media associated with the Austronesian expansion; for example an enveloped cross motif on Lapita pottery from the Santa Cruz islands (Green 1973).

Recent work in Vanuatu indicates that rock art is a particularly long-lived tradition. Depictions of

Fig. 95
Engraved fish design on a beach-rock exposure at Malap, east Erromango. Scale: 10 cm.

Fig. 96
A complex enveloped cross motif on the Siligi boulder, central Maewo. The design is some 12 cm in diameter.

European ships at engraved sites on Ambrym (Speiser 1923, 1991), Maewo (Regenvanu 1992), Erromango (Roe 1992b), and at a painted site on Maewo, demonstrate the continuation of rock-art production at least until the 18th century.

Obtaining more information and greater precision in the dating of rock art in Vanuatu will be difficult, and will require either the recovery of art in sub-surface datable contexts, or the direct dating of organic components in pigments using accelerator mass spectrometry (cf. Loy et al. 1990). Given the proven extension of the rock-art tradition into the period of European contact, a re-evaluation of the limited oral testimonies regarding rock art is also required.

Conclusion

Few of the rock-art sites in Vanuatu possess any accompanying documentation that sheds any light upon the purpose or meaning of the designs. The Aname boulders in Aneityum were reportedly used as a fishing shrine (Inglis 1887), but, despite the suggestions of the early missionaries, no other ritual or religious purpose of rock-art sites has ever been demonstrated. There are indications from Aneityum and Erromango that rows of cupules act as tally devices, while on Maewo the complex geometric forms at the Malangulgul site are interpreted by local informants as designs whose copyright is restricted to particular lineages. The north-west Malakula cave sites, which are particularly rich in their design catalogues, are all featured in myths relating to the 'road of the dead' (Deacon 1934b).

The problems of investigating meaning in Melanesian art generally (Forge 1979) are exacerbated in the case of rock art by the longevity of the tradition and the likelihood that its symbolic meaning has changed through time. Even where the designs remain constant in form and may be recognised and named by informants, the meaning of them, if any, cannot therefore be ascribed to purely prehistoric art. Although the meaning and purpose of rock art in Vanuatu may remain elusive, it remains a valuable artifact worthy of fuller investigation, and has importance as an indicator of cultural relationships and as testimony to the rich symbolic and artistic heritage of Vanuatu.

Fig. 97
A group of cupule marks at the Malap beach rock site, east Erromango. Scale: 10 cm.

Fig. 98
Anthropomorphic figures of the profile style in blue-black pigments at the Abeialau cave site, north-west Malakula. The figures are positioned high on the cave wall and are approximately 60 cm in height.

Fig. 99
'Double-ended' hand stencils at the Yalo cave near Tenmial, north-west Malakula. Scale: 10 cm.

Chapter II
Men's art, women's art

An Agricultural Art: Taro Irrigation in Vanuatu[1]

Matthew Spriggs

[1]. References to taro irrigation in Vanuatu can be found in Spriggs 1990b. See also Bonnemaison 1974 for a description of irrigation on Maewo.

The largest pre-20th century artifacts found in Vanuatu are undoubtedly the irrigated garden systems that occur on several of the islands. Often constructed of large stones as well as earthen embankments, their terraces sometimes cover entire hillsides and take their water supply from streams several kilometres away, bringing it to the gardens in canals which are skilfully constructed to follow the contours. In terms of technical achievement, they represent perhaps the apogee of Vanuatu traditional science. The crop grown is taro (*Colocasia esculenta*), one of the major Pacific root crops. Taro is a water-loving plant and responds well to irrigation. Indeed, a swampy habitat is presumed to have been the home of its wild ancestors in the South-East Asian and New Guinea areas.

The yield per hectare is considerably higher under irrigation than in rain-fed gardens in a similar environment. In some of the drier parts of Vanuatu, taro could not be grown successfully as a staple crop without irrigation. Even in areas where rainfall is usually sufficient for good crop growth, irrigation is used both as a safeguard against occasional drought and, what is more important, to promote higher yields.

In several parts of Vanuatu (and in neighbouring areas such as New Caledonia and Solomon Islands), flights of previously used irrigation terraces can be seen on the hillsides. We might be tempted to see these as abandoned remnants, witnesses to a once numerous rural population and of interest now only to the archaeologist. In fact they form, in most cases, a permanent infrastructure that could be brought back into productive use at any time with comparative ease. This permanency is of crucial importance, as it lessens any future labour input necessary for their reuse. In some parts of Maewo where the original coastal populations died out because of introduced diseases, the hill peoples have moved down in the last sixty years and brought the terraces back into production.

On Aneityum, many now-uninhabited valleys are covered with the remains of stone-lined terraces for dry-land and irrigated gardens. The latter were fed by water from springs, or from canals up to 5 kilometres in length and crossing major watersheds. In addition, the lower courses of many of the rivers and streams on the island exhibit evidence of course-straightening and are lined with stone revetments. The straightening and lining of the rivers would have meant greater efficiency in shifting water into the sea during periods of exceptional rainfall caused by seasonal patterns or occasional cyclones. In dry-land terraced gardens on hillsides, and sometimes around spring-fed irrigated gardens, there are networks of stone-lined storm drains with a similar function – they are designed to prevent gully erosion and swamping or slumping of hillside gardens during heavy rainstorms.

On the coastal plains, the difficulties of circulating water were solved by leading the canals along the top of earth embankments before letting the water down onto the flattest areas, which could not otherwise have been irrigated. Some of the embankments or aqueducts were up to 4 metres tall and hundreds of metres long. The technological sophistication of these systems shows a detailed understanding of engineering and water-control principles, and an effective response to the dangers of erosion caused by gardening on the unstable soils of steep hillsides.

There are two main types of traditional irrigation found in Vanuatu: true irrigation and swampland cultivation. True irrigation refers to diversion of water from its source to the fields. Swampland cultivation techniques generally consist of the management by ditching of freshwater swamps, where the aim is not complete drainage to create a dry environment for planting, but only to control the water table within required limits.

True irrigation in Vanuatu

The dams which divert water from the streams are made of loose boulders so that excess water can filter through. They are usually no more than 1 metre tall, to allow easy repair, and are designed so that in floods they wash away and prevent floodwaters from damaging the canals and gardens. Sometimes water is diverted almost directly from a stream into the garden area, but more usually unlined or stone-lined canals up to several kilometres in length are necessary. Found in association with such canals, or in place of them, are pipelines of bamboo, coconut, pandanus, or tree-fern trunks, which themselves may be of some length.

Three methods of applying water to the crop are found in Vanuatu: paddies or pond-fields, simple flooding, and furrow irrigation.

Pond-fields resemble Asian rice paddies, and indeed may have an ultimately Asian origin. They are the commonest form of irrigation used in Vanuatu and occur today in the Banks, Santo, Maewo and Pentecost. Early European visitors' accounts and some archaeological remains suggest that they were formerly more widespread and once occurred also on Efate, Erromango, Ambae, and perhaps Nguna and some other islands. They are also common in other parts of the Pacific.

The fields consist of flat terraces with an earth, wood, or stone-faced bund or embankment. The planted area on the terrace is an artificial pond through which water is kept constantly flowing, usually about 5 to 10 centimetres deep. After planting, the major task is weeding, which is usually necessary about three times during the twelve- to eighteen-month growing period for taro. Soil type, nutrient supply, availability of land, and the labour needed to clean out the soft mud from the fields at the end of each planting cycle are factors which determine how many years a field can be kept in continuous production. In northern Maewo, eight to ten years use is common, followed by three to four years fallow period on the best soils. On less fertile soils, three to eight years use with five years fallow is more typical. If yields decline, then a mulch of dry banana and breadfruit leaves can be trodden into the pond-field, and this is said to allow a further two plantings before it becomes necessary to rest the

Fig. 100
Taro garden furrows, made by Tamadui, Itanytmere, Ingarei valley, Aneityum.

Fig. 101
Taro terraces, Naviso, Maewo.

field. Replanting does not take place until all the taro plants have been harvested. Then the soft mud is cleaned out and thrown onto the bank. All remaining roots, half-rotten pieces of taro and other debris are removed before the next crop is planted.

On the east coast of Maewo, the gardens are on very stony, coralline soil, and in some areas only one cycle of planting takes place before a fallow period of up to seven years. The coral rubble from which these terraces are constructed gives added scope for the aesthetic sense of the gardeners (fig. 101). The almost blindingly white terrace walls, relieved here and there by a dark-grey or black stone of different origin, contrast with the cool green of the gently waving taro leaves. Further contrast is given by the different shades of green of other food crops planted on the banks, and the purple and red of crotons and cordylines.

In simple flooding systems, water is led to the upper edge of the garden and then circulates down, usually with simple wood or stone barriers to slow down the flow. These act to control erosion and trap sediment. This technique is quite common in the New Guinea highlands, and is reported in Vanuatu from south Malakula. In a variation on this practice, small terraces are constructed directly in small stream beds. There is no permanent field infrastructure and gardens have to be made completely anew after each fallow period. At most, only two cycles of cultivation are possible before a long fallow.

In furrow irrigation, water is applied to the ground in small, shallow furrows from which it soaks laterally through the soil to soak the area in between, where the taro is planted. In the Pacific, I have only ever seen this system in use on Aneityum (fig. 100). It appears to have been a unique invention there. The soils of Aneityum are generally of very poor fertility. They are also unstable and subject to erosion. In other parts of the world where furrow irrigation is used today, it is generally in areas where the land surface is moderately steep and irregular. It ensures uniform wetting and limits erosion. The canals and terraced garden plots on Aneityum provide a permanent infrastructure, although the individual furrows must be redug with every planting. In 1980, a furrow irrigation garden on the island was recommissioned after having been abandoned for more than eighty years. Under the dense forest vegetation covering the area, the canal and terraces remained largely intact and were brought back into use with minimum effort.

After a fallow period and vegetation clearance, the garden area may be tilled or left as it is. The taro is planted, then the furrows are dug about one month later. The growth period is about twelve months. Kava (*Piper methysticum*) is planted between the taro. After harvest of the taro, the furrows are blocked off and the kava is harvested dry after two to three years. An extended fallow period is then instituted, but it is said that when the island's population was much higher and land was in more demand, a fallow of as short as three years was normal.

Swampland systems

Taro is often seen planted in naturally wet areas such as swamp edges and alongside streams or ditches. More intensive swampland use often involves creating 'island beds' by digging channels around the edges of usually rectangular plots to create a network of 'islands' raised above the water table. The spoil from the ditches is used to raise the level of the planting beds.

Aneityum again provides many examples of such systems, and they are widespread elsewhere in the Pacific. Taro takes about twelve months to mature in the taro swamps of Aneityum. After the harvest, the soil is turned over, mulched with green leaves from selected plants, then replanted. The mulching allows continuous use of the swamp plots for an indefinite period without fallow. Most of the taro now grown on Aneityum is grown in these swamp gardens (*inhenou* in the Aneityumese language), and the furrow irrigation gardens (called *incauwai*) are very rarely made. At present population size, the swamps are able to provide for almost all the needs of the population.

A dying art?

In some parts of Vanuatu, and more so in many other parts of the Pacific, there has been a decrease in, or even total abandonment of, taro irrigation. The causes include substantial population decline through foreign diseases in the 19th and early 20th centuries, and, more recently, urban migration and the general change to a cash-crop economy based on copra and cocoa, which competes directly for labour and land. In some areas, alienation or seizure of productive land by European settlers, and the breakdown of traditional patterns of leadership that formerly had a role in the organisation of traditional agriculture are aggravating factors.

As the populations of Pacific island states continue to rise at a rapid pace, more intensive forms of agriculture will be necessary to feed them. It would indeed be misguided if tried and true techniques, developed over thousands of years and adapted to local soil and climatic conditions, are ignored when searching for solutions to the problems of adequate food supply. For instance, the yields of taro on Maewo are some of the highest ever recorded for the plant anywhere in the world, comparable to those obtained by commercial Hawaiian farmers using heavy fertiliser supplements in conditions of semi-mechanisation. Every time an old taro farmer dies without his or her knowledge being passed on to a new generation, we are tearing another vital page out of the book of how to feed the fast-growing populations of the Pacific.

Pottery and Potters of Vanuatu

Jean-Christophe Galipaud

The volcanic islands of Vanuatu contain few clay materials capable of use in pottery-making. Clays do, however, exist, abundantly in some islands, as J. Garanger and G. Ward have shown. These authors have demonstrated that in the group's central islands, as well as in the Banks, an original sort of pottery, named 'Mangaasi' after one of the villages of the west coast of Efate, was intensively used as early as 1000 BC, or in other words, at the same period as Lapita pottery elsewhere in Melanesia.

More recently, when carrying out research on Malo Island, just south of Santo, Hedrick confirmed that Lapita-style pottery existed in Vanuatu as in other areas. Pottery of this type had already been found on Efate (Hébert 1963-1965c), and more recently on Erromango as well (Spriggs and Wickler 1989). This initial diversity of ceramic production is noticeable in the islands right up until the arrival of the Europeans and even later, since a few villages along the west coast of Santo still keep this milleniums-old tradition alive.

Islands with pottery, islands without pottery

It is difficult to establish what the distribution of pottery throughout the islands was. On some islands, potsherds are numerous and visible; on others, they are less so, and on some no fragment or other trace of ceramics has ever been found.

After more than thirty years of sporadic research, the islands of Vanuatu are still little known, and we cannot assume that present sites of archaeological evidence, either of a general kind or more particularly of pottery, truly represent ancient use of these artifacts. Discoveries made in the last two years by the Vanuatu Cultural and Historic Sites Survey (VCHSS) team bear this out.

From the Banks Islands to Efate, one frequently finds fragments of prehistoric pottery. This is particularly the case on the big islands (Santo, Malakula and Pentecost) where the extremely weathered ancient volcanic substratum is rich in composite clays (kaolinite, halloysite), and iron and manganese oxides, and thus supplies the raw materials. On at least two of these islands (Santo and Malakula), the fact that some sites contain whole pots suggests that pottery was still being made quite recently (fig. 102). Some authors have even suggested the pottery of Malakula was made on Santo and then distributed by means of exchange as far as South West Bay (Malakula), and even the Shepherd Islands and Epi (Speiser 1923). The women of Wusi, on the west coast of Santo, have relearned an art which had disappeared at the beginning of this century.

On Pentecost, members of the VCHSS project team have collected sherds from several areas of cultivated land in the north and east of the island. The absence of sherds on the surface and in eroded areas near the sea seems to argue that these materials are ancient.

On the islands of Ambae (Aoba) and Ambrym, there is only sparse evidence of the use of pottery in ancient times. Speiser (1923) records sherds buried under several metres of volcanic sediment. The intense volcanic activity in this part of the islands makes it difficult to find ancient remains, which are very quickly covered by the rain of ashes. The paucity of potsherds, however, does not necessarily mean there are none.

On the islands south of Efate, the situation is quite different: with the exception of a few fragments of pottery found on Erromango, it appears that pottery was never used or made there. Efforts by Shutler (1968), Groube (1975), and Spriggs and Wickler (1989) to uncover traces of this ancient industry on Anatom and Tanna, and then Erromango, did not produce the results they hoped for. Nevertheless, the eight sites containing pottery eventually discovered on Erromango (Spriggs and Wickler 1989) may push back the limits of existing evidence.

Archaeological excavations in the Banks Islands (Groube 1972, Ward 1979), on Malo (Hedrick n.d.), and in the central islands (Garanger 1972a) have enabled us to situate these widely-dispersed remains chronologically. These researchers have grouped the decorative styles into a single style called Mangaasi, characterised by incised and applied decoration.

Appearance and disappearance

The Avunatari site, on Malo, dates from early in the first millennium BC and marks the first appearance of pottery in Vanuatu. As elsewhere in Melanesia, the pottery is of the Lapita style.

The last vestiges of 'prehistoric' pottery, found on Efate, may date from the 16th century (Garanger 1972a). Again, this is 'Mangaasi' pottery. Ward (1979), in the light of the results of his research in the Banks Islands, disputes these dates as too recent and puts forward AD 1000 as the approximate date when pottery-making was abandoned.

Fig. 102
Ceremonial pottery.
Meltmes site, south Malakula.
Vanuatu Cultural Centre, Port Vila.

We do not know when Lapita pottery disappeared, but we can reasonably situate it around the time of Christ, based on our knowledge of other Lapita sites in Melanesia and western Polynesia.

The date of Mangaasi pottery's appearance (600 BC on Efate; 800 to 400 BC in the Banks) shows that both Lapita and Mangaasi pottery were being made in Vanuatu before the birth of Christ.

This situation is comparable in every way with what we know of other parts of island Melanesia. Lapita is not, as may previously have been thought, the only milestone marking the progress of settlement through these islands. The existence of pottery like that of Mangaasi in Vanuatu, which was made from a very ancient period, shows the diversity of settlement and the difficulties of interpretation.

The incised decorations and applied reliefs appear throughout the chronological sequence, from start to finish, and are often found on the same pot. Applied decoration, however, tends to become rarer, and decorative designs poorer, in more recent times.

The persistence of Mangaasi pottery and the slow development of its forms and decoration are signs of

Fig. 103
Fragments of prehistoric pottery, Malo Island:
b, c, d, e, f, h, i. Incised and applied decorations, Mangaasi style.
a. Scale design.
g. Lapita dentate design.

Fig. 104
Mangaasi pottery, applied decoration.
Vanuatu Cultural Centre, Port Vila.

social stability; the similarity of decorative techniques in islands as far away as New Britain, or even New Guinea (Gorecki, p. 62, this volume) evidence a capacity for exchange and diffusion of ideas.

One style, or several?

Mangaasi pottery was defined by Garanger (1972a: 124) after the excavations he carried out in Efate in the 1960s. It is characterised by its decoration, which consists of incisions and applied reliefs (fig. 103a, b, d, e, f, g, h; fig. 104), and by its shape, generally spherical or ovoid, with a wide mouth decorated by a flat or flaring lip.

The classic Mangaasi style is, of course, that of Efate and the Shepherd Islands, but one finds not only similar techniques but also similar decorative designs in the northern islands. The potters of Wusi, on Santo, still use these designs. Listening to their descriptions, one realises that these abstract geometric patterns (checkerboard, chevron, zigzag, and so on) are, to them, perfectly concrete representations of the nature that surrounds them: palms, breadfruits, pigs' teeth, mats, and so on.

On a few islands we find decorative patterns produced by different techniques which can therefore not be compared to those just described. The question has arisen whether or not they should be considered part of the Mangaasi style. José Garanger prefers, in his study, to exclude them, and we shall do likewise, as the originality of some of the decorative techniques points to different cultural networks.

The commonest decoration, found everywhere from Malakula to the Banks Islands, is done when the pot is being shaped. The paste is pressed with the thumb as it is turned. The pattern, a series of 'scales', appears in relief on the outside of the pot (fig. 103c). As in the case of most of the descriptions which follow, we have little information about these patterns other than the geographical area in which they are found.

On Pentecost, a recently uncovered fragment is decorated with excised geometrical designs, similar to some present-day New Guinea pots (fig. 105). This decorated sherd is, for the moment, the only example of the technique in Vanuatu.

Other incised pottery has been found which is unlike the Mangaasi style in its lack of applied reliefs, its different shape and its type of decoration. This pottery, many examples of which can still be seen at traditional sites in South Malakula, is cylindrical with a pointed base. The crudely incised patterns on the belly are not very stylised and are sometimes even quite figurative (human or animal likenesses). These pots are sometimes of great ritual power; they were placed in graves to house the dead person's soul.

The potters of today

Except in New Guinea, very few groups went on producing pottery after their first contact with the white man. The tradition persists on Santo's west coast, on Choiseul in the Solomon Islands, and in a few Fijian valleys, though now for the benefit of curio dealers.

It appears that, in Santo, the technique did not come unscathed through first contact with the European world at the end of last century. Jean Guiart (1956a) and Elizabeth Shutler (1968) were privileged, in the wake of Speiser, to observe the details of pottery making. Their accounts, with several years' interval between them, give a good idea of the techniques used. Speiser, at the beginning of this century, mentioned the names of two villages where pottery was being made: Wusi and Pespia. Only one of these, Wusi, now survives. A coastal village, it appears to have been abandoned shortly after Speiser's visit, and later resettled by west-coast clans who revived the tradition.

The different authors collected different information. It is interesting to compare their observations, as this shows the relativity of certain procedures with respect to the final result, and the technical choices favoured by different artisans.

According to Guiart (1956a:45), the potters find their raw material (*tanolo*) on the banks of a river south of Wusi, and they sift through it carefully to remove any impurities; according to Shutler (1968: 15), they extract the clay from a place near the village, and it is full of impurities which temper the clay. The cleaned, well-kneaded clay (Guiart) is then stored in a shady place. Shutler writes that the impurity-filled clay is used immediately, after moistening and kneading on a sheet of bark.

At the time of Speiser's visit, two different

Fig. 105
Fragments of pottery, decorated with geometrical excised designs, found on Pentecost.

pottery-making processes were used in Pespia and in Wusi (1923: 232).

In Pespia, a long roll of clay was coiled and attached to the extremity of a bamboo cylinder about 12 centimetres long. Other rolls were then added, one after the other, to form the belly of the pot. While this was being done, the potter turned the bamboo cylinder between her legs, in a way reproducing the movement of a potter's wheel. The base, a circular sheet of clay, was finally attached to the rest before the whole pot was removed from the bamboo base. Pottery made in this way retained a base of conical shape.

In Wusi, pots are made by moulding a ball of clay the size of a fist. This simpler technique than the one described above is the only one observed by Guiart and Shutler. The ball of clay, hollowed out with the fist and then moulded on the knee, forms the rough basis of a pot. The sides are built up with the help of a paddle and an anvil; that is to say, by striking the outside of the vessel regularly in an upward motion with a small wooden or bamboo paddle, while holding the inside with a flat stone or sometimes the hand. When the pot has been shaped, the potter flares the mouth with a turning motion and smooths the resulting edge between two fingers (fig. 106).

Wusi pots are small bowls or basins 14 to 28 centimetres in diameter and 12 to 18 centimetres in

Fig. 106
Pottery-making at Wusi. The potter, Vira, applies the red clay-slip on the lip of the pot. North-west Santo.

Fig. 107
Pottery-making at Wusi. Drying the pots before firing. Magic leaves (centre right) ensure the operation's success.

Fig. 108
Pottery from Wusi.

height. After drying in the shade for some time, they are decorated with applied or incised patterns and then covered with a red slip (fig. 106). This slip, made of iron-rich clayey earth, comes not from Wusi, but from a valley in the interior, and is obtained in exchange for pots. After further drying, the pots are fired.

The firing, the last but decisive stage, is done with particular care. The prohibitions observed in the process are all intended to prevent the pot from cracking in the fire. Magic leaves (fig. 107) are used for additional protection. This is the most delicate stage of the operation. In Melanesia, many factors are involved in the making and firing process, over which the potter has no control but which nonetheless determine the success of the enterprise: the nature of the clays and tempering material, the thickness of the pot, the residual humidity at the moment of firing and, of course, temperature and length of firing. The potter takes innumerable precautions, using empirical knowledge based on long experience. For example, in Wusi the slip and the clay are mixed with seawater. The salt acts as a flux; in other words, it promotes fusion of the clays at low temperatures.

The hearth is also prepared with the same preoccupation in mind. It is done in two separate stages. First, a small fire is lit on a platform of smooth river stones. When the stones are hot, the fire is scattered and the pots to be fired are arranged upside down on the stones. Preheating the hearth reduces the risk of poor diffusion of heat at the base of the fire.

Dry coconut-palm fronds and broken bamboo are used for the fire proper. They are piled up on top of the pots and stood upright in bundles around the hearth, with the tips meeting at the top.

Firing is done at dawn, to avoid anyone coming to stir up the fire, which would make the temperature rise too fast. Firing is rapid and the heat intense. While the fire is burning away, the potters prepare another platform of stones nearby, and as soon as the last flames have flickered out, they carry the still red-hot pots there. The pots are then sprinkled with seawater into which arrowroot (*Maranta* sp.) has been grated. The purpose of this is to make them more watertight.

These techniques, well-described by a number of researchers, are not exclusive to Santo. They were used with little variation in New Caledonia shortly before the arrival of the Europeans, and are still in use in New Guinea.

While the decorations, and to some extent the shape, bear the symbols and marks of the individual or group, the manufacturing technique, through the empirical knowledge it contains, refers back to a more ancient cultural ground that is common to all the potters of the Pacific.

Vanuatu's potters, ancient or modern, are no exception to the rule. Our knowledge of Vanuatu's prehistoric pottery is still very fragmentary. There is no doubt, however, that it is part of Melanesian pottery as a whole, the origins of which are now put at 5600 years ago in north-east New Guinea (Swadling et al. 1989; Gorecki et al. 1991).

Fig. 109
Ancient pottery, Olpoï style.
North-west Santo.

The Feminine Art of Mat-weaving on Pentecost

Annie Walter

1. See Bolton, p. 114, this volume, for the different types of mats in Ambae.

Mats printed with purple designs are made and exchanged on Pentecost, Ambae, Maewo, and the small island of Tomman. In northern and central Malakula, mats are dyed a uniform red, without any design. We know little about the origins of the art, although it is undoubtedly connected with the settlement of the Pacific Islands and the exchanges which took place between different peoples. Central Pentecost mythology attributes the origin of weaving to the Raga of the north, and of dyeing to the Sowa.

Whatever the origins of the art, the Apma women of central Pentecost work every day on making these long mats with their purple designs. They are works of art, and an object of pride to these women. They are also symbolic objects representing the feminine principle, and embody the soul of the people.

Different kinds of mats

On Pentecost there are three kinds of mat:[1]
- The *sese* (fig. 110), 4 metres long and 79 centimetres wide, are printed with white designs on a purple ground, and decorated along their whole length with a long, thick fringe. The ends are decorated with a finely woven open-work edging finishing in little plaits.
- The *tsip* or *malmal*, small mats for clothing, measuring 1.2 metres by 30 centimetres, are printed with red designs on a white background, which immediately indicates a different technique from that used for *sese*. *Tsip*, a women's garment worn around the hips, are wider than *malmal*, a men's garment worn as a loincloth. The former usually have no fringe at the ends, but are decorated with an open-weave border extended to the sides with fringing. The latter have a similar open-weave border and little fringed braids at each end. Some *malmal*, known as *tsip malmalhang*, are worn only by men of high rank, and are made in secret by those women who know the complex process required for their making. Their characteristic features are woven strips at each end, which are further extended by fringed braids. The *malmalhang* may be left white, or have white and red strands woven in together. This second type is reserved for the highest chiefs.
- *Butsuban* mats are sleeping mats with no printed purple designs. They are of medium size (2 metres by 70 centimetres), and are

Fig. 110
Sese mat with red designs on white background (*wakit kere* pattern); decorated lengthwise with thick fringes. Collected by Speiser between 1910 and 1912.
Central Pentecost.
Basel, Museum für Völkerkunde.

THE FEMININE ART OF MAT-WEAVING ON PENTECOST ▼ 101

Fig. 111
These patterns are organised in squares (the most common), in broken lines (the most complex), in bands, or around a small central design.

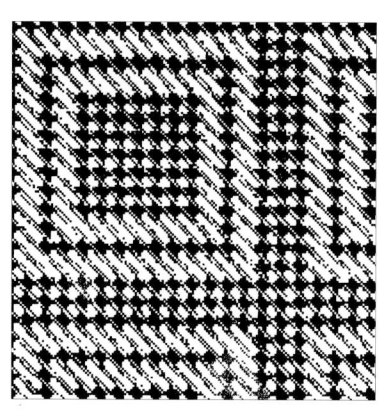
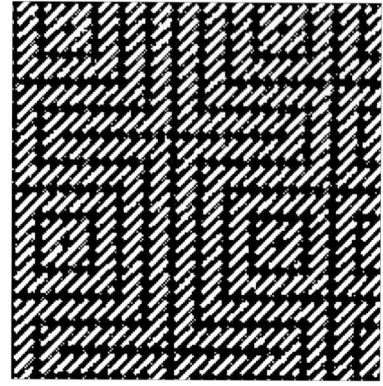

Square patterns

Broken line patterns

Band pattern

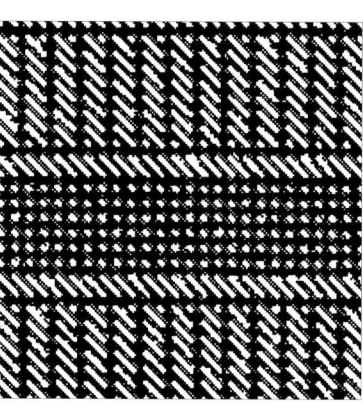

Eye pattern

decorated with a simple open-weave border and little fringes, often dyed, at each end.

Mat weaving and woven designs

All these mats are made out of pandanus leaf (*Pandanus tectorius*). Each woman has her own trees planted all around the village and reproduced by means of cuttings. The leaves are gathered green, held in the flames of a fire to soften them and then cut into narrow strips. These strips are then soaked in fresh water and bleached in the sun. The longest strips are kept for weaving *sese*. Once the strips of pandanus leaf have been bleached and softened, they are stored for several months in a dark, damp corner of the house.

The making of all mats, irrespective of the type, is based on the same technique. They consist of two parts joined together by a central seam, and the main body of the mat is woven diagonally, while the open-weave borders are woven parallel to the seam.

The weave generally used is a 1/2, 1/3, 1/4 or 3/4 twill. Simple and twill plaiting, and even fancy weaves, are also to be found. These weaves are used to make various complex patterns in the mat. All the women know four or five designs, but the best weavers are able to do about twenty, each one of which has a number of possible variations. This range of designs is used for any type of mat.

The designs are arranged in squares (the most frequent arrangement), in strips, in broken lines (the most complex), or around a small central design (figure 111). The names given to the designs refer to an element of nature (stone, water), the name of the woman who first used it (Angeline) or, more often, the name of a plant (pandanus, cycad, cabbage, bamboo).

The simplest designs are handed down from mother to daughter, the most complex from an expert to a beginner (figs 112, 115). Learning the complex designs is a matter of personal discovery, in that each weaver is free to learn new ones, though only the best will seek to increase their knowledge. When a woman teaches a new design to another, it means she implicitly recognises in her the qualities of a good weaver: a taste for doing a good job, perfect technique, and the skill which produces a flexible mat with a regular pattern, perfectly smooth and

Fig. 112
T*sip* mat, with fringes, collected by Speiser between 1910 and 1912. Central Pentecost. Basel, Museum für Völkerkunde.

Figs 113, 114
Mat weaving.

with no defects. Years of practice and consistent interest in the art of weaving are needed before a woman can achieve some of the complex designs. This means that in the handing down of skills, much social interplay takes place between the women.

The same goes for the elaborate open-weaves used to ornament the borders of each mat. The borders, placed at each end of the mats, can be wide or narrow, and more or less open. The finest are used on *malmal* and are reminiscent of the finest lace.

Three different techniques may be used for the lengthwise border of the mats. According to the first (*tsinkin boswos*), the strands of leaf are taken out towards the edge of the work so they can be used to make the fringes of a *tsip*. The second (*tsinkin bobol*) technique is to fold the strands back towards the middle of the work and leave a plain border. The third (*tsinkin wet*) is to fold the strands towards the outer edge, but in the opposite direction, thus making it possible to add a fringe to *sese*.

The side band can also be of three types. It can be plain (*bong rubale*), or made of little points (*bong sosok*) or tiny scallops.

The four corners of the mat and the central seam usually end in a little braid. Here, again, there are two sorts of braid. One is simple (*watsinetsine mirit*, eel's intestines), while the other, more complicated braid is not used by all the women (*wagune*). Some mats have little braids across their whole width.

Once the mat is woven, a fringe is added by shredding the strands left free beyond the border.

Dyeing and printed designs

The purple designs on *sese* and *tsip* are obtained by a reserve dyeing technique. There are two variations of this, one for *sese* and the other for *tsip*.

Mats are dyed in batches at dyeing sessions lasting a whole week, which occur once or twice in a woman's life. Each such occasion is a big event in the village and an important date in the life of the woman who organises it.

A week before the date fixed for the dyeing, the mats are washed and scattered with little leaves (*Astronidium aneityense*). They are then rolled up into bundles of five, tied with string and immersed in a natural basin in the coral plateau filled with seawater. This treatment disinfects the fibres, colours them a very pale yellow and allows the red dye to take better. After four days, the mats are removed from the seawater, rinsed in fresh water and dried in the sun.

The big *sese* mats are rolled around a big bamboo stem with a lengthwise slit in it, into which the fringes are inserted. These fringes have first been tied together in bunches with a strip of pandanus, which is impermeable to the dye (*wowori* or *Pandanus cominsii*). More strips of pandanus tie it in place. Then a mask, cut from the bark of a *fehi* banana tree, in which a design has been cut with a knife, is applied and fixed to the mat. Because the strips of banana bark are narrow, four masks are needed for each mat, each being ornamented with a similar design. Then a long cord (*katalvit*) plaited out of *bourao* bark is tightly wound around the mat and its masks. This cord takes the dye and leaves no mark on the dyed mat. Modern string, however, which is sometimes used, will leave parallel white lines over the whole surface.

Tsip are also attached to a bamboo stem, but a smaller one. Strips 1 or 2 centimetres wide cut from the stem of a musacea (*Heliconia indica*), and then scraped are applied to the mat to produce geometric designs (figs 116, 118). The stem of this plant is impermeable to the dye and thus produces white motifs on a red ground. Strands of pandanus hold the sticks in position until the design is completed. Then a *katalvit* cord, thinner than the one used for dyeing *sese*, is wound around the *tsip*. The strips of pandanus can then be untied.

When it has been prepared in this way, the mat is plunged into a vat of boiling water in which powdered dye has first been diluted. Formerly, the vat was made out of the bark of certain trees (*Pangomia pinnata*, *Calophyllum* sp., *Alphitonia ziziphoïdes*, *Antiaris toxicaria*, *Pterocarpus indicus* or *Trema orientalis*), but nowadays it consists of a sheet of metal folded in two. The wooden vat would be filled with seawater, but the metal one is filled with fresh water. The old kind of vat was very sensitive to the heat of the fire and was therefore placed at a distance of 1 metre above it; it was not very watertight, and this meant it had to be topped up continually. It was also small and mats had to be dyed twice. All these disadvantages have disappeared now that metal vats are available, but everyone agrees that the colours obtained are not so beautiful and the designs are less clearly marked.

The powdered dye is obtained by scraping the bark of the *Ventilago neocaledonica* (*butsu laba*). The powder is put into the vat of water and then sprinkled on the mat.

After the mat is put in, the vat is closed for four hours, during which the fire is kept going under the metal sheeting. The liquid must be kept simmering but must not be allowed to boil too hard, so as not to damage the masks or shift them out of position. The mat is then removed from the dye bath (fig. 120), drained, unfastened from the bamboo, brushed, shaken and placed to dry. Another mat, a big *sese* or a small *tsip*, is then plunged into the vat.

In former times, women were in charge of every stage of the weaving and dyeing process. Recently, men have taken over one of the important stages of dyeing, that of cutting *sese* designs in banana bark. The right to make these designs is acquired through an initiation which involves a sponsor, drinking a substance which ensures the initiate will immediately know all the traditional designs, and a pact with the spirits of the forest. This pact is renewed for every dyeing session by a gift of food from the artist to the spirits.

Fig. 115
Mat weaving.

Figs 116, 117, 118
Laying of *kal*.

Fig. 119
Large *sese* mat. *Bakap*, to mask areas to remain uncoloured, has just been applied.

Fig. 116

Fig. 117

Fig. 118

Fig. 119

Forty-seven different named designs have been recorded on large mats and there are variants of all of them (Mabonlala 1991).

The designs printed on *tsip* mats are made by the women without any initiation, but after a long apprenticeship with a teacher. At every dyeing session, the artist in charge assembles one or more helpers to whom she gradually transmits her knowledge. When these apprentices have mastered the technique and know the many existing designs (twenty-three recorded and numerous variations, Mabonlala 1991), they can if they wish become fully-fledged artists and take part in dyeing sessions as '*kal* placers' (*kal* are the little sticks made from *Heliconia indica* stems). They are then paid and in their turn train a new generation of apprentices.

Once dyed, drained and dried, the mats are taken to the river, where they are carefully washed in fresh water. Then they are placed to dry in the sun on the bank, face down to prevent the sun from bleaching the delicate dye.

At this stage, a paste made of turmeric (*Curcuma longa*) is rubbed on the spaces left white by the strings, to colour these spaces yellow.

Fig. 120
The mat is removed from its dye bath.

Fig. 121
The reserve will appear white on the dyed mat once the *bakap* masking has been removed.

Fig. 122
The young bride and her aunts (*wawa*), covered with a *sese* mat.

Fig. 123
Mats given to the bridegroom's family by that of the bride.

The mats are then folded and kept in trunks or large baskets out of the light until the time comes for them to be exchanged at a big ceremony.

Mat symbolism

Some of the *tsip* designs indicate the social status of the woman wearing them and must therefore have been bought by her at a special ceremony conferring on her the corresponding rank in the social hierarchy. Examples of such motifs are *sum* (the beads), *butsu metakal* (the sun) and *biribiri wala* (the little cucumber).

Some *sese* designs have special significance. For example, the *kamatkel* (harpoon) motif is supposed to attract other mats, and for that reason, a mat decorated with this design is always placed first in the large basket where mats are stored. The *ulun kataptap* (cut the design) motif is the one an artist makes first at the start of each weaving session. It then reactivates memory of all the other designs, a memory conferred on her at her initiation.

Other designs have language value. The *sipbalil* (orchid) design symbolises the vanity of one who has succeeded in an important enterprise generally reserved for one of higher rank than him. The design honours the success of the enterprise but reproves the one who took it upon himself to undertake it.

A dyed mat is first and foremost the menstrual blood of women, the feminine principle of the universe, the symbol of the lineages which give women in marriage. It is in symbolic opposition to the curved pigs' teeth which represent men's reproductive substance, the masculine principle of the world and the lineages which give men.

Social organisation is based on a dualistic classification coupled with a system of grades by which men make their way up a hierarchy, and where the marriage system is based on the exchange of women between two matrilineal moieties and on virilocal residence, so lineages are both givers and receivers of women. Hence the direction in which red mats and pigs' teeth must be exchanged is fixed at every marriage. The woman's family will give the mats, the man's family the pigs. The first dyeing organised by a couple is, in fact, organised by the husband's mother, who, as soon as possible after the marriage, will dye the white mats brought as a dowry by her daughter-in-law. Should she delay at all in doing so, the whole village will take it as a sign the woman was opposed to her son's marriage. This is a serious affront which the bride will hold against her and which will feed village gossip for several years.

When a woman has succeeded in getting together a large number of dyed mats, she organises a *kau* ceremony. Wearing the attributes which indicate her rank in society (comb, chicken feather, bracelets and woven mat clothing decorated with a particular design), she dances around her mats, piled in their hundreds on long bamboo poles, each carried by two women. This ceremony is a moment of great prestige for the woman concerned, as the many songs composed on the occasion make clear. The mats celebrated in this way are then exchanged when one of her children takes a grade.

The reason why women take such great care and devote so much time to making these red mats is that the mat represents that feminine principle of which they are the natural bearers, a principle which is praised and venerated at all ceremonial exchanges, which thus become a reactualisation, a hundred times repeated, of reproduction and of social life made possible and comfortable. Their responsibility is therefore to master as best they can the techniques of weaving, and then to make mats as abundant, as beautiful and as delicate as the fertility of women.

Dyed designs on Pentecost mats

Alfreda Mabonlala

Fig. 124 Dyed designs on *sese* mats

Ulun kataptap: cutting out
When the artist cuts out the reserve shapes for dying *sese* mats, he first of all makes the *ulun kataptap* design. This design wakes in him the memory of all the other designs.

Ulun tsinen sohak: the banana tree
The *sohak* banana (*Musa troglodytarum*) is not an ordinary banana. The fruit of all other bananas grow downwards, but these grow upwards. A design appears when you cut one of the fruits across. This is the design reproduced on the mats.

Wakit kere: sideways glance
It was evening, and the men were on their way to the *nakamal*. A young boy took a kava root (*Piper methysticum*) and went to join his friends at the *nakamal*.
On the way, he met a very beautiful young girl. He greeted her and they talked for a while. The girl was shy, and looked at the young man out of the corner of her eye while she talked to him. He said goodbye, and the girl went back home, while the young man went on his way to the *nakamal*. As he drank his kava, he thought constantly about the girl's beautiful face. When the kava was finished, everyone went home.
The days passed, but his meeting with the young girl stayed with the young man, and he wanted to see her again. But it was too late, the girl was dead. In his house, he suffered great sorrow, so much that he made a drawing of the young girl, just as she was when he saw her for the first and last time. He drew two crescent moons, for her eyebrows, and a heart shape, for her face, her eyelids, one eye looking sideways, and her mouth. He called the drawing *wakit kere*.

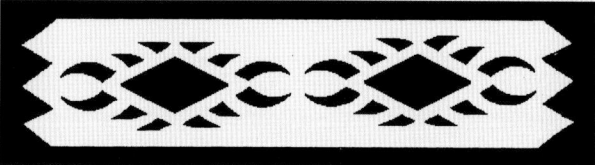

Bwihil nan ut lewahan: the ocean bird
This ancient design is widely used in decorating ceremonial mats. Its significance has, however, been forgotten.

Wul: the moon
The design represents the full moon (in the middle) surrounded by two crescent moons and moonbeams. This is a very old and widely used design.

Fig. 125 Dyed design on *tsip* mats

***Sum*: the beads**
The term *sum* now means beads and jewellery in general. Mats with this design can only be worn by women with rank in a graded society.

***Gereban*: in single file**
The term *gereban* means a series of things or people placed one behind the other. It can be roughly translated as 'in single file'. It is also a feminine first name.

***Butsu metakal*: the sun**
This design is made with two different plants: masks made out of *bega* (*Heliconia indica*) provide white lines, while those made out of the *melbogon* banana (*Musa* sp.) allow some of the dye to pass through and produce pink lines.

The precise meaning of the name is 'sun head'. The term *butsu matakal* is also the name of a green scarab beetle.

***Kalin tsinvin Livelani*: Livelani's *tsip* designs**
Livelani was the first woman to make this design on a *tsip* mat. It has been called after her ever since. Many *tsip* designs are named after the woman who invented them and used them for the first time.

Biribiriwala
This design represents the seeds of a small cucumber cut lengthwise. It is a design belonging to women of rank in a graded society.

Tahigogona's Sisters: Women, Mats and Landscape on Ambae

Lissant Bolton

One of the stories about Ambae's origins tells that the island was created by the culture hero Tagaro. He was travelling from Maewo to Santo, taking yams to feed his pigs there. His canoe turned over in rough seas, and from it he created Ambae. From a distance, this is how the island looks, like a large upturned canoe, the long dome of the dormant volcano, Manaro, creating the curved bottom of the canoe. To the north and south of the island the land falls precipitously from cone to sea like the sides of the canoe, while to the east and west – the bow and stern of the boat – the land falls more gently to some plains. Ambaeans live on the coastal plains, and on the lower slopes of the volcano, in districts which radiate around it.

As another story tells it, pandanus first grew in the southern district, at a place called Lolodomai, Lolovoli. The nine sisters of a man called Tahigogona took the leaves from the tree, and from it wove mats which they sold to people who lived around about. But the nine sisters argued among themselves about who got the most pandanus. Tahigogona intervened. He broke nine branches off the tree and gave one to each of his sisters. He told them to go up to Manaro, and each to follow a different line of hills down into a different part of Ambae. He warned them they might be killed, but perhaps they would meet a man who would indicate a piece of land on which they could plant their pandanus. Perhaps some of the sisters were killed, but some were given places to plant their pandanus and so brought mats to the district they had come to, to Nduindui, to Walurigi, to Lolovinue. Their descendants, members of the same matrilineal descent association, can be found in all the districts of Ambae, and in all these districts women weave mats.

This story draws attention to several relationships or interconnections, particularly those between women, mats and landscape. Mats are centrally important to contemporary Ambaean life, and it is through women that they appear, in that women weave them, and in that over time women have developed new mat types. The story also reveals the links and the separation between the different districts of Ambae, and it reflects on the way in which women move across the landscape, taking their skills and resources with them. Men may trade for mats, but women take and teach skills to each other, introducing new mat types into other districts. To be able to describe Ambae mats, it is important to understand the nature of the interconnections between women, mats and the landscape of Ambae. In this discussion, I describe Ambae mats by considering these interconnections.[1]

---

1. This paper is based on fourteen months fieldwork carried out in Vanuatu, predominantly on Ambae, from July 1991 to August 1992. The research was implemented under the auspices of the Vanuatu Cultural Centre. It was supported by a grant from the Emslie Horniman Anthropological Scholarship Fund, Royal Anthropological Institute, and by a grant from the Wenner Gren Foundation for Anthropological Research. I would like to thank Wenner Gren and the Emslie Horniman Trustees for their support, and to thank the board of the Vanuatu Cultural Centre which gave me permission to undertake the research.

Ambae mats

In English, 'mat' refers to a coarse fabric used as a protective surface of some kind – as a floor covering, or as a surface on which to sleep or sit. The word mat has been incorporated into Bislama, and Ambaeans use the term, when speaking Bislama, to describe a number of kinds of objects women weave from pandanus. In Ambaean languages, however, there is no single word for all these different objects. In east Ambae, three separate terms distinguish them: *gwana*, *maraha*, and *singo*. Of these, *gwana* refers to mat-like objects that are most like mats in the English sense. *Gwana* are placed on floors, sat and slept upon. They are also worn as clothing and can be used as slings in which to carry things (and children) on one's back. They are, furthermore, used as items of exchange and are important in a number of ritual contexts (figs 126, 127).

The other mat-like objects Ambaean women weave are never used as a protective surface. *Maraha* is the name for a category of objects that are used as items of exchange, and that are used to wrap the dead. There are many different kinds of *maraha*, but all of them are large, from 4 metres to 100 metres long, and between 0.5 metres and 1 metre wide. *Singo* are small, finely woven mats which are used to symbolise and confer status, and are understood to be inherently powerful, capable of causing harm to those who mishandle them.

Ambaeans do not, however, use the Bislama term *mat* indiscriminately to refer to all the 'mat-like' objects that women weave from pandanus. It is used specifically as an umbrella term to refer to *gwana*, *maraha* and *singo*. I use the English 'mat' here as a term of convenience in the sense in which it is applied in Ambaean Bislama.

Women also weave another mat-like object from pandanus, known in east Ambae as *wasmahanga*. A *wasmahanga* is worn by men, folded over a belt and hanging from it, either at their front or back, to indicate achieved status in the graded pig-killing system known as *hungwe*. This is not a *mat*, Ambaeans say, because although women weave it, they do not use it. It goes by another road, and is used only by men (fig. 128). *Gwana*, *maraha*, and *singo* are woven by women and used by them. Men also use all the objects in these three categories, although in some cases they use them differently to women.

Fig. 126
Gwana mat, with *vulé* (moon) pattern, worn by women. Collected by Speiser between 1910 and 1912. The pattern is still in use.
Ambae.
Basel, Museum für Völkerkunde.

Fig; 127
Women of Lolovoli wearing *gwana* mats, the central one of which bears a *vulé* pattern. Dance performed at Saratamata in 1992. South-east Ambae.

Fig. 128
Singo tuvegi men's mat, probably used to indicate a grade in the *hungwe* system. Collected by Speiser between 1910 and 1912. The pattern is no longer in use, but the name *butovundulé* is still known in east Ambae. Ambae.
Basel, Museum für Völkerkunde.

Mats are, therefore, absolutely identified with women, not only as their sole producers, but also as their users. Each woman has her own store of mats that she has woven, or received in an exchange, which she generally keeps in a big basket, known as *tangbunnir*, slung from the rafters of her house or her kitchen. Men also own mats, which they have acquired, and which they give, in several kinds of exchanges. But it is women who dominate the exchange of mats, and exchanges of mats mark all the traditional formal occasions of Ambaean social life. Without a mat to contribute, a woman would be ashamed to attend.

Today, mats dominate exchanges. In the eastern district of Longana, for example, as many as 1500 mats may be exchanged at one marriage (fig. 129). The sight of women pouring onto the ceremonial ground, carrying great baskets of mats on their heads, is a most dramatic and impressive one. When they reach the centre of the ground, they let the baskets fall from their heads with a satisfying thud, expressive of the labour they have invested in their contribution to the exchange, and unfold and lay out the mats in great heaps. Men, having made a small initial foray onto the ground to lay out several of the most valuable *maraha* as their contribution, sit on the sidelines and watch the piles of mats grow. Women say with pride and satisfaction that it is they who make such occasions, that men just sit at one side and drink kava. As the custodians of mats, women perceive themselves also as being the custodians of tradition.

There are more than fifty different named mat types woven on Ambae. (I use the term 'woven', although in a technical sense mats are plaited. In Vanuatu, loom weaving was formerly used only in the Banks Islands.) These types are usually distinguished on the basis of their woven form rather than on the patterns subsequently applied to the mat in the dyeing process. Characteristics which define mat types include their length and width, and the presence or absence of a central seam running down the length of the mat. They are also defined by the ways in which the edges of the mat are resolved – in various fringe and tassel types, or with various kinds of selvedges. Mats are also distinguished by the presence or absence of in-weave designs in the body of the mat, and by openwork decorations woven into their ends. Although it is only appropriate to include such designs on certain mat types, however, it is a matter of the weaver's skill and personal preference whether or not she does so, and which designs she includes.

The exception to this are *singo*, which are characterised by the use of an overweave in the body of the mat, which sets out a named design that is subsequently outlined in the dyeing process. It is this overweave which gives *singo* their dangerous potency (fig. 130). Only certain women weave *singo*, and other people (women and men) purchase the *singo* they require from them. Women who want to acquire this skill must pay a *singo* specialist to teach them, and the skill is often handed down through families, from mothers to daughters, and sometimes from husbands' mothers to sons' wives.

Although it is the woven form that distinguishes mat types, it is nevertheless the case that nearly all mats are dyed. They are dyed one colour only – red. Formerly the dye was obtained by grating the bark of the root of a vine, *langwe* (*Rham. ventilago neocaledonicum*; botanical identifications were provided by Sam Chanel, ORSTOM, Port Vila), which grows wild and is also cultivated. This produced a reddish-brown shade, the colour of dried blood. Today, women use a commercial dye, supplied by local trade stores, which creates a range of vivid magenta

Fig. 129
Women presenting mats in an exchange marking a marriage in east Ambae, 1991. On such occasions, mats are presented by being laid out on the ground in a specific order based on the named type category to which they belong.

Fig. 130
Margaret Solomon weaving a *singo* mat, incorporating the overweave stitch which confers a dangerous potency to the mat.
Lovonda, east Ambae, 1991.

shades. Women assess these shades critically, always endeavouring to achieve a darker colour. In parts of the Longana district, for example, women use the colour from carbon paper to darken the store dye. Although trade stores also provide dye in other colours – green, yellow, blue – mats should always be red. A woman who is in a hurry to produce some mats and uses another dark colour, like blue, because there is no red available will be criticised, and the mats considered less valuable. Such other-coloured mats are rare.

It is the dyeing that completes a mat and makes it new. It is not the case on Ambae, as it is in many

Fig. 131
Singo tuvegi mat, collected by Speiser between 1910 and 1912. Pattern woven with applications, known in the north of Ambae as *mataitalai*, and in east Ambae as *vovaho*. Basel, Museum für Völkerkunde.

parts of western Polynesia such as Samoa, that certain old mats are highly valued and individually named. On Ambae, a new mat is valued more highly than an old mat, and at an exchange towards which women have had the opportunity to work, such as a marriage, many new mats should be given. A woman may weave mats for more than a year in anticipation of her brother's marriage, but even the oldest of these mats will be defined as new at the marriage exchange if she has dyed it in the preceding week (fig. 129).

Maraha are dyed a single block of colour by being briefly immersed in a bath of boiling dye, but *gwana* and *singo* are dyed using stencils. There are two stencilling techniques. One of them, called *bwagavi*, is used on *gwana*; the other, known as *gigilugi*, is used on *singo* and on one *gwana* type, *sangulé*. In both cases, the mat is first bound tightly around a log cut from a light wood, which is kept specially for the purpose. The stencil is then firmly bound over the mat around the log, using a rope made of wild hibiscus (Malvaceae: *Hibiscus tiliaceus*), through which the dye can penetrate. In the *bwagavi* technique, the stencil is cut from a banana spathe, which has been prepared by being scraped thin. In the *gigilugi* technique, small pieces of leaf stem (Musaceae: *Helicona indica*) are used to build up the design. While the *bwagavi* technique is one every woman uses, the *gigilugi* technique is only known to some. It is used principally in the production of *singo*. In this case, the stencil is built around the design already woven into the mat with the overweave stitch.[2]

There is a catalogue of different patterns that can be used on the mats. Each pattern is suitable for use only on certain mat types. In the case of *singo*, it is the design (created in the weave) by which the mat is named, but for *gwana*, the choice of patterns is a matter of the dyer's preference. Some women know only a few patterns, while others have a wider range. Two patterns appear most frequently on the most common types of *gwana*; that is, on *gwanvivi* and *gwanvuvulu*. The *vulé* (moon) pattern is often used on *gwanvivi*, while the *matanaho* (rising sun) pattern frequently appears on *gwanvuvulu*.

The inventory of mat types in use on Ambae has changed over time. This is evident from the study of museum collections, and from women's comments. It seems both that certain mat types found in museum collections are now no longer made on Ambae, and that there are mats being made and used today that are not to be found in museums, and that are innovations whose history is remembered. Overall, the inventory of mat types in use has grown through this century, as has the volume of mats given at each exchange. Whereas marriages in times past would involve the gift of only two or three of the most valuable *maraha* – known as *navhangavulu* in Longana – it is now not uncommon to see fifteen being presented.

Mats and the social landscape of Ambae

With the exception of the people in the two western districts of Walaha and Nduindui, Ambaeans organise themselves into two exogamous matrilineal moieties, known as Tagaro and Merambuto. From their mothers, they inherit their social character: the moiety affiliation is the axis on which all a person's relationships turn. From their fathers, Ambaean men inherit land. As is the case elsewhere in Vanuatu, Ambaeans identify themselves in terms of the place they come from.[3] Marriage is virilocal, so that while, in general, a man lives all his life on the land on which he was born, a woman moves at marriage and takes her identity from her husband's place. Thus persons identify themselves in terms of the place they come from, and is also located by the moiety and family affiliation which they obtain through their mothers.

The distinction between east and west Ambae is based partly on locally perceived linguistic and cultural differences between the western districts and the rest of the island. It also reflects the geographical barrier of the volcano, the steep northern and southern sides of which are much more lowly populated than east and west. Local terminology divides the two western districts from the rest of the island through a distinction between east and west Ambae, which I follow in this paper. Allen (1969:50) reports that people in west Ambae regard the east Ambaean matrimoieties as the true Ambaean custom, which they once had, but have since lost. In west Ambae, land a man inherits land from his father and marriage is virilocal, but people do not inherit social identity from their mothers in the form of moiety affiliation.

West and east Ambaeans speak separate, though related, languages, and share many similar cultural traits. Both languages have many dialects. While the mat categories and many individual mat types are the same in all districts of Ambae, as are the ways in which they are used, different names are applied to some mat types in different districts. Thus in west Ambae, people recognise their term *rosso* to apply to the mat category known in the eastern districts as *maraha*, but in east and west alike, women weave a *gwana* called *gwanmavuté*.

In the past, inhabitants of different districts kept separate from each other, and people did not often marry outside their districts. Tahigogona's warning to his sisters that they might be killed when they entered another district is an apt reflection of the former relationship between the districts. Even today, Ambaeans often fear to encounter poisoning and sorcery in another district. Formerly, however, men made trading expeditions to other districts, and one of the principal objects of their trade was mats. The island is about 40 kilometres long and about 12 kilometres wide at its broadest point, so the distances travelled on these expeditions were not great, although the terrain was often quite difficult to traverse. Marriages from district to district are still uncommon, although they now occur more frequently than they did.

While many mat types occur throughout Ambae, there are some mats that are or were only woven in certain districts. This is particularly true for different kinds of *singo*. Several districts were the sole producers of certain *singo* types. Formerly, for example, only some women in Nduindui had the right to weave a *singo* known as *mataitalai* (fig. 131), which in many parts of Ambae is worn to indicate achieved status in the pig-killing system, or *hungwe*.[4] In the past, men from the northern district of Lombaha, for example, regularly made trading expeditions to Nduindui to obtain *mataitalai* for their participation in the *hungwe*. Today, however, women in many places weave *mataitalai*.

Even where individual mat types are woven in many districts, it is generally recognised that they may have an origin place at one particular point in the Ambae landscape, which women may or may not know. Often the women in a village or area know from which village a new mat type was brought to their area, but do not necessarily know where it came from beyond that. In some cases the origin of a particular mat is well-known. The *maraha* type known as *vatungulé*, for example, is known to derive from two stones lying in a creek called the Waisala, in south-eastern Ambae. There are two long stones lying side by side in the creek, and there are two *vatungulé, vatungulé mwera (vatungulé*

2. In fact, these dyeing techniques are used widely in north Vanuatu, although there are variations in their distribution and application. In central Pentecost, for example, both the *bwagavi* and the *gigilugi* techniques are used, but there mats are never dyed a single block of colour. By contrast, mats are dyed a single block of colour in Malakula. In central Pentecost, the *gigilugi* technique is never used to outline in-weave patterns, except on the borders of the mat (see Walter, this volume).

3. This identification of person and place on Ambae is discussed by M. Rodman (1987:34-41). It is, more widely, characteristic of all ni-Vanuatu, implicit in the Bislama term *man ples* (Bonnemaison 1986c:232-235, 391-419; Jolly 1992b:342).

4. W. Rodman gives a detailed description of the *hungwe* in his thesis *Men of Influence, Men of Rank: Leadership and the Graded Society on Aoba, New Hebrides* (1973). A briefer account occurs in Blackwood's paper 'Rank, exchange and leadership in four Vanuatu societies' (1981).

5. This contrasts with the situation in central Pentecost, where men dye the mats that women weave. There (see Walter, this volume), men dye using the *bwagavi* technique when the mat is to be dyed in an iron dye bath. Men in central Pentecost, however, never use the *gigilugi* technique, even when an iron dye-bath is to be used.

man), and *vatungulé vaviné* (*vatungulé* woman). The length of each of these is supposed to reproduce the length of the stones (about 20 metres and 12 metres respectively). But while most east Ambaeans know that *vatungulé* derives from this place, nobody I encountered was able to tell me a story which explains how the mat developed.

Women, men and mats

Some Ambaean men comment that while women weave mats, it is men who know about them. To the extent that this is true, it is true from a male perspective. The mats that men know about and are interested in are those mats that are used in various ritual contexts in which men have an interest. Thus, for example, when a girl is sent by her family to her husband in marriage, her fathers place a particular kind of *gwana*, known as *gwanhunhun*, on her head. By association with a particular story, the pattern on the *gwanhunhun* sometimes conveys a message to the groom's family, usually on the theme of respect and fidelity within the marriage. The girl is unaware of the message that covers her head, although some women know such messages are sent.

Some men also know the traditional stories about the origin of mats, and know the histories of particular mat types, most notably those of *singo* and *maraha*. The histories generally record how a man used a mat type innovatively, introducing it into a particular context in a way that enhanced his renown and that of the mat type. Thus the value or importance of *vatungulé* was enhanced some generations ago by a man called Tarilama, who came from east Ambae. When taking a rank in the *hungwe*, he arranged for a woman to present him with *vatungulé*, and by this innovation made *vatungulé* more important.

The value that men place on mats is evident in that they made trading expeditions to acquire them. Men also used to commission particular *singo* from certain women, and would formally present themselves to watch the mat being woven, and to talk to the weaver about it. Men were never directly involved in the production of mats, however, assisting in neither the weaving nor the dyeing of them.[5] Men do not have any detailed knowledge about mat types, weaves and patterns.

The body of knowledge women hold about mats thus comprises technical knowledge which is exclusive to them, knowledge about some uses that are common to women and men alike and some that are gender-specific, and knowledge about the origins and histories of mats. Men and women can and do know origin stories, although those that know them generally only know one or two such stories. Women also have a particular body of knowledge related to a sequence of ceremonies that celebrate their skill and effort in producing mats, and through which a woman enhances her rank and status.

These ceremonies, known as *huhuru*, are explicitly compared with the *hungwe*; *huhuru* is the *hungwe* of married women. In these ceremonies, a woman dyes a suite of *maraha* she has woven, and commissions a *singo* specialist to dye a *singo* that the specialist has woven in advance for the occasion. The mats are then presented to the woman's husband. There are grades for this ceremony, which are created by the kinds of mats used in it, and a woman who takes all the grades is said to become respected and honoured in the same way as a man who has taken many grades in the *hungwe* (cf. also M. Rodman 1981: 97). The *huhuru* ceremonies are one of the main avenues through which men acquire large numbers of the *maraha* they need to give in exchanges.

Mats, women and landscape

One of the *maraha* often used in the *huhuru* ceremonies is a type known in the eastern district of Longana as *navhangavulu tavalu*. *Navhangavulu* are the highest grade of *maraha* in most parts of Ambae. They are very long mats, up to 100 metres long, and about 0.5 metres wide (*navhangavulu* means 'ten lengths', referring to how its length is measured). A *singo* from the subcategory *singo maraha* is joined to the end of these mats to complete them. There are two types of *navhangavulu*, *navhangavulu vinvinu* and *navhangavulu tavalu*. *Navhanagavulu vinvinu* is woven with a central seam that runs the full length of the mat, creating two panels, one each side. *Navhangavulu tavalu* has no central seam, and thus only one panel. The story of this mat illustrates both the control held by women over the innovation of mat types, and the ways in which women carry knowledge and skills about mats around the island, as Tahigogona's sisters first carried the pandanus.

The mat was created by a woman who lived at a small place called Lovuinbangataue, a little inland from Navonda in the Longana district. This woman was looking after a tusked pig that her husband, Vire Tavire, was to use when he took a grade in the *hungwe*. When a man kills a pig, his wife should give a *navhangavulu vinvinu*. One of the pig's tusks was broken, however, and the woman worried that it was inappropriate to give a *navhangavulu vinvinu* when the pig had only one tusk. It occurred to her that the solution was to weave the *navhangavulu* with only 'one side', one panel to match the one tusk, so that the one panel and the one tusk would be equivalent to one whole, one *navhangavulu vinvinu*. *Tavalu* means 'one side', *vinvinu* means 'joined'. She did so, and the new *maraha* type she thereby created has now spread widely throughout Ambae. In Longana, it is now more commonly woven than *navhangavulu vinvinu*.

Navhangavulu vinvinu was a mat type woven in most districts at that time, although in most places it is known by another name, *sawea*. The introduction of what is known in these districts as *sawea tavalu* can still be partially traced. Thus in the northern district of Lombaha, in the village of Lowainasasa (a place about 15 kilometres from Navonda), the introduction of this new mat occurred within living memory. It was brought to Lowainasasa by two women who married from the village of Tavalawarigi, which is about 5 kilometres east of Lowainasasa, closer to the Longana district. The second of these women, Lilian Mala, is still only in her late forties, so she must have introduced the mat about twenty-five years ago.

In the village of Sakao, in the south, women also remember the introduction of *navhangavulu*. They formerly wove various *maraha* types, but did not weave *navhangavulu* at all. Once again, the introduction was made by a woman who married into the area. In this case, a woman from the Longana district, Nomi Kwoilala, married a man from a village some kilometres south of Sakao, Lovunimbori. She introduced *navhangavulu* to Sakao probably within the last ten years, when she wove a *navhangavulu* for a Sakao woman who was undertaking her second *huhuru* ceremony.

The pace of such introductions has been increased by the rise in the incidence of inter-district marriages, but the practice has always occurred to some extent, as Tahigogona's sisters married men in the districts they entered, walking down the hills from Manaro. The story of the innovation and introduction of *navhangavulu tavalu* illustrates the continuing importance of mats, and women's creative control over them. It also illustrates the dynamism of the contemporary mat complex on the island.

The reference to place as the location of identity on Ambae is therefore relevant not only for people. Among other things, it is relevant for the identification and significance of mat types. Mat types can be distinguished both on the basis of the places where they originated or the places from which they have lately come, and on the basis of the places where they are now made. Mat types, like women, can move, changing their district affiliation as they are introduced into new places, and lost in others. It is through women themselves that these alterations occur. Women stand at the centre of the landscape of Ambae mats as Manaro stands at the centre of the island itself.

Fig. 132
Ureparapara, Banks Islands.

Woven female waistbands of northern Vanuatu

Kirk W. Huffman

According to ancient versions of origin myths from Longwengwea and Lolopuepue, Ambae, when Tagaro the Creator made the *ragmwehu,* the first men, he then changed one of them into the first woman. For her, he made a waistband of the leaves of the *tupe* creeper, and ordained that from henceforth women should wear such waistbands, *tupeki.* He took a wife, Tebisui, and eventually decided to demonstrate his approval of her by having her fully tattooed to indicate her high and sacred status. He thus made her what is called in some areas of Ambae today a *bure,* a sacred, fully-tattooed woman – the beauty of whose tattoos could only fully be seen if she was wearing *tupeki.* Less than a dozen of these *bure* survive today on Ambae[1] because the tattooing tradition there was finally stopped by the missions in the 1920s, but the wearing only of *tupeki* disappeared ages ago as other spiritual, ritual and material influences (before the white man's arrival) developed the complex and dazzling women's woven and dyed mat-world. Throughout the world, fashions develop and change, and so with the *tupe/tupeki*. From a simple 'cord' it developed into beautifully woven and dyed pandanus waistbands, tied at the front with its tassels hanging down (see the two *tupeki* from Ambae, cat. no.1900.198, from the collections of the University Museum of Archeology and Anthropology, Cambridge). By the time the white man began to stumble clumsily through the Pacific, the beautiful mats manufactured and worn by the women already had an ancient and respected history, although women would sometimes in those days wear only *tupe/tupeki* when inside their house, and mats when they were outside. Then probably came the stage (like today) where mats only were worn, but sometimes (or at least ideally) still with a woven waistband, because elders with a full knowledge of the myths might consider it 'nakedness' without even a symbolic waistband, at least in certain rituals.

Such woven and dyed ritual female waistbands were also originally manufactured and worn in Maewo and northern Pentecost (such as waistband from the Raga-speaking area of northern Pentecost in the above Cambridge collections, cat. no. 1920.476), and also areas 'where Tagaro ruled' and where the waistband-mat history may have been similar.

It seems that the female mat costume tradition may not have reached northern Maewo by the time Europeans first appeared in the area, and it had definitely not reached the Banks Islands, where, up until at least the 1870s, most women wore solely a small woven band around their waist, sometimes doubled, and called in some areas *pari* or *hopare*. Today's Bislama term *parpar* – to 'wrap abound the waist' or anything worn around the waist (that is, a verb and a noun) – may come from that area.

Tagaro's counterpart in the Banks Islands, Qat, born from a stone mother on Vanua Lava, created the first woman, Iro Vilgale, and married Iro Lei, but I do not know if Qat ordained women's original costume as Tagaro is said to have done in parts of Ambae, although this might be likely. Female body tattoos (full tattooing for women of high status) was one of the ritual and artistic characteristics of the areas dominated by Tagaro and Qat, and forms of female waist-straps seem to be an associated cultural feature. Dyed and undyed examples were made, ranging from the beautiful, intricate, blazing-white examples collected by Speiser in January 1912 from Ureparapara (fig. 132; see Vb 4235, 4233, 4232, 4230, 4234 and 4231) to the spiritually-powerful female status designs of the red-dyed examples collected by Speiser on Gaua in December 1911 and January 1912 (figs 133, 134, 135; see illustrations of these waistbands from the Basel collections, cat. nos Vb 4213, 4215, 4216, 4218, 4220, 4222, 4228 and 4238). The designs are similar to many elements of the incised designs of certain of the bamboo, cane or reed ear-ornaments from the Banks and Torres (see also p. 240, this volume), but are more exclusively ritual, spiritual and status-oriented, as are the linked female body tattoos, associated board paintings, carvings and women's sacred hut decorations from women's status rituals in various areas of the Banks Islands. The spirit face on the decorated Ambae waistband in the Cambridge collections (cat. no. 1900.198) is indicative of the connections, economic, ritual and mystical, that once joined these areas.

Such decorated waistbands were produced in the Banks Islands until World War II, and it is obvious that they were ceremonially oriented, and not just worn to have the tied tassels hanging in front for modesty: as soon as European cloth became available, they were worn over the cloth, particularly at ritual times. Production of such important female waistbands has almost completely ceased now in Ambae, Raga, Maewo and the Banks, particularly because of the diminishing traditional cultural trade process in the women's sphere between the above areas, and also partially because of an emphasis on interest on woven and dyed mats in the former areas, to the detriment of the numerous other types of women's woven materials that were produced and circulated in these parts of northern Vanuatu. Such change of emphasis also, to a certain extent, extends to some aspects of the world of men. For example, Ambae was once an island with a rich tradition of mask, ritual-object and spiritual (wood) carving production, which also has almost completely disappeared. But these forms only 'sleep', and can be reawakened if there is the will and the respect. A stunning (and almost completely unknown to the outside world) type of large wooden spirit-power image is still produced (and hidden) on a nearby island which obtained rights to do so by ritual

Figs 133, 134, 135
Gaua, Banks
Islands.

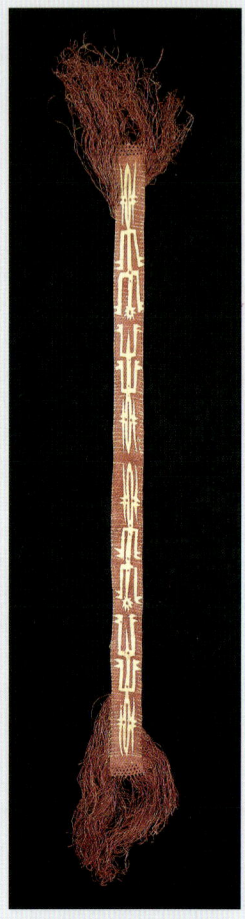

payments to copyright holders on Ambae, where production ceased towards the end of the last century.

I would like to apologise to ni-Vanuatu women of the above areas for – as a male – having written this short and simplified article. But I have written it with a particular purpose in mind, in the hope that ni-Vanuatu women reading it will regain an interest in another aspect of their intricate cultures; to show them that, for example, such waistbands are also, like mats, an item of importance that can mark their identity in the world; and as an encouragement to the new group of female Vanuatu Cultural Centre fieldworkers, led by Jean Tarisese and advised by Dr Lissant Bolton, to help in the reawakening of the production of such items. In some areas of Vanuatu it is acceptable, and sometimes traditional, for men to 'open the gate' for certain women's rituals; I humbly view this note in that sense.

1. A special study of some of the last of these *bure* has been made by Nadia Kanegai, of Ambae-Maewo descent. The booklet, profusely illustrated by Fidel Yoringmal, is written in Bislama: *Bure blong Ambae*, published in 1994 by the Vanuatu Cultural Centre. The study and publication was kindly funded by the Australian government's South Pacific Cultures Fund and the Australian High Commission in Port Vila, and was begun in 1985.

Arts of Language and Space, South-east Tanna

Lamont Lindstrom

The material culture and art traditions of the Tannese appear simple and unelaborated. No-one erects choruses of finely carved slit-gongs in his village; no-one constructs elegant *nakamals*, or men's houses; no-one carves figures of wood or sculpts volcanic tuff; no-one models his ancestors in intricate creations of mask and puppet. But Tanna's apparent artistic barrenness is deceptive. There exist several rich if less visible domains of intense creative endeavour on the island. People's imaginative efforts focus on the immaterial arts of language and of spatial relations.

Tannese elaboration of language and space, rather than of wood and stone, must be understood in context of the island's religious and political systems (see Guiart 1956c). Men may possess one or the other of two sorts of traditional chiefly titles (*ierumani* 'ruler' and *iani nīteta* 'spokesman (of the canoe)', in the Nīfe or Kwamera language of southeast Tanna; see Lindstrom 1986). These two titles are Tannese reflexes of Polynesian sacred and talking chiefs. The force of island titles, however, is situational and variable; local political relations are notably egalitarian, among adult men at least. The absence of an effective class of traditional chiefs or of any other sort of permanent hierarchy on the island vitiates one of the common functions of art (figs 136-139), to symbolise political hierarchy. Tanna's title system has only minor effect on the island's corpus of material artifact. A man with a title, along with his wife and children, for example, might wear several additional feather plumes during island exchange and dance celebrations, such as *nakwiari* and *nieri* feasts; and he may insist on a variation of the common diamond motif on traditional tapa belts (*katoti*) that men once employed to tie up their penis-wrappers (*ninhum*; *nambas*, in Bislama).

Within Tanna's egalitarian political arena, however, individual claims to chiefly titles and the details of entailed rights are always open to public discussion and ongoing negotiation. This hones people's interest in rhetoric and in the arts of debate; island discourse characteristically is decorated with figures of speech, including traditional as well as fresh metaphors and parables (*nagkiariien ruvsini*).

Tanna's religious system is also egalitarian. Although many Tannese have been Christian for several generations, and others ascribe to a variety of local religious cults (the most famous being the John Frum Movement), almost no-one has lost faith in the imminent presence of island ancestors. All men are ultimately responsible for communing with and propitiating their own ancestors, and most do so daily by spitting out their last sip of the

Fig. 136
Offering of pigs sacrificed during the *toka* ceremony celebrated at Iwel on 25 and 26 August 1994. The dead pigs form a row in the direction of the road of alliance from where the guests to whom the pigs will be donated will arrive.

Fig. 137
A woman's face decorated for the *toka* dances. The art of the body decoration is closely linked with the art of dancing.

Fig. 138
An important man of Tanna (and his son) is transported, accompanied by songs, on a stretcher carried by men. They are sitting across the pig that they are going to offer to their allies. Iwel, 1994.

Fig. 139
Flute player with traditional headdress. South-west Tanna.

Fig. 136

Fig. 137

Fig. 138

Fig. 139

evening's shell of kava (the Pacific's traditional drug substance, *Piper methysticum*). This spitting is a form of ancestral libation (Lebot et al. 1992). The contemporary absence of a class of traditional priests on the island also vitiates some of the symbolic functions that art fulfils elsewhere.

The Tannese do not make plastic representations of their ancestors or of other island deities, such as the culture heroes Karapenumin and Mwatiktiki (the Polynesian Mauitikitiki). Instead, they locate their gods in singular rock formations and in other prominent features of the landscape (Bonnemaison 1986c:78). People commonly claim to encounter ancestral spirits regularly, either in their dreams, while intoxicated on kava, or in person. It may be that this active, mundane presence of ancestors in people's consciousness and in their conversations substitutes in part for the variety of plastic ancestral images that artists carve and sculpt elsewhere in Vanuatu. Given their genius with language arts, the Tannese instead represent their ancestors orally, in stories and in everyday conversation.

As a society possessing only muted and contingent structures of hierarchy, the Tannese have no spectacular traditions of art that might display relations of inequality. They do, however, fabricate and sometimes decorate a variety of lesser artifacts. Historically, these once included finely ground stone and tridacna (giant clam) shell axes and adzes (*paha*); long, elegant, cylindrical throwing stones (*kauas*) pecked from soft volcanic stone; scattered petroglyphs and other rock art; tortoiseshell earrings (*nīprinei*); shell necklaces; and stone pendants (*kwanari*). The latter include nephrite, or greenstone, pendants (*kwanevir*) (fig. 140), which may have originated in some lost quarry on Tanna but more likely were imported from New Caledonian sources (Aubert de la Rüe 1938).

Contemporary artifacts include a range of woven and plaited objects, produced mostly by women. These are baskets (*tīnīrup*); mats (*kafete*), fine and course; feather plumes (*kaio*); and fibre skirts (*rous*) made from the inner bark of the hibiscus tree (*H. tiliaceus*) and coloured in bright checkerboard patterns with imported dyes. Other woven artifacts – these made ordinarily by men – include the basket-like walls of local houses (*napwīr*) that are fashioned of bamboo slats or sections of wild cane; and long,

Fig. 140
In the centre, man with penis-wrapper, photographed by Aubert de la Rüe, around 1935. Middle Bush, Tanna.

horizontal trellises of cane (*nīfetafata*) that support cultivated yam vines and runners. The Tannese also tie short lengths of bamboo into panpipes (*tarheinau*), and they make longer bamboo flutes (*kwataratara*) as well. They fabricate coconut-shell kava-drinking cups and armbands (*kwatikinapuei*) (fig. 141), the latter often simply incised.

Occasionally, men make tapa belts (*katoti*) from the inner bark of banyan and other trees. They paint

Fig. 141
Coconut bracelet. Tanna.
Basel, Museum für Völkerkunde

Fig. 142
Women during *toka* dances. They wear long dresses of coloured fibres, which are a recent innovation of Tanna custom. Iwel, central southwest Tanna, 1994.

these belts, which are esteemed exchange gifts presented during *nakwiari* festivals, in patterns of black and white diamonds and triangles. The main Tannese canvas, however, is the face. Some Tannese women and men sport small facial and body tattoos (*natatau*), but the paramount island tradition of body adornment consists of impermanent, and more brilliant, face painting. Men, women (fig. 142), and children alike paint their faces in dazzling reds, yellows, and blacks for important dance festivals. Traditionally, people employed powdered volcanic clays of various colours, and also imported red ochre from the neighbouring island of Erromango. Nowadays, people oil their face with Johnson's Baby Oil (rather than traditional coconut oil), and then decorate themselves by dabbing imported powdered dyes onto their faces. Designs vary, although most involve a series of coloured planes created by first bisecting the face horizontally, and then vertically. Black or yellow lines start at the ears and cut across the cheeks to the bottom of the nose, separating an unpainted lower face from a painted upper. Next, one or two vertical lines run upwards along the ridge of the nose, bisecting the upper face into at least two planes that are coloured in red, or sometimes yellow. Women, typically, paint their faces in more elaborate fashion than do men (fig. 137); many of the latter are satisfied with just the basic painted framework or, more simply, a single line across the forehead. The island's foremost style of body art, is thus, in harmony with its other artistic traditions, likewise impermanent and immaterial.

The ritual exchange festival is the primary arena for display of dance and song – the island's most common artistic productions. People have a repertoire that comprises a variety of circle dances (*nupu*) and also several line dances (*toka, nau, kosusiva*) that they perform during major exchange festivals. Line dances include deft mimetic performances. One or two dancers emerge from the larger group to present the themes of a song in inventive pantomime, imitating a wide range of lyrical topics ranging from the flight of seabirds, to landslides, to contemporary boxing matches.

Song accompanies all dance, and each local group possesses a treasury of songs. These serve in part as historical archives that preserve the names and deeds of the group's ancestors. As people dance, they sing. And as they sing, they accompany themselves with handclapping and by stomping their feet in time, using no other musical instrumentation to support their performance. The volcanic soils of Tanna, however, reverberate with almost ringing tones and the island itself serves as a sort of immense drum upon which people dance.

The structure of dance, and the arrangement of island dancing grounds, disclose an aesthetic of space. People perceive their cultural landscape to be organised by two conjoined primary structures: kava-drinking clearings (*imwarīm*) within the forest, and a lattice of 'roads' (*suatuk*) that link these clearings together (see Bonnemaison 1986c). The model of clearing and road – of centre versus periphery – is a powerful aesthetic archetype that structures many of the ways in which people arrange themselves spatially. Moreover, the two components of this paradigm take on a series of broader cultural meanings that are organised dualistically. The centre connotes masculinity, culture, high status, and speech; the periphery, in opposition, evokes femininity, nature, lower status, and silence.

Culturally, kava-drinking clearings are the most significant spaces on the island, and are swept clean of all vegetation, in counterpoint to surrounding field and forest. In the past, men's houses stood at these centre points, surrounding by a perimeter of hamlets in which slept women and children, and a more distant periphery of the community's garden and forest lands.

The same aesthetics of space also govern events that take place upon kava-drinking clearings themselves. Men meet here each evening to drink kava, and the community as a whole convenes at clearings to debate local issues and problems, to exchange ritual gifts, and to dance. During public meetings, for example, participants organise themselves according to the island's spatial aesthetics. Active speakers come into the centre of the clearing; male auditors collect around the periphery close to where the particular 'roads' that they might control intersect the clearing; and women and children in the audience, who do not ordinarily possess the right to make public statements, sit on the outer edge of the perimeter, where clearing fades into forest.

When people meet to exchange goods, they likewise situate themselves along certain arcs of the kava clearing's perimeter according to the location of converging roads. The two principals of the exchange arrange the goods that they are giving away (kava, raw and cooked pigs, tubers and tuber puddings, baskets, mats, bark skirts, 2-metre lengths of cloth, and blankets) in the centre of the clearing. They present these goods in carefully constructed, heaped displays customarily composed of a regular series of layers running from cooked food at the bottom to baskets and bark skirts on the top.

The same spatial aesthetics govern how people dance *nupu*. Men as a group rotate counterclockwise in the centre of the clearing, surrounded by a periphery of skipping women, who spin around the encircled men. Tannese yam gardens, also circular clearings in the forest, exhibit a similar structure: people plant prestigious, ritually male yams (*Dioscorea* spp.) in the centre of the garden clearing, and surround these with plantings of symbolically feminine taro (*Colocasia esculenta*) and other crops (Bonnemaison 1986c).

Although the Tannese do not possess a notable heritage in the plastic arts, they share with most people of Vanuatu a theory of artistic invention and a traditional system of copyright, both of which govern artistic production everywhere in the archipelago (Lindstrom 1990). Traditional copyrights, or patents, protect valued knowledge, including

Fig. 143
Recent photograph of a young custom man with a traditional male hairstyle.
Central south-west Tanna.

songs, myths, histories, genealogies, and herbal cures, as well as artistic motifs and carving designs. Only people who possess a copyright can make legitimate public use of copyrighted knowledge, whether this is the public repetition of a lineage's genealogy, the performance of a particular song, the beating of a slit-gong rhythm, or the reproduction of a carving motif. A dance team celebrating a feast, for example, must ask permission to sing a song that belongs to a neighbouring group. If someone misuses copyrighted material (for example, appropriates someone's carving design, or plagiarises someone's kava magic), copyright holders may protest and demand compensation.

Traditional copyright also restricts the public narration of myths and histories that relate local events of the past. On Tanna, rock formations and other notable geologic features mark the sites of important past events. People not associated with a particular local group lack the right of public repetition of its copyrighted histories and myths. Although individuals inherit and control primary copyrights, other residents of a locale have vested rights of knowledge repetition, narration, and performance. Over time, this copyright procedure in effect brings into existence a number of geographic *œuvres* on Tanna: the organisation of knowledge according to place rather than according to the identity of an author, or a school of authors.

The ultimate investment of copyrights in local groups reflects Tannese theories of artistic production. Islanders do not share powerful European presumptions about the existence of individual creativity. Personal creativity, rather, is muted as a theoretical discourse that might account for the origin of novel products and design. The Tannese do not cite individual intellect, brilliance, aptitude, flair, or personal talents to give their artistic products authority. Instead of the mysteries of European individual genius, Tannese artists cite several types of external authoritative sources to explain and legitimate novel artistic productions. These external authorities include a range of spirits, ancestors, and also persons (and nowadays written texts) who come from beyond the local community. Artists who produce novel objects, designs, songs, or stories maintain that they merely pass along a revealed message or idea from an external source.

Islanders thus do not explain the production of art in terms of an artist's personal talents, genius, or creativity. Local epistemology seeks authorities, not individual authors. Individual creativity, in fact, is devalued *vis-à-vis* external inspiration as a means to legitimate artistic productions. One's own ideas are never as good as information externally received. People account for the production of new songs, for example, in these inspirational terms. A songsmith dreams up a song, or acquires it by somehow overhearing ancestral or spiritual voices. To encourage an ancestral revelation, in fact, some songsmiths may retire to spiritually active forest glades, drink kava, sacrifice a fowl, and settle back to await lyrical inspiration.

Rather than foregrounding personal creativity to lend authenticity to their art, the Tannese intimate instead that they are revealing products taught them by their parents, whispered to them by spirits when they are intoxicated with kava, or revealed by ancestors in dreams. Recently, however, the traditional depersonalisation of artistic production has been undercut as some islanders encounter European theories of individual creativity at school, and in the programs and institutions in Port Vila and beyond that encourage individualised island arts for Western consumption.

The Tannese may lack noted art traditions but this by no means implies that they are artless. Their attention instead engages the less material arts of speech, debate, face paint, song, and dance, and a refined cultural aesthetic governs the flow of sound and movement throughout everyday experience. This, in part, involves an aesthetic of space that people use to cultivate their island, and their inhabitation of this island, so that Tanna itself stands as their paramount artistic production.

The 'Decorated Cloth' from the 'Island of Good Yams':[1] Barkcloth in Vanuatu, with Special Reference to Erromango

Kirk W. Huffman

Aside from a few scattered references, the production and use of barkcloth of various types in Vanuatu has gone almost unmentioned in the ethnographic literature. Its production and use, however, domestic and ritual, was relatively widespread, from Aneityum to the Torres, but particularly in central and southern Vanuatu from Tongoa southwards. The major production centres of what in Polynesia would be called 'tapa'[2] were in the area from Tongoa southwards to Efate (and its offshore islands), and the island of Erromango. A few scattered examples of barkcloth from these areas are found in museum collection in Europe, but the biggest (and best) collections are at the Australian Museum, Sydney, and, to a lesser extent, at the Museum of Victoria, Melbourne, and the Museum of Mankind, London. The Australian Museum has twenty-six Vanuatu barkcloths in its collections: eighteen from Erromango (six acquired from members of the Robertson family; Reverend H.A. Robertson was a Presbyterian missionary on Erromango from 1872 to 1912); six from central Vanuatu (two acquired by the Robertsons); one from Santo (unknown area); and one beaten barkcloth belt from Tanna. The Museum of Victoria has two superb central Vanuatu barkcloths, collected by J.W. Lindt between 1889 and 1890. The Museum of Mankind has at least seven Vanuatu barkcloths (four of them pictured in Speiser 1991): four from Erromango, a superb one from Efate, and one mysteriously labelled a Tannese 'burial cloth'.

Production of barkcloth died out rapidly in central Vanuatu, with the introduction of European cloth in the last quarter of the 19th century, and in Erromango in the first quarter of the 20th century. Its production in the form of beaten barkcloth belts for male hierarchy and ritual purposes survives today only on the island of Tanna.

In southern Vanuatu, rough beaten barkcloth belts and sometimes hairstraps (for men with the extended braided ritual hairstyle known, for example, in Narhak (Whitesands) language of east Tanna as *iatuawai*) were found on Aneityum, Aniwa, Futuna, Tanna and Erromango. On Futuna and Aniwa, the barkcloth belt was called *hlava*, on Erromango *netoetngi* (Sie language), and on Tanna, variations of the Narhak word *tut'h* (for example, *tut'h katoti* in Nininife (Kwamera) language of south-east Tanna). European leather belts, usually taking the language name for barkcloth belts, rapidly replaced the traditional straps (usually for holding up the traditional male item of daily attire – unless a more basic fibre cord was used around the waist – except on Erromango, where the penis-wrapper

1. This article is dedicated to the people of Erromango (not, of course, the *real* name of their island, which is Nelokompne).

 Captain Cook first called the island 'Erromanga' after his stop there on 4 August 1774: during the melee near Potnarvin, confronted with people who were probably Sorung-speakers from the Rovilian district, he was (according to *his* journal) given a yam. According to the Erromangans today, Cook was presented with types of food, and was repeatedly told '*armai n'go, armai n'go*' ('This (type of) food is good'), which the latter assumed was the name of the island.

Fig. 144
Barkcloth belt collected by Speiser in 1912.
Tanna.
Basel, Museum für Völkerkunde.

Fig. 145
Other barkcloth belts collected by Speiser in 1912.
Tanna.
Basel, Museum für Völkerkunde.

hung down, as in the traditional Kanak *bagayou*). This did not occur on Tanna, however, where the barkcloth belts are still produced for ritual use and where painted red and/or black (often dentate) designs indicate the wearer's status in the complex social hierarchy (figs 144, 145; for an example of a Tanna barkcloth belt with crosshatch designs, see Speiser 1991, pl. 43, no. 2; *tut'h aben* with black designs, *tut'h meta* with red and black designs; see also Guiart 1956c:85). It is important to note that on Tanna it is the *men* who produce and decorate the barkcloth straps. The most valued form of Tannese pig, the rare hairless type known as *kepwia* in the language of the Lenakel area of west-north-west Tanna (and *pukah kipwia* in Nininife (Kwamera)), also has the right to wear the black decorated barkcloth strap of the type known as *tut'h aben* in the former area, when in ritual use, befitting its bigman status. Such a pig is a beautiful sight to see, with its face painted red, like a 'chief', as it is led across the dancing ground in presentation rituals from bigman to bigman. (It is interesting to note, however, that the Tannese, like Aneityumese, Aniwans and Futunans, do not value tusker pigs as do ni-Vanuatu in central and northern Vanuatu. In 1990, one old

Tannese 'chief' was amazed to hear that Malakulans and Ambrymese valued tusker pigs – he had never heard of them, despite circular pigs' tusks having been on the Vanuatu flag since 1980 and on the currency since 1982.)

There are indications that rough barkcloth sails and types of thick and finer barkcloth sleeping mats were originally produced on Tanna, but it seems these rapidly disappeared with the spread of woven leaf materials and the introduction of 'white man's' cloth and blankets. The barkcloth sleeping mats would have been made by women.

Fig. 146
Detail of Efate barkcloth corner with highly decorated border. Paris, Musée national des Arts d'Afrique et d'Océanie.

Fig. 147
Detail of Efate barkcloth with border and feather fringe. Stuttgart, Linden-Museum.

2. The word 'tapa', a term which in Polynesia generally refers to beaten barkcloth, in many cases made from the bark of the paper mulberry tree, was almost unknown in Vanuatu until the 1980s, but has now become incorporated by some into Bislama as the general word for barkcloth, as no general word existed before (although there are many local language terms).

3. For an example of this Efate type of barkcloth, with feather end decorations, see Speiser 1991, pl. 78, no. 9 (Museum of Mankind coll. cat. no. Oc.1898, 0704.5, don. J. Jennings, 1989).

4. For language terms in these three paragraphs, I am indebted to Willy Roy Tarisaliu of Purao, Tongoa (formerly Vanuatu Cultural Centre fieldworker for the Tongoa-Shepherds region), via the intermediary Karl Waldebäck, who provided the terms for me in 1993.

5. Thanks to the late, beloved Chief Graham Kalsakau for those terms, given to me on 30 October 1980.

Just north of Tanna, Erromango had a highly developed and complex variety of decorated beaten barkcloth types for wear, display and ceremonial purposes, produced by women for women. This will be dealt with later in this section.

Central Vanuatu, from Tongoa to Efate, was the area of production (by women) of many types of beautiful fine barkcloth, of types which would be familiar to many Polynesians today. Traditionally, men in central Vanuatu would wear this kind of tapa cloth around their waist and between their thighs, or in a breechclout style. There were regional stylistic and status variations for the costume versions. Depending on the wearer's status and the occasion, the barkcloth could be dyed yellowish, or 'ochre', with types of turmeric dye. This dye could come off quite easily, as W.E. Giles found after a delegation of chiefs from Emae (Emwae) island visited the brigantine *Bobtail Nag* in 1877, and left the seats and tables of the boat stained yellow after their departure. Also in 1877, in Sesake village on Emae, Giles noted the blood-stained, yellow-coloured tapa *sulus* of two Finonge men hanging from a tree, a sign that they had been killed in a recent fight. In some parts of Efate, men would wear a mat or barkcloth breechclout (or series of them), with a barkcloth breechclout or pubic covering. Brenchley, passing through Efate in 1865, even saw some women wearing yellow-coloured barkcloth around their waists and thighs, with the typical female Efate woven tail hanging from the belts at their backs. These beautifully woven and dyed, tasselled, miniature buttock mats were the origin of early European stories of 'tailed women' on south Efate. On Ifira Tenuku (Fila Island), they were called *totapi*. The late *olfala* Daniel Kalorib Senior, of Ifira Tenuku, said they also had a functional purpose, in that Ifira Tenuku women, traditionally not allowed to physically chastise misbehaving children, could slap them with their tails (for example, see Speiser 1991, pl. 46, no. 6).

Other types of barkcloth or tapa were produced – rougher, larger types for sleeping mats, and finely decorated thin barkcloth with feather decorations along the two narrower ends (figs 146, 147). The latter were important for ceremonial purposes, as part of marriage payments, fines and chiefly rituals. The fine base of this cloth was white, and was coloured, or rather painted, with resinous yellow, brown or reddish geometric patterns, the final finish giving it a sheen like varnish. Undoubtedly, these large and valuable items were circulated and exchanged widely throughout the region.[3]

General language terms for barkcloth or tapa throughout central Vanuatu included:
- *namarove* in Namakura language (spoken, for example, on large parts of Emae, Tongoa, and on Ewose (Awoh), Falea, Tongariki, Buninga, Mataso, and part of Emau);
- *navilnakau* in Nakanamanga language ('north Efate', Leleppa, Moso, Nguna, and parts of west and north Tongoa); the specific Nakanamanga term for the yellowish-coloured male dress barkcloth was *soki mimi*;
- *nasias* in the Polynesian languages spoken by a small group of speakers at Makatea, on east Emae, as well as on Imere Tenuku (Mele island) and Ifira Tenuku (Fila island), south Efate.[4]

On Ifira Tenuku, the male barkcloth worn round the waist and between the legs was called *massi* (cf. Fiji, *masi*): when one bolt of *massi* was wound and worn, it was *temassi*; if more than one was worn it was *amassi*.[5] According to one myth, the ancestors of the Kalsakau lineage brought the right of *massi* to Ifira Tenuku. When Dr S.M. Lambert was leaving Vanuatu after his 1925 anti-yaws campaign, he was presented with an old, rare roll of tapa cloth by Reverend Fred J. Paton. Paton told him the roll was collected (somewhere) on Efate, and the earliest missionaries there said this tapa piece was 'worshipped'. The tapa was double thickness, very fine, with a velvet texture, shell-scraped – not pounded – and covered with fine, reddish feather designs. When Lambert later showed the cloth to Queen Salote of Tonga, she and her advisors indicated to him their belief that it was a rare and ancient 'royal' cloth from Futuna (cf. Wallis and Futuna).

European trade cloth rapidly replaced the central Vanuatu barkcloth as a costume and ceremonial item: in the final two decades of the 19th century, it was still being produced on Nguna, Emae and Tongoa, and its production probably hung on in the Purao area of Tongoa until the death of the great then-chief Tarisaliu in around 1925; it is in this area that the most detailed knowledge of its production still exists. The last man with a detailed knowledge of Irifa Tenuku *massi* was probably *olfala* Pastor Sope, who died in the late 1970s.

With the disappearance of valued barkcloth in central Vanuatu, an interesting cultural evolution has taken place. After passing through a period when European trade cloth took its place, as costume and in ritual, the last thirty years or so has seen a stage when the woven mat materials – for example, mats with feathered end tassels like the earlier ceremonial barkcloth – has replaced the *kaliko* that replaced the barkcloth. By the late 1970s, male and female waist coverings were being produced and worn for certain ritual dances – again, replacing the *kaliko* that replaced the barkcloth. While the elders in Purao – and possible elsewhere – retain the knowledge to make and use their beautiful barkcloths, it would be important for them to assist in its revival before they die, taking their knowledge with them.

Northwards, throughout the rest of Vanuatu, production of barkcloth was rarer, particularly in the major mat-producing areas such as Ambae, Maewo, Pentecost, and the areas where matted spider-web 'cloth' was (and is) used as a base for much material (as in south Malakula). Production of a light, thin, stretchy type of whitish-yellowish barkcloth was often used as a base (stretched over a light wooden frame, for example) on which to paint or place ritual materials, such as in certain male secret societies from Ambae, and certain masks from one small area of southern Malakula. Such a base is still used for certain of the *nahonata* masks, and certain of the end tassels of the beautiful *fakas rossa* hand-held dance batons for 100-day funerary rituals in the *Sungwandaga*-speaking area in central Maewo. Fine, soft barkcloth sleeping mats, *ta'mbagha m'bar*, were at one time produced on Vao, probably for high-ranking men and ritual purposes, and variations of this type were probably originally found throughout north-east Malakula.[6] An isolated area (inland) in west-north-west Santo produces a type of lightweight barkcloth as a kind of mosquito netting. Certain of the ritual objects associated with the *tamate* societies in the Banks Islands have a type of barkcloth stretched on a frame as a base for the painted mask or figure. A large, nearly triangular sheet of yellowish barkcloth, of unknown use, from the Torres is in the collections of the University Museum of Archaeology and Anthropology in Cambridge, UK.[7]

Production and use of types of barkcloth may have been more widespread – language terms for it (*gavu* in south Maewo, *gagavu* in Mere Lava, *malsam* in Mota Lava, and *siopa* in Mota) that were often immediately applied to European cloth when it arrived[8] may indicate an earlier, more widespread production of cloth-like material, as in the south-eastern Solomons.

Barkcloth on Erromango

Erromango has had an extremely complex and tragic history since the arrival of the white man. Rapid depopulation, combined with external and internal factors, resulted in the disappearance of four of the possible six languages extant at the time of first contact, and the extinction of numerous cultural traits. The last conversions to Christianity were in the 1930s, and today the whole population speaks (variants of) what is now called Sie (formerly Yoku, or variants of Enyau), while half a dozen very elderly Ura-speakers survive.[9] Thus, most of the language terms given in the following section will be in Sie, but slight differences may reflect local or historical variations, or the linguistic origin and history of a particular informant.[10]

The general term for (undecorated) beaten barkcloth was *n'mah-itse* or *n'mas-itse* ('barkcloth, beaten'). Made all over Erromango, its early main production centre was in the Ralefati district, a Ura-speaking area of north Erromango. Its manufacture held out to the first quarter of the 20th century in Unepang district (of the original Sorung-speakers), up to Pongkil in Loitnateman district of the Yoku-speaking (now called Sie-speaking) area in south-west Erromango. There was a slight, short-lived revival of barkcloth-making in south-west Erromango during World War II, due to a lack of European cloth in that area. The last area of irregular production – during the 1940s – was in the South River area. The barkcloth was produced by women, and was of different types: a rough, strong kind as a floor 'mat', slightly finer types as sleeping and 'blanket' mats. These were undecorated. The most famous kind of barkcloth, which has survived in museum collections, is the beautiful decorated type worn by

6. Vianney Atpatoun of Tolamp (Tonlamp), Vao, produced a sheet of this in 1984, probably the first in generations.

7. The specimen (cat. no. 1912.22.25) measures 500 cm x 71 cm x 13 cm, and was donated by the Reverend Durrad in 1912.

8. The presence of a small group of Tongans, traditionally dressed, living on the small island of Kwakea for two years in the 1840s, may have had some linguistic influence on terms of barkcloth.

9. Besides the linguistic publications, cf. William Mete's 1979 tape-recordings of the last surviving Ura-speakers (in the Vanuatu Cultural Centre's audiovisual collections).

10. The information in this section is based partially on scattered published 'morsels', but mainly on discussions over the years with Erromangans, and particularly with James Nobuat Atnelo (born 1935) of Pongkil, south-west Erromango, Cultural Centre fieldworker, especially during the month he spent at the author's house in 1984 during the Vanuatu Cultural Centre '"Tapa" blong Vanuatu' exhibition preparations.

Fig. 148
Barkcloth from Erromango. London, Museum of Mankind, British Museum.

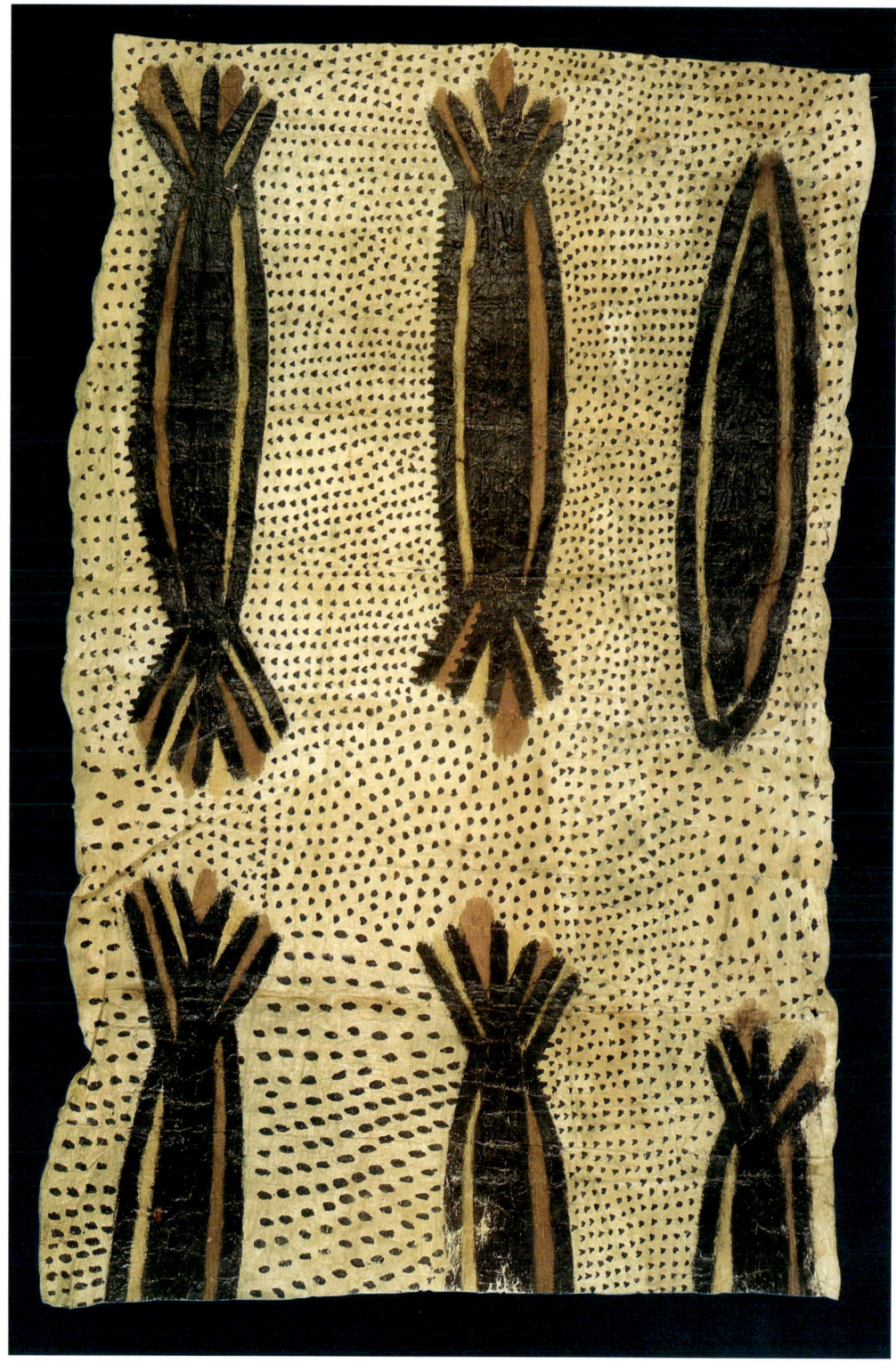

Fig. 149
Erromango barkcloth.
Sydney, Australian Museum.

THE 'DECORATED CLOTH' FROM THE 'ISLAND OF GOOD YAMS' ▼ 135

Fig. 150
Erromango barkcloth.
Basel, Museum für Völkerkunde

women across their shoulders, or draped over one shoulder and across the breasts (figs 148, 150). This type was used mainly for ritual and ceremonial display, and as part of ritual payments (as, for example, part of bride-price payments). An undecorated type was also worn by women when, for example, working in the gardens in cool weather, or in which to carry their babies. There was much *nevasi* (trade) in these barkcloths along predetermined trade routes.

During rituals, women would put on their best *nomblat* (the Erromangan type of voluminous leaf skirt made of pandanus, *burao* (*Hibiscus tiliaceus*), or a type of split banana bark) and their best decorated barkcloth, but the most voluminous *nomblat* and the most 'flash' barkcloth were usually worn by *nasimnalam* (the wife of a chief) married to a *fan lou* (chief; also *natemong* in Sie, and *yarumne* in Ura), or *fan lou nusian* (high chief). Sometimes dozens, or hundreds, of these decorated barkcloths would be hung from long bamboo or wooden poles radiating, like the rays of the sun, from the base of 30-metre-tall *nevsem* towers built for *nehekar/nisekar* chiefly alliance rituals, or burnt *en masse* in a similar situation for chiefly funerary rituals. These ceremonies died out by the late 19th century and most people on Erromango have little knowledge of them. Sempet Naritantop first heard about these funerary aspects around 1986, from possibly the last surviving Erromangan to see them, an extremely ancient woman who broke into tears when reminiscing on the beauty of the spectacle.

There were various terms for these beautiful decorated barkcloths: *n'mah norok* and *n'mah norolat* may have referred to particular sizes, but by the end of last century, the most widespread general term for them was *n'mah neyorwi* ('cloth, decorated (beautiful)'). But fashions, all around the world, change, and so on Erromango: particular styles of designs would come into and fall out of fashion, and the same thing would happen with the terms used for these cloths. Before the white man arrived, the 'fashionable' term was *napnungun neko* ('the tracks (marks) of the *neko*'; *neko* was the general term for a barkcloth beater); when this name fell out of fashion, the cloths's 'in' name became *neko neyorwi* ('the decorated (or beautiful, or "flash") *neko*'). These fashionable changes in designs and names are similar, for example, to concepts among Cuna Indian women of Panama and north Colombia, world-famous for their beautiful, multicoloured appliqué cloth breast-coverings, originally body paints that, with the introduction of cloth, became two-colour geometrical *mola mugan*, and have now become multicoloured, multilayered, multi-design *mola*.

Materials

The barks (often inner barks) of at least seven different types of root tree, bush, or creeper/vine were used to make the barkcloths, depending on the type, colour and texture required. Originally the barks were cut off with a stone adze (*nelit orao*), later with bamboo (*nao*), and, after the arrival of white-man goods, with knives (*nao itungo*; literally 'bamboo (knife) that comes from a long way away'). The types of bark used were from:

- *n'm pang*; *nabanga*, *Ficus* spp.: if the bark of the tree was used, a *young* tree was chosen, as its inner bark did not break so easily. More commonly, the inner bark of the *young* aerial roots was used (for the same reason). The technique with the aerial roots was to cut them at the top first and then cut the lower end when it was lying on the ground. After heating over a fire, the outer bark was cut off, and the inner bark sliced longitudinally, cut off and rolled up for later use.
- *natong*; *natongtong*, mangrove, *Rhyzophora* and *Sonneratia* spp.
- *nema ema*; unknown type: for a type of white cloth.
- *ponku*; unknown type, possibly *Ficus adenosperma*; the roots are used: also for white cloth.
- *nomut*; unknown type of vine or creeper; the bark is used when the plant is as thick as a man's arm.
- *naomova*; unknown type; grows short 'like *burao*' and produces soft barkcloth 'with holes: like a thick cotton shirt'.
- *nuwo*; unknown type; bark from the roots is used.

Other types of bark may also have been used. Bark types were never mixed; only one type of bark was used for each cloth.

There were three types of hardwood barkcloth beater, the general term for which was *neko*, and there was a short and a long version of each type:

- *neko orong*, with wide longitudinal grooves. The longer version was *neko nongun orongo* ('the *neko* with big teeth').
- *neko firo'h*, with narrower longitudinal grooves. The longer version was *neko nongun firo'h* ('the *neko* with small teeth').
- *neko denyung*, with incised crosshatching. The longer version was *neko nowatnin' denyung* ('the *neko* with *denyung* roots'; *denyung*

Fig. 151
James Nobuat Atnelo of Erromango with a piece of decorated barkcloth he made with one of his barkcloth beaters. Port Vila, 1984.
(Photo: Kirk Huffman)

is the cane grass *waelken*, *Miscanthus floridulus*).

The 'beater' *neko* was made of *nokesam*, a hardwood which can take a high polish. As a base on which to beat the bark, a round, smooth log, *nampou*, about 30 centimetres in diameter, 1.5 to 3 metres long, and with its bark removed, was used. *Nampou* was not just the term for this base, but also for the special type of wood used for it, which gave off a soothing, medicinal smell when beaten.[11]

11. *Nampou*: *huremi* or *waetwud* (*Alphitonia zizyphoides*), whose leaves and sap are used as a medicinal rub for sore muscles on Erromango, and whose liquid can be drunk medicinally. Its cleansing smell is like a mixture of creosote and wintergreen.

12. *Nohorat*: *yelotri*, the Indian mulberry (*Morinda citrifolia*). Its inner bark provided red dye, while its roots provided yellow.

13. For *navelah*, see Speiser 1991, pl. 78, no. 11. The term *navelah* traditionally also more properly refers to the rare material of the objects.

Fig. 152
Tapa cloth donated to the National Museum of Vanuatu on the occasion of its opening, 1995. Erromango.

Preparation

The basic making of (an undecorated) cloth would normally take three to four days. The strips of rolled bark to be used would be soaked overnight in *nu wohon* (fresh water), taken out the next morning, placed on the *nampou* and rhythmically beaten. Normally two (or sometimes more) women would do this, one on either side of the log, each with a small wooden bowl (in the shape of a canoe) filled with fresh water beside her, and a small reed whisk to liberally sprinkle the bark to keep it moist while beating. There were special songs for the beating. As many strips of cloth as were to be used in the final object were separately beaten on this first day. *Neko orong* was mainly used on the first day, with a bit of *neko firo'h* towards the end of the day. The *neko* was always kept wet. Those strips beaten on this day were then hung up to dry.

The second day was for 'doubling' the cloth, thickening it by beating together several layers (prepared the previous day) laid at different angles. The same procedure (but often with different songs) was used, the cloth again being sprinkled with water and the *neko* perpetually moistened. On the second day, *neko firo'h* and *neko denyung* were used. When the doubling was finished, the cloth was again hung up to dry.

The third and final day was for 'joining' the cloth, to make it longer. A series of 'doubled' cloths were interleaved at their edges, sprinkled with water and beaten with moist *neko firo'h*. The complete *n'mah itse* was finally beaten with *neko denyung* to 'finish it off', which was done when the joins could no longer be seen. The final cloth was then hung up to dry completely. If it started to separate during drying, it was taken down again, beaten with moist *neko denyung*, rehung, and left to finish drying.

Decoration

If the cloth was to be decorated, to be *n'mah neyorwi*, the desired design was drawn upon it in charcoal while it was still damp before its final drying. When it was finally dried, the dying process could begin. The most commonly used colour or dye was *nohorat*, from the bark of tree of the same name; this could provide yellow or red.[12] Ashes, water and scraped *nohorat* were strained through a coconut-spathe filter into a container, and the cloth was dipped into this mixture. When the cloth was taken out, the charcoal design had absorbed the colour and the rest of the cloth regained its normal hue. Other colours, such as black and blue-green, could be obtained from the sap of other types of wood, roots or leaves.

The designs were mainly pictorial (figs 148-150), not geometrical as in central Vanuatu barkcloth. Erromango barkcloth depicted animals, fish, birds, plants (ordinary and spiritual aspects), ritual, ceremonial and historical events, people, spirits, stars, the sun and the moon, and sometimes scenes, objects or events given by *potnimpris* (the ancestral spirits) in *nemeviag* (a dream). In effect, the designs could be *netaiyi*, a form of writing. One puzzling design, a series of joined triangles or globes (as in the famous design on display in the Vanuatu Cultural Centre, on loan deposit from the Australian Museum), represents physical and spiritual aspects of *nobuan ieva*, a sacred type of bush, tabu to cut. *Nobuan ieva* (or *heva*) grows to around 2 metres tall. The 'fruit' grows annually in a 'joined', extended bunch, so that if the bush has, for example, five joined bunches, one knows that it is five years old. This bush obviously formerly had great ritual significance. It grew originally only in southern Erromango, although some is now growing near the mission station in Potnarvin. I suspect it may have something to do with *nen taviar walevat*, ritual sun 'power' associated with southern Erromango. Other, rarer designs can represent *naveleh* or *norei*, sun and crescent moon, the rare and unique Erromangan fossilised clam shell, or quartzite clan-money used in ritual, bride-price and blood/peace payments.[13] A design on one unique early cloth may represent a different type of chiefly status currency, now completely disappeared, a woven male waist strap upon which dozens of *nempati* (small pigs's canine teeth) were sewn.[14]

N'*mah neyorwi*, produced by women for women's wear, were also *noute*, 'cargo', objects of value, and as such were also used in trade, ritual exchanges and ceremonial display. Production of this beautiful barkcloth gave women increased status and prestige within their own and neighbouring groups, and the wearing of a beautiful one could really help to make a woman a *fah nahiven*, 'woman of substance'.

The traditional male penis-wrapper of Erromango, *yelau*, which hung down (and was not strapped upright as in other areas of Vanuatu) sometimes to knee length and, rarely, for particular chiefs, to the ankles, was normally made of the fibrous *burao* bark, or of *nagarie* (*Cordyline terminalis*) leaf. For particular chiefs and occasions, though, it could be made of *n'mah itse*. The long history of the wearing of *yelau* finished in the mid-1980s, when the last *yelau*-wearer, an old man in the South River area who wore one hidden under his cloth *parpar*, died.

In 1984, the Vanuatu Cultural Centre planned a small, temporary display of Vanuatu barkcloth ('"Tapa" blong Vanuatu') with Erromango barkcloth borrowed from the Robertson collection at the Australian Museum (cat. no. E12394) and an Efate barkcloth from the Museum of Victoria, in Melbourne. In preparation for this, James Nobuat Atnelo, one of the then two Vanuatu Cultural Centre fieldworkers on Erromango, toured his island to find the last three individuals with detailed knowledge of barkcloth production and use. After James gathered information from each individual, each, in turn, died. James then came to Vila for a month for the duration of the exhibition (fig. 152). The exhibition was officially opened on 28 June 1984 by the then president of Vanuatu, His Excellency Ati George Sokomanu, who gave the opening speech, followed by speeches from Chief Andrew Namel (representative chief of Erromango in Port Vila), Chief Graham Kalsakau (chief of Ifira Tenuku), and Mrs Grace Molisa, representing the Cultural Centre board of management and ni-Vanuatu women, producers of the barkcloth. The exhibition generated intense interest among ni-Vanuatu (so much so that the then prime minister, the Honourable Father Walter Lini, and most of the government ministers, who were due at a meeting on Paama on the day of the opening, asked for a special viewing of the barkcloth early on the Sunday morning before their departure), and wide media coverage. James Nobuat was present each day to explain aspects of Erromango barkcloth to the hundreds of ni-Vanuatu visitors. The plan was for him to return to Erromango at the end of July 1984 and organise a group of women there to revive the production of barkcloth. Sadly, the night before his departure from Port Vila an accident resulted in in him having to have a leg amputated,[15] thus nipping the project in the bud. It is now hoped that the recently founded Erromango Cultural Association, supervised by the Vanuatu Cultural Centre and through its dynamic Erromango Cultural Centre fieldworker Jerry Taki, can continue this important project.

The Efate barkcloth returned to Melbourne, but the Erromango cloth has remained on display in the Cultural Centre (thanks to the Australian Museum and its board of trustees agreeing to place it there on a long-term loan and deposit agreement) in a specially constructed, waterproof display case. It has served as an inspiration to many ni-Vanuatu, most lately seen in the large tapestry version of it produced by young female Erromango artist Juliette Pita and exhibited in the special Nawita Association of Contemporary Artists' (see Regenvanu, p. 311, this volume) display held in the capital in November 1994. Certain earlier writers (for example, Speiser 1991:240) have postulated that the presence of barkcloth in certain areas of Vanuatu can be traced to Polynesian influence,[16] and, although this may be true in certain instances at a particular time in history, it may not necessarily always be the case. Production and use of beaten barkcloth of many types was found traditionally throughout many areas of Melanesia, a completely normal development in populations of such ingenuity. The Polynesians have

14. The design I refer to is on the right of the cloth pictured in Speiser 1991, pl. 78, no. 4. This cloth, in the Museum of Mankind in London, is Ms List 10, part of Q78.0c.543, collected by Brenchley in 1865. Mineral dyes (for face painting) were traded from southern Erromango to northern Tanna to there purchase the numerous small pig canines for the woven 'money', or status, belts.

15. No Erromangans will be surprised at this accident, nor the rapid deaths of the three informants mentioned earlier. This all ties into a pattern typical of the island, and which has a particular explanation which I will not divulge out of respect.

16 For example, did Roy Mata pass through Erromango before arriving on Efate, as some myths indicate? Stories also exist on Erromango of an intrusive Polynesian population group, eventually defeated in war by the Erromangans, the survivors pushed into the Mount Rantop area (bounded by Potnarvin and Traitor's Head in eastern Erromango).

developed the production of a particular kind of complex beaten barkcloth, widely known to the outside world as tapa, and back-voyaging influences undoubtedly injected certain types of material and ritual traits back into parts of Melanesia, but who is to say that the origin of Polynesian barkcloth may not lie somewhere in the ancient barkcloth traditions of Melanesia, through which the Polynesians passed on their relatively recent migrations further into the central and eastern Pacific?

Haircombs

Kirk W. Huffman

Haircombs, like flowers in Vanuatu, were traditionally usually an item of male attire, the latter often being more status-related than the former. Incised bamboo haircombs (for example, fig. 153, from Tanna, with designs similar to some of the barkcloth belts from the same island) were widespread, particularly in areas where the penis-wrapper was traditionally worn, although there was some overlap. The largest bamboo combs were those worn by Big Nambas males in north-west Malakula, who continued to wear these on the high plateau in that area well into the 1970s. These were much larger than the similar *ninger'r* bamboo combs worn by the neighbouring Batar'nar peoples and the numerous styles of north-eastern Malakula (for example, fig. 156). Hardwood combs were widespread in central Vanuatu (for example, fig. 157, from Efate, probably a chief's comb), parts of southern Malakula (figs 162 and 163), Malo (fig. 164, from northern Malo), and parts of Santo (figs 158, 160, 161, all from south-western Santo, and fig. 159, tipped with pigs tails, from north-east Santo). Haircombs are still quite widely worn in Middle Bush Santo.

A type of plaited comb consisting of hardwood points plaited together with prepared twine of coconut fibre or *burao* was found in northern-central Vanuatu from central Pentecost, northwards and westwards through Maewo, Ambae (fig. 166), and into southern Santo. This type of comb survives in the Apma-speaking area of central Pentecost, where it is called *bwalavwih*. There, the wooden points are usually from the interior of the tree fern, and are called *mau vwilih*. The plaited cord binding is called *bwele rava* if of *burao* fibre, but can be made of coconut fibre (*tsinsinan kulakül* in Apma). The tradition of making these plaited combs had almost died out in central Pentecost until in the 1970s *olfala* Linoh (*kastom* name Wadan) of Baksal began reteaching their making, supported by the Catholic mission station at Melsisi.

Another type of plaited – and strapped – wooden-point comb was found throughout much of the Banks Islands (fig. 165, probably from Gaua), a style showing links with the Solomon Islands.

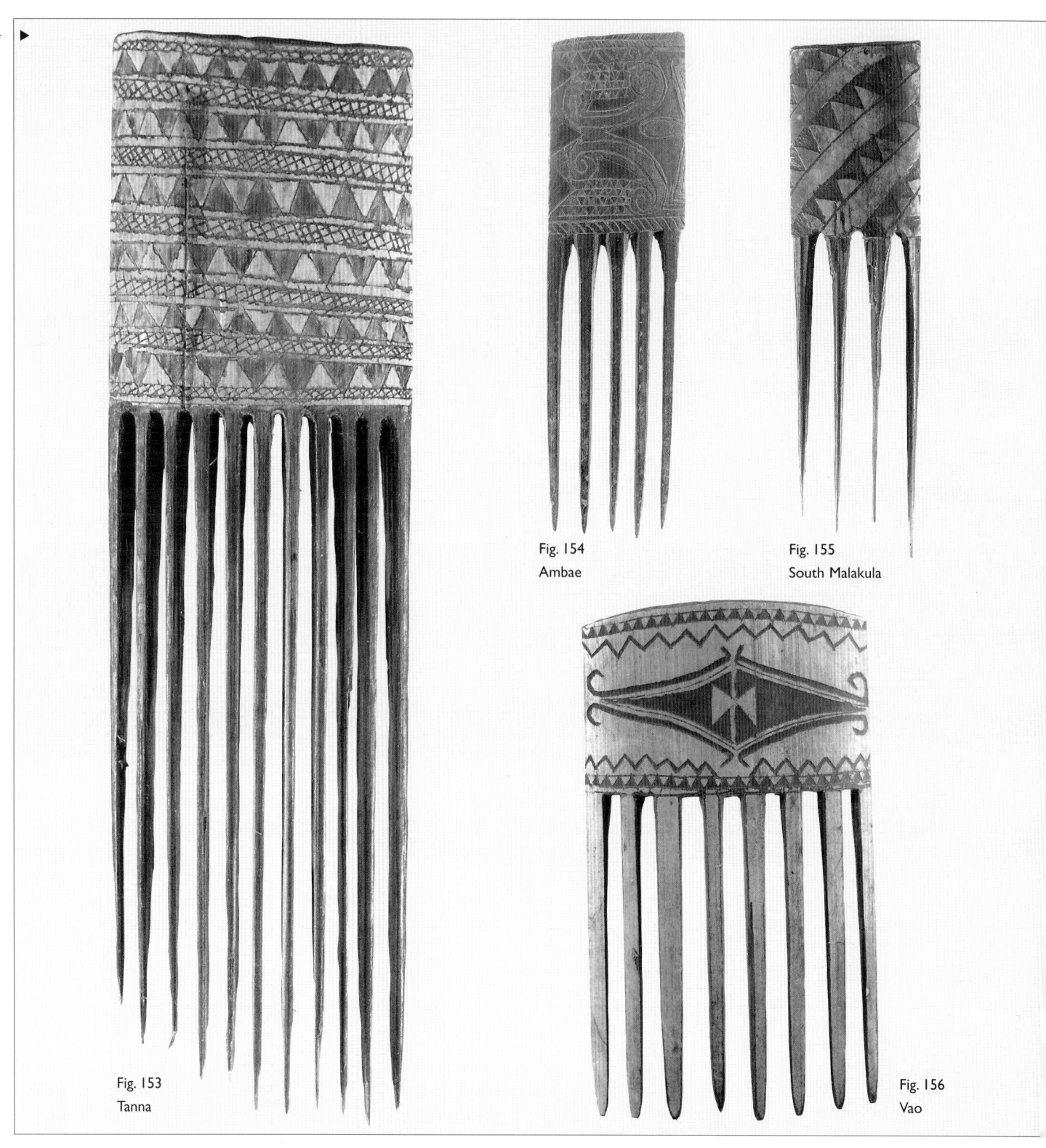

Fig. 153
Tanna

Fig. 154
Ambae

Fig. 155
South Malakula

Fig. 156
Vao

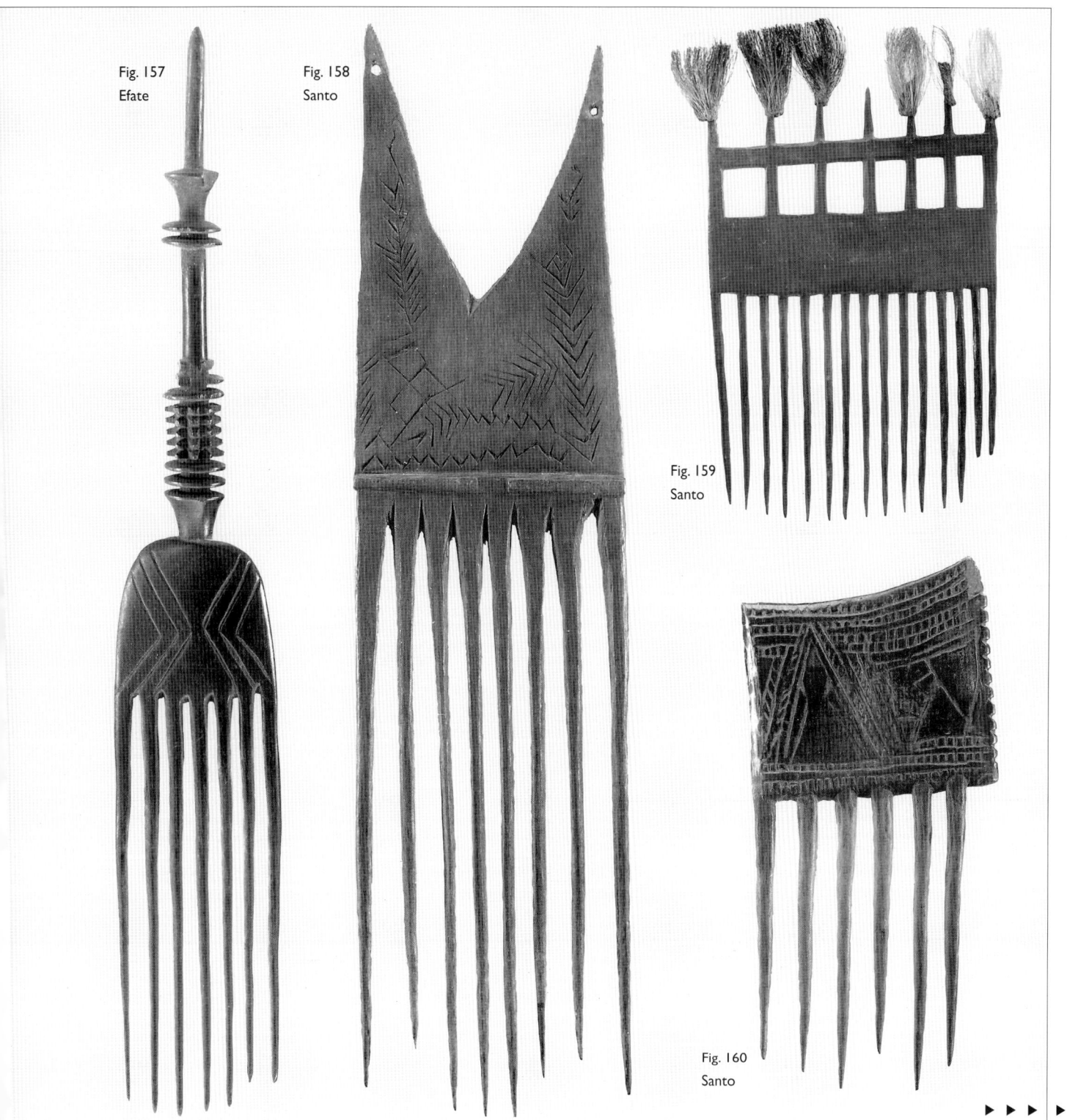

Fig. 157 Efate

Fig. 158 Santo

Fig. 159 Santo

Fig. 160 Santo

HAIRCOMBS ▼ 143

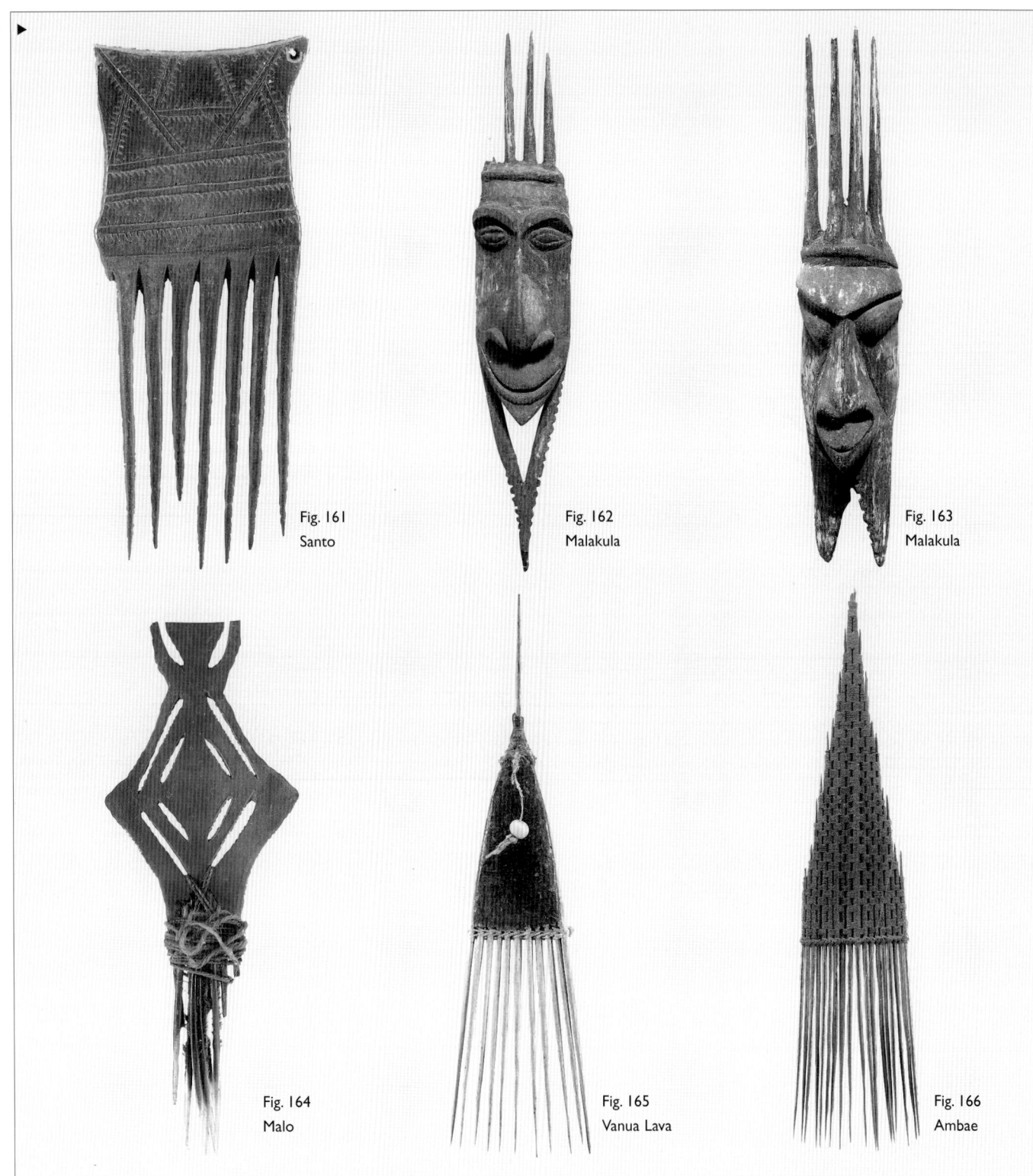

Fig. 161 Santo
Fig. 162 Malakula
Fig. 163 Malakula
Fig. 164 Malo
Fig. 165 Vanua Lava
Fig. 166 Ambae

Music in Vanuatu

Peter Russell Crowe

Indications of ancient music and dance practices may be cautiously inferred from archaeology and by comparison with the ethnographic record. Musical instruments were made of perishable material, bar those of shell (for example, conches) or pottery. Skeletal ornaments in tombs suggest an anticlockwise direction may have been preferred in circle dances for a long period. Pottery vessels may have been at the origin of the Malakula *temes nainggol*, 'ancestral voices', nowadays bullet-like, hollowed wooden cylinders, used to amplify bamboo aerophones. Malakula musicians saw resemblances to the blowing of the Australian didgeridoo on a visit to Fiji, at the inaugural South Pacific Festival of Arts, 1972.

The most recent language classification (cf. Tryon, p. 172, this volume) correlates with the well-known presence of planted, giant slit-gongs south of a line between Espiritu Santo and Malakula, south of Ambae, cutting through central Pentecost at Melsisi (Apma-speakers) in the Central Vanuatu subgroup (including Emwae, Epi and Efate).

Myth states that Maewo is now in *marama rua*, 'second rebirth'. The prehistorical record of Vanuatu might well match references in song texts, as also shown in gesture (dance), the ritual calendar, and ideas about prerequisite elemental presences for human existence (that is, to have stone, wood, water, fire, plants, birds, creatures ...). Perhaps there is also a case for Maewo as the springboard of eastbound voyages towards Fiji (or 'Mamalu'), enshrined in myth and song, and backed up by place-names and linguistic features (cf. Crowe 1991, where musical examples for this relationship are discussed).

In more recent times, de Bougainville reported hearing slit-gong ensembles on 'Lepers' Island' (Ambae), taking them for 'native messages'. Around 1850, Bislama began its development as a lingua franca, now important in modern musical idioms. Some early missionaries left useful records of ritual (for example, Dudley's 1860 *Mota Journal*), and the best of them did remarkable work (for example, Dr Codrington's *The Melanesians* of 1891, and Codrington and Palmer's *Mota Dictionary* of 1896). Of particular musical interest are the works of Layard (1928, 1942) and Deacon (1934b). There is by now a long list of references – much of which has some relevance to contextual studies of music and dance (for example, McLean 1995).

There have been few properly ethnomusicological studies of Vanuatu put in print, and the discography remains scant and obscure. The first re-

Fig. 167
Slit-gong. Drawing by Mikloucho-Maclay, 1879. Tasiko, Epi. Mikloucho-Maclay 1950-1954, vol. 5.

cordings were made by Layard (Clausen 1958), and Deacon bemoaned his lack of equipment when discussing the south-west Malakula *temes nainggol* ensembles:

> The total effect is unlike anything I have ever heard, except some Japanese records of Japanese orchestral music ... So far I have found it hopeless to try and record [notate] the music. It is altogether too unlike anything I am used to; moreover, it is orchestral in character and therefore really needs a phonograph to do anything with it. It is a powerful form of art. (Deacon 1934b:392 n.)

There is (now) virtually no traditional polyphonic choral singing to be heard, and nobody can be sure if there ever was. Some singing in parallel thirds from Paama has been adopted into customary Ambae song-dances, like the *sawagoro* form (possibly derived from 'campfire singalongs'), but Layard (1942) notated some parallel-third passages in Atchin songs. While there are few traditional 'harmonies' where combining sonorities are musically regulated, there are many kinds of ensemble or 'orchestral' musical spectacles demanding a polyphonic-like performance, having operating principles of synchronisation and specificity in the parts. These are present in slit-gong ensemble music, where polyrhythm seems dominant, but is also ordered by contrasting pitches. The ensemble music with *temes nainggol* heard by Deacon included singing and hand-gongs, which he thought was 'in the manner of a part song', and where at times

> ... the cylinders burst into a kind of musical pyrotechnics, with trills punctuated by horn-like notes on the small high-pitched cylinders and backed by a continuous deep note on the larger ones, interrupted now and then by scale-like passages and sometimes rising to a prolonged climax in which all the cylinders merge into a long-drawn harmony or discord. (Deacon 1934b:391-392)

The tall (up to 6 metres, above the ground), vertically-planted wooden slit-gongs were once found everywhere south of the 'Crowe-line' (cf. Clark 1983). Nineteenth-century pictures (for example, the sketches of Mikloucho-Maclay, such as fig. 167, and also early photographs) often show numbers of them grouped as miniature forests (fig. 168). Specimens from Efate, Malakula (figs 170, 185, 187) and Ambrym (fig. 184) have reached museums worldwide as artistic carvings rather than practical musical instruments. Despite widespread inter-island voyaging in the past, the idea of making such gongs was not pursued outside this area, neither to the

Fig. 168
Slit-gongs, photographed by Lindt, 1891. Leleppa Island, north-west Efate.

neighbouring northern, nor to the southern islands (Erromango through Tanna to Anatom). Upright gongs, standing on their own, are unique to central Vanuatu, indeed for all Oceania. In border areas, some longish gongs may be used horizontally (fig. 171) and then propped up for specific ritual points (for example, during women's ululations in Bunlap circumcision ceremonies).

A preference for anticlockwise directionality goes with the high incidence of circling dances, wherein directional movement 'follows the right-hand side', and is related to ideas of male 'hardness' versus female 'softness'. This principle extends to the playing of slit-gongs of all types, which are always struck on the 'right-hand' side – obvious when they are stood upright. Horizontal gongs are turned with the slit facing a seated player, who strikes the upper lip. Such gongs should be seen as if toppled tree trunks with the roots (earth) to the right, the leafy crown (sky) to the left: the upper lip conveys 'message', the lower lip ('left-hand') would be 'nonsense'. The idea of 'correct direction' is learned, and is shown in children's dances and games, where clockwise directionality may be tolerated, up to a certain age. Some Banks Islands *mago* 'dances' are performed by men in a circle in which a number of steps are taken anticlockwise, and then there is a turn to go clockwise, then anticlockwise, and so on.

Singing, dancing and playing instruments are all in the realm of oral tradition, which includes mnemonic formulae. 'Non-literate' ni-Vanuatu have prodigious capacity of memory. The late George Boe of Maewo claimed and then proved to know more than 1000 songs and 200 myths. Rather than being conservative (unchanging), Vanuatu oral tradition is dynamic and adapting. One operating principle is 'getting away with breaking the rules', referring to a deeper 'rule', being 'capacity to reinvent'. Thus ritual forms can undergo gradual but visible alteration over time. Repertoires are retained in units (for example, songs with fixed texts), but their uses (for example, in ritual sets) may involve chang-

Fig. 169
Recent photograph of a ritual ceremony. Interior of south-west Malakula. The face style of the slit-gong comes from south-central Malakula.

1. In Vanuatu, slit-gongs are often called slit-drums, especially when referring to the small horizontal specimens, sometimes made from bamboo.

ing plans. Rigidity of form is more apparent where 'custom' is in jeopardy; for example, with the advent of a cash economy. Potential capacity to lead singing or dancing, also to be seen as 'creativity' (as in 'contracts to perform'), is as much valued as the possession of a stock of specific items (repertoire). A common act before the revival of a song, dance or instrumental item is 'straightening it' first, in the mind of a performer. This involves revision of text and context appropriate to the coming performance. For such reasons, much traditional music and dance is in a constant state of change, and the 'antiquity' of any item is not always shown by any feature (sonorous, gestural), but by its contextual position. Was this capacity inherent among the original voyagers who became the ni-Vanuatu? Presence or absence of polyphony, or the steps of a 'scale', is unreliable as to 'antiquity' in a given repertoire (in contrast with Euro-Asiatic notions of 'complexity', in a supposed 'evolution'). We note, though, that many children's songs are based on 'fanfare' (do-mi-sol) melodies.

Musical instruments

Ni-Vanuatu have produced a large number of blown and struck instruments, but only one or two are plucked or scraped. Most are biodegradable because they are made of vegetable or animal material. Stones, shells, bones, ivory and pottery are the most durable materials. The following is a necessarily incomplete sound-maker list.

Wood

Known hardness of trees determines selection of species for different purpose-made slit-gongs (which are also 'Helmholtz resonators', in that pitch will rise as the the slit widens, for a given capacity) (figs 184, 185, 186, 187). In the 'upright' area, trunks are dressed to regular cylinders and ornamentally carved. In the 'horizontal' area, natural forms are retained, so that any pitch variations on an instrument can be musically exploited, and are usually without carving, except for handles.[1] Beaters are selected for size, balance and weight from hard or soft woods, or butt-ends of coconut fronds.

Temes nainggol resonators are made from softwoods, but activated with blown bamboo or reed tubes. A membrane drum (perhaps a kettle-drum type) is reported from the Banks and Maewo (*na olo*), but is a secret instrument. Myths typically say a primordial woman invented the slit-gong but did not produce sonorous 'meaning' or beauty with it, so the men took it over to show what could be done. The buttress-roots of trees are carved into large concussion plates, struck by bamboo, often placed over holes in the ground (fig. 188).

Bamboo

Diameters and inter-node lengths of different species permit varied products from small, hand-size panpipes to medium-size, multi-voiced slit-gongs of two or more nodes, too big with which to dance – but hand gongs (one node) are carried and played by dance-leaders. On Maewo, a portable pentatonic xylophone is recalled, but no playable specimen remains. Split, dry lengths of bamboo, put in bundles on forked supports, may be struck by several players for 'snare-drum' rhythms for Ambae dances.

The bamboo aerophone (figs 172-183) is known everywhere, in several guises: a V-notch end-blown flute, one node, two or three holes at the bottom, played with arms and hands fully extended to the waist; a transverse, twin-node, centrally blown 'bamboo (flute) to satisfy two women at once'; a long (1.5 metre) transverse 'shoulder flute', which was in use on Ambae; bundle-pipes or panpipes; and a type of side-blown trumpet (conch substitute).

'Aeolian' bamboos are suspended from upper branches of a banyan tree on Maewo or Motalava, to whine in the wind as ghost-voices. On Malakula and in the Banks, the reticulation of weird, ghostly sounds via bamboo pipes was brought to a fantastical fine art (cf. Deacon 1934b).

Leaves, seeds, fruit, roots

Dried umbrella-palm fronds are scraped on stone make *tamate* 'tabu spirit' sounds on Mota. Pentecost Apma-speakers roll coconut-leaf fronds into a simple 'oboe' to imitate fowl. Hand rattles of dried seed pods are in use at Naviso. Ankle rattles are made with *pangium* pods tied with coconut sennit. Ambrym's musical bow employs a vine cord. Humming tops are made from seed pods. Halved coconut shells are 'clopped' on the ground in games. Shark rattles came via Santa Cruz.

Shells

Leg-rattles of sea snails, cowry and other small shells were used in the Torres and Banks groups. Conch

Fig. 170
Dancing ground, Vao Island, with slit-gongs, megaliths and pig-tusk presentation racks. Photographed by Speiser, 1910. North-east Malakula.

Fig. 171
Horizontal slit-gongs, photographed by Speiser in 1910. North-west Santo.

Fig. 172
Decorated flutes.
Pentecost and Ambrym.
Basel, Museum für
Völkerkunde.

Single Bamboo Flutes

Kirk W. Huffman

Fig. 173 Two flute-players on the beach at Ranon, photographed by E. Aubert de la Rüe, 1935. North Ambrym.

Although the island most famous today in Vanuatu for the production of single bamboo flutes is Ambrym, such flutes, with their many local variations, were originally made throughout almost the whole of Vanuatu. Normally with only two holes at the lower 'playing' end – ideally in line with the nock of the upper blowing 'mouth' – there were, and still are numerous stylistic and functional differences in these flutes (usually played by men) around Vanuatu, from the undecorated relatively shorter flutes of Tanna, played vertically with bent arms, to the longer, beautifully incised ones from Ambrym, played vertically with fully stretched arms. Many Ambrym flutes have a 'knocked' double projection at the lower end, representing the mouth of a certain fish. Ambrym's particular artistic bent has resulted in elaborate incised designs covering many of the flutes with stylistic representations of natural and spiritual aspects, from marine motifs to the garden world, to interlaced spirit and *rom* faces to rarer designs of an erotic nature. More stylised and less elaborate incising is found in southern Pentecost. From central Pentecost northwards through to Ambae and Maewo, undecorated flutes are found, often with a third playing hole underneath and behind the lower playing end, while, for example, northern Pentecost also has a smaller flute with three playing holes aligned at the lower outer end, 'for training the fingers of young men'. A few very elderly males in northern and central Pentecost and northern Ambrym use a long, double-ended, single flute played horizontally from the middle.

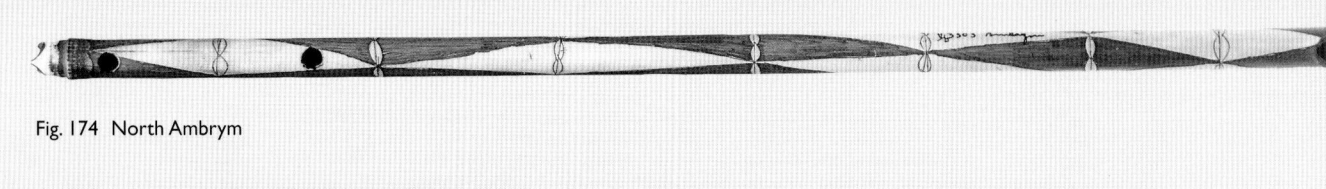

Fig. 174 North Ambrym

Fig. 175 Pentecost

Fig. 176 Ambrym

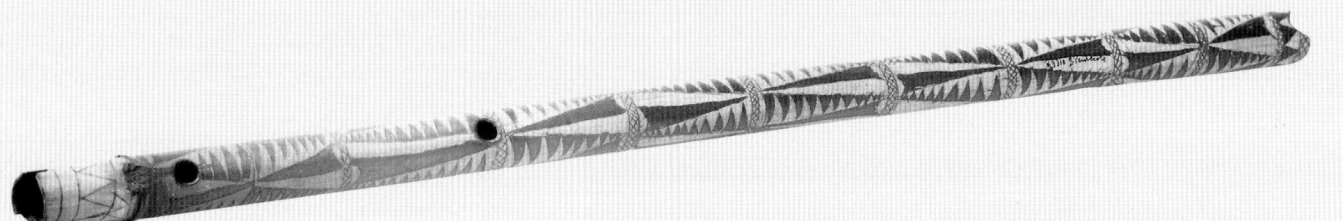

Fig. 177 Pentecost

Many flutes are played for general entertainment or relaxation, or in conjunction with the telling of a traditional story, or with the making of a particular sand-drawing or even string figures. Other types, or tunes, can be used, for example, to assist love magic, to promote sprouting of yams or, like the four-holed flutes played by women in parts of the Banks Islands, during the yam harvest. Other types can be used in restricted aspects of funerary rituals.

As with sand-drawing in Vanuatu today, there is a slightly growing tendency for the particular type of decorated single flute from one particular area of the country to gain 'prominence' and even to be considered, by some ni-Vanuatu and outsiders, as a sort of 'national' type. There is no national type of flute; there are numerous variations, and it is important for younger ni-Vanuatu from every island of the country to approach their elders with respect, to learn the manufacture and use of the particular types of flutes their ancestors were given or decorated for their own cultural areas.

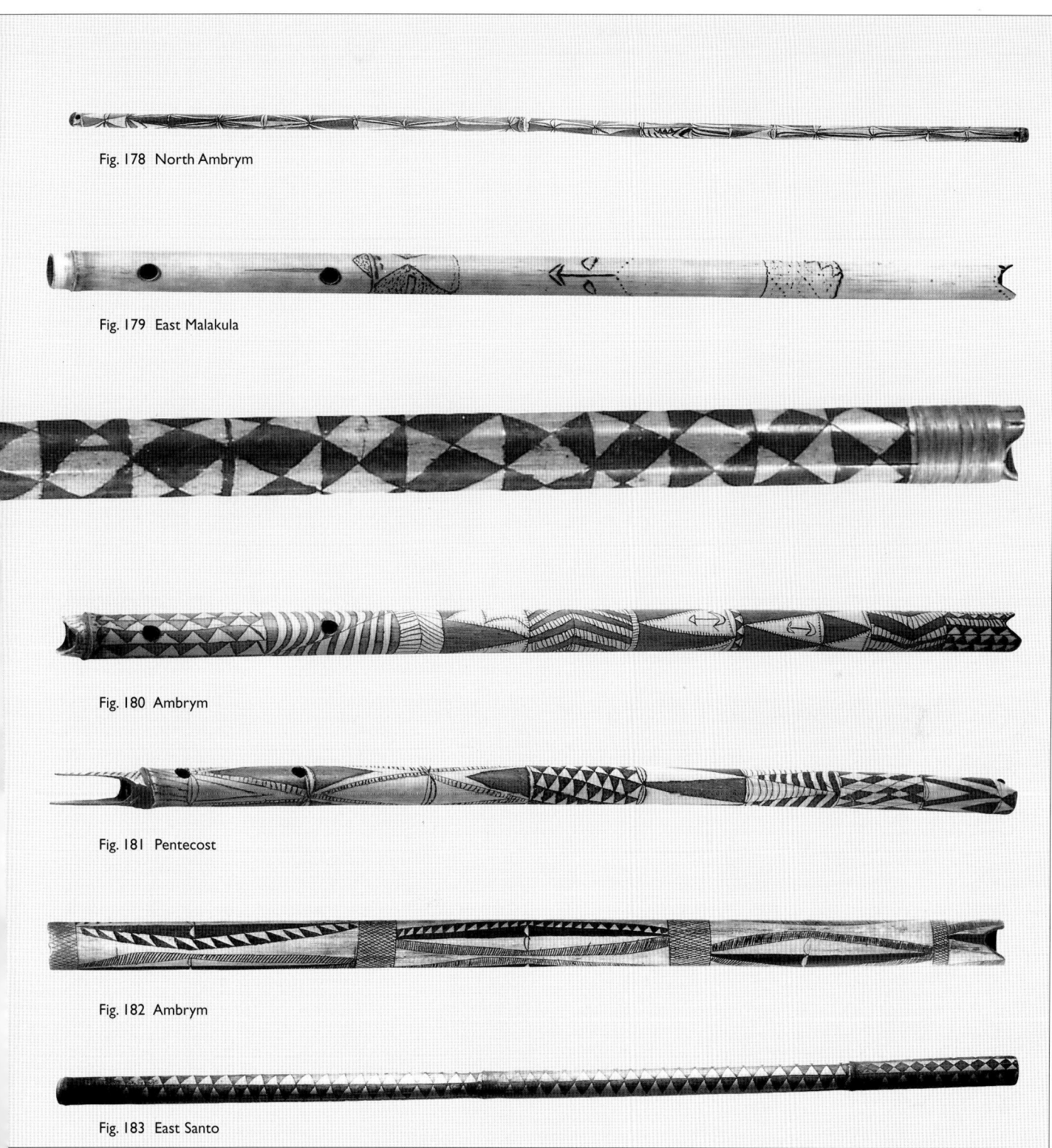

Fig. 178 North Ambrym

Fig. 179 East Malakula

Fig. 180 Ambrym

Fig. 181 Pentecost

Fig. 182 Ambrym

Fig. 183 East Santo

Fig. 184
Slit-gongs.
North Ambrym.
Paris, Musée
national des Arts
d'Afrique
et d'Océanie.

154 ▼ MEN'S ART, WOMEN'S ART

Fig. 185
Small polychrome two-faced gong, seen from the rear.
Vao, north-east Malakula.
Paris, Musée national des Arts d'Afrique et d'Océanie.

Fig. 186
The same slit-gong, showing the two faces on its front.
Vao, north-east Malakula.
Paris, Musée national des Arts d'Afrique et d'Océanie.

trumpets are made from several seashell species (*Triton, Strombus, Fusus, Cassis*), end- and side-blown.

Knowledge of, and adaptation to, the particular biocultural environment of Vanuatu – by means of song, dance and ritual – has depended on oral-gestural transmission. The Vanuatu Cultural Centre began a conservation program in 1976, and by 1992 had forty-six local fieldworkers using audio-visual recording devices, many of them for music. For instance, Jeffry Uli recorded forty-five minutes of the *Qat Baruqu* ceremony of 5 January 1976 at Ngota, Maewo, as fieldworker and participant. The ceremony had not been performed for twenty years (cf. Track 19, Vanuatu CD – Crowe 1994b)

Dangers from earthquakes and volcanic eruptions have always been present. Virgin forestry, mineral and fishery resources are diminishing. Some low-lying islands (for example, Torres group) risk swamping by rising sea levels as the ozone layer depletes. Monoculture, as agricultural policy, locally reduces the variety of resources to fully carry out rituals. For example, cash cropping of coconuts on western Ambae (Nduindui district) led to problems in raising pigs, a major factor in abandoning the *huqe* 'pig-killing grade rites', in the 1930s (cf. Allen 1969), but happily the slit-gong ensembles there have kept up their extensive *huqe* repertoire (the *surara* is Radio Vanuatu's call-sign).

Musical performance

Symmetry in design is omnipresent in most forms of music. There is a high degree of 'redundancy', shown through the use of repetitions or balancing

Fig. 187
Large slit-drum (detail).
Atchin Island, north-east Malakula.
Paris, Musée national des Arts d'Afrique et d'Océanie.

phrases in songs and instrumental pieces. Thus verse or litany forms are recurrent. They depend on both the repetition of gestures (as in dance in a limited area), and on the twin concepts of self-contained lines (textual) and phrases (melodic). Iterative forms may result from a required ordering (lists), or priorities of significance.

Free or continuing variation is a formal tendency only in certain long narrative songs such as the 'banned' *tanumwe* of Ambae, wherein the narrated or sung 'events' may be fairly unpredictable, and transcribed melodies are difficult to segment because of an apparent lack of repetitions ('lines'). These songs deal with 'technical incest' (intra-moiety love affairs, more kin-distant than that between cross-cousins), not supposed to happen in the new 'enlightened' society. Such songs are usually long (often ten minutes), seem rather unrhythmic, and are performed with 'absence' of posture (that is, floppy, relaxed). But they are felt to be highly affecting songs of 'sorry' (fate, vulnerability), and their rare performances attract profound local attention. Rhetorical and narrative structure is also a determinant in longer-song symmetrical structures, taking a holistic rather than segmental view. Non-danced versions of many songs may be performed too.

Conventional classification by scales shows a familiar pattern of:
- 'fanfare' (triadic) melodies;
- high incidence of anhemitonic tetra- and pentatonic types; and
- many hexa- and heptatonic types seeming like sections of the 'European' diatonic scale.

'Chained thirds', with alternations minor or major, are frequent in sets of three intervals on four notes; for example, A-C-E-G. The presence of chained perfect fourths is notable on Maewo, where there is a clear pivot point around a semitone step; for example, D#-G#-C# <> D=G=C= (ascending order, range a major 13th). This exists, and it is most unusual, alongside all the other scales mentioned above in the list above. These pitches refer mainly to songs, there being few fixed-pitch instruments except for flutes.

Use of the word 'pitch' (rather than 'scale') is deliberate, because chains of intervals exceeding whole-tones puts the notion of 'steps' into doubt, especially when they become as large as fourths (giving an impression of aural pendulum-motion). One might speak of 'melodic-templates' instead.

Body-based binary pulsation dominates the dancing, subdividing in twos or threes. Solo song (without regular gestures; for example, sung in a sitting position) tends to 'additive' groupings (in combinations of twos and threes as if 'Bulgarian' rhythms, but non-isometric), in *parlando rubato*. Some slit-gong pieces (Ambae, Raga) make play with the *hemiola* (3x2-2x3) in compound-time passages; Malakula ensembles employ elaborate codings for long rhythm-sets, which at first may seem quite aleatoric, as in Walarano gong-raising rituals. Rhythm-sets are often in *ostinati* – that is, extensible subsets, with some unpredictable combinations occurring in crossover passages from one subset to another.

A big range of tempo is in use, from *adagio* to *presto*. Controlled *accelerando* is quite frequent; less often the *rallentando*. Some songs may be sung slowly in *parlando rubato* in one context, and sung and/or danced quickly in *tempo giusto* in another; in the first, text dominates, in the second it is the spectacle. In the *parlando rubato* manner, the singer says he or she is 'pulling' the song (or the text).

Ni-Vanuatu often show keen rhythmic skill, flexibility and invention, and this cultural achievement is certainly related to healthy diet, supple physique and capacities for endurance, especially in rural areas (outdoor life), as much as to compositional creativity. In bringing music to life, the idea of 'being together' (in sync) and of performing with good style (vigour, knowledge) is important. There were, for example, more than 300 terms of critical appraisal of Mota music and dance performance: for singing in or out of tune, for being 'slack' in rhythm or incorrect in tempo, as well as terms of appreciation for skill and for achieving subtlety, or splendid effects. Examples are: *liñai*, 'sound, voice, taste, way of life, manner'; *nunuai*, 'the mental impression of sound or force … taken to be real'; *sito!* 'the cry in the *mago* to mark the change in the song which the dancers are singing to themselves'; *qaui*, 'knee, a turn in a song', thus *qau as?* 'be behind at the turn' (Codrington and Palmer 1896).

At Saranabuga (west Ambae), a method of teaching slit-gong rhythms was devised by the late Samuel Lengge, of 'finger drumming' – that is, to tap with the fingers of both hands on a bamboo pillow or hand-gong, skeletal versions of the ensemble items (five gongs). Apprentice drummers learn the items' apparent form (or gestalt*)* like this, and in rehearsals are expected to discern their parts within the whole, and elaborate them. '*Save*'-systems, like the expert systems so dear to the planners of artificial intelligence, are held by ni-Vanuatu *kastom* men as codes (see Crowe 1990b).

In east Ambae slit-gong ensembles, the largest gong is called *ratahigi,* the middle gong *simbegi* and the small gong *valagi*. The ensemble is likened to a voyaging canoe, where the gongs are 'captain', 'helmsman' and 'crew' respectively – the 'crew' may be several small gongs – and on the dancing ground the *ratahigi* controls the ritual sequencing (items, stops and starts), the *simbegi* directs the speed of the items in sync with the dancers, and the *valagi* provides rhythmic embellishment.

Ways to learn in any environment involve memory of things heard, seen and sensed ('felt'), but have a particular character in an oral tradition. No doubt enculturation starts in the womb, and the 'matriality' of the familial world is probably impressed already on the newborn infant. As a child grows, its memory will record experiences, but according to expanding but subconscious codes, and these will include myriad sonorous and gestural details. It is rather difficult to record or memorise experiences that do not fit into patterns, so we postulate here that music, dance and language acquisition run analogously and in parallel, and that the power of memory shown by many ni-Vanuatu is directly related to oral and visual means of transmission, flowing with little impediment. Literacy-oriented schooling tends to put interference into the traditional processes and introduces a reliance on mechanical means (books, tapes, pictures) of recording information.

Fig.188
Men beating a flat board covering a hole with bamboos, accompanied by a horizontal drum resting on forks. Photographed by Speiser in 1910.
Ureparapara, Banks Islands.

The Boars of Bali Ha'i: Pigs in Paradise

William Rodman

The hunt in the rainforest

It is wartime, and Lieutenant (jg) James Michener stands on the deck of a transport ship, the *Cape Horn*, anchored in Luganville Channel. He gazes out across the ocean, and sees on the horizon the faint outline of a volcano. It rises from a real island, but in his mind he conjures another island into existence, one he names 'Bali Ha'i'.[1]

> 'What's this killing pigs, Billis?' Fry asked. 'Well, they're holy pigs, sir.' 'Holy?' 'Yes,' Billis replied. The young native shook his head in agreement. 'But you see, sir, they aren't really holy till they're dead.' (Michener 1964)

The 'real' Bali Ha'i has been known by many names – Leper's Island, Aoba, Omba, and now Ambae. There, on a cool and bright May morning a quarter of a century after the end of World War II, I joined a group of men on their way to hunt tusked boars in the rainforest. For weeks, a slit-gong had burst the early morning stillness of the village where I was staying. The message of the drum was that a major rank-taking ceremony was imminent, a pig-killing in which ten valuable tusked boars would die. Now it was two days before the event.

We were thirty men, and we had as many dogs, all thin, quick and scarred, obedient to their owners, wary of everyone else. These were pig-hunting dogs, not pets. A festive air prevailed as the hunters strolled through a succession of coconut plantations, toward the hills and the deep brush. As we entered the forest, the light became pale, almost green, and we split into groups of two or three men, some with dogs, some without. I set off with the young chief who was to take rank. The two of us moved quickly along narrow jungle paths, out of sight of the other men.

He motioned with his hand: look, over there. Three pigs lay in a dust wallow about 9 metres (30 feet) from the track. One was a boar of great size – maybe 200 kilograms (450 pounds). We carried no weapons with us, and I felt very vulnerable. Suddenly, my partner whistled – loudly – to signal the other hunters. The pigs twitched, grunted, but did not move from the wallow. Terror must have been written all over my face. The young chief grinned broadly. 'Rest easy,' he said. 'The others will be here soon.'

Soon, indeed, I heard dogs yipping, and men scrambling through dense brush. Then everything began to happen quickly. The dogs burst through the undergrowth, alarming the pigs, which squealed and charged off in three directions. The pack set off in hot pursuit of one of the pigs – the

---

1. Vanuatu's National Tourist Office (*Visitor to Vanuatu* n.d.:15) describes Ambae as Michener's 'Bali Ha'i', a claim that David Stanley reiterates in the *South Pacific Handbook* (1989:645). In fact, Bali Ha'i could only be a composite of several of the forty-nine Pacific islands Michener visited during World War II. Some elements of Bali Ha'i's physical setting evoke Bora Bora, while the details of pig-raising and rank-taking found in the chapter entitled 'A Boar's Tooth' in *Tales of the South Pacific* seems to me to be derived from a mix of Malakulan and Ambaean *kastom*. Ambae is the only volcanic island that can be seen from Luganville, where Michener served as a

big tusker. In minutes, the dogs had cornered the boar against a fallen banyan tree. Men were shouting as the dogs did their work, keeping the pig in place. The dogs snapped at the boar's genitals and nose. The boar kept moving its lowered head from side to side, responding to threats, trying to see its tormentors on all sides. Several times, it charged forward a few paces, then retreated back against the tree. One of the hunters slipped behind the banyan, a jungle vine noose in his hands. He reappeared squatting like a bush spirit on the tree, behind the pig. Two other hunters crouched low in front of the boar, one to the left, the other to the right. They too held liana nooses in their hands. The dogs continued to harass the pig. Then the time was right: the hunter perched on the banyan slipped his noose over the boar's head and jerked sharply upwards. For just a second or two, the pig's front hooves left the ground, time enough for the two men facing the boar to throw their lines. The loops tightened and held. All three hunters yanked their ropes and the boar lost its balance. It fell, squealing and kicking, and other men from the party of hunters dashed in among the dogs and secured the tusker's hooves with strong and supple vine.

The hunters made a makeshift litter from sturdy branches cut from nearby trees. They rolled the boar onto the litter, which six men hoisted onto their shoulders with great effort. We set off for our home village in a joyous, singing, joking frame of mind, sportsmen after a good match, a small victorious army with a prize captive. Once back in the rank-taker's hamlet, the boar was enclosed in a small wooden pen. There, it would spend its last days. The rank-taker rewarded us all with kava and food and, as darkness fell, we remembered moments from the day's hunt, and they told me tales of other, more dangerous times.

Matters of pedigree and place

It really bothered the old Ambaean chief who adopted me into his family that so many white men believe that the fine tusked boars of Vanuatu are European in origin. Pigs were my late 'father's' passion and a source of his considerable power. He had made a lifetime study of them and he knew that their beginnings lay here in the Pacific, perhaps even

Fig. 189 Tusker pig. Amok, north-west Malakula.

right here on Ambae, the ancestral home of the god Tagaro. Yet over the course of his lifetime, a white planter, two missionaries, and several government officials all told him more or less the same story, that Europeans first brought pigs to these islands on their sailing ships and trading vessels. Some even asserted as an obvious and irrefutable fact that Captain James Cook introduced pigs into the Pacific on his voyages of exploration.

My 'father' was closer to the truth about the origin of pigs in Vanuatu than the Europeans he asked. In terms of their origins, Melanesian pigs are of the place, or at least of the Pacific rim: they are not descendants of European swine. Throughout most of this century, scientific writers have trended toward the view that pigs in Vanuatu are *Sus papuensis*, a distinct species that – as the name implies – originated in the area of Papua (Baker 1929a; Harrisson 1937; Layard 1942). Opinion now is changing, but not in the direction of a European origin for Melanesian pigs. The most recent authoritative view is that pigs in Vanuatu are not a separate species, as the name *Sus papuensis* implies, but rather a hybrid, the result of cross-breeding *Sus celebensis* and *Sus scrofa* (Groves 1981, Jolly 1984).

publications officer in 1943 and where he wrote *Tales of the South Pacific*. In addition, Ambae – like Bali Ha'i – was a 'forbidden island' to US Navy personnel during World War II, a prohibition that may have originated in Ambae's designation as 'Leper's Island' on navy charts. My opening paragraph is an imaginative reconstruction based on available information. For additional information concerning Michener's war service in the New Hebrides and other parts of the Pacific, see Hayes (1984) and Michener's autobiography (1992).

Fig.190
Domenico Bule Vakha, the highest-ranked man in the traditional hierarchy, Apma region, photographed with a *lipsal* grade tusker pig in 1978. Central Pentecost.

Any consideration of the physical nature of pigs in Vanuatu must take into account two striking facts. First, tusks are a product of culture rather than a given of nature. The magnificent tusked boars (fig. 189) used in rank-takings and other ceremonies in Vanuatu would not develop their tusks without human intervention in natural biological processes. Second, there are more intersex pigs in Vanuatu than anywhere else in the world (Baker 1929b:62). Both the production of tuskers and the existence of significant numbers of intersex pigs have major implications for *kastom* and culture in Vanuatu.

Behind the figure of the warrior-chief on the national crest of Vanuatu is a full-circle tusk. The symbolism of the crest points to the value and importance that ni-Vanuatu place on tusked boars. It also expresses the idea that tusks are a sign of the leader and a substance on which leadership is based (fig. 190). Europeans tend to think of the value of a pig as residing exclusively in its flesh; pigs are walking pork chops, protein on the hoof. Ni-Vanuatu see things differently. Most would tell you that, indeed, pigs are good to eat, but they also would say that the most valuable pigs are not the biggest, but those

with the best-developed tusks. This is vividly illustrated in the local laws of east Ambae. There, in 1984, chiefs set the price of a live full-circle tusker (*ala tawasiri*) at VT18 000. They assigned a dried and intact skull of a circle tusker only slightly less value: VT16 000. Either can be used in ritual; one is as good as the other for the achievement of rank or the payment of debts. That there is a difference of less than US$20 between a live tusker and the intact head of a dead one makes a statement about the relative value of tusks and flesh.

The operation that leads ultimately to the growth of tusks is simple and pragmatic. A shoat of about one year of age is caught and secured with a strip of jungle vine or rope. The owner forces a short wooden stick between the pig's jaws and, working as fast as possible, uses a hammer and file to knock out its two upper canines. The 'rubbish teeth' are thrown away, and the two cavities are packed with soft earth and leaves to staunch the bleeding. In the years that follow, the two emerging lower tusks are free to develop unimpeded into full circles that, optimally, re-enter the mandible close to each tusk's own root.

It takes seven or eight years for a boar to develop full-circle tusks (fig. 191). Relatively few pigs attain this ideal. Some starve to death when their tusks begin to re-enter their jaw bone. Others with developing tusks are used for a variety of purposes, including rank-taking ceremonies, as wedding gifts, or as death-feast offerings. To raise circle-tusk boars, a ni-Vanuatu must have patience, solvency, luck, and sons without need of bride price.[2]

There are three well-established sexes of pigs in Vanuatu: male, female, and intersex. An intersex animal is simply one that combines features of both male and female. All earthworms and snails are true hermaphrodites, but the trait occurs only rarely among mammals. Even the best-known example in Europe may not be familiar to many readers – the freemartin, or sexually abnormal heifer (Baker 1929a:115). In some places in northern and central Vanuatu, however, intersex pigs can be found in almost every village of any size. A zoologist who made a study of intersex pigs counted 125 specimens in a day in one location alone, the aptly named Hog Harbour on Espiritu Santo (Baker 1929b:62). What exactly did he see?

Intersex pigs can grow tusks in the manner of

boars, but their external genitalia range from 'nearly the female condition to something approaching the male' (Baker 1929b:57). On Espiritu Santo, Ambae, and other islands, local languages include words for intersex gradations of maleness and femaleness. Dissection, however, reveals that intersex pigs in Vanuatu completely lack a uterus and vagina, a trait that serves to distinguish them from similar pigs found occasionally in Great Britain and Europe (Baker 1929b:56). Intersex pigs cannot reproduce. Instead, certain sows inherit a tendency to issue intersex offspring; Ambaeans believe that one in four piglets born to these sows will be an intersex.

Intersex pigs are valued because of their uniqueness and relative scarcity. The limited number of sows capable of producing a single intersex in a litter, combined with the fact that intersex pigs can duplicate any stage of tusk development common to boars, ensures that the available supply never approaches the demand for them. In the past, they were valued items of trade, from west Ambae to Santo (Weightman 1989: 290), and from northwest Malakula (a place where people had no use for intersex pigs) to Malo (Harrisson 1937:26). Even today, the ceremonial destruction of ten such animals in rank-taking rites generates uncommon interest, spreading from clubhouse to clubhouse, across islands, and even across the sea between islands.

'A chief feeds his pigs': metaphor versus practice

There are more than 70 000 pigs in Vanuatu, on average about three pigs for every rural household. On one island alone – Tanna – there are 16 000 pigs.[3] Many, perhaps most, of these pigs are neither feral nor completely domesticated. Valuable boars are kept in enclosures, but other pigs (including boars with crescent tusks) roam at will through brush, forest and plantations, foraging for roots and refuse. At dawn, and again at dusk, pigs appear near the household of their owners, snuffling, ever watchful for dogs, waiting for their owners to feed them. They favour scraps of cold, cooked taro, rotting papaya and bananas. Most days, they just get coconuts, split and tossed in their general direction.

'A chief feeds his pigs,' my ni-Vanuatu father often told me in the serious voice he used when he was trying to teach me an important life lesson. Metaphorically, he lived up to his ideal: he was self-reliant and he looked after his followers' welfare. In practice, the only pigs he fed were a few valuable full-circle tuskers he kept in a stone fence a little distance away from his hamlet. These he babied with mashed papaya and grated coconut, while his wife split coconuts to feed to the rest of his pigs.

This unequal division of labour is common in Vanuatu and, indeed, most of Melanesia. So often is the daily care of pigs the chore of women rather than men that Jolly (1984:82) playfully suggests that for the sake of accuracy we should speak of 'pig wifery' rather than 'pig husbandry' in Melanesia.

The ownership of pigs is gender-based in some Vanuatu societies, but not in others. In south Pentecost and among the Seniang of Malakula, all pigs are the property of men (Jolly 1984:88; Deacon 1934b:197). On east Ambae, however, women can and do own pigs (which nonetheless are considered, in general terms, men's wealth), just as men can own valuable pandanus mats, the 'currency' of women. Deacon (1934b:197-198) describes a situation in Lambumbu, on Malakula, that may occur elsewhere in the group. There, a woman has pigs of her own as well as guardianship of her husband's pigs. She can do as she likes with her own pigs, but not with those of her husband. She is, in effect, a trustee rather than a co-owner of her husband's pigs.

The place(s) of pigs in Vanuatu

The ethnographers who worked in the New Hebrides in the first four decades of the century tended to be conservative in

2. In very rare circumstances, boars develop tusks more elaborate than a single full circle. When Queen Elizabeth II visited the New Hebrides in 1974, the government gave her as a gift a full double-circle tusk (Weightman 1989:292). Harrisson (1937:25) and Layard (1942:241) saw three-circle tuskers on Malakula.

3. The pig population of Vanuatu was enumerated in 1983, as part of a general agricultural census. The figures I cite from the census are noted in Weightman (1989:199).

Fig. 191
Double-circle pig tusk, collected by Speiser in 1911.
Ambrym.
Basel, Museum für Völkerkunde.

style, cautious in their generalisations, little given to overstatement. Yet listen to the way they describe the place of pigs in Vanuatu. For Speiser, 'the pig is the standard of value and all other values are related to the pig' (1990:246). Layard simply found it 'impossible to describe any aspect of Small Island culture without reference to pigs' (1942:240). Deacon made the discovery that pigs are the 'keynote of the Malekulan character' (1934b:17). And the most experimental and poetic of early ethnographers, Tom Harrisson (1937:24), evokes the voice of a man of Matanavat, Malakula: 'Pigs are our life and our progress,' he writes as the native. 'Without pigs we should only exist. Our pigs are power.'

What was true before is true today. It is hard to overstate the importance of pigs for the vast majority of people who live in the rural areas of Vanuatu. Without pigs (and especially tusked boars), *kastom* in Vanuatu simply could not continue to exist.

According to a former Director of Agriculture, Livestock and Forestry, 'the best village pigs are to be seen in Tanna' (Weightman 1989:300). On Tanna, as on other islands in the southern part of the group, pigs are used in a wide variety of food exchanges and traditional payments, including bride price, circumcision, compensation for wrongdoing, and ceremonial performance. Yet it is in the north, in the area of Ambrym, Malakula, Malo, Espiritu Santo, Ambae, Pentecost, and Maewo, that the 'pig complex' of Vanuatu reaches its true height of development. These are islands where rank associations often called 'graded societies' in scholarly literature have persisted through time or been revived. Graded societies vary in form, but all are based on the idea of a social hierarchy consisting of ranks scaled in terms of relative prestige. To achieve a new rank, an individual (or, in some societies, a kin group or local group) has to accumulate and dispose of boars with tusks in particular stages of development. The better the tusks, the higher the grade, and the greater the rank-taker's or rank-taking group's prestige. The achievement of each rank alters a man's or a group's status permanently. The highest ranks in the graded society are reserved for men who accumulate and kill a substantial number of boars with full-circle tusks (figs 192, 193, 194).

Tusked boars represent social, political and economic capital for individuals engaged in graded-society activities. Alliance and sponsorship are ideas central to rank-taking. To achieve a new rank, a person cannot simply raise a herd of pigs and then slaughter them; in fact, on east Ambae, there is a rule that an individual may not kill more than three of his own pigs at a rank-taking. The other seven pigs to be used in a rank-taking ceremony must come from other people. At ceremonies, donors present pigs to a rank-taker, and these pigs are always new loans or repayments of prior loans. A presentation is a symbolic political statement, a message to all about relations of respect and alliance between the donor and recipient. So there is a sense in which bestowals of pigs are like votes of support in a political campaign. In another sense, however, presentations of pigs are investments that must be repaid. How much profit can an investor reasonably expect to make? This question is difficult to answer, as most ni-Vanuatu do not regard a transaction involving pigs as a closed event with a predetermined yield. There is a general cultural understanding on east Ambae that a loan of one tusker should earn a

Fig. 192
Man of high rank, photographed by Speiser in 1911.
Tongtong Mal, Port Vato, west Ambrym.

return of two of the same quality or better. This is a guideline, not a firm rule. The bottom line of the economics of rank-taking is that a recipient of boars must repay his debts, but the rank-taker – not a donor – sets the terms and timing of repayment.

Since I first began fieldwork in east Ambae in 1969, I have attended twenty-six rank-takings, including one occasion on which 100 tusked boars were killed. Less than 5 per cent of the pigs I saw used in rank-takings were raised on other islands; the vast majority were born in the district in which they were killed. Ethnographic literature suggests that earlier in this century, trade in boars was of great political and economic importance throughout the northern islands. In some places, boars were traded for shell money, and in other places they were traded for women (Harrisson 1937:399-400). Layard (1942:253) reports that Malakulans organised great sea voyages to Ambrym, south Raga and Ambae exclusively for the purpose of obtaining fresh supplies of pigs. Bonnemaison (1979, 1985a) writes of well-defined and rigidly controlled trade routes in the northern islands, and tells how the exchange of pigs between chiefs led to more general conditions of alliance and peace between peoples of different cultures and islands (figs 195-199).[4]

European traders in the 19th century found ways to exploit the New Hebridean 'pig complex' for economic profit. They traded local peoples on Tanna a few yards of calico for 100 pounds of pig, then set sail for Erromango and Espiritu Santo to barter pigs for sandalwood. Not all the pigs that Europeans acquired remained in the islands. In one year alone – 1865 – Europeans shipped 8000 pigs from the southern New Hebrides to Queensland in Australia, a trade which Harrisson says 'upset the very foundation of native culture and currency' (1937:141).

Holy pigs

The novelist James Michener paints Bali-Ha'i as a South Seas paradise; the ethnographer John Layard proclaims the region 'a paradise for pigs' (quoted in Jolly 1984:83). Michener's character named Luther Billis, a US Navy entrepreneur with an interest in native culture, explains to a superior officer about pigs in paradise, that 'pigs is their religion. They keep pigs the way we keep churches. The rounder

Fig. 193 Pig-killing club, collected by Guiart, 1949. Lele, west Ambrym. Paris, Musée national des Arts d'Afrique et d'Océanie.

Fig. 194 Pig-killing club. Malakula. Stuttgart, Linden-Museum.

Fig. 195

Fig. 196

Fig. 197

Figs 195, 196, 197, 198, 199
Carved stones for pig magic, mostly collected by Guiart.
Ambrym.
Paris, Musée national des Arts d'Afrique et d'Océanie.

the pig's tusks is, the better the church' (Michener 1964:241). At first glance, ethnographic literature on some societies in Vanuatu appears to support Billis's vision of 'holy pigs (that) aren't really holy till their dead' (Michener 1964:240). For example, Jolly (1984:82, 93) relates that 'pigs are often accorded a religious reverence' in south Pentecost; there, people believe that sacred power expands with each grade. Huffman (1976:417) states that the Mbotgo't of Malakula believe that the spirits of the pigs a man kills during his lifetime await him in the afterworld. Layard pushes the identification of man and boar to an extreme not found elsewhere in ethnographic literature on the region. In Malakula and the Small Islands, he tells readers, the sacrifice of tusked boars has replaced the sacrifice of human beings.[5] He clearly means for his readers to take the word 'sacrifice' literally, as a religious act. According to Layard (1942:258), a key element in the belief system of the Small Islanders is the notion that boars have souls. They believe that the soul of the boar passes into the body of the sacrificer at the instant of the animal's death. It is only through the sacrifice of boars that a man can achieve life after death (Layard 1942:241). So Michener's Luther Billis had it wrong: pigs don't become holy after death; the point is that men become sanctified through the death of pigs.

Good Anglicans do not believe that pigs have souls. For rank-takers on east Ambae, the rewards of pig-killing are of this world, not the next. Yet these rewards are of the spirit as well as of the material world.

There is a rough magic in rank-taking that is hard for Europeans to understand. For one thing, the way in which rank-takers kill boars runs counter to conventional European sensibilities. Before intensive contact (and maybe even today in a few

164 ▼ MEN'S ART, WOMEN'S ART

Fig. 198

Fig. 199

places), rank-takers used a wooden, knee-shaped hammer to kill pigs. Today, most men dispatch their pigs with the blunt end of an axe, aimed straight between the eyes. The pigs are tied securely to wooden stakes; this is no contest between man and beast, as some regard a bullfight. Where, then, is the magic?

Once, I saw a man kill pigs in the midst of a storm, in pelting rain, lightning flashing across the sky. The weather did not seem to matter to him. He was as joyful as a bridegroom, a man radiant with energy, his every movement clean and precise. At some rank-takings, the pigs die hard, screaming like babies, afraid and in pain. This time, the boars made hardly a sound as they died tethered to stakes embellished with bright green and scarlet croton leaves. All I could hear was thunder and the sound of steel on bone.

When the last boar died, the young chief shouted out the new name he had chosen for himself. This is a privilege that accompanies the achievement of a new rank. I recognised the name he shouted. It was

4. On east Ambae today, pigs continue to have strong symbolic associations with the cessation of hostilities and, more generally, with peaceful behaviour. After independence, members of rival political parties – bitter enemies for several years – exchanged pigs to re-establish harmonious relations. One of the most important legal principles in east Ambae is *boe tamwata* ('pigs of peace'), the right of a chief to collect pigs from wrongdoers for breaches of the law within the chief's territory.

5. Speiser (1991) also proposes that pigs replaced humans as graded-society sacrifices. Neither he nor Layard (1942) present much evidence in support of their theory of the origins of pig killing.

Fig. 200

Fig. 201

Fig. 202

Fig. 200, 201, 202
Magic stones used for unknown purposes. The first two come from Pentecost, the last from Malo.
Fig. 200: Basel, Museum für Völkerkunde.
Figs 201, 202: Paris, Musée national des Arts d'Afrique et d'Océanie.

the name of one of his ancestors, a great warrior who died around the turn of the century. He roared out the name of his forefather, and the wind howled back, and I saw on the ceremonial field, there in the mud with ten dead boars, a man that ritual and history had renewed.

Sometime after nightfall, the storm ended and people gathered in a nearby village. Lights were lit against the darkness; kerosene lanterns, cooking fires. I saw the rank-taker on the edge of a ring of light, dignified in his bearing yet smiling with his eyes as a circle of his kinsmen and friends danced in his honour and sang the old songs in the language of the place.

Chapter III
The art of relating

Dialect Chaining and the Use of Geographical Space

Darrell Tryon

With a population of something around 150 000, Vanuatu has one of the highest language densities in the world, for there are more than 100 indigenous languages spoken in this archipelago, all of which are members of the great Austronesian or Malayo-Polynesian language family (Tryon 1976, 1995). This gives a ratio of something like one language per 1500 inhabitants. The languages with the highest numbers of speakers, on Ambae, Pentecost and Tanna for example, have fewer than 10 000 speakers, while many of the languages of Vanuatu have fewer than 300 speakers.

Within the Austronesian language family, however, the languages of Vanuatu are tiny languages in terms of numbers of speakers and geographical range, yet they constitute almost 10 per cent of all Austronesian languages.

In addition to the indigenous languages, the metropolitan languages English and French are spoken and taught in Vanuatu, and to a lesser extent Vietnamese, Hakka Chinese and Tahitian are also spoken. The national language of Vanuatu is Bislama (known in French as *Bichelamar*), an English-based Melanesian pidgin, the lingua franca of the nation, spoken by almost 100 per cent of the population.

Of the more than 100 indigenous languages, three are Polynesian (Futuna-Aniwa, Mele-Fila and Emae; see fig. 204), known as Polynesian Outliers (since they lie outside the Polynesian Triangle). These languages are the result of back-migrations from Polynesia, approximately 800 years ago.

Language subgrouping

It is appearing increasingly likely that the languages of Vanuatu belong to a single higher-order Vanuatu group which splits into two major subgroups, North-Central Vanuatu and Southern Vanuatu. The North-Central Vanuatu group divides into Northern and Central Vanuatu as indicated in the tree diagram below (fig. 203).

The major division between North-Central and Southern Vanuatu occurs between Efate and

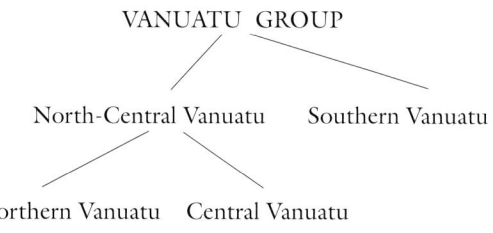

Fig. 203 Principal linguistic subgroups of Vanuatu.

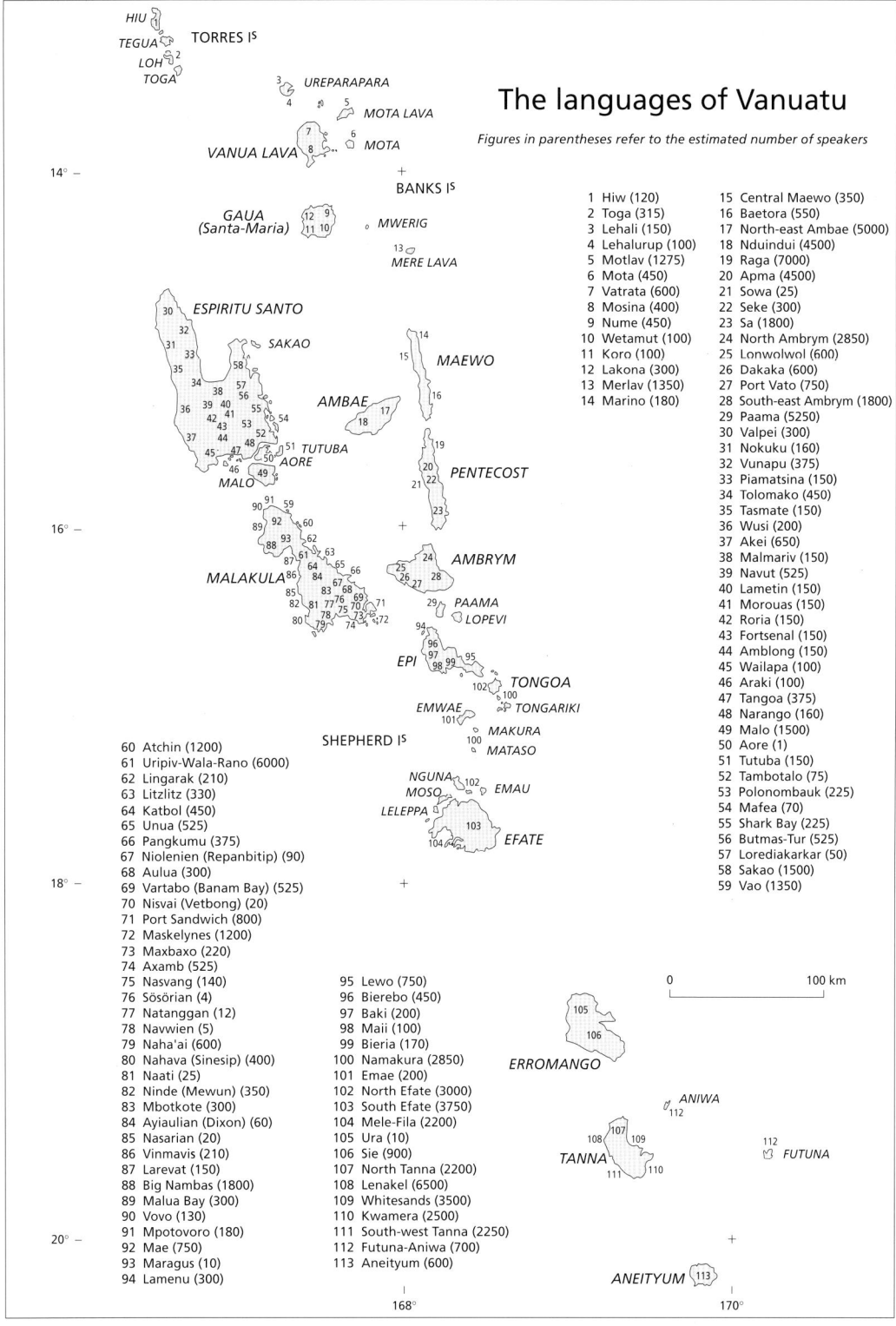

Fig. 204 The languages of Vanuatu

Fig. 205
Shell money, collected by Speiser in 1910. Southwest Santo.
Basel, Museum für Völkerkunde.

Erromango (see fig. 206). In linguistic terms, however, there are a number of shared lexical innovations (exclusively shared vocabulary items) between the North-Central and Southern subgroups. Indeed, Lynch and Tryon (1985) have proposed a Central-Eastern Oceanic subgroup, which includes all of the languages of Vanuatu within a single higher-order subgroup, splitting at a lower level into a North-Central and a Southern group.

The Southern Vanuatu subgroup includes all of the languages south of Efate with the exception of the Polynesian Outlier Futuna-Aniwa. Of particular interest, however, is the North-Central subgroup, which divides along a line which runs between Malakula and Santo in the west and cuts through northern Pentecost in the east (fig. 206). The Northern Group includes all the languages of the Banks and Torres islands, Maewo, Ambae, northern Pentecost and Santo. Within this group, the languages of Santo probably constitute a subgroup on their own. The Central Group consists of the languages of Malakula, central and southern Pentecost, Ambrym, Paama, Epi, the Shepherd Islands and Efate, with the exception of the two Polynesian Outlier languages Emae and Mele-Fila. The line just described corresponds to an interesting division in terms of material culture:

1. a. To the north of the Santo-Malakula line, mats are worn traditionally.
   b. To the south of that line, *nambas* (peniswrappers) are traditionally worn. This includes the Southern Vanuatu subgroup. The wearing of the *nambas* is associated with circumcision. (It should be noted, however, that central Pentecost is a transitional zone in terms of traditional mat versus *nambas* wearers).

2. a. To the north of the Santo-Malakula line, the graded society (*sukwe*) is matrilineal, while to the south that society (*manggi*) is patrilineal. The graded society involves rank-taking based on the sacrifice of tusker pigs. (Indeed tusker boars, with excision of the upper eye teeth, are cultivated only in the area of the graded society).
   b. In the Southern Vanuatu subgroup, south of a line running between Efate and Erromango, there is no graded society.

3. a. To the north of the Santo-Malakula line, drums are horizontal, while to the south, as far as the limit of the Central Vanuatu subgroup, they are upright.
   b. In the Southern Vanuatu subgroup, there are no slit-drums.

4. Speiser (1923) reports that the distribution of a number of other material culture items corresponds to the tripartite division of Vanuatu languages, as follows:
   a. The use of shell and feather money (fig. 205) exclusively in the Banks and Torres.
   b. The use of mat money in Maewo, Ambae and north Pentecost.
   c. The fact that no spears are used in the Northern Vanuatu subgroup (bow and

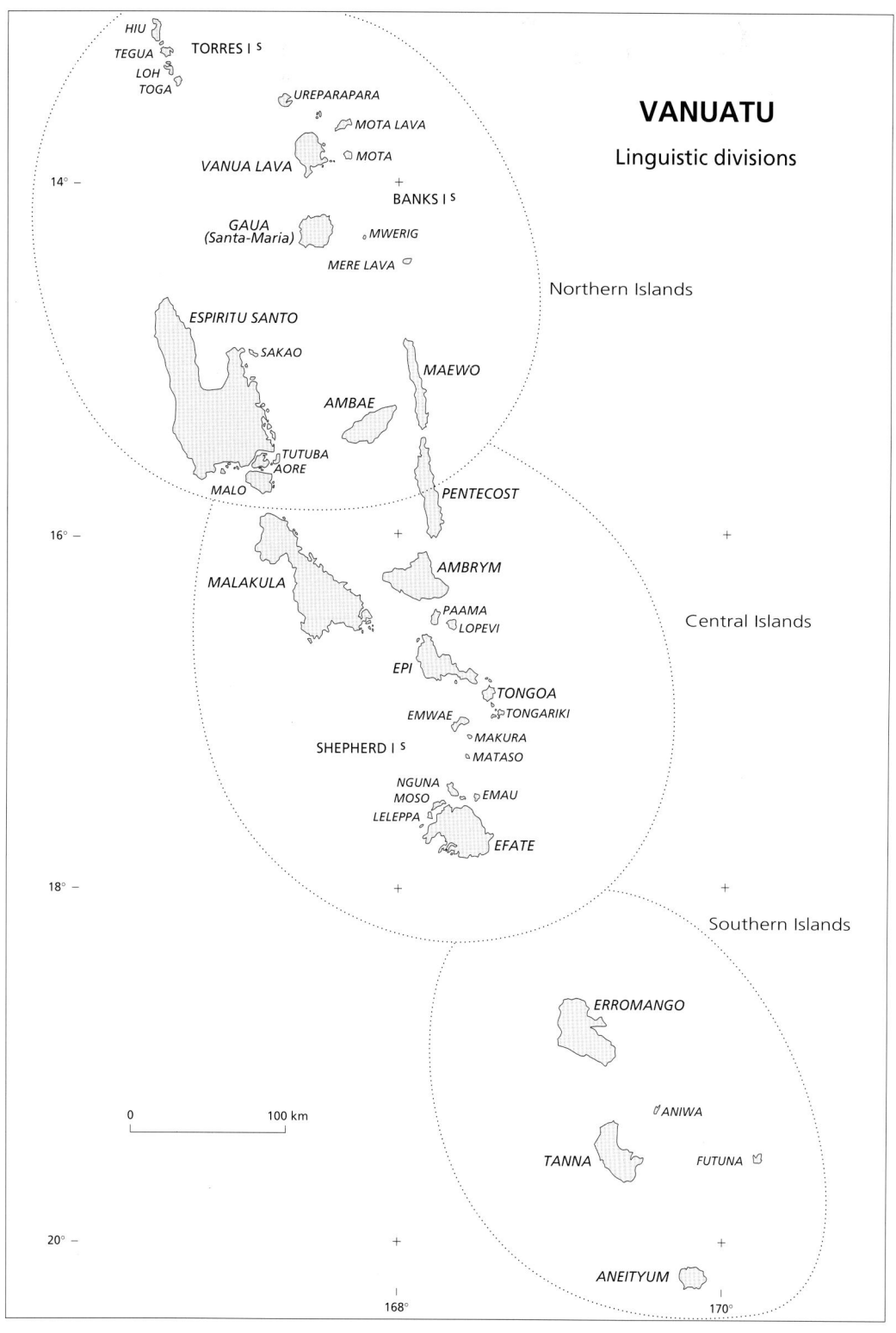

Fig. 206

DIALECT CHAINING AND THE USE OF GEOGRAPHICAL SPACE ▼ 173

A web of connections

Joël Bonnemaison

In a linguistic chain, languages become increasingly diversified the further they are from the point of origin. Languages are juxtaposed like dominoes, but as the line lengthens they take on more and more dissimilar forms. Linguistic fragmentation, then, does not mean sharp breaks or splits, but an alignment of languages along a path, each segment of which, though original in itself, is linked to a greater or lesser degree with its neighbours. It follows that it is more appropriate to talk of linguistic chains or progressions than of boundaries or areas. In this context, any attempt at mapping Melanesian languages and the areas in which they are used is a challenge. It is in terms of relationships and contacts, rather than of boundaries, that the linguistic map of Vanuatu must be drawn. The earliest observers' impressions were particularly ill-founded, in that wherever they looked they found only watertight divisions and difficulties of communication. The lack of a central language radiating its influence over a wide area, or of a prestige language, reflects equality among different languages and among different local societies, rather than true heterogeneity. In fact, individual speakers have little difficulty understanding their neighbours' language; more often than not, they speak to them in their own language, and in turn understand theirs without great effort. Step by step, such a system of communication can work over a considerable distance. For this reason, Bislama is, in fact, only used between speakers from widely separated communities, and is rarely used between people from the same island, with the exception of the larger islands of Malakula and Santo.

So behind the notion of linguistic fragmentation, we begin to see the image of a chain which strongly counteracts the impression of scattered and unrelated cultures one might gain from a cursory approach. While no one language dominates these islands, there are concatenations of languages, in which some links act as junctions between different systems (cf. fig. 211).

If we look at the map of traditional sea links, as revealed by shared linguistic features and trading relations recorded by oral tradition, we see that there are no really abrupt breaks in the archipelago's system of internal communication (fig. 174).

Though with varying degrees of ease, communication from north to south has almost always been possible provided one followed the orderly sequence of mutually intelligible languages, without omitting any of the necessary links.[1]

The picture which emerges is one of a web: a pattern of autonomous points linked by threads of relationship. Each point represents a language and also a local society, of varying size. The language's autonomy is commensurate with the political autonomy of the social group, while the extent of mutually intelligible relations with its neighbours is a measure of the degree to which it is open to the outside world, or in other words, of its more or less central position in a fluid system of relations.

In the web of relations thus formed, the points where the most threads converge stand out and indicate central nodules, knots where the web is more densely woven, allowing communication between segments which otherwise would remain separate. The knots where strands of the

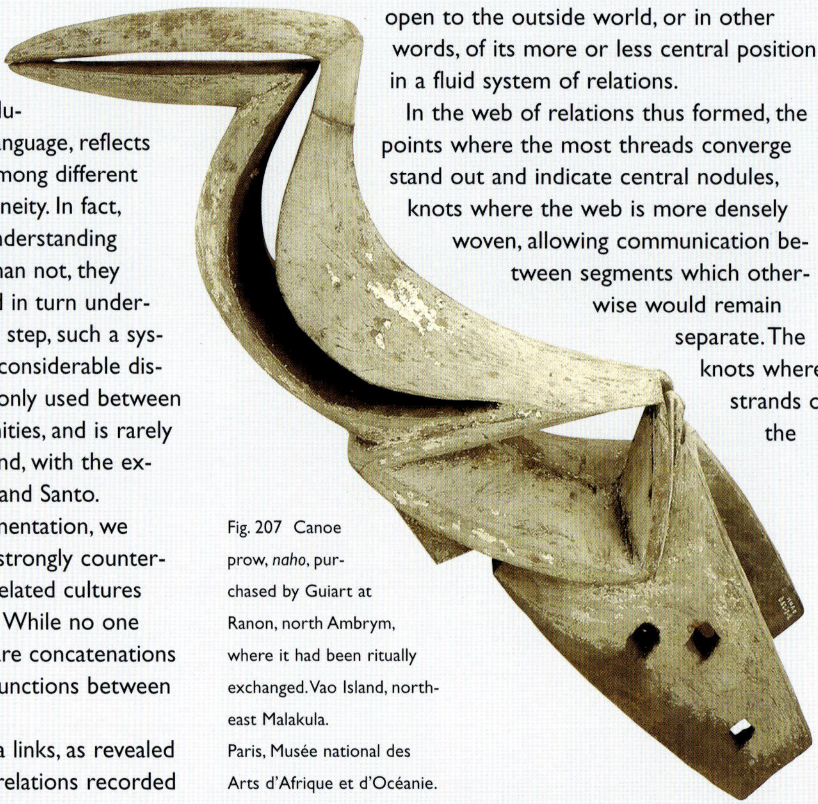

Fig. 207 Canoe prow, *naho*, purchased by Guiart at Ranon, north Ambrym, where it had been ritually exchanged. Vao Island, north-east Malakula. Paris, Musée national des Arts d'Afrique et d'Océanie.

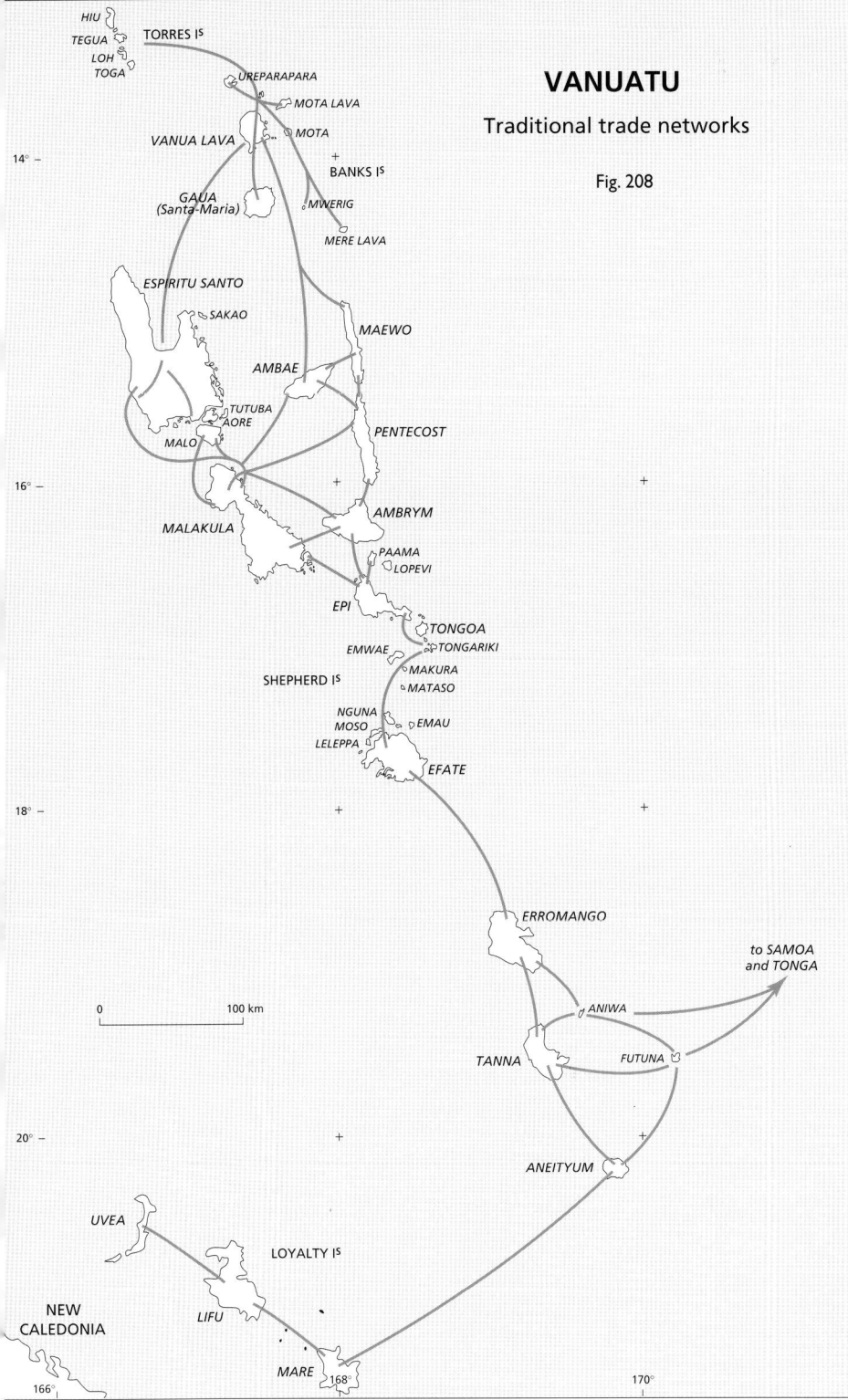

VANUATU
Traditional trade networks
Fig. 208

network meet form a hub in the system of relations, a crossroads where contact, exchange, cultural creativity are all likely to be more intense.

Such a 'web of connections' favours a network type of system of relations. Intelligibility along lines of small juxtaposed segments of a path is characteristic of a multi-centred cultural space. The archipelago does not seem to be ordered according to a centre or a hierarchy of centres producing peripheries, but according to a network whose mesh is sometimes wide and sometimes tightly woven. In such a system, the extent or size of the islands counts less than their position relative to each other. Topology is the primary datum.

This 'network society' seems to have been a response to an essentially political preoccupation. Each local society sought to preserve its autonomy in a dialectic between linguistic intelligibility and unintelligibility. The partial intelligibility of its language made relations with its neighbours possible; its relative impenetrability protected it from those neighbours at the same time. A local group may perfectly well make its language incomprehensible to its neighbours if it wishes, and, conversely, make it easily understandable if it wants to communicate with them.

1. See also the various texts dealing with traditional relations in Vanuatu: Guiart 1956d; Bedford 1973:57; Vienne 1979; Bonnemaison 1979; and Cabalion 1981. All these make clear how dense the exchange networks were.

A WEB OF CONNECTIONS ▼ 175

arrow instead), with the exception of Santo, where Speiser reports that throwing spears were used with a spear-thrower. In the Central Vanuatu subgroup area, thrusting spears were used, while in the Southern subgroup, throwing spears and spear-throwers were used as in Santo.

Language and dialect chaining in Vanuatu

While the family-tree model presented above gives a clear picture of the main subgroups of the Vanuatu languages, with significant geographical matches in terms of material culture and social organisation, it fails to represent graphically the areal diffusion, contact and links that existed and took place around the archipelago. This diffusion is, though, represented in Tryon (1976). In this study, the principal diagram from which is reproduced in figure 209, chains of languages and dialects and even subgroups appear, based on percentages of shared basic vocabulary.

Language chaining

Languages have often diversified by dialect differentiation which has occurred as a language has spread geographically so as to be spoken in more than one settlement. The linguistic evidence that a group of communalects has arisen from dialect differentiation consists of:
1. innovations shared by all members of the group;
2. innovations which link communalects in a chain or network. In a chain, language/dialect A shares one or two innovations with B, B with C, C with D, and so on. This situation occurs because an innovation may arise in any communalect of the chain and spread to its neighbours, so that the geographical domains of various innovations may overlap.

Chain is commonly used to describe the situation where communalects have spread along a coastline, each related most closely to its neighbours on either side. *Network* is preferred where communalects are scattered over a land area or archipelago, having neighbours on more than two sides and often sharing different innovations with several of these.

In Vanuatu, in addition to the dialect chains described above, there also exist chains of languages such that Language A shares a relatively high percentage of common vocabulary with Language B (say in the order of 60 to 70 per cent), that between Languages B and C the same situation obtains, while between A and C the percentage is significantly reduced, as is the case with dialect chains.

In figure 209, languages sharing between 50 and 80 per cent are considered to be separate languages, but still members of the same subgroup. Membership of each subgroup is indicated by a rectangle, all of the languages enclosed within the rectangle being members of the same subgroup. In other words, all of the languages within any given rectangle share at least 50 per cent common vocabulary with any other language inside the rectangle. This lexicostatistical classification produces some interesting results when represented graphically. The membership of many of the subgroups overlaps, as indicated by the overlapping rectangles and circles in figures 209 and 211. The subgroups themselves are based not only on shared lexicon, but also on shared grammatical features. Thus most of the subgroups and their constituent languages in Vanuatu are bound together in interlocking chains.

In the far north, for example, we have a subgroup which contains all of the languages of the Banks and Torres islands; another the languages of the Banks Islands and Maewo; another the language of Merelava in the southern Banks, plus Maewo, Ambae and north Pentecost; yet another embraces the languages of Ambae, south-east Santo and north-east Malakula. The chains of subgroups run on and on further south, as illustrated.

An examination of the North-Central Vanuatu diagram shows considerable and extensive chaining, extending unbroken from the Torres Islands as far south as Paama. Other chains link most of the languages of Santo, while a good number of the languages of Malakula are also linked in the same way. It is noteworthy that each of these chains is linked by Vao in north-east Malakula, which suggests that linguistically at least, Vao was a kind of crossroads through which much of the traffic linking Santo, Malakula and eastern Vanuatu (Maewo, Ambae, Pentecost and Ambrym) passed.

While most of the North-Central Vanuatu

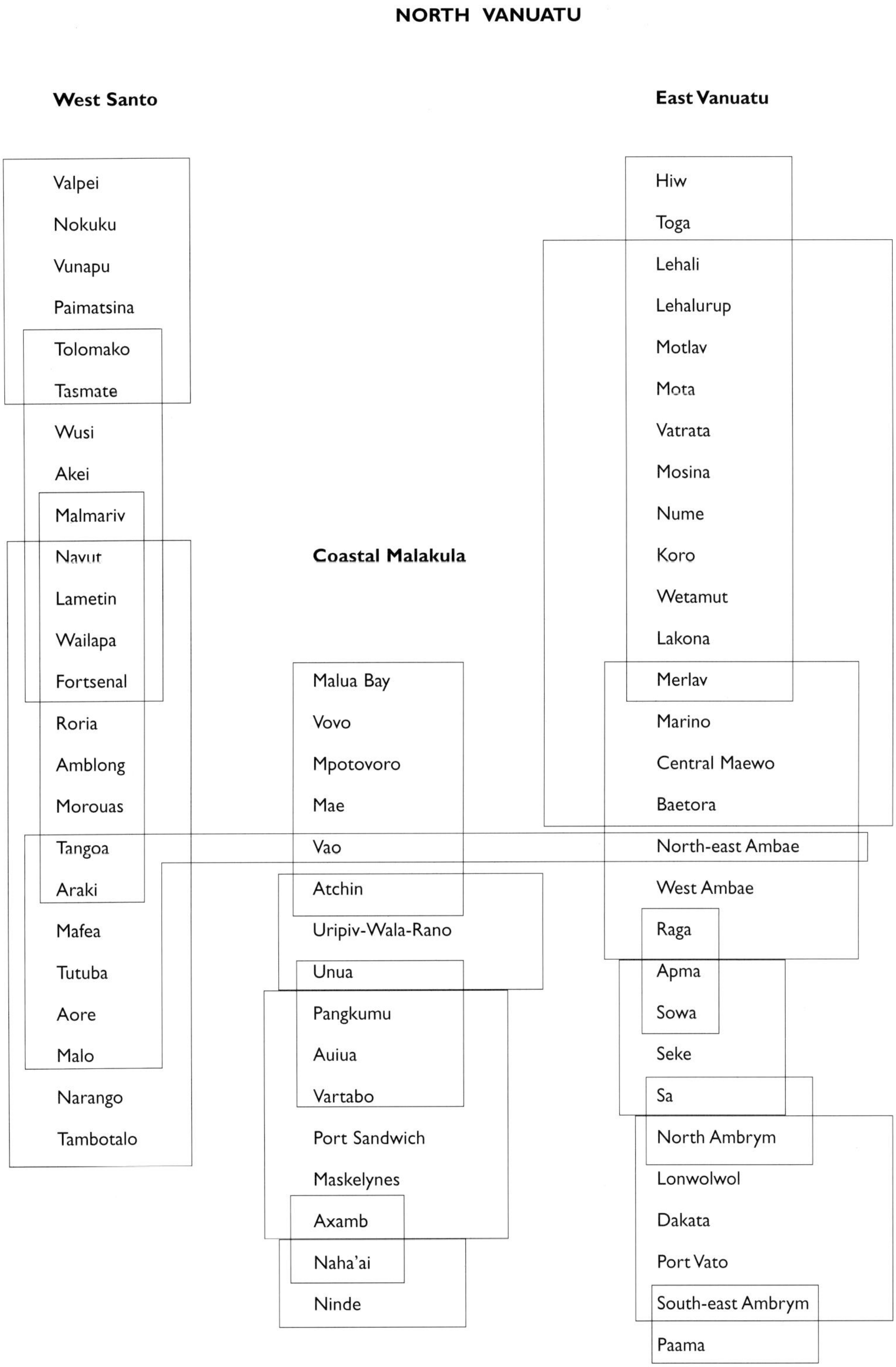

NORTH VANUATU

Fig. 209 Language chaining in Vanuatu.

West Santo

- Valpei
- Nokuku
- Vunapu
- Paimatsina
- Tolomako
- Tasmate
- Wusi
- Akei
- Malmariv
- Navut
- Lametin
- Wailapa
- Fortsenal
- Roria
- Amblong
- Morouas
- Tangoa
- Araki
- Mafea
- Tutuba
- Aore
- Malo
- Narango
- Tambotalo

Coastal Malakula

- Malua Bay
- Vovo
- Mpotovoro
- Mae
- Vao
- Atchin
- Uripiv-Wala-Rano
- Unua
- Pangkumu
- Auiua
- Vartabo
- Port Sandwich
- Maskelynes
- Axamb
- Naha'ai
- Ninde

East Vanuatu

- Hiw
- Toga
- Lehali
- Lehalurup
- Motlav
- Mota
- Vatrata
- Mosina
- Nume
- Koro
- Wetamut
- Lakona
- Merlav
- Marino
- Central Maewo
- Baetora
- North-east Ambae
- West Ambae
- Raga
- Apma
- Sowa
- Seke
- Sa
- North Ambrym
- Lonwolwol
- Dakata
- Port Vato
- South-east Ambrym
- Paama

DIALECT CHAINING AND THE USE OF GEOGRAPHICAL SPACE ▼ 177

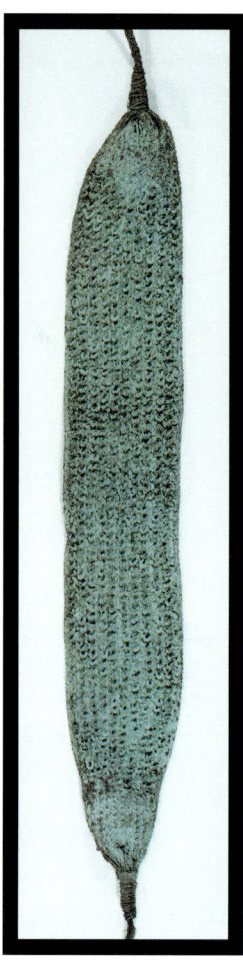

Fig. 210
Man's ritual headband, woven with incorporation of valuable pearl shell painted with green ochre, obtained as an exchange object. Collected by Speiser in 1910. South-west Santo. Basel, Museum für Vökerkunde.

languages are included in figure 209, so representing the extensive dialect and language chaining that characterises this part of the south-west Pacific, a number of languages, especially those in eastern Santo and in the interior of Malakula, are much less conservative lexically, having replaced basic vocabulary items at a faster rate than their neighbours. While they are excluded from the overlap diagram, their membership of the North-Central Vanuatu subgroup is vindicated by other criteria, as indeed is that of the languages of Epi and the Efate-Shepherds group (see Tryon 1976:80).

As far as the Southern Vanuatu subgroup is concerned, the languages of Erromango, Tanna and Aneityum constitute separate subdivisions, without the inter-island chaining phenomenon which characterises the North-Central subgroup (fig. 211).

Chaining and trade networks

All of the islands of Vanuatu which are contiguous are linked by trade networks that link every island from the Torres to Aneityum. This traditional trade networking is illustrated in figure 208. It is evident that this trade network bears a close resemblance to the language/dialect maps in this paper.

Indeed, Speiser says that it is natural to investigate which items of material culture have coextensive areas of distribution, but that very few items are coextensive in Vanuatu (although, as we have seen above, there are some important exceptions) – what is significant is that Speiser remarks that items of material culture are found overlapping in a quite irregular pattern. This, of course, implies multiple contacts between more than just two communities, which is significant in explaining the interlocking and criss-crossing language and dialect subgrouping patterns observed.

Speiser (1991:229) says:

> For each craft there was an island where it had attained a particular vigour and the objects in question were accordingly esteemed and traded by the natives of other islands.

Trading was not confined to the inter-island network, however. There was a vigorous intra-island trade and well-established trade networks, especially on the bigger islands of Malakula and Santo.

The objects traded were many and varied, with one natural set being those products available and produced near the sea and those restricted to inland areas. Bonnemaison (1974) has documented this in some detail for Ambae and Maewo. Another type of object traded in well-established networks concerned traditional life and its associated ceremonies. A selection of these includes the following:

1. Pigs: The most important objects in Vanuatu traditional life were pigs, especially tusker pigs, the hard currency of most of the country. They were traded far and wide, as their sacrifice is the basis of all progress and advancement in the graded society, or *nimanggi*. Pigs were traded almost everywhere. In the Banks Islands, for example, pigs were traded by other adjacent islands for shell money, especially on the island of Rowa (Reef Islands). They were also traded between the Banks Islands and Santo and Maewo, and so on further south between neighbours and not so near neighbours are far south as Malakula. They are also known to have been traded between Erromango and southern Efate, and between Tanna and Erromango.

2. Wives: The next most important exchange item which involved contact between contiguous and sometimes more distant speech communities was the women who were exchanged in marriage alliances. Thus, for example, the people of Epi exchanged pigs and yams for women from south-eastern Malakula. Exogamous marriage rules made it mandatory in many areas that wives be sought outside the local community.

3. Ochre and colouring materials (fig. 210): Ochre for paint was widely traded. Much of it originated in Santo and Malakula, and was traded with Ambae, Ambrym and Epi. In the south of the group, it was traded by the Erromangans with the people of Tanna, in exchange for pigs and white seashells, often the *Ovula ovum*. Speiser reports that red earth pigment was also traded to Tanna by the Aneityumese. (Indeed, wives were also exchanged between Aneityum and the Kwamera area of south-western Tanna.) At the same time, a black

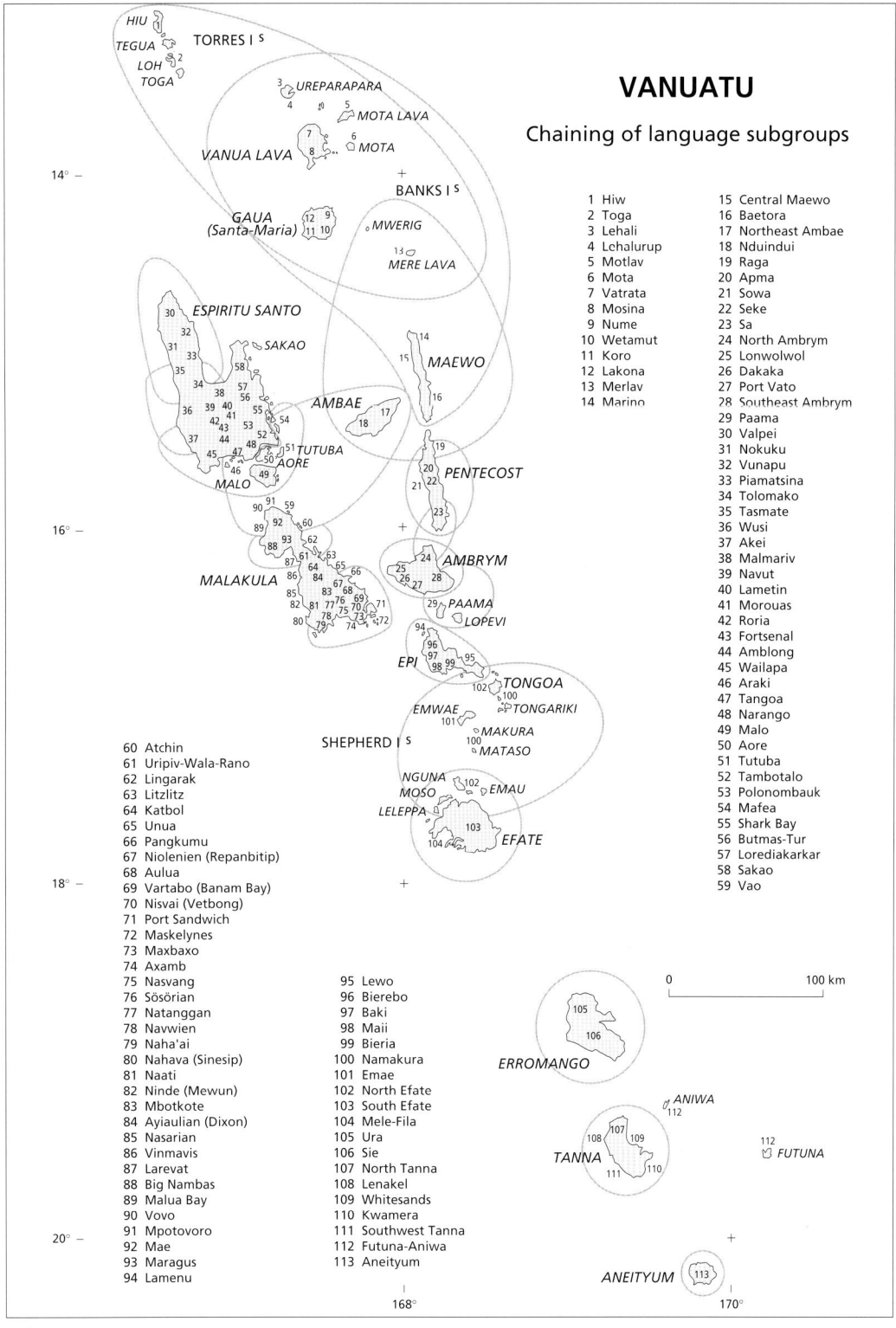

Fig. 211

VANUATU

Chaining of language subgroups

1 Hiw
2 Toga
3 Lehali
4 Lehalurup
5 Motlav
6 Mota
7 Vatrata
8 Mosina
9 Nume
10 Wetamut
11 Koro
12 Lakona
13 Merlav
14 Marino
15 Central Maewo
16 Baetora
17 Northeast Ambae
18 Nduindui
19 Raga
20 Apma
21 Sowa
22 Seke
23 Sa
24 North Ambrym
25 Lonwolwol
26 Dakaka
27 Port Vato
28 Southeast Ambrym
29 Paama
30 Valpei
31 Nokuku
32 Vunapu
33 Piamatsina
34 Tolomako
35 Tasmate
36 Wusi
37 Akei
38 Malmariv
39 Navut
40 Lametin
41 Morouas
42 Roria
43 Fortsenal
44 Amblong
45 Wailapa
46 Araki
47 Tangoa
48 Narango
49 Malo
50 Aore
51 Tutuba
52 Tambotalo
53 Polonombauk
54 Mafea
55 Shark Bay
56 Butmas-Tur
57 Lorediakarkar
58 Sakao
59 Vao
60 Atchin
61 Uripiv-Wala-Rano
62 Lingarak
63 Litzlitz
64 Katbol
65 Unua
66 Pangkumu
67 Niolenien (Repanbitip)
68 Aulua
69 Vartabo (Banam Bay)
70 Nisvai (Vetbong)
71 Port Sandwich
72 Maskelynes
73 Maxbaxo
74 Axamb
75 Nasvang
76 Sösörian
77 Natanggan
78 Navwien
79 Naha'ai
80 Nahava (Sinesip)
81 Naati
82 Ninde (Mewun)
83 Mbotkote
84 Ayiaulian (Dixon)
85 Nasarian
86 Vinmavis
87 Larevat
88 Big Nambas
89 Malua Bay
90 Vovo
91 Mpotovoro
92 Mae
93 Maragus
94 Lamenu
95 Lewo
96 Bierebo
97 Baki
98 Maii
99 Bieria
100 Namakura
101 Emae
102 North Efate
103 South Efate
104 Mele-Fila
105 Ura
106 Sie
107 North Tanna
108 Lenakel
109 Whitesands
110 Kwamera
111 Southwest Tanna
112 Futuna-Aniwa
113 Aneityum

mineral powder was also traded between Maewo and Ambae, and also between Pentecost and Ambrym.

4. Pottery: This was traded from west Santo to Malo, down to Vao and along the coast of east Malakula, across to Epi. There was also extensive trading in items other than pottery between Epi and Efate, so extending the network.

5. Mats: These were traded between Maewo, Ambae and Malakula. There were frequent trading trips between the Small Islands of north-east Malakula (Vao, Atchin, Wala, Rano) and west Ambae and Pentecost. Some of these trips were part of male initiation rites (see Layard 1951), the Malakulans trading high-quality pigs for the Ambae and Pentecost red mats. Speiser reports that red dye (for mats, *nambas* and wigs) was also required on Malakula and south Santo, being brokered to both of these areas through the small island of Vao, on the north-eastern extremity of Malakula (fig. 212). Vao mats were also traded with Ambrym, as indeed were the *nambas* made on the island of Wala.

6. Songs: Songs were traded over great distances too, very commonly between south-eastern Malakula and Ambrym, and also between south-eastern Malakula and Epi (as indeed were wives).

On one level, there is a striking similarity between material culture and the major subgroups of the languages of Vanuatu, a number of important cultural items being limited in their distribution to particular linguistic subgroups; for example, the mat-wearers (the Northern Vanuatu subgroup) and the *nambas*-wearers (the Central Vanuatu subgroup); the use of horizontal drums (the Northern group) versus upright drums (the Central group). Such linguistic and sociocultural matching even extends as far as spear-types, see above.

On another level, there is a high degree of correspondence between the language/dialect chains and their directions and linkages, and the established trading networks; Vao, for example, is a known trade-broking house and at the same time finds itself at the centre, almost like an axis, linking together a number of language/dialect chains coming from different directions. That Vao is known to have acted as a kind of middleman in trade terms, and that this emerges plainly from an examination of the chaining diagram, raises the question of whether it occupied a central trade role because of its linguistic position or vice versa.

It should be stressed that this paper is only an impressionistic first look at a question which is the subject of a fine-grained, longer-term study by me, but one which promises much in contributing to our knowledge of population and language movements in Vanuatu and, by extension, in island Melanesia as a whole.

Sociolinguistic considerations

None of the 100-plus indigenous Vanuatu languages are currently taught in schools, though forty-one of them have been reduced to writing, mostly for evangelical purposes, and often many decades ago. Many of the scriptural translations are largely forgotten, out of print or unobtainable (Tryon 1979).

The Anglican Church (Church of Melanesia) selected one of the indigenous languages, Mota, from the Banks Islands in northern Vanuatu, as its lingua franca. This language was used throughout the Anglican dioceses in Vanuatu and the Solomons until 1931. A mission newspaper, *O Sala Ususur* (*The Story Road*), was written in Mota and distributed throughout the Anglican mission area from 1896 until after World War II. While Mota was used as the mission lingua franca, scriptural translations were also made in other vernacular languages within the Anglican area – for example, Toga (Torres), East Ambae (Ambae) and Raga (Pentecost) – and since the demise of Mota as the mission lingua franca, there has been an ongoing translation program in many of the languages of north-eastern Vanuatu.

In the area controlled by the Presbyterian Church, there was an active translation program into the local vernaculars, with little attempt to impose or devise a mission lingua franca, with two exceptions: Aulua was used as a lingua franca in south-eastern Malakula, and an Efatese koine devised by the Reverend Daniel MacDonald in the late 19th century, replaced finally by Nguinese (North Efate), in the Efate-Shepherds area.

Fig. 212
Penis-wrappers from north Malakula. Collected by Speiser between 1910 and 1912 on the Small Islands of north-east Malakula. Basel, Museum für Völkerkunde.

The Catholic Church also used a number of vernaculars for evangelical purposes, for example Sakao (north-east Santo) and Vao (north-east Malakula). Other missions followed suit, for example the Church of Christ (west Ambae), the Seventh-Day Adventists (Atchin, Malakula) and the Reformed Presbyterian Church (Big Nambas, Malakula). Apart from biblical translations, however, there is little or no material published in the Vanuatu vernaculars, apart from religious or pious literature used for evangelical purposes. At the same time, Bislama was considered an unfit language for such translations until finally common sense prevailed and the first religious publication in the language, the *Four Gospels in Bislama*, *Gud Nyus Bilong Jisas Krais*, appeared in 1971. Since that time, Bible translations in the local Vanuatu vernaculars have proceeded apace in individual regions, while Bislama has undergone a period of rapid expansion and development, especially in the immediate pre- and post-independence years.

The languages of Vanuatu: the future

Since independence in 1980, there has been an impressive cultural revival throughout Vanuatu, and at present few of the languages appear in immediate danger of extinction. Nonetheless, the small number of speakers of many of the languages must put their survival in jeopardy, especially those with fewer than 300 speakers, because for some time now there has been a growing number of multilingual villages and centres where the smaller languages are doomed to disappear within one or two generations.

Perhaps the greatest threat to the indigenous languages is posed by Bislama, an English-based pidgin, the national language of Vanuatu. Ni-Vanuatu children, brought together for educational purposes, tend to use Bislama among themselves, rather than one of the languages of education, English or French. As a consequence, there is a very noticeable Bislama component in the lexicon of many of the local vernaculars, especially among younger speakers. More disturbing is the replacement of a number of grammatical features in local languages by Bislama equivalents. Compounding this disturbing tendency is the habit of some parents to address their children in Bislama rather than the local vernacular. While this may be natural in the case of parents coming from different language areas, increasing urbanisation is taking a heavy toll as languages spoken around these centres reflect the increasingly heavy inroads made by the national lingua franca. As Vanuatu gains greater access to the electronic media, the threat to the rich linguistic patrimony of the country will become even greater. On the credit side, however, it is widely recognised that ni-Vanuatu are fiercely proud of their languages and culture. It is this which guarantees the continued flourishing of the great majority of the languages of Vanuatu for the foreseeable future.

Trading, Cultural Exchange and Copyright: Important Aspects of Vanuatu Arts

Kirk W. Huffman

... An incessant interchange of things and ideas, the firm roots of tradition always sending out new branches on the evergreen tree. New influences going from island to island, drifting in from faraway groups, drifting out again. (Harrison 1937:69)

The vast subject of trading, cultural exchange and its related aspects, a topic of profound importance for ni-Vanuatu, has been relatively little dealt with in the academic literature,[1] but is essential for an understanding of Vanuatu societies, their arts and material culture. No cultures are static, and Vanuatu was and is no exception: the ebb and flow of relationships with neighbouring cultures and islands formed part of an intricate process which has continued, in a modified form, to the present day.

Because of Vanuatu's great linguistic and cultural diversity, it is often very difficult to generalise about cultural matters. Two major points that stand out, however, when viewing this topic historically:
1. the vast scope, potential rapidity and intensity of inter-group and inter-island economic and cultural exchange, and;
2. the importance of women as a factor in establishing many of these links.

Within the short space available, I will not raise the topic of an eastern Melanesian 'cultural continuum' linking, by possible regular or intermittent contacts, the south-eastern Solomons and northernmost Vanuatu, eastern north-central Vanuatu with the western part of Viti Levu (Fiji), and southern Tafea district with the Loyalty Islands (New Caledonia). I will concentrate instead on the 'inland sea' area of northern-central Vanuatu. This area comprises the major islands of Malakula, Epi, Ambrym, Pentecost, Maewo, Ambae, Malo and Santo, and their numerous smaller associated islands (fig. 213).

This area has been chosen because it is one of the most prolific areas of Melanesia in the production of the material arts, which are widely represented in museum collections around the world. It is also a core area for the men's social ranking systems known generally in Bislama as *nimanggi* (which have innumerable local variations and, very often, associated women's ranking systems), and for a complex system of cultural copyright covering certain items of material culture, visual art, rituals, music, song, dance, myths and ideas. This 'copyright' system recognises certain individuals, groups or areas as the proper owners of cultural items, the rights to which can be purchased, sold and resold over large areas in the perpetual spiritual and

---

1. Noteable exceptions being Joël Bonnemaison (1985b) and Jean Guiart (1990).

material drive upwards and outwards towards increased social height, prestige, power and influence in the world of the living and the world of the ancestral spirits. The more basic levels of the system (for example, for food staples) could involve 'silent trading', barter, and exchange, while the middle and higher levels could involve complex business deals with payment in money mats, stringed shell-money and/or pigs (*Sus papuensis*), the latter involving a complex concept of values depending on the type of pig (female, male, castrated, tusk curvature, and intersex) and notions of 'pig credit', loan, interest and compound interest. This *bisnis pig* brings one potentially into the higher, more powerful and sacred levels of the copyright system and can concern topics and rituals that are tabu in nature, and therefore cannot be fully described or can possibly only be hinted at in this article. As so many of these concepts still exist in Vanuatu, these prohibitions must be respected, even by outsiders. 'Breach of copyright', or lack of respect for it, could, and can, even today, result in imposition of fines, 'correction' by magic, sorcery, or even death. Breaching of the sacred knowledge system can even result in cultural destruction: several copies of R.H. Codrington's *The Melanesians* circulated secretly in the Banks and Torres Islands shortly after its publication in 1891, and this was a factor in the disintegration of much ritual life, particularly for the *tamate* secret societies in the Banks Islands.[2] The publication was thought to reveal many secrets, and was believed to make freely available – to those who did not have the right to it – information that normally had to be paid for.

Establishment of intra- and inter-island links: exchange, markets and trade of 'non-ritual' commodities.

As with so much in Vanuatu, women were often at the basis of the establishment of many trading links which were then normally organised and controlled by men. Such connections could have a basis in fact, or have a mythical origin conceptually as true as the factual one. Selected examples will be given from the areas chosen.

In the larger islands of the area, such as Malakula, there were large 'saltwater' and 'bush' populations. Inland peoples needed coastal produce and vice versa. As the normal relationship between such groups could be hostile, a peaceful link or *rod* had to be made and this was normally done by the exchange of women between the two groups concerned; that is, a woman from the bush area would be sent to the coast (in marriage), and a woman from the coastal group sent inland (in marriage), thus establishing the *rod* along which trade and other items could flow. Ni-Vanuatu will often say, '*From we long fasin blong kastom woman nao emi pis, woman emi go festaem, nao i wokem "rod", baebae i nogot faet.*'[3] As the two groups involved often spoke different languages or dialects, such primary exchange was useful to also have someone from one's own language group within one's trading partners in the early stages. Children of these 'exchange' marriages would grow up learning both languages, and because ni-Vanuatu are excellent linguists, future linguistic communication provided only minor problems.

In the southern part of the Ninde-speaking Mewun area of South West Bay, Malakula, there was regular trade with inland peoples of the Mindua area, particularly those owing allegiance to the *nakamals* of Amimindua, Loh'taha and V'nembanganimbie. Following links established by the exchange of women, the trade began of yams, water taro, bananas, freshwater eels and freshwater shrimps from the inland for shellfish and other coastal products. Following such links established by women, Ninde-speakers further north along the coast around *nakamal* Loh'bongalo had their own trade connections inland, to which they provided shellfish and smoked fish, and with whose inland products they traded northwards along the coast in bamboo rafts (*nogunbua*) to Dixon, Tisvel, Vinmavis and Lambumbu, where Loh'bongalo had other 'roads' established by women. The Nindespeakers had no canoes until recently. Similar bamboo rafts, called *nawangk ambu*, were used for short-distance coastal trading by the Nahava-speakers of Seniang district just south of South West Bay.

Further northwards, there was a highly organised, 'semi-silent' type of trading between the coastal Lambumbu peoples and those inland, taking place during the slack season between yam planting and harvest. The Lambumbu would travel by canoe to specific coastal passages and wait in their canoes

2. Codrington's book can now, however, be a source of cultural inspiration for ni-Vanuatu involved in cultural revival in the Banks and Torres.

3. 'Because in "custom" women represent peace, they go ahead first and make the "road" (connection, or link) so there will be no fighting'.

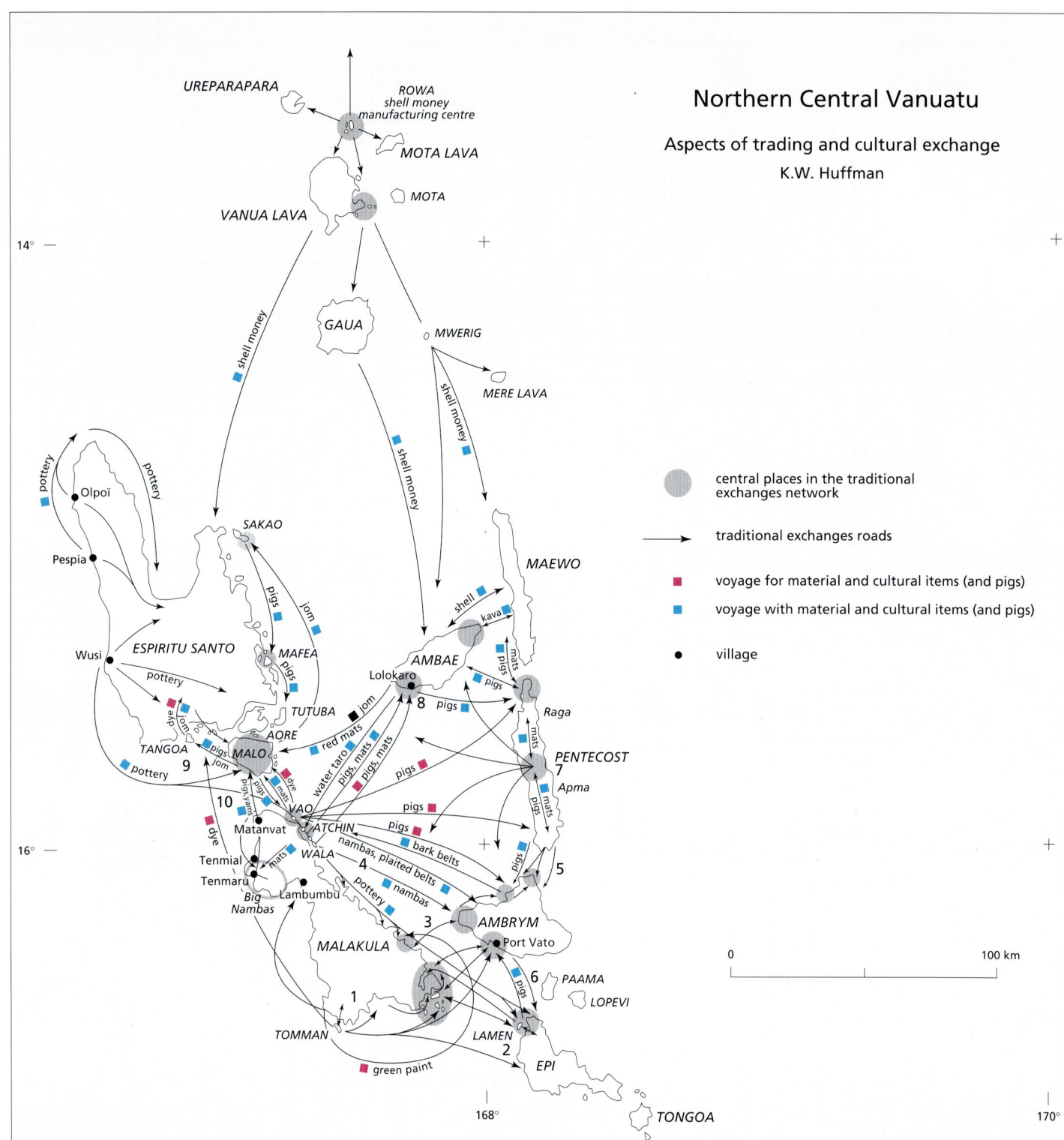

Fig. 213 *Local language,* **Bislama.**

1. **Periodical exchange sites:**
   Pul savi ('to pay for', 'to meet') in Nahava language.
   Na save in Naha'ai language. These exchanges took place in the Wien region, especially at Ranrombat, near Farun: bows and arrows, nasal sticks, clubs, taro, and so on.
   Niseyei : exchanges at Lambumbu.

2. **From Lamen to Nevia (a beach near Lamap) in *walava* canoes:**
   Pigs from Lamen for 'strong' yams.
   From Lamen to Ambrym: to seek pigs (used for purchasing women.
   Lamen: *wabo* ('silence'), double-prowed war canoes (fore and aft).

3. **Links between west Ambrym and east Malakula (*fren*/roads):**
   From Craig Cove to Banam Bay.
   From Sesivi to Port Sandwich.
   From Port-Vato to the Maskelynes.
   Pigs from Ambrym for food from Malakula.

4. **Links between north-west Malakula and Ambrym:**
   From Vao to Ranon: **nambas** and woven belts for pigs and bark belts.
   From Vao and Atchin to Ranon: sale of *maghe ne mal gelte* (for *maghe ne kuman*).
   From Wala to Craig Crove: **nambas** and woven belts for bark belts (exchanges also carried out by intermediaries from Banam Bay).
   From Vao to north Ambrym: purchase of women.
   Canoes from north-east Malakula: at Vao, *nuwak wala*; at Atchin, *na-ak wala*.

5. **Links between north Ambrym and south Pentecost, limited for north Ambrym to the regions of Olal-Harimal, Fandang, Falibeur and Parereo:**
   North Ambrym needs consisted of special baskets, money mats and funerary mats, clubs, *lira*, mineral paint, *ye*, with and nickel and copper base (green) and *ling* (blue).
   North Ambrym trading canoes: *bulbul*; also *bulbul lini* (made of **nangae** wood, *Canarium indicum*).
   South Pentecost canoes: *Bülbül*

6. **From Ambrym to Epi:**
   Food purchasing (rarely, however, as Epi magic was feared), and red mineral paint (*weyang*).

7. **Central Pentecost:**
   Exchanges of mats, pigs and women with Ambae, Maewo, Ambrym and Malakula.

8. **From north-east Malakula to Ambae :**
   Atchin went to Meterepo, Vao went to Natarimboë (on the piece of land called 'Vao' inland, above the Lolomwele passage, west of Lolokaro).

9. **Araki:**
   Purchase of men's aprons, *ro'o* (woven and dyed), made on Ambae and paid for with hermaphroditic pigs (**narave**).

10. **From Malakula to Malo:**
    Purchase of mats, bark belts and clubs, for pigs. The exchange system of north-west Malakula (Big Nambas) made it possible for them to obtain red dye from south Santo, which passed through intermediaries in Matanvat, Malo and Tangoa.

Fig. 214
Watercolour of north-east Malakulan trading canoes. Painted by Norman Hardy in 1895. Probably Wala Island.

while inland peoples brought and left taro and other inland products on the shore, which the Lambumbu would pick up after the inland peoples had retired. Ten days later, the Lambumbu would return and go onshore with predetermined amounts of fish, shellfish and other coastal products. These market exchanges were called *nisevei* in Lambumbu.

Such types of silent or semi-silent trading were pursued essentially by groups potentially hostile to one another, or who had no links (yet) established by marriage exchange of women. In south Santo the islets of Tangoa and Araki, although having 'proper' trading links with some areas, also had silent trading partners in other areas on the mainland. 'Bush' people would come down to a specified clan-boundary area on the coast with such items as yam, taro and arrows, place the items in specified heaps and retire a distance. The 'saltwater' people would then approach and place by each heap a specified amount of smoked fish and coastal products (for example, salt water in bamboos), pick up the bush products and retire. The inland people would then pick up the coastal produce.

Back in south-west Malakula, the Nahati-speakers of the Wilemp area had established a *rod* with the Mbotkote-speakers of Lendamboï, in the mountainous interior, by an exchange of women. Men from the Wilemp *nakamal* of Lor'meo would go inland and send a message up for the Lendamboï people to come down. Trading of different items was done at different sites – highland taro for lowland 'strong' yams at Lawemelau, and pig exchanges at Naitek Nambuas. The survival of this particular link was instrumental in the gradual introduction of Christianity into the interior during the 1980s. Many of these inland-coastal exchanges involved also, for example, shellfish items needed in the interior, not just for food, but for ritual purposes: Lendamboï needed *natavwi* (conch shells) for graded rituals and *nambulgaig'r* (nautilus) for funerary rituals. Similarly, Nisvai-speakers of the interior Malesif area had trade links with the northern tip of Port Sandwich in south-east Malakula, an interior 'market' at Baksave, and a need for similar shells for rituals.

Similar coastal-inland relationships pertained throughout the other large islands, each with their own peculiarities and specialities. 'Heavier' cultural trading, though, was often done by canoe.

Trading canoes

Large outrigger trading canoes travelled widely throughout the area until the latter half of the 19th century (fig. 214), trading for and with foods, pigs, money mats, baskets, clubs, pottery, mineral paints, dye, rituals, and so on. Inter-island trading links often followed connections originally established through women, population movements, or mythological connections. The death knell of these major voyages was the arrival of the blackbirding ships (fig. 215), from the 1860s onwards, which would often not hesitate to kidnap the large crews of any trading canoes found in their paths. From the end of last century, many missionaries tried to dissuade or prohibit their coastal converts from voyages associated with pig trading, and from the late 1920s the condominium government tried to stop inter-island canoe voyages in north-central Vanuatu, ostensibly to prevent increasing canoe accidents but also later possibly to prevent the spread of John Frum movement ideas (from Tannese leaders imprisoned at Lamap in south-east Malakula), which had already spread following traditional trade links from south-east Malakula into west, south-west, and then north Ambrym.[4]

By the time of early contact with the white man, only single-hulled outrigger canoes were being used, but stories exist of earlier, large, double-hulled canoes; for example, *nuwak gheru* of Vao, and the type called *rue rue* in north Pentecost. Most areas still have smaller outrigger canoes for several persons or a slightly larger version (for example, south-west Malakulan *nawangk mbarangkin* from the Nahava-speaking area of Seniang; *nanang mbarangin* from the neighbouring Naha'ai-speaking area around Tomman; the *wàlava* of Lamen Island, north-west Epi; and the *bulbul* of north Ambrym and *bülbül* of south Pentecost), but these are now rare. The large trading canoes that could hold up to forty people (of the type called *nimbwembeu* in the Nahava-speaking area of south-west Malakula, or the Vao *nuwak wala*, Port Sandwich *nuangk wala* and the Lamen Island double-ended fighting canoes *wabo*, 'silence') had almost all died out by the beginning of this century. The last-mentioned of these types were more 'sacred', involving rituals in construction and launching similar to entry into the graded system, taking on of a personality and name, and even having mortuary rituals performed for them when their days were over. Women were excluded from their construction and forbidden to travel in them.

In large canoes like these, intrepid voyagers followed their *rod* in the complex series of interwoven but controlled links that covered the whole area. For each item, craft, pig type or ritual characteristic, there was a major island, which became thus a focal point for trade in its specialities. Banks Islands shell money (*nasum*) was traded southwards from its manufacturing centre on Rowa (Reef Islands) into eastern Santo, Ambae, and from there to Maewo. Red pottery from west and north-west Santo followed trade links to Malo, Vao, along the east coast of Malakula to northern Epi. Pottery possibly

4. Missionary, trader and government (condominium) pressures combined to reduce the frequency and extent of ni-Vanuatu trading expeditions from the late 1920s: the missions to reduce trade in the cultural sphere (which they equated with 'heathenism'); the (European) traders to try to stop growing ni-Vanuatu initiatives in trade in 'European' trade items; and the condominium to do a combination of both, with a special concern for safety. These pressures increased in the 1940s.

Fig. 215
Blackbirding ship recruiting in the Pangkumu area, east Malakula. Photographed by J.W. Lindt in 1890.

Fig. 216
Young girls wearing their necklace and waistband shell money (*jom*) wealth. Photographed by Speiser in northern Malo between 1910 and 1912.

produced from the clay source of Venbetakmo in the hills near Lakatoro on the coast of east-north-east Malakula was probably traded up and down the coast, possibly even reaching into the southern interior, where I collected sherds (*netenau*) of lipped pottery at approximately 600 metres on Mount Navwalasakien, well inside the Mbotkote language area, in 1976. Examples of the earlier 'sacred' type of cylindrical or conical pottery (*naamboi* in Nahava language) are not restricted to south-west Malakula as originally thought, but are found over most areas of the island.

The island of Malo served an important function as a manufacturing centre for stringed shell-money, *jom* (fig. 216), and as 'middleman' in a complex trading system for mat dye between north Malakula and south Santo. Malo *jom* were particularly fine and greatly desired in neighbouring areas where shell money was accepted for pig purchases, bride price, and status display. From the main manufacturing centre at Avunambakura, in north-west Malo, *jom* circulated within the island and was then taken up by canoes on trading voyages as far north as Sakao (Lathi) Island (and the mainland opposite), in north-east Santo, in exchange for *narave* (intersex pigs: *ndre* in Sakao), essential for Malo graded rituals and highly valued in east and south Santo, Ambae, Maewo and Raga. Returning from Sakao, the Malo canoes made trading visits to Mavea and Tutuba islands.

The Big Nambas peoples of north-west Malakula needed regular supplies of *ni* leaf, source of the dark-red dye for their woven pandanus-fibre *nambas* (*navai*) and female mat skirts (*nahei p'h p'h*; fig. 217) and head mats (*nahei p'arei*), but *ni* and the *lepaè* vine grow best in south Santo. As the Big Nambas only had bamboo rafts for short coastal trips, a complex trading chain became established to obtain the *ni*. Pigs, tusker pigs and yams were taken from Tenmaru (At'nmarao) to coastal peoples at Matanvat and Tenmial. The latter, having canoes, then traded across to the Alehilao-speakers (now extinct) of south-west Malo. Trade connections within Malo converted these goods so that Malo areas having connections north-westwards then left with *jom* and intersex pigs to exchange them for the dye leaves with partners on Tangoa, who had trade links with those on south Santo who had rights over the leaves. When packets of the *ni* leaves finally arrived back at Tenmaru in the Big Nambas area, a series of interlinking exchange markets were held at points along the Tenmaru boundaries, at Aplendar P'h'par for Tenamit and the Batarmül area, at Epek'm't for Amah/Amok, and at Pwipaièn for Ondowalo and Nevinalah. Trade from Tenamit to Mahawe was at Menevet Iüd. Control of this trade was in the hands of the Big Nambas hereditary chiefs.

Vao canoes also traded with Malo for the leaf dye. The volume of trade south Santo-Tangoa-Malo-north Malakula was so great that by the 1930s certain European traders attempted to involve themselves by cutting out the Tangoa and Malo middleman and dealing directly south Santo-north Malakula. This killed off the indigenous trade system.

The peoples of the 'Small Islands' off north-east Malakula – Vao, Atchin, Wala, Rano, Norsup, Uripiv, Uri – and the mainland peoples at Pinalum and Tautu, were the sea travellers *par excellence* of the area, and called themselves 'the Sea People' (*mwere n'das*, Atchin). Their large 'winged' (the Vao term for sail, *ga'mban*, means 'wing') sailing canoes, with woven mat sails dyed red, flew themselves along the coast of Malakula as far south as the Maskelynes, Lamen, north Epi, west and north

Ambrym, Pentecost, Maewo and Ambae. (It is quite possible that a smaller version of one of these canoes, some say from Wala, was in Port Sandwich at the time of Captain Cook's visit in 1774.) The driving force behind this was the trade in pigs (1500 required for a *maki-ru* ritual on Vao in 1892, 200 for a similar *maki-ru* on Vao in 1986), rituals and other trade items. Each of the Small Islands had specific links with particular areas for particular items: Vao traded woven penis-wrappers and tasselled status belts with north Ambrym for bark belts, and pigs for pigs; with Pentecost for pigs (an area just inland from Loltong would exchange a Vao circle-tusker for ten smaller pigs, a good trade); to Maewo for pigs and rituals; and to Ambae with chickens and pigs for woven mats, *biok* (a type of water taro), pigs and rituals. Wala canoes (sometimes through middlemen at Duen, Banam Bay, south-east Malakula) traded penis-wrappers, woven straps, and pigs for bark belts, pigs and ritual exchange with Craig Cove (west Ambrym). Atchin traded with Ambae, Maewo and north Pentecost (these three areas being known on Atchin as *wenu si Tahar*, the 'Land of Tahar', Tagaro), particularly with Ambae, with pigs for mat skirts (Atchin *nambar*), pigs (particularly the double-circle tuskers called *ruk waru* in southwest Ambae, giving thus the similar grade title in Atchin grade rituals) and rituals. Often at the same time as regular pig-trading expeditions to Ambae, young men from Vao, Atchin and Wala voyaged there for important initiation rites all centred around the area of Lolokaro in south-west Ambae.

At the same time as the Sea People were flying out in their winged and bird-figure canoe-prowed ships, a similar intensive and extensive system, centred around south-south-west Malakula, in the Nahava- and Naha'ai-speaking areas, was sending its large *nimbwembeu*-type canoes northwards to Lambumbu and eastwards, with much stopping and inter-trading, along the south coast of Malakula (with canoes from south and south-east Malakula) to the Maskelynes, north-west Epi, and as far as Ambrym, Ambae and Santo (for mat dye). Large trading markets (*vul savi*, 'pay/come together', in Nahava language; *nisave* in Naha'ai language) for the peoples in the south-south-west were held in coastal Wien area, particularly at Ranrombat (near Farun). Taro, bows and arrows, nose sticks, clubs, and a particular type of nut whose juice was used in the process of skull elongation, were among the items traded. The 'heavier' side of this extensive trade system was, though, the pig trade involved in eventually purchasing ones way 'back home' up the numerous steps of the many differing south Malakulan *nimanggi* public graded systems, or in the purchase of entry into the non-graded, potentially more secret varieties of the *nalawan*-type societies. Mineral colours essential for the innumerable types of body painting and ritual objects of these ceremonies came from all over, each particular area having access or rights to different colours.

South-east Malakulan traders, with partners, intermediaries, groups or men acting individually, from the Maskelynes, Lamen, and north-west Epi, funnelled trade items, pigs, rituals, song, dance, art styles, and magic along their routes, and so into western Ambrym (and vice versa).

Fig. 217
Big Nambas women from north-western Malakula, 1992.
(Photo: David Becker)

Figs 218, 219, 220, 221
Male social-status body decorations with shell beads, originally shell money.

Fig. 218
Waist belt of high social status, tied in front with decorations worn at the back.
Ureparapara, Banks Islands.
Basel, Museum für Völkerkunde.

Fig. 219
Male armbands.
Left: Ambrym; right: Malakula.
Basel, Museum für Völkerkunde.

Fig. 218

Fig. 219

In the 'copyright system' area, almost everything could be sold and almost anything could be bought (figs 218, 219, 220) – a whole series of rituals, or one particular ritual or aspect of it, particular types of masks, slit-drum styles, body-painting codes, mythical cycles or sections of them, dances, or songs. Those purchasing the rights to them from the copyright owners could then resell to other buyers. In this way, items from different areas could combine in varying patterns in other areas and, with acceptable modifications and embellishments, be sold further afield. A type of ritual 'police' (for example, the *nitupat* of the Ninde-speaking area of south-west Malakula) enforced the correctness of adherence to a ritual of a particular area at a particular time, and its possibility of variation. The rituals themselves were, and are, thought to have a power and spirit of their own that urges them to get up, move to other areas, to stay there for a while, and then move on (as in the case of *luan* rituals from the Port Sandwich area in their voyages to areas of Ambrym). The ritual does not (necessarily) disappear from its place of origin, but expands itself spiritually – through the intermediary of men.

Although Ambrym had its own series of 'indigenous' or very ancient rituals (for example, *fenbi*; see fig. 221), these were added to, extended and embellished by purchase along established 'roads' from areas of Malakula, the Maskelynes and north-western Epi. Purchase of titles/steps and associated items in the men's graded system from areas of east-south-eastern Malakula added to those already existing in west Ambrym, and there was a gradual flow/resale of the latter and others up to north Ambrym. The south-east Malakula-west Ambrym cultural exchange process was incredibly complex, involving intense reciprocal exchanges, items being purchased and repurchased several times over generations. Much discussion still goes on today between these two areas as to rights and obligations, but there does seem to be general agreement that at least three of the higher 'stone' *Nimanggi* grades came from south-east Malakula to west Ambrym. The purchasing routes for these grades were as follows:

- *Maghe ne mal*: Port Sandwich (south-east Malakula – but probably with its origin much further north) to Melbür (near Sesivi, south-west Ambrym) to Craig Cove (west Ambrym) to Fanü to Ranon (north Ambrym), and from there eventually to north-east and south-east Ambrym.
- *Loghbaro* and *vetnemweleun*: from Burbar (south of Weso Bay, east-south-east Malakula) to Labül (between Malver and Baïap, west Ambrym) to Wakon (Dip Point, west Ambrym), back to other areas of west Ambrym then up to the Olal area in north Ambrym.

Maghe lon bul is an Ambrym grade, but there are two varieties, one of which came from Malakula.

The more sacred *luan* on Ambrym was a fusion of elements that came in from Burbar (east-south-east Malakula) to Ponbarite (near Baïap, west Ambrym), from Port Sandwich to Melbür (near Sesivi, south-west. Ambrym), and from the Maskelynes and Lemaru (north Epi) to Port Vato (south-west Ambrym). From west Ambrym it followed links up to north Ambrym.

It seems that the spread of these elements from Malakula to Ambrym took place within the relatively recent past. One lineage from Boletaurakon (Lele, west Ambrym) traces its descent back sixteen generations from the present day – and the first male in this line to purchase the grade *mal* was Malsangelap of the sixth generation. To give an indication of the rate of spread from west to north and then to south-east Ambrym, one should note that by the time the first European missionary arrived in south-east Ambrym in 1903, only one man in the whole area had reached the grade *mal*.

Regarding the famous and beautiful Malakulan and Ambrym vertical slit-drums, an artistic chain runs throughout the two islands. The closest similarity of the west and north Ambrym slit-drums were to those of the Port Sandwich area. Purchasing of rights and particular styles continues, particularly in north Ambrym.

West Ambrym (and associated) cultural elements spread widely into north Ambrym through kinship and pig trade links. North Ambrym also had particularly close trade and cultural links with 'Sosok' (the north-east Malakulan islands of Vao, Atchin and Wala) and 'Ra' (south Pentecost), recognising 'Tamis' (Lamap, Port Sandwich area) as the origin for *luan*, and Sosok for the purchase of *maghe ne mal gelte* for *maghe ne kuman* (not associated with general graded rituals). Initiative for the trade connections between Sosok and north Ambrym were left to the former – the landing spot on north Ambrym was predetermined, the timing not. Large canoes from Atchin landed regularly at Ranon, north Ambrym, for trade, searching for *bumto* (north Ambrym circle-tusker pigs) and to sell, on the landing beach, *maghe ne mal gelte*, involving an Atchin

Fig. 220
Pen, male armband of shell and coconut-wood beads, indicating acquisition of a ritual not associated with the graded system. Collected by Guiart in 1949.
Lele, west Ambrym.
Paris, Musée national des Arts d'Afrique et d'Océanie.

Fig. 221
Akorbu garter worn below the knee, indicating acquisition of the male rite *fenbi*. Collected by Guiart.
West Ambrym.
Paris, Musée national des Arts d'Afrique et d'Océanie.

Fig. 220

Fig. 221

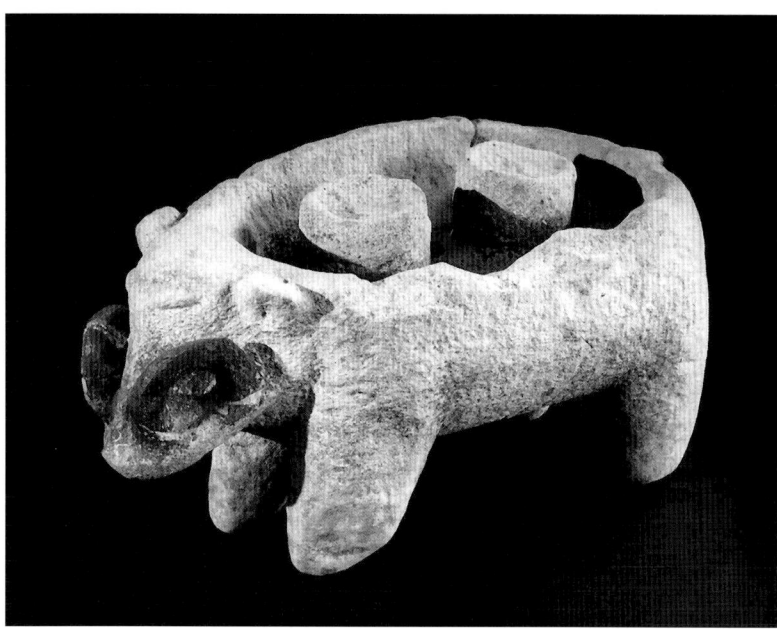

Fig. 222
Stone kava-preparation bowl in the form of an intersex pig. Collected by Meier and Stähelin in 1934, and said to be from Ambae.
Basel, Museum für Völkerkunde.

solip (canoe prow). This then gave the north Ambrym purchaser the right to use a canoe prow in the ritual *maghe ne kuman*, which was said to have been brought to Ranon by a 'high' woman from Ambae. This is one of the reasons north Ambrym called Ambae *vere ne vehen* ('Land of the Woman'). There was also a north Ambrym-Sosok-Ambae connection involving women for wives, but aspects of this cannot be spoken about.

Canoes from Vao also sold rituals involving the canoe prows, and trade in pigs and rituals continues today between Vao's Netsara Veèn/Venü (and *Singon*) and the north Ambrym bush village of Fanla.

North Ambrym trade with south Pentecost followed kinship and *rod* links from Olal, Harimal, Parereo, Fandang and Falibeur, to links particularly in the Bay Martelli area of south Pentecost. Ambrym needed taro, yams, mineral paints, small money and funerary mats, clubs, and pigs from south Pentecost. South Pentecost needed pigs from the *ta beir* (*man Ambrym*) but also sold rituals. One lineage in Parereo, north Ambrym, claims the right to 'pull' the famous land-dive ritual *naghol* from south Pentecost, and the ritual has been performed at least twice there at Ranme Naghol this century – once in the 1920s and lately in 1983. A step from the south Pentecost graded rituals, *warsangül*, with the associated *tip* dance was planned at a ritual near Fantan in 1992.

South Pentecost Sa-speakers followed kinship roads and trading links through Seke and Sowa-speaking areas into the large Apma-speaking region of central Pentecost. Trade was brisk in dye roots, mineral colours, pigs and mats: the large Sa money and funerary mats, *badji'enriri*, were particularly in demand. Central Pentecost was, and is, a major centre for dyed red mat work, which was traded all over Aruaru (Pentecost), and with women and pigs, to Ambae, Maewo, Ambrym and Malakula. These 'roads' still exist today, except for that with Malakula. *Tsip* are the female mat skirts and small money, *sese* the longer money mats. These money mats are entirely interchangeable as currency, mats for pigs, pigs for mats, and mats for male and female status-ceremony payments, as are the recently revived *tjuwun* long funerary mats. Central Pentecost mats were and are in great demand in Arato, Raga (north Pentecost) where trade 'roads' brought pigs, clubs, and ritual styles for the Apma mats and food staples. North Pentecost, producing red mats itself, funnelled vast numbers of mats and pigs out in a perpetual mat, woman, pig and ritual trade and exchange following kinship, ritual and mythological links on south Maewo and east Ambae. It is said that this incessant trade, also including kava, linked populations and *ratahigi* ('big men', leaders) to minimise fighting.

Maewo, 'Land of Light', northern home of kava and the culture hero Tagaro, was and is a power centre guarding and emanating spiritual force. Tagaro's home at Ghombio contains his stone map of the islands 'in which he works' and through which his light spreads – Maewo, Ambae, Pentecost, Malakula and Ambrym. At least sixteen different varieties of kava are recognised on Maewo, about ten of which are used regularly and can be traded. Male and female costume and money mats were more commonly undyed shining white, with a tendency towards finer openwork at the ends. Red-dyed mats tend to be traded in from Pentecost or Ambae. The need for *kwari* (circle-tusker pigs) for *nasumbwe* (Maewo male grade-taking), or for similar rituals for a woman to become *motari* (a 'high' woman),[5] took Maewo men on voyages to Raga, Ambae, Navu (Malakula), Sugu (Tutuba) and elsewhere; water taro, mats, pigs, kava, magic, ritual and mythical cycles brought back the required goods.

Ambae represents Tagaro's upturned canoe.[6] It is still widely famed today as another centre for fine woven and dyed mat work. As in Maewo and north Pentecost, this is all regular women's work, providing the costume and money mats that form the basis (with pigs) of complex monetary, exchange and graded systems.[7] Eastern Ambae's links were mainly with Maewo and north Pentecost, with shell beads and shell money, pigs, kava and mats perpetually circulating. Ambae produced particularly fine tusker-pigs, and also required *narave*. Parts of (particularly western and south-western) Ambae served also as production centres for islands to the west and south-west for particular woven items not required on Ambae, but produced specifically for use in neighbouring cultures. Examples were the small woven and dyed male pubic coverings traded to the small island of Araki, south Santo, and there called *ro'o*; payment from Araki was one *narave* for a large bundle of *ro'o*. A special woven and dyed, very small mat was also produced as a penis-wrapper and sometimes traded, for example, to Wala (north-eastern Malakula) as a special-purpose *nambas*, there called *man-masangk*. Some of the Vao *mangau* (funerary and money) mats were also sometimes produced. Much of the production, though, was of normal Ambae dyed male and female costume mats, sometimes with special designs for the areas to which they were to be traded (for example, to Malo, or to the Small Islands off north-east Malakula). Such trade normally involved the other islands coming to west or south-west Ambae rather than the contrary, although large Ambae trading expeditions often visited Malo.[8] The most outstanding example of this was the complex, regular trade system from Vao, Atchin and Wala to the now mostly depopulated area of Lolokaro, in south-west Ambae. Starting out as trade voyages to the Lolokaro area for dancing-mats and pigs, there developed a more sacred and parallel purpose, that of a type of pilgrimage/initiation for recently-initiated young males of the Small Islands. Because of still-existing north-east Malakulan tabus, that aspect will not be described. It can be said, though, that Wala began the voyages, rights to which then spread to Atchin and Vao. North-east Malakulan myths attribute the origin of the voyages to south-west Ambae, to a Wala man Nimbel ('hawk') travelling by magical means to Lolokaro to obtain a fine Ambae mat skirt (*nimbar*, Wala) for the Wala girl he loved. Various versions of the myth exist in north-east Malakula. The Lolokaro version attributes the origin to the arrival of a shark man, *Kangwalevo Mbal-Mbal*, from Malakula, and his taking back to Malakula of a girl from Lolovat and her *bargare* red mat-skirts. Such 'doubled' origin stories are common, and indicate the primary importance of women in the establishment of trade and ritual links. Each north-east Malakulan 'small island' came to have its own landing beach in the Lolokaro area: Wala near Lolovat, Atchin at Meterepo, and Vao at Natirimboè.[9] Another landing place was at Kwowosaenat. These trade and initiation voyages came to an end in the late 1920s. By this time depopulation had devastated the Lolokaro area, and 'local assistance' – and mats – were no longer available.

Lolokaro survivors today trace the cause of the depopulation to another trade link – that went wrong. A high-ranking man of Lolokaro, Natnaquari, had pig-trading links with an area in north Pentecost. His Pentecost partner wanted to marry his daughter, but ended up killing her and trying to kill Natnaquari. In retaliation, Natnaquari managed to capture a Raga 'tabu man', Mol Ravae, brought him back to Lolokaro and killed him. Mol Ravae's 'power', though, caused the area to be depopulated, and the bush covered it up. And so the area remains today.

This short peek into a few of the aspects of the trading systems of a particular area of Vanuatu began in Malakula, has followed a counterclockwise direction like the growing right-hand tusk of a tusker-pig, and has come back full circle. I have only touched the tip of the yam-heap, but this paper does give an idea of the difficulties in really identifying 'origin locality' for many of the Vanuatu artifacts in museum collections around the world. Much is not what it seems – all are links in a complex series of chains. When shown a photograph of the famous 'Ambae stone pig' (fig. 222) from the Basel Museum collections in 1985 (see Guiart 1963a:213, pl. 205), an aged Lolokaro survivor immediately

5. Terms in Sungwandaga language from central Maewo.

6. And is the 'real Bali Ha'i' from *Tales of the South Pacific* (J. Michener, pers. comm., 1984); see Rodman, this volume.

7. An exception is the Sa-speaking area of south Pentecost, where women weave the mats and men do the dyeing.

8. The desire to re-establish this link (and to encourage Malo males to again wear mats) was exemplified in a ritual presentation and speech by Ambae chief James Tambe to the Malo delegation from Avunatare at the 2nd National Arts Festival, held on Santo in June 1991. Chief James presented the Malo leaders with the Ambae type of male apparel mat known on Malo as *vuhru*, and enjoined them to revive it. When worn, these dyed mats are known as *vualamalisi* (west Malo) or *valvalis* (south-east Malo).

9. There is still an area of land called 'Vao' near Natirimboè, in the bush just above Lolomwele passage west of Lolokaro. Mangrove trees at Natarimboè today mark the 'friendship' of north-east Malakula and south-west Ambae.

Fig. 223 Janus-headed club, a variant of the type of famous club collected during Cooks visit to Port Sandwich in 1774. Collected by Guiart on Ambrym in 1949. Paris, Musée national des Arts d'Afrique et d'Océanie.

recounted the story of Nambilak carving such a stone pig (*narave*) at Matanmwando, in south-west Ambae, and eventually taking it to north-east Malakula. Such stone-pig kava bowls are unknown in the rest of Ambae, but are known, exist, and are kept hidden around north-east Malakula.

Did the member of Captain Cook's crew who collected the beautiful Janus-headed club (fig. 223) in Port Sandwich, south-east Malakula (where they are called *mwemwe p'h'mandre*), in July 1774 (now in the Pitt-Rivers Museum, Oxford; see Kaeppler 1978:249, fig. 543), realise that even then he was collecting a rare type of high-status club that signified links for south-east Malakula-west Ambrym-north Ambrym-south Pentecost? Did Cook's men who left a pair of (Tahitian) dogs (unknown in Malakula until then, and thought to be pigs) in Port Sandwich then realise they were involved in a trade eventually resulting in the rights to use a figure of a dog as the gable-end symbol of the *nakamal* of Barboli, near Lamap? Could early European traders in rifles envisage that their 'killing-sticks' could be transformed into the beautiful *nambong natluo* ('barrel', 'musket') dancing poles for *nalawan nampah* rituals revived in the Ninde-speaking area of south-west Malakula in the early 1980s?

One could go on almost indefinitely. The answer is not to deluge Vanuatu with expatriate anthropologists; the answer is to support Vanuatu's desire for cultural continuity, development and revival, while respecting its tabus. In many areas of Vanuatu, *kastom* is alive and well; in many areas it is under threat from new fundamentalist missionary sects, or potential logging activities; and in others it is only 'sleeping', waiting to reawaken and fly like the sacred hawk that inspires high-ranking men. Sometimes *kastom* can pose problems for 'development'. During the national census held in May 1989, the census office in the capital, Port Vila, sent a series of messages over the national radio to the peoples of Pentecost asking the men to please remain at home to be counted. The 'problem' was that so many of the men were away following trade links through the island on the perpetual *bisnis pig* circuit. This is a good sign. Who outside of Vanuatu knows that in 1980 the people of Atchin carved and launched a 15-metre traditional trading canoe (of the rare *na'ak nemang* type) – and sailed it by the stars and currents all the way to Papua New Guinea? Or that the people of Ranon launched a new *bul bul* canoe in February 1993? Or that chief Rupert Garae of Atavoa/Siwoi, east Ambae, has now killed 1000 pigs? That a variant of the long-lost *chubwan* rituals began again in southern Pentecost in 1990? That *mansip* rituals were performed again in Lamap, south-east Malakula in 1992 for the first time in perhaps sixty years? Vanuatu has managed to confuse and confound anthropologists for 100 years, and has managed to retain many of its secrets. Let us hope that it continues to do so.

The author would like to thank the hundreds of ni-Vanuatu friends, and especially the Vanuatu Cultural Centre fieldworkers and staff who have helped me over the years; it would take an entire book to list all your names. Many are now dead: may their spirits still dance. Thanks go also to those white men and women in Vanuatu and overseas who have helped; none are forgotten.

Kiamu, the Southern Canoe

Michel Aufray

In the far south of the archipelago lies Aneityum, or, more accurately, Anecom.[1] The name means 'place of the *necom* tree',[2] and refers to a toponym which early navigators took to be the name of the island as a whole, traditionally known by its inhabitants as Kiam or Kiamu.

Captain James Cook fixed the position of the island on 21 or 22 August 1774, during his second Pacific voyage, after his visit to Tanna. The Spaniards Alessandro Malaspina and Jose Bustamente y Guerra, and later the Frenchman D'Entrecasteaux, also sailed off the island without landing on it. In 1827, Dumont d'Urville described Anatom as seen from on-board ship, but was unable to land because of rough seas. The first contacts between Europeans and the people of the island probably took place in about 1830. At that time, a sandalwood ship under Captain Lawler and Lieutenant George Ward Cole anchored at Port Patrick, in the north of the island. The crew, mostly natives of Tahiti and Rotuma, raided the native plantations. Two sailors were killed in confrontations with the islanders. Anatom later became a whaling station, and then a sandalwood station, particularly after 1844, when James Paddon set up his store on the small island of Inyex, off the village of Anelxauhat, which he acquired in exchange for an axe, a blanket and a few beads.

The arrival of the white man had tragic consequences for the local population. Smallpox, influenza and measles epidemics brought in by European vessels decimated the island's population in a few years. This high death rate was accompanied by a drop in the birth rate as a result of the labour trade, which took able-bodied men away from the island. The population fell from an estimated 4000 in 1848, to 713 in 1876, and 192 in 1949.

Along with this massive depopulation, the cultural substratum crumbled after 1848 as a result of the island's evangelisation by Presbyterian missionaries. Fundamentalist pastors John Geddie and Thomas Powell established a sort of theocracy. They devoted themselves to rooting out the traditional culture which they considered to be inspired by the Devil, and in its place laid down a code of Christian laws. Not only were ceremonies and rituals prohibited, but also some traditional techniques.

The land of the living

Though the new Christian order sometimes met with resistance from traditional chiefs, the ancestral culture was practically wiped out. For this reason, our knowledge of social life on the island before the arrival of Europeans is limited to the accounts of a

1. This name has been variously spelt. The two commonest variants are Anatom on French maps and Aneityum on English-language maps. In this article, to reproduce *anecom* names, we have used a slightly modified form of the traditional spelling adopted in the 19th century by Protestant missionaries in their translations of the Bible. We thus have the following equivalences:

Bible	Modern spelling
<j>	<c>
<d>	<d>
<c>	<x>
	<g>
	<ny>
	<pw>
	<mw>

2. Unidentified tree.

3. Spelt Anelgauhat or Anelgaohat on maps.

4. *Naputu* means 'a person who is killed on the death of another', whereas *nases* means 'strangulation'.

5. Unidentified river fish. Literally 'water shell'.

few missionaries and navigators, and data collected in recent years by archaeologists and ethnolinguists. Oral texts and a vocabulary have been collected. This data provides us with a glimpse of what Anecom's social system and culture once were.

The origin of Aneityum's inhabitants is recounted in various versions of the same myth: a man named Warariki and a woman named Riu landed on the island and settled at Exdootxe near Inrero mountain. They came into possession of the stone which allows man to reproduce. It is called 'the stone of the beginnings of man'. Warariki and Riu gave birth to two boys called Necom and Nidinecom, 'sap of the *necom* tree', then two girls called Tisianecom, 'flower of the *necom* tree', and Wanecom, 'fruit of the *necom* tree'. They married among themselves. One of their descendants, Pinakai, set up the chiefdom and the rites for installing chiefs.

Territorial organisation of the island appears to have been identical with that of Tanna as described by Bonnemaison (1986b, 1986c). On the one hand, the island was divided into strips of territory, *umwa*, running uphill from the seashore to the highest peaks. On the other hand, these territories were structured into canoes, *neixau*, which meant both a space made up of places and the social group living there. These 'land canoes' commemorate the community's initial voyage and settlement of the land. The name of the island's main village, Anelxauhat,[3] is a reference to this: literally, it means 'place of the stone canoe'. The canoe metaphor was also present in the kava ritual. The doubled-handled wooden bowl used to prepare the beverage was called *nelxau amuny*; that is, 'drinking canoe'. The symbolic form of this object underlined the bonds of solidarity between men descended from the same canoe and taking part in the same ritual.

According to Spriggs (1981), the island was made up of about sixty canoes grouped into seven political territories attached to a central chiefdom. According to Inglis (1882), there were six districts, three in the south and three in the north, grouped into two big chiefdoms, that of Anelxauhat and that of Aname. For this reason the island was compared to a hut supported by two posts. In addition to these divisions, the island fell into two economic groups: the people of the shore, *nop u wun cop*, and the people of the interior, *nop u tohou* or *nopwa elxau itohou*, who exchanged the produce of the sea (fish, turtles) for that of the forest (timber, vines, fruits and root vegetables).

The political organisation, no doubt influenced by neighbouring Polynesian groups, seems to have been comparable with that of the other southern islands of the group. It was characterised by a system of hereditary titles and a certain amount of social stratification. The principal terms used were: *natimarid*, 'chief', or *natimi alpwas*, 'big man, chief'; *nasositai u natimarid*, 'servant of the chief'; *nop itap* or *natimi itap*, 'priest' or 'magician'; and *nop an peke*, 'people of the land, subjects'. This model, however, was in no way autocratic and retained enough flexibility to allow room for competing claims to such social positions.

When the chief was installed, he was carried on a litter, *nahat*, by four men. One man, *inyaupo u natimarid*, fulfilled the function of 'stepping stone' and helped the chief climb into the litter. Then the people gathered round the procession would throw rocks, sling-stones and spears at the chief, which he had to dodge. If one of these missiles found its mark, it was an ill omen, and meant that some time in the future he would be vanquished in war. After this ritual, the chief organised a big feast for his subjects, in which he could not take part.

The Aneityum people maintained relations with neighbouring islands. The people of Futuna, *Inpeke an has*, 'the land of evil', would come to Aneityum to get mineral pigments used in tattooing; the Tannese, *Inpeke ran ma*, 'land of the branch of the breadfruit tree', held that Aneityum was the dwelling-place of the ogre Semsem or Semosemo. Contacts with the Loyalty Islands and the Isle of Pines were also frequent. In those islands, a banana clone still bears the name Kiam. Oral tradition also has it that a man by the name of Magkia settled on Maré, while a Maré man, Laline, established himself on Anatom. Similarly, a certain Naruwa, from Aneityum, founded a clan on Lifu. Stories and songs also refer to the landing on the island of people from Civic, or in other words, Samoa.

The first missionaries were struck by the custom of strangling widows, *naputu* or *nases*.[4] When a man died, his brothers had a duty to strangle his widow. This blood price enabled the children to inherit the dead man's land. The killers had only a few days in

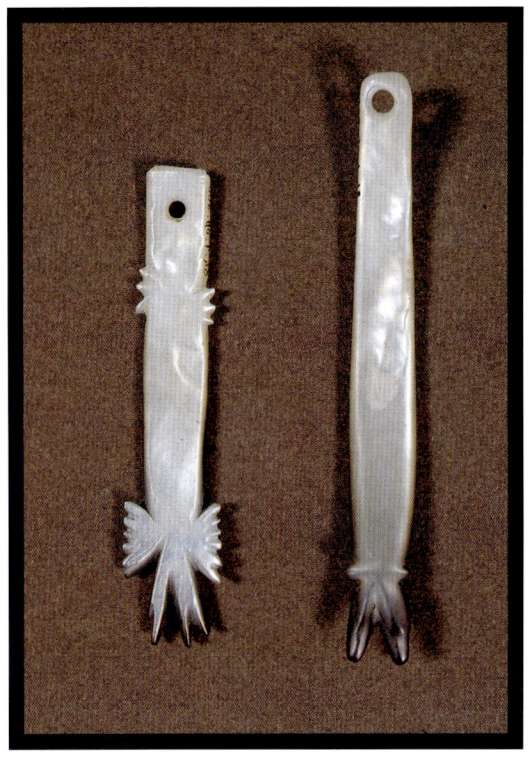

which to carry out their task. When this had elapsed, they lost all their rights. Sometimes the woman's close relatives opposed the execution. Members of the family would then stand legs apart above the woman as she lay on the ground. Through this simulation of childbirth, the woman became a little child again and could thus escape her persecutors.

The land of the dead

In former times, there were two types of burial. When a chief was being buried, the corpse was interred except for the head, which was left protruding above ground. A small hut, in which a man had to stay by the dead chief, was built over the grave. A basket containing taros and *nipcin wei*,[5] a freshwater fish, was hung in the hut. The mourner was to eat this food while looking the dead man in the eyes. If he turned his eyes away, he was put to death by the warriors waiting outside the hut. After finishing his meal, he had then to make an incision with his thumbnail in the dead man's head, along a line down the middle of the forehead and nose to the mouth, to hasten decomposition. When the head had become detached from the trunk, the mourner carried it to a sacred place in the bush, where the skull of another chief who had died previously had been placed. This skull was pushed out of the way with the head of the chief who had just died. Thus he succeeded his predecessors.

It appears that the other type of burial, *netheso an cop*, 'sea burial' was for commoners. The corpse was carried on a litter to the coastal cliffs. If it was necessary to go through enemy villages, these would allow the cortège to pass. Once at the seashore, the dead man's relatives would put on him an armband made of coconut shell, *nethado*, and various plants. The body was weighted down with stones and thrown into the sea from the top of the rocks. One man had to jump into the sea with the body to make sure it came to rest on the seabed. Back on land, the diver was not to stay on the shore, but to live hidden

Fig. 224
Mother-of-pearl pendant.
Futuna.
Chartres, Musée
des Beaux-Arts.

Fig. 225
Mother-of-pearl pendant.
Futuna.
Chartres, Musée
des Beaux-Arts.

Fig. 226
High-ranking Kanak
hairstyle, 19th century.
Paris, Musée
de l'Homme.

6. Baskets containing plants to be used for magic purposes.

7. Name of the dead ancestor protector of Napwau.

8. *Myzomela cardinalis*, Meliphagidae, the cardinal honeyeater.

9. *Araucaria cooki*, R. BR., Araucariaceae.

10. The island of the dead, *Umwai upni*, literally 'good, pleasant, place', was off the east coast near Anhacenpeke, 'the other side of the land', spelt Nétchinimbéké on the IGN map.

in the bush so as not to see the dead man's remains devoured by sharks.

The spirits of the dead, *natmas*, were carried by the sharks to their dwelling places at sea. These were islands all around Anatom, which the living could sometimes glimpse early in the morning. At Isia, on the east coast, the island of the dead was called Ralau. There grew a banyan whose leaves were associated with a sea fish, *nopom erin pak*, 'banyan leaf mackerel'. When these fish are plentiful, people say the spirits of the dead are sweeping the leaves of their banyan.

Sometimes the living strayed into the land of the dead. The latter would welcome them by offering them uncooked food, bananas and sugar cane. They were not to touch the peelings, because with these the dead made fires whose smoke forced the living to close their eyes. When they opened them, they would find themselves on Anatom again.

A number of songs refer to this journey to the country of the dead (see inset below).

Material culture

Archaeological excavations carried out by Matthew Spriggs since the 1970s have made it possible provisionally to date the earliest traces of human occupation of the island at 2000 BP. By the 12th century, the islanders had developed a highly elaborate agricultural irrigation system. Terraces and distribution channels were built for the cultivation of taro, the island's principal resource. More than 130 names of clones have been recorded. Petroglyphs have been found almost everywhere on the island. On the other hand, no trace of pottery has been discovered to date, nor have we been able to find any words in the language for earthenware pot or clay modelling.

The name of Aneityum is rarely mentioned in works on Oceanic art. Most objects have disappeared, usually burnt when the missionaries arrived. In their iconoclastic frenzy, they destroyed especially the wooden or stone statuettes, *natmas imai*, 'images of the dead', mentioned by the first explorers, which seem to have been connected with the cult of the dead.

Except for basket making and mat weaving, traditional crafts have disappeared. A number of terms designating tools, weapons and everyday objects are, however, still in the vocabulary. This vocabulary gives us some idea of Aneityum's material culture.

Ayeg pok Pwarua	Let us put the Pwarua out to sea
Am acxei xat tran	And attach the baskets[6] to the boat.
Is ethag napwat tran an topuwahou	In the middle of the ocean the mists have swallowed up the boat.
Wat excomexcom is apos ak Nakau	You, pilot Nakau, could no longer see clearly in front of the boat,
Am alany pan uhup pwar arowei Napwau	You cried out and called Napwau.
Is aidyen wat top aworakosen	Then he turned round and worked some magic.
Wat iogi se am arowei Narinowei	When he had finished he called Narinowei.[7]
Is auyag nadiat im la inretcei u won	The day began to dawn and light appeared in the east
Im law inhox tran ethan exce xop	And the humming bird[8] began to sing under the purple pine trees.[9]
Nekra apahaf an peke rumwai upni	We were all going to the land of happiness.[10]

Chapter IV
The art of power

Graded Societies and Societies Based on Title: Forms and Rites of Traditional Power in Vanuatu

Joël Bonnemaison

Two broad types of political power are found in Vanuatu (fig. 227). In the northern islands, from the Torres to Epi, chiefdoms are founded on a hierarchy of grades: men of power come to the fore through competition of an economic sort. In the central and southern islands, chiefdoms are partly hereditary, partly elective, and based on titles, rather than achievements. They are, to some, extent reminiscent of the pyramidal power structures characteristic of western Polynesian societies.

The makers of tradition

The 'graded hierarchy' is simple in theory and complex in practice. It is as if it were a part of the Melanesian genius to take the model it receives, as it spreads from place to place, and complicate it as much as humanly possible to put a local stamp on it. The system consists in formalising access to local political power by establishing a series of hierarchical grades. For every grade there is a corresponding rank which confers the right to wear certain insignia and ritual ornaments (figs 228, 229, 230). This rank is obtained by passing an economic test; the higher the grade, the more complex and demanding the test. The grade-taker must pay for all the rituals connected with the grade, and sacrifice pigs to a value proportionate to the rank he is taking.

When Europeans first had dealings with these islands, this power system held sway over a large part of the north and northern-central islands. It still exists to a large extent in islands like Ambae, Pentecost, Maewo, some parts of Ambrym and Malakula, where it is even going through something of a renaissance.

The system brings with it a certain amount of social mobility; any man can be a candidate for the highest grades and climb the rungs of the hierarchy one by one, as long as he has the support of those dignitaries who hold the keys to power, and shows enough energy and talent. While all members of the social body take at least the lowest grades, however, few reach the highest. Members of influential descent groups undeniably start off with a better chance of success than ordinary men, because they have the economic wealth, consisting of the all the loans granted them by their kin, and an extensive network of relationships. It does not by any means follow, however, that they will rise automatically to the highest grades: the old chiefs only give their support if they feel their sons or grandsons are worthy successors.

This chiefly power is therefore neither entirely hereditary nor entirely elective, but is, in the last

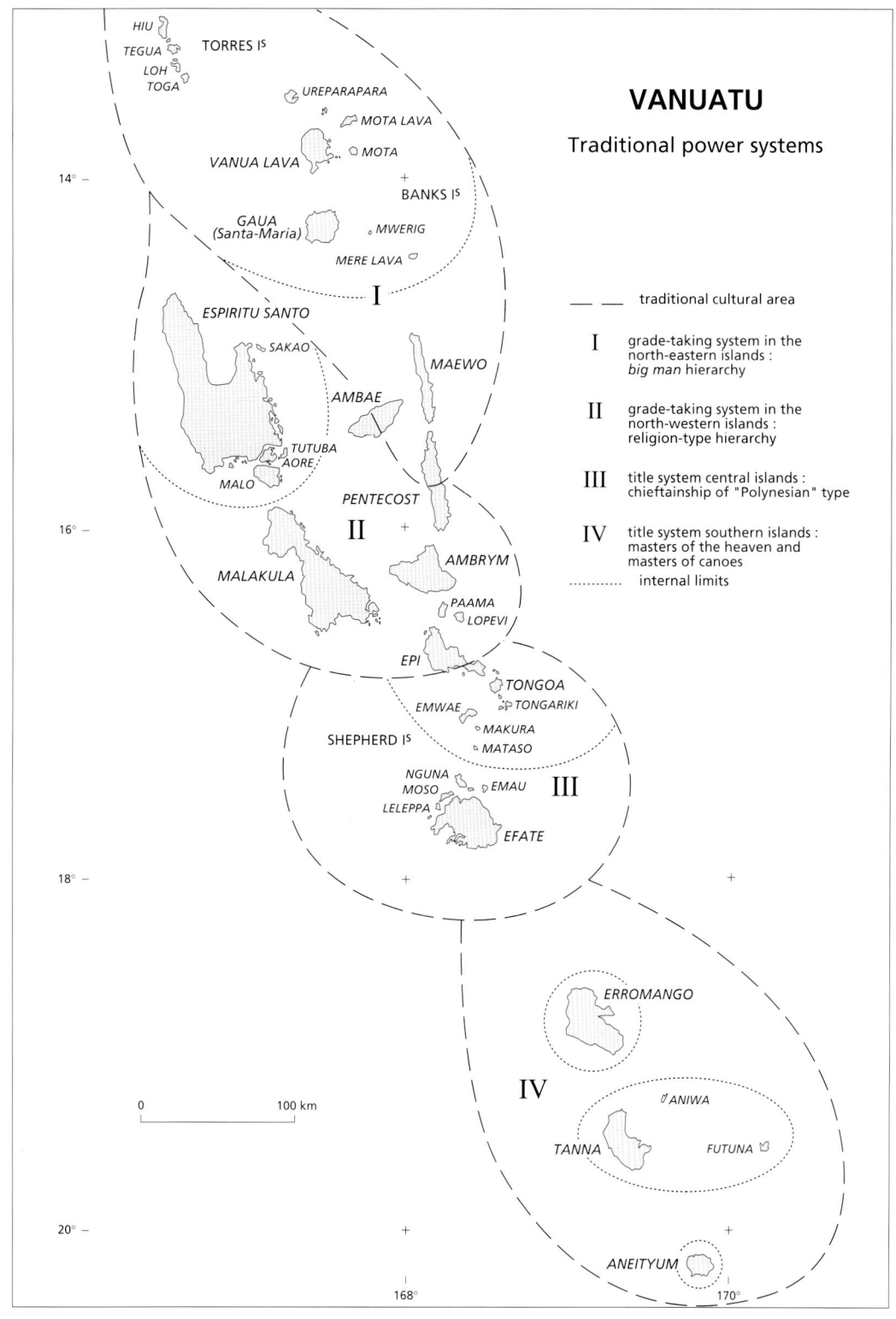

Fig. 227

GRADED SOCIETIES AND SOCIETIES BASED ON TITLE ▼ 201

Fig. 228
High-ranking man with ritual insignia. Grade-taking ceremonies ceased, because of epidemics, shortly after the visit of the photographer Lindt in 1890.
South coast of Santo.

succeeding through his ability to get on with people, through his human and social qualities, in gathering around him men who will support him, the candidate for high rank creates around him the consensus which will carry him naturally to power. He must, consequently, be generous and sociable towards the men of high grade above him, as well as to those of low grade who support him.

The rituals, the number of grades and the trials candidates have to go through vary from island to island and from one cultural area to another. Each local system can be broken down into three broad levels, each including a number of grades. On the bottom rung of the ladder we find the common people, or 'men of gardens' (in Bislama, *man blong karen*), rooted to their territory; in the middle come the local chiefs, leaders of small residential groups, elders of the descent group segment; and last, at the top, we have the men of the highest grades, who dominate or control exchange relations. Thus they hold a form of traditional economic power, based on the interplay of debts and the social advantage one can derive from it.

On Ambae, these chiefs are called *ratahigi*, which means 'fathers'. One after another, their grade-taking successes have shown everyone their qualities as leaders and the magical power vested in them; in other words, the *mana* described by Codrington (1891), without which there can be no great men and no great deeds. These men of high grade are protected by and intimate with supernatural beings (Allen 1972). They are close to the sacred and communicate directly with the ancestors.

These 'fathers of tradition', the men of high grade, are above all the masters of traditional ritual and exchange, both within the territory and beyond it. This position gives them the right to overstep common men's laws and perhaps even to forge new laws, make or remake tradition, and codify the rituals around which society is built. I once asked a Pentecost man of high grade what *kastom* (tradition) was (fig. 231). He replied with sublime arrogance: 'I am *kastom*.'

Men of high grade do not, however, embody pure political power in the sense in which we generally understand the word 'chieftainship'. They undoubtedly have every means of becoming 'leaders', if their natural authority and charisma lend themselves to it,

analysis, won by competition. The qualities a chief must have are those usually required of a Melanesian 'big man': he must have the personality of a leader, be a good public speaker and a 'winner' in whatever he undertakes. In a way, taking a grade is the political seal of approval of successes achieved elsewhere, in the social and economic field. By growing rich through the manipulation of debts and counter-debts, by demonstrating a calculated generosity, by

Fig. 229 Armbands of an important man, with beads of European origin, purchased by Guiart in 1963.
Mèndu, south-west Malakula. Paris, Musée national des Arts d'Afrique et d'Océanie.

Fig. 230 Grade armbands with beads of European origin, collected by Speiser between 1910 and 1912.
Left: south-west Santo. Right: Gaua, Banks Islands. Basel, Museum für Völkerkunde.

but it is not necessarily something that goes without saying; in the last analysis, it depends on their personal qualities.

Furthermore, in traditional society, the grade system is not the only means of access to power: great warriors can also become big men; magicians and sorcerers can exercise a feared and respected hidden power; secret societies, which constitute the secret, magical counterpart of graded societies' public rituals, represent another road to power.

Each grade system, rather like the archipelago's languages, has its own characteristics and general characteristics common to all the others. The cultural chain pattern is found more or less everywhere; neighbouring regions in frequent contact transmit cultural elements to each other which, however, as they pass from one to another, are more and more likely to become differentiated and, sometimes, to be inverted.

There seems an obvious relationship between the *suque* of the Banks Islands (Codrington 1891, Vienne 1984), the *hungwe* of Ambae (Allen 1972,

Fig. 231
Ceremonial pigs about to be sacrificed or exchanged during a ritual. Large sese mats in the background. Central Pentecost.

GRADED SOCIETIES AND SOCIETIES BASED ON TITLE ▼ 203

Wooden and bamboo food knives from northern Vanuatu

Kirk W. Huffman

Fig. 232
Malo

Wooden and bamboo knives for food preparation, eating and other purposes were widespread throughout the whole of Vanuatu. In many areas of the country these rapidly disappeared with the introduction of white man's knives in the 19th century, but their use continued in certain areas – in some until the present day – either because of isolation, ritual significance of the traditional knives, or particular cultural attitudes to the meaning or use of foreign iron or steel. In some parts of the country even today it can be forbidden, or frowned upon, to, for example, use iron or steel knives in association with yam, or with certain types of taro, depending upon the local culture. In the southern islands, sharp bamboo knives were used for many purposes: on Aneityum there were called *nawu;* on Futuna and Aniwa, *mat'chira;* on Tanna, *nau* (all areas); on Erromango, *nao* (Sie language). These, however, mostly named from the term for bamboo, were the type most easily replaced by European metal, and the local language terms for the new European knives – or bush knives – reflected local and foreign attributes. Thus a metal knife on Aneityum became known as *nawu tonga* (as even the first white men seen on Aneityum were called *nupu tonga*); on Erromango, they became *nao itungo* ('bamboo, it comes from a long way' ('foreign')).

As one moves further north, although one still finds bamboo knives, wooden knives associated with food became more

Fig. 233
Big Bay, Santo

common; it is therefore common to find a different terminology for knives associated with food. In the Sa-speaking area of south Pentecost, the general term for knife is *ai,* but the special wooden type for breadfruit preparation is called *aït.* In north Ambrym the general term for knife is *ayi,* but the special wooden knife for cutting and serving *laplap* is *asi:* Daniel Hanghangkon (who died in 1982), of Magham, north Ambrym, carved several beautiful, highly decorated *asi* in the late 1970s.

Among the Big Nambas of north-west Malakula, the ordinary term for a wooden (and now metal) knife is *tali,* also *talei.* Fine bamboo knives, for food cutting and also for carving, are known as *tali lamu.* A special wooden knife, however, if used for cutting and eating the food of the powerful hereditary Big Nambas chiefs, would be called *taliet* or *taleiet,* and could have been decorated, though no examples survive. Among the neighbouring Batarnar, the common term for knife, *ni rind,* becomes *ni-sip* when referring to wooden knives for food. On Atchin, off north-east Malakula, the general term for knife is *ni-sip,* but the proper form for the wooden knife used for cutting food pudding (for example, *nalok*) is *kiki,* also *ne-kik.* The proper term for the special bamboo knife used for cutting and serving pudding (for example, *nalok palu'ulen*) is *ne-tsi,* (although the term *ne-sip* is now often used, but this is a 'borrowed' term that came to Atchin from Wala probably in the late 19th century). *Ne-tsi* can look almost exactly the same as *utus*, the small Atchin bamboo knife for cutting *waelken* (Bislama for a type of cane), but as the function is different, so can be the name. For the cutting and serving of special *laplap* or *nalot* (that is, pudding) in an Atchin men's sacred house (*amal/hamal*), however, a human thigh-bone knife (*pelok*) could be used, or specially carved wooden knives whose intricate handles could signify the user's rank status (either *mal* or *melteg*) or particular attributes. Enlarged versions of these wooden knives could also be used as ritual decoration in *naleng* dances, the blade being stuck into the wearer's *tsemtsem* (the leaf/fibre headdress worn in *naleng*), leaving only the carved handle to be seen sticking out as decoration. A fine example of one of these can be seen on the photograph opposite page 360 in Harrisson (1937); in this example, with its carved male figure handle, the knife would be called *kiki tsünöb*, or *ne-kik tsünöb*. There were sometimes projections (*boro'n*, 'ears') at the base of the blade. Similar variations on the style would have existed throughout the Small Islands off north-east Malakula.

From this area northwards, one begins to encounter more elaborate carving styles for these wooden food knives, particularly those for men of rank to be used in the men's houses. An example of a *simba* from Malo (fig. 232) has a carved hole, surrounded by fine dentate carving around this section's outer edge, in the portion separating the blade from the handle. The hole represents the *buru* (cooking oven) in the *rombu* (men's hut), the notched decorations (*gundugundu*) emphasising the importance of the *buru* and its food. The presence of only one hole, or fire, in the knife indicates the owner was probably of the first or lowest rank in the *sumbwea* (men's graded system in northern Malo), with rights to eat only from the lowest fire (terms in Auta language).

On Santo, carved wooden knives were more common in north-western Santo (for example, fig. 233).

Museum collections of these types of knives have tended to concentrate on the intricate examples from the Banks and Torres islands. Here design of handles was intimately linked with the owner's status in the *sukwe* (Banks) and *huka* (Torres) men's graded systems, where status was purchased by lengths of stringed shell-money (*nasum/nisim*) and pigs. Although there is much sharing of styles between the two areas, befitting the cultural links and ranking connections, those from the Torres tend to be longer (some

Figs 234, 235, 236, 237
Torres Islands

Fig. 238
Ureparapara

Fig. 239
Banks Islands

up to 65 centimetres) and thinner than those from the Banks (usually about 35 to 45 centimetres), and those with long, thin handles bordered with fine, geometrically-cut edges are only from the Torres (figs 234-237).

Many Banks knives, and some of the Torres ones, have a hole (figs 238, 239) or series of holes in the handle, representing the sacred fires or ovens inside the men's house (Banks: *gamal/gamel*; Torres: *g'mel/gomoi*), thus indicating the owner's rank. Others have the handle intricately cut out in a design based on the human figure, each section also representing a separate fire. In both styles, each section is separated by a carved ridge indicating the dividing barriers (of bamboo, wood or stone) separating each fire inside the hut. On Mota, these barriers are called *tingting i'av*. It is, difficult, however, to discern the owner's exact grade from looking at his knife: there is much variation in the ranking systems in the Banks, and some grades were 'doubled', in the sense that men of two different ranks could eat at the same fire. In general, however, the knives could not consist of more than eight or nine sections, because this was the maximum number of grades in the 'lower' *sukwe* before one reached the determining, or 'decisive', ninth or tenth grade, *nemel/nemwel/mele* (in Bislama *namele*, *Cycas circinnalis*), the major and first 'high' grade, beyond which few passed. The men's ranking system had mostly died out in the Banks by the early part of this century, the last rituals taking place just before World War II (although there are now plans in Vanuatu to revive it), social power shifting to the Church and to the *tamate* societies of the *salagoro,* so it is difficult to correlate now exact social status with the early knives in museum collections overseas. In general, however, the rule of thumb would be that the higher one's rank the more segments one would have on the handle of one's food knife (*nem' tema'a* on Mota Lava, *metegess* in parts of Vanua Lava).

Increasing complexity of handle design once one had reached *nemel* grade – or even those just below it – may mean, however, that in some areas one restarts the handle sections from one, with more complex human or spirit additions to the handle finial (fig. 240), as those of this grade and above ate on slightly raised stone platforms (in the men's hut), above those of lower rank. These men were the *tavus/mele* (Mota Lava), 'men who have hit, or killed, the *mele'*, of status like the northern Pentecost or east Ambae *rata higi*. On Mota, such high men were *wetuka* ('those who are close to, or have reached, the sky'). Handle designs by this step and above, could represent other ritual aspects of status, because by the time one made *nemel* grade, at least on Gaua, one may have had carved as many as ten large tree-fern *wotomaragae* male spirit figures for the ceremony, and (on Ureparapara) one had the right to wear a 'two-flap' (fore and aft) *malo saru* chest-covering for one's ritual. Aspects of these may be reflected in the handle design of one's knife; for example, a knife from Vanua Lava (illustrated in Speiser 1991, pl. 22, no. 15), whose handle consists solely of a solid spirit figure with the blade appearing from the head rather than from below the 'waist' or 'legs', as is more usual. The figure has big ears: this may tally with the rank (called on Mota) *k'p'woro k'p'woro lava* ('ear ear big'), which had an associated female spirit tree-fern

Fig. 240
Ureparapara

figure with big ears. This rank was the third rank above *nemel*. If the handle of the knife, then, does represent this female spirit, the carved waistband and 'hanging attachment' (?) may represent the typical Banks Islands woven female waist-strap, with the tassels tied and hanging in front, the normal position.

Thus it is interesting to speculate if the knife from Gaua (illustrated in fig. 241, length 35 cm) is linked with the following grade, the fourth after *nemel*, and called *womataloa* ('eyes of the sun') on Mota, which there had associated with it a (male but sexless) tree-fern carving with Janus faces and a long straight bust. The following grade, *welgan* (on Mota), had an associated male spirit tree-fern figure ('born' on Vanua Lava) of now unknown style, but the grade-taker had the right to wear a *malo saru* of four flaps (cf. fig. 244). The fifth grade after *nemel*, on Mota *wetaur o maligo* ('he who catches the clouds'), had an associated male spirit tree-fern figure holding a sphere above his head, with the stars, moon and sun painted on it. The last and highest (Mota) grade, *tikangwono*, had an associated female spirit tree-fern carving, and the grade-taker had the right to wear a *malo saru* with five flaps.

At this point, I may be thought to be digressing from the topic of food knives, but this is not the case. Such objects (like sand-writing or sand-drawings) do not exist in a cultural vacuum; they form part of an extremely sophisticated series of ritually connected links. As it was accepted practice in the Banks for a miniature of the grades associated spirit tree-fern figure to be carved on the top of the rank-taker's 'baton', and representations of it incised on the wearer's bamboo or cane ear-sticks (cf. fig. 259), it

seems possible that the same would pertain to the individual's eating knife. To make the situation more complex, one should consider the possibility that Banks Islands *tavine motar* ('women of distinction'), of high rank in the associated women's *sukwe*, would also have had their own wooden food knives and range of designs.

Many knives of those of highest rank may have been interred with their owners (who were buried in their *malo saru*), unless the owner, before death, had made (on Mota) *vatavata varvarnanao*, a verbal last will and testament to share out some of his worldly goods. But an *etvusmel* (Mota Lava, singular of *tavusmele*) does need eating equipment and spiritual food on his way to *panoi*, the world of the dead, so many of the most intricate knives would probably have followed that road. But examples may exist in the unstudied corners of museum collections overseas, so may I humbly request that Museum curators search their collections and send photos or sketches of the more intricate knives they may possess to the Vanuatu Cultural Centre? This will allow the Cultural Centre to photocopy and distribute these to northern Vanuatu to assist in revival of certain of these styles.

I dedicate this short and incomplete note to the people of the Banks and Torres, and particularly to Eli Field of Vanua Lava, Cultural Centre fieldworker and probably Vanuatu's most prolific woodenknife carver today, who has rescued many styles from oblivion.

Fig. 241
Gaua, Banks Islands

Fig. 242
Mage ne wurwur grade sculpture, collected by Guiart in 1963. Painted by Naïm Balbal, Neuha. Wilit, north Ambrym. Paris, Musée national des Arts d'Afrique et d'Océanie.

Bonnemaison 1972, W. Rodman 1973) and the *bololi* of southern Maewo and northern Pentecost. In this geographical area, traditional relations appear always to have been close; common cultural archetypes and sociological models can be traced from island to island and from place to place. When it comes to details, there are numerous local variants, but the essentials remain the same. These societies are organised into matrilineal moieties, whether these have an explicit name (as in Ambae, Pentecost and Maewo) or not (as in the Banks; Vienne 1984). Grade hierarchies coexist here with secret societies whose initiates alone control the world of magic and communications with the dead ancestors (*tamate*). Masks are the insignia, as it were, of an initiate. Lastly, the whole of this area shares myths referring to the same 'civilising heroes', the most important of whom is Tagaro or Tagar, creator of the night and the islands, and who is constantly invoked in rituals.

The area from the Torres to north Pentecost used to form a sort of Oceanic Mediterranean throughout which rituals and cultural innovations were constantly being transmitted. The prevailing grade system shows a similar structure underlying a myriad local particularities. The number of grades varies from ten to fifteen and for the highest, the number of pigs killed can be very great, more than a hundred animals for the highest ranks. The same dances are danced during all the rituals.

Essentially, the graded society in this part of Vanuatu takes the form, today at least, of a competition of an economic nature. The ritual seems to have grown away from what were probably its original religious and mythological sources. Its very complexity partakes more of ostentation and a quest for personal prestige than of a desire to participate in a sacred ritual. Thus emphasis on the individual and his personal qualities is what characterises the competition of the graded society in this area. The man of high grade is first of all someone who, to achieve his goals, has received help from the ancestors and the support of their magical power, but who nevertheless does not identify with them. To some extent he is a big man in the sense defined by Sahlins (1963): a man of weight and renown, rich and generous, whose influence reaches beyond his local group and who appears in the eyes of all as a hero as much as a political leader.

Another more heterogeneous cultural chain can be identified from south Santo (especially the coastal regions), Malo and Malakula to Ambrym and, in various forms, on into Paama and south Pentecost. There are more similarities between the Maki of the small islands off north Malakula (Layard 1942), the Nimangki (Deacon 1934b) of southern Malakula, and the Mage of Ambrym (fig. 242; Guiart 1951), than there are differences. The characteristic features of this geographical area are a patrilineal kinship system and the omnipresent slit-gongs, hollowed out of tree trunks and erected at dancing grounds. Similarly, the Pentecost Jump, or land-dive ritual, in which young men plunge from a high tower with their feet attached to vines, above a crowd of dancers and onlookers, is part of a first yam harvest ritual which was once to be found in Ambrym, in south-east Malakula and south Pentecost.

In this area of cultural continuity, grade-taking ceremonies are marked by more complex rituals which often reveal a feverish preoccupation with display. The religious aspect, particularly in south Malakula, is very marked. As he rises, the man of high grade becomes a supernatural being, hedged about with numerous tabus and kept carefully apart from the world of the 'living'. He takes his meals alone and lives in the sacred solitude which is the mark of his rank. In short, rather than a big man or a hero, the man of high grade here is a man who has joined the community of his ancestors; he no longer lives with men but is already in the company of the gods (fig. 243).

In the Seniang society of south-west Malakula, A.B. Deacon (1934b) counted thirty-two different grades, divided roughly into two classes: the first accessible to ordinary, 'common' men, the second reserved for men of power. To accede to the lower ranks, each grade-taker carves a statue in tree fern, symbolising his admission to the grade, which is then left on the dance ground. For the intermediate grades, the carving is surrounded by rows of small upright stones. Lastly, for the highest grades, tall stones are erected. 'The use of stones in the Nimangki seems to be of significance: it is always associated with taking the highest grades' (Deacon 1934b:273).

In this type of society, the carved tree-fern statues

Fig. 243 Once they have died, high-ranking men are represented in effigy. This consists of the overmodelled skull of the deceased, and a body made of vegetal elements. It bears the insignia of the man's rank. These *rambaramp* are kept in the men's house. Custom practised only in south Malakula. Paris, Musée national des Arts d'Afrique et d'Océanie.

The path of peace

In northern Ambae, the myth of origin of the Malauhi lineage explains the meaning of the graded society, or hungwe, and it is explicitly identified as a 'path of peace' enabling societies to overcome their divisions and internal quarrels, and to move on to a higher order and civilisation.

One day near Longana a man by the name of Gasinamoli made a strange discovery. In the heart of a tree called 'Malauhi', he found a boy child. The *malauhi* is a valuable tree with very hard wood which is used to make house posts and weapons. Gasinamoli brought up the child he had found and called him 'Garobani'; the child was as obstinate and tough as the wood of the tree in which he had been found.

As soon as he was grown up, Garobani became a formidable warrior. His delight in warfare knew no bounds, he provoked fights wherever he went and was responsible for the death of many adversaries. This fighting was troublesome to his father Gasinamoli who had recently entered the *hungwe* and was very active in the traditional trade in tusked pigs; the continual fighting prevented him from trading successfully. Neighbouring villages, fearful of Garobani, refused to have any dealings with him.

Gasinamoli asked his son to stop the fighting but his son said 'I have too many enemies now; I am no longer able to stop the wars I have started'.

Gasinamoli went to fetch a sacred stone he used as a pillow, which had been consecrated according to sacred rites. He told his son to break it and to take a piece of it and a *mambu* pig's tooth to every village where he had killed a man. Garobani set off on a long journey of peace throughout not only the territory of Longana, but also Lolopuepue and Lolovenue country. In every village he handed over the piece of stone which was to serve as the foundation of the new law of peace. This law was called '*Tamati vatu*', in other words, the 'stone of peace' and it was as solid as rock. Whoever offended against the law of stone risked instant death.

So peace was established over north-west Ambae and Garobani was able to devote himself to trading in pigs, *bisnes long pig* in Bislama. He was as fervent a seeker after riches as he had formerly been a warrior. He bought ritual ornaments and costumes and lent them for grade-taking ceremonies. In exchange he was given the mats and pigs with curved tusks which enabled him to prepare to take the highest grades himself and buy more ornaments. These included the multicoloured strings of beads or shells which he went to Malo to obtain and which were worn as bracelets on the arms and wrists or as anklets, the mats made of long red fibres which are worn around the waist and reach down to the ground, and the headdresses reserved only for men of the highest grades, which command a very high price and circulate from group to group and even from island to island.

Garobani very soon became a man of high rank; everyone honoured him and obeyed him; he lived in peace. One day he said to his father, 'The path of peace is better than the path of war; why didn't you tell me so before?' But Gasinamoli replied, 'Before it was as if you were mad, you were always running off and you thought of nothing but fighting; you would not have listened to me.'

Ever since, Garobani and his descendants have kept their word, and followed the law they set up. They have gone as far in the way of peace and trade as they had before in the way of war.

As told by Moses Gnere of Lolopuepue, north-east Ambae, in Bonnemaison 1986b, 1986c.

---

set up on a platform are also associated with the highest grades. It seems that here there was a mingling of the cultural tradition of tree-fern statues and that of stone monuments.

Early this century, it seems that the graded society model was not found everywhere in the northern islands. The anthropologist Speiser, who reached central Espiritu Santo in about 1910, states grade ceremonies were unknown to the mountain people there. In the varying complexity of graded societies, the fact that the institution took longer to reach some places than others, being entirely absent or existing only in rudimentary form in some particularly isolated inland groups, indicates that this form of power was still only in its infancy when Europeans first came to the archipelago.

From this, one may deduce that there used to be another social system, but one which it is difficult to reconstitute. When questioned on this point, most informants almost everywhere refer to the not very distant time before the introduction of the grade system in negative terms: before graded societies, fear, war and virtually perpetual 'barbarism' reigned; the people thought about nothing but slaughtering each other. Chiefs were the most feared warriors or the most powerful sorcerers; it was impossible in those days for anyone to travel or exchange goods at any distance from his home territory.

By creating a new hierarchy, grade-taking rituals and the pig exchange created a new order which prevented a war of all against all and the risk of deadly chaos inherent in war. They laid the foundations of a new society based on exchange and co-operation. From then on, men of high grade were 'pig chiefs' (*ratahigiboi*, in the north Ambae language), and not warrior chiefs: the social ethic now valued skill in negotiation and generosity in exchanges. When discussing the Banks Islands *suque* (fig. 244), Vienne (1984) points out that values of the graded society are in opposition to egalitarianism and individualism, insofar as it is the 'way of peace' as distinct from force, war and sorcery, which are ways of individual interest. This idea, according to which the graded society is an instrument of civilisation, an art, creator of peace and exchange within societies where previously there had been only war and famine, can also be found in various forms in most of the islands of Vanuatu.

Fig. 244
Malo saru garment, woven by men, marking one of the highest grades in the *suque* system. Ureparapara, Banks Islands.
Basel, Museum für Völkerkunde.

Fig. 245
Chief of Mele Island, wearing on his chest a symbol of chieftainship, with an armband, both signs of his status, photographed by Gaillard in 1887. South-west Efate.

Power through name

South of an imaginary line passing south of Malakula and through the south-east peninsula of Epi Island, power is no longer to be won through competitive grade-taking; it is 'received' at the same time as a custom name, which is a title forming part of a hierarchy of titles. The theoretical structure of power in this area is not linear, as in graded societies, but a pyramid. A highest title of 'chief' (fig. 245) crowns an ordered set of lower titles all owing allegiance to the chief.

Members of a local residence group hand down the same set of personal titles from generation to generation within the framework of kinship relations. In the Shepherd Islands, most titles nowadays are transmitted from father to son, usually the oldest son. According to individual cases, however, there are other ways of transmitting a title within the descent line or even, through adoption, outside it.

These ranked societies which predominate in the centre and south of the archipelago seem to be older than the grade systems. They are a variant of the general central Oceanian model. The social organisation into three 'classes', based on a chief, a sort of 'court' grouped around him and related to him by ties of personal allegiance, and a broader category of 'commoners', is reminiscent of the Polynesian model of Samoa and Tonga. In fact, the political structures of the central and southern islands seem to have received some cultural influences from the east, which were then readapted and diversified according to the modes of thought and cultural structures of the Melanesians.

If the oral traditions of the central islands are correct, the theoretical principles of the ranked society were introduced by Roy Mata, hero and legendary chief of Efate and surrounding islands. Roy Mata, according to this tradition, arrived with a fleet of canoes from north-east of Efate through Manuro Passage, and established his sway over the whole island. He set up a matrilineal kinship system with descent groups between whom warfare was declared impossible, installed the principal chiefs of the island and bestowed titles on them. These chiefs were bound to him personally by oaths of allegiance.

This arrival by canoe fits into what Garanger has described as the westward 'ebb' of some central Oceanian groups shortly after AD 1000. Other movements of this type have been recorded in the oral traditions of central and southern Vanuatu, particularly the small southern islands of Futuna and Aniwa off Tanna, which have a Polynesian language, and the oral tradition of which mentions ancient and sustained relations with a place they call Tongatapu. Roy Mata was, then, the most prestigious and successful of conquerors among the canoe people from the east. His 'royal' status seems to have died with him, but the system of personal allegiance symbolised by the hierarchy of titles still remains.

Ranked societies can also exhibit the same pattern of a chain of places along which there occurs a progressive differentiation of sociocultural systems originating at a single source, and of a single cultural model. There are, in fact, numerous local variants. The central islands (Efate, the Shepherds, and southern Epi) form a single cultural and sociological universe, but it cannot be described as uniform throughout. The five southern islands (Erromango, Tanna, Aneityum, Aniwa and Futuna) also form a cultural world of their own, and the influence of the ranked society is found here too, but in considerably altered form.

In Tongoa (in the Shepherd Islands), local society is divided into the commoner class (*nare*), and the noble class (*wotalam*), but in reality this produces a three-tier arrangement not unlike the graded societies. On the lowest level of domestic households, nuclear families and the smallest territorial units is the title of *nare*. A number of *nare*, by forming alliances based on common residence, group themselves together in a *varea* (dancing ground) or a *kamal* (men's house; see fig. 246). In other words, they form a political group dominated by a middle-ranking title, a small local group of a few dozen people at the most, a hamlet. These *varea* are, in fact, segments of patriclans consisting of a few closely related families.

The intermediate rank, where a first level of power comes into play, is made up of the *varea* chiefs; these men are already 'nobles', masters of a certain share of the political arena. Some of them are considered *wotalam* in the full sense of the word.

The *wotalam* are the 'big chiefs', who bring several local groups under their political authority together in a larger territorial framework. In other words, several small local groups come together through their common allegiance to a big *wotalam*, or *wotalam mata*, to form a broader local group whose power transcends immediate bonds of locality and kinship.

The geographical area of ranked societies corresponds to an organisation of space which brings out a definite territorial structure. In such societies, the islands are divided into political territories arranged in strips running from the shoreline towards the central spine. In the central and southern islands, everything points to the existence of stronger organisations, a more firmly asserted control of society and territory, at least in principle.

In ranked societies, political rankings and bonds of allegiance have a territorial dimension. When he takes a title, a man also takes a place or network of places, a 'road' which confers rights and obligations; conversely, the social status incorporates a territorial identity embodied in certain clearly defined places and pieces of land taken as a whole. This is undoubtedly the outstanding structural feature which distinguishes graded societies from ranked societies. While grades form a purely social hierarchy which rises upwards into the heavens, so to speak, and has no formal connection with the system of land tenure, titles form a social hierarchy which spreads horizontally in space and is rooted in the territorial earth. In the central and southern islands, there can be no title which is not also a gateway into a piece of land, a social place and a horizon full of alliances.

Because a title refers to a place of origin which is itself part of a chain of places of origin within a political territory, it represents the inheritance of land. Social identity merges into geographical identity and this limits social mobility; the social order is fixed by the prior order of places which reproduces it exactly as it stands from generation to generation. Looked at from this point of view, territorial organisation reflects social organisation: each parcel of land or piece of space is one element in a fixed structure taking a title as its reference. Conversely, each title refers to a space – in practice, to several. Thus it is impossible to read the social structure other than as part of the structure of land tenure.

Those who possess the land are the *nare*, commoners; that is to say, those who work it. The 'big chiefs' only exercise their power through the system

Fig. 246
Men's house in the shape of an upturned canoe, photographed by W. A. Lucas in 1899.
Ifira Island off south Efate.

Fig. 247
Man returning from garden, carrying his tool for digging holes for planting taro. Interior, south-west Tanna.

of political relations. They do not own the land any more than they distribute or control land tenure. Control of land, divided in an egalitarian way between group members and sometimes even in inverse relation to political status, places a de facto limit on the big men's power. It is as if this limit, which the carefully maintained dispersal of holdings further reinforces, has been consciously sought after and desired by the society as a whole.

The traditional tangle of land-holdings is such, in fact, as to make it impossible to put together a large domain, thus making any war of territorial conquest pointless. Land was the material support of cultural identity, the ground to which descent lines were anchored, and the economic space which ensured household autonomy and survival, but it could not, at least in principle, become the object of power relations. In this way, ranked societies also define themselves as 'paths of peace'; their response to the dilemma of peace and war is not to prohibit war, but to banish and confine it outside 'land', that is to say outside the cultural, emotional and physical sphere where rootedness, human survival and freedom are played out.

The festivals instituting titles play the same role as does grade-taking further north. They used also to be the occasion of complex, ostentatious exchange ceremonies in which networks of debt and counter-debt were woven. As in the north, the scale and grandeur of the rituals vary according to the importance of the title. For the highest, men with high-ranking titles from all over the island travel to take a personal part in conferring the title. In this way they show their approval, and several of them will place their hands on the head of the new chief. In these cases the festivities are equal in complexity, in the number of participants to be fed and in the abundance of the gifts which must one day be reciprocated, to the higher grade-taking rituals in northern societies. Dozens and dozens of valuable pigs are sacrificed, while several years of preparation are needed to accumulate the wealth and food which will be exchanged and consumed by the allied groups.

When a young man acquires a title at the *nahel-nale* ceremony, his father, biological or otherwise, who holds the title he is going to transmit to him, officiates with the *wotalam*, head of the men's house and of the original canoe he is attached to, sometimes accompanied by other *wotalam*. By laying on his hands, the *wotalam* proclaims himself in the eyes of all to be the 'lord' of the man he is elevating. In return, the man who is thus acquiring the title acknowledges himself to be the 'subject' (*nakainanga*) of the first. At regular intervals he will pay him the *nasotonga*, a gift consisting of valuable pigs, to which the chief will respond with a symbolic counter-gift of a small pig of lesser value. Every year the subject will also plant in his garden a crop of ceremonial yams and vegetables (*novaka ariki*) for his chief, which will be taken directly to the latter's personal store.

This theoretical scheme is complicated by criss-crossing allegiances and trans-territorial relations.

Most titles, in fact, allow of several allegiance relationships both within and beyond the territory where the title-holder lives. Often the social position of a man varies according to the direction in which he turns. He will pay a gift to the east, but will receive one from the west; he will be subject and chief in turn. The allegiances binding titles one to another, not only within an island but also beyond it, from southern Epi to the island of Efate, thus becomes an extraordinarily complex web of relationships whose threads cross and cross again without end. Each of these relations perpetuates an alliance stretching like a road over land or sea, along which wives and ceremonial goods can travel. Here again the principle whereby power is exercised through the control of routes is revealed; the higher the title, the further the geographical relationships extend.

These complex allegiances are recorded in myth. The canoes which left Efate on their colonising adventure arrived in scattered groups; most of them found already settled groups along their route, with whom they negotiated the payment of tribute or dues entitling them to pass, which recognised the prior status of those who had arrived first.

A title embodies the sum of all relations created in the course of its history over the routes it has followed, and some are an asset, others a disadvantage. The man who assumes a title, from one generation to another, must take on all these relations in his turn. He is thus caught in a web of allegiance and lordship which stretches beyond his territory, his island and sometimes even his memory. But there is always someone to remind him of his distant obligations and nothing is lost or forgotten. The islands are living records.

A structurally similar social system is found in the five southern islands of Vanuatu, with titles distributed in space, each of which refers to clusters of places, to land-holdings and to a social status. The man without a title is a man without true traditional power.

On Tanna, the myth of the canoe reveals the metaphors of social organisation. Each local group is categorised as part of a canoe, or *niko*, which in turn refers to a territory and a 'stock' of titles. At the prow of the canoe is its emblem, or *yremera*, the man who, in rituals, has the privilege of wearing the headdress of sparrowhawk feathers. In his person he

Stamba rod
The Founding Voyage

When the people of Efate saw that grass was beginning to grow again on the ashes of Kuwai volcano, and it was starting to be covered by a bush called Tongoa, which gave its name to the island, they decided to resettle it. Over a period of time a series of small groups set off, to arrive at the spot where they are now settled after complex adventures and wanderings. Each of the present-day *varea*, or dancing grounds, of Tongoa thus has its origin in a precise place on Efate whence it set out on a voyage of territorial conquest, all the significant details of which have been recorded in the founding story. The dancing ground has its origin in a canoe which has a name, an internal organisation, traditions, a symbolic emblem, magic powers, a chief and a helmsman. The myth records the places where the canoe called on its voyage, the landing on Tongoa, the wanderings through the island, which was either already inhabited or in the process of being settled by other canoes, and last of all the final settlement in one place and the creation of the first territory. Each dancing ground's tradition recalls the route the canoe followed and perpetuates it in the form of alliances.

The place where a group has now put down roots – in a *gamal*, or common men's house – near a *varea*, or dancing ground, is thus the destination of a journey which, however, is not necessarily over yet. Around the men's house, the territory is laid out, and each of its land-holdings is connected with one of ranks of the men in the canoe which made the founding voyage. Consequently, each local group reproduces on land the society formed for the sea voyage; its true territory, far more than the present site of settlement, merges into the route the canoe followed and the various alliances formed at that time.

Fig. 248
Setting reed climbing supports in place on a yam mound in a garden in south-west Tanna.

Fig. 249
Tapa belt with triangular motifs in black and red (*tut meta*). Belts symbolise political power. The black belt (*tut apen*) is worn by the masters of the heavens (*iremera*), the red and black belt by the masters of the canoes (*yani niko*). The one who wears the belt 'pulls the men behind him'. The triangular motifs seem linked to the skin of the snake, a magical being associated with the hero Tangalua, who is also known as Tangarua or Tagaro on many other islands of Oceania.

sums up the group's honour, but his power is founded more on prestige and display than on political authority properly so-called. In the stern of the canoe sits the helmsman, who sets and holds the course. He is the *yani niko*, or 'voice of the canoe', who commands in the name of the 'lord', seated in the bow. His hidden power is often the stronger. Last, in the middle of the canoe, is the agrarian magician, or *naotupunus*, who, through his work in the gardens and his magical filiation with the Polynesian god of food, Mwatiktiki, feeds the other two. The *naotupunus* is also referred to as the 'belly' of the canoe. All titles on Tanna refer back to one of the three functions of Tannese society, which situates them in a hierarchical relationship *vis-à-vis* traditional social organisation (figs 247, 248). Of the three functions, that of 'the voice of the canoe' (*yani niko*) is politically the most essential, since he assumes traditional control of land tenure and guardianship of the territory. *Yani niko* clans (fig. 249) are male clans, while middle, or *naotupunus*, clans have symbolic female status. The importance of the last of these, however, is just as vital as the two others: they are the masters of fertility, they control and reproduce life.

This simple account gives some idea of the cultural richness of the islands of Vanuatu. The variety of forms of political power engenders the diversity of artistic and ritual forms which accompany them. Each island claims to be unique, different, the master of its own power and customs. Each local group guards its traditional heritage jealously and keeps watch to make sure nobody copies it without their knowledge, whether it is a type of mask, a style of carving, the design of a woven mat, a dance or a song, or the specific ways of achieving status by taking grades or of conferring titles. This gives rise to a profusion of cultural forms, a rainbow which makes Vanuatu what may be a unique place of artistic creation.

Traditional Housing and Architecture of Vanuatu

Christian Coiffier

The people of the various islands of Vanuatu live in a wide variety of housing. Villages comprise small family groups of a few dozen people grouped together in hamlets and bound by a network of trading and marriage relationships. Each hamlet has its own characteristics depending both on geographical situation and the local social structures. Until recently this kind of housing arrangement was still the norm throughout almost all of Melanesia. That diversity is now giving way to a general standardisation. Colonisation and Christianisation brought new designs, hand in hand with new ways of life. A distinction must also be made between coastal villages whose present economy is based on coconut plantations, and mountain bush villages with an economy based entirely on bush-clearing and gardening. In mountainous islands, villages are built on the plateaux or cling to the slopes. In Santo, there are villages (fig. 250) up to altitudes of almost 300 metres (Aubert de la Rüe 1945:117). For the last century, inland populations have tended to migrate to the coastal zones.

Hamlets usually consist of a few dozen houses gathered around a dancing ground where, especially in the northern islands, stands a set of large slit-gongs. The dancing ground is often surrounded by big banyan trees, as in Tanna (Bonnemaison 1986b, 1986c). In the northern islands, the men's meeting house, or *nakamal* in Bislama, often stands near the dancing ground, surrounded by a fence of stakes and various plants (cordyline, croton, cycad), and sometimes by low stone walls. Family dwellings with their small gardens are also fenced to prevent pigs destroying the root crops. There is a very distinct opposition between private, individual, feminine space and the public, collective, masculine space of men's houses. Most buildings in Vanuatu are built directly onto the ground according to a rectangular plan, with a double-sloping roof. In the northern islands and Malakula, we find buildings raised on piles, usually for storing root vegetables. All these buildings are relatively low, so space inside is limited. They are subdivided by woven partitions to separate the two sexes, when they live together. Mats are spread on the beaten earth floor and furnishings are rather rudimentary. Doorways are usually low and further reduced by a threshold to prevent pigs from getting in. Houses are frequently windowless. Many utilitarian or ritual objects are kept in the roof, on shelves or stuck into the thatch.

As in Melanesia as a whole, many varieties of plant materials are everywhere in evidence: banyan roots, split bamboo, areca-palm and tree-fern stems. In the north, roofs are usually made out of sago-palm leaves, *natangura* (fig. 251), while in the south, coconut leaves and reeds are used. In the past, stones were also used on many islands, as on Nguna, where villages had defences made of enormous blocks of lava (Aubert de la Rüe 1945:121). The construction of a family or communal house involves all or some of the rest of the village community. The division of labour is according to sex, age and the social hierarchy.

The types of architecture in Vanuatu can be classified into three distinct categories, corresponding to geographical areas (Coiffier 1988). The northern type (Torres, Banks, Santo, Ambae, Maewo, and northern Pentecost) is characterised by buildings in the form of a hall with a double, slightly sloped roof coming down almost to the ground. In the central islands (Malakula, Ambrym, and central and southern Pentecost), houses have a rounded 'apse' at either end, while the southern type of building (in Efate, the Shepherds, Tanna, and Aneityum) is oblong with a ribbed roof coming down to ground level. Hybrid forms combine the three types, sometimes with outside influences.

The northern islands

Housing in these islands has changed considerably in the past century, but it cannot be examined apart from the still-current political organisation of the graded societies: *suque* in the Banks Islands, *hungwe* on Ambae and *bolololi* in southern Maewo (cf. Bonnemaison, this volume). The originality of the traditional architecture of the northern islands lies in the use of stones as building materials. This technique used to be found in Polynesia, in the construction of the *marae*, as well as in Micronesia, in Palau, Yap and Guam. Buildings were usually constructed on broad platforms made of blocks of coral or volcanic rock. They followed a grid pattern in which the men's house was placed at right angles to the family dwellings, with low walls and stake fences surrounding the villages. In mountainous areas, houses were built on piles sunk into stone platforms (fig. 252). On Vanua Lava, some houses had real foundation walls.

Each village had one or two *nakamals* placed side by side. They were divided up by means of bamboo poles laid on the ground to form as many

Fig. 250
House in mountain area. Interior of Santo.

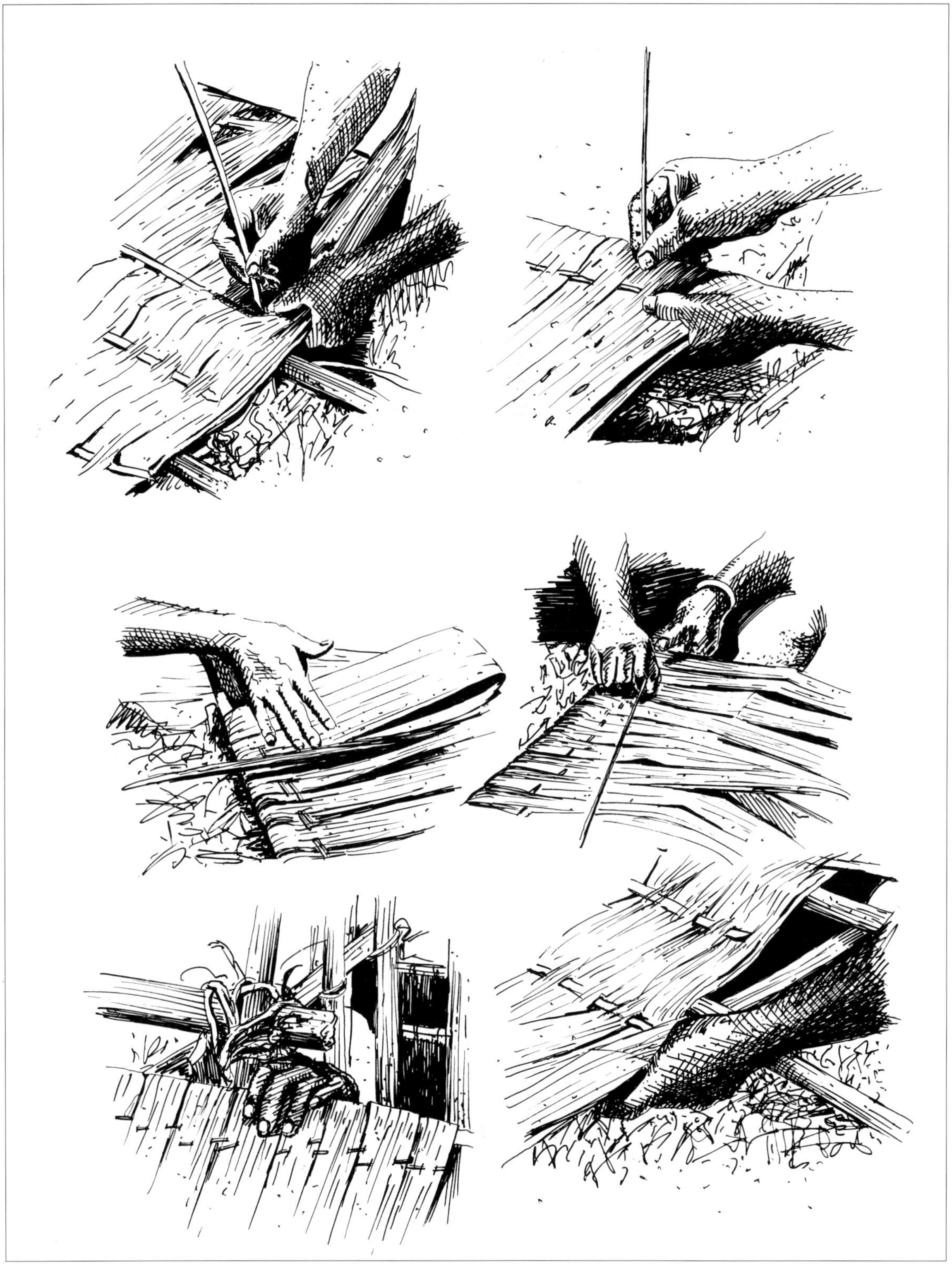

Fig. 251
Roof construction methods for traditional houses.

Fig. 252
Upright post of a men's house with carved beam at end. Collected by Speiser between 1910 and 1912.
Tolomako, north-west Santo.
Basel, Museum für Völkerkunde.

compartments as there were grades (fig. 253). Some of them were very large: the *nakamal* in the Santo village of Nedjets was 56 metres long (Speiser 1991, pl. 10, no. 5). The side posts were sometimes fixed on a slant (Guiart 1958:27; Speiser 1991, pl. 13, no. 8), as in the ceremonial houses of the Kwoma and the Ngala of the Sepik Valley in Papua New Guinea (Hauser-Schaublin 1989, figs 175-181).

Family houses were divided crosswise into a sleeping space and a cooking space, in which the hearth, surrounded by large stones, held great symbolic importance. There was a door in each gable, the masculine end facing the dancing ground and the feminine end facing the bush. There were also special buildings serving as kitchens and food stores. The length of a house depended on the social status of the owner and could be extended when necessary. A man of high grade had his own house in which he lived with his several wives and their children. Women had to live apart in special small huts when menstruating.

Some houses of woven materials, of which the average size was 10 by 4 by 3 metres, were in the shape of an overturned canoe (fig. 254; Speiser 1991, pl. 12, no. 8, and pl. 18, no. 2). The frame was tied with strips of bark or woven coconut fibre prepared by the women (Vienne 1984). The walls were made out of split bamboo and the double-sloping roof covered with 1.2 by 0.7 metre 'tiles' made of a layer of three or four sago-palm leaflets placed one on top of the other. Banyan roots were used as ridgepoles or beams, and bamboo for the rafters (Torres Islands). Ridgepoles were covered with bunches of grass bent over a reed and held in place by heavy branches. In times gone by, roofs went down practically to ground level (Vienne 1984:140).

Malakula and Pentecost

There are very obvious differences between the social structures of northern and southern Malakula. In all the communities of this large island, however, segregation of sexes is strictly observed. Male society is divided into a number of hierarchical groups, each with its corresponding privileges and tabus marking its prestige. Men of different grades cannot eat together, nor sit or sleep side by side. The taking of each grade involves special rituals during which wooden carvings and stone monuments are erected and various plants planted. The higher in the social hierarchy a man goes, the greater his prestige and authority in his village, but he also finds himself under an obligation to redistribute the wealth he acquires. When a man of high grade grows old, the power of his magic and the tabus with which he is surrounded often oblige him to live like a recluse in a house apart from the rest of the community (cf. Bonnemaison 1986b, 1986c).

Villages are situated on high ground and usually consist of several hamlets, each defining itself in relation to its men's house, which embodies a clan's prestige. It is the place where men meet to drink kava (*Piper methysticum*), and, inside, it is divided into as many compartments as there are grade levels in the society. The largeness of the men's house at Vao (fig. 255; 25 by 7 by 5 metres) required a dozen central posts (Layard 1942:441; Speiser 1991, pl. 15, no. 1). In southern Malakula the men's house was built on an anthropomorphic model: the central post at the front was masculine, and the one at the back feminine (Deacon 1934b:33-34).

A hamlet is made up of three distinct spaces: the central dancing ground (figs 256, 257); the men's house (*gamal*), forbidden to women and uncircumcised children; and family dwellings scattered around the perimeter. Beyond the village, there are gardens with woven reed fences forming a maze of little alleys. Large hamlets may have two parallel *gamals* standing side by side, always built on the highest ground. Each family has several buildings, including a storehouse of woven reeds for root crops. Pigs are sometimes kept in the rear portion of the dwelling house. A household's group of buildings is sometimes enclosed by hedges of plants and little walls of coral blocks (as in the islands of the northeast). On Vao, the men's path goes through the dancing grounds, whereas the women's path studiously avoids them. (Layard 1942:69). This peculiarity is also found in the Sepik villages of Papua (Coiffier 1982). Slit-gongs carved with human faces sometimes stand in the middle of the dancing ground, surrounded by a large number of upright stones.

Building a house involves the collaboration of related clans and many distributions of food at various stages of the work. It is done under the direction of

Fig. 253

Fig. 254

Fig. 253
Interior of a men's house, with slit-drum in foreground, photographed by Speiser between 1910 and 1912.
West Santo.

Fig. 254
Two dwelling houses, the one on the right on a stone platform, photographed by Speiser between 1910 and 1912.
Ureparapara, Banks Islands.

Fig. 255

Fig. 256

Fig. 255
Men's house, *gamal*, with rack for pigs' jaws, large stone as ceremonial seat, and hawk as roof-peak carving. Photographed by Speiser between 1910 and 1912. Peterhul, Vao, north-east Malakula.

Fig. 256
Dancing ground with low stone wall and small ceremonial houses to shelter pigs destined for grade ceremonies. Photographed by Speiser between 1910 and 1912. Atchin Island, north-east Malakula

the elders, who decide how big it will be. The men fell and prepare the trees of various species to be used for pillars and beams, and bamboos for the frame. The women make do with plaiting coconut leaves for the walls. The roof is covered with overlapping 'tiles'. These 'tiles' are made of sago leaflets one on top of the other, folded back lengthwise over reeds. The leaflets are kept folded by bamboo pegs. Ties are made of vines or coconut fibre, and vines are also used to take measurements. The pillars and lengthwise partitions are put up first to mark the dimensions of the building. When a ridge carving is finally placed on the end of the ridgepole, the structure is finished. In northern Malakula, this carving (*ponarat*; fig. 258) is made out of a tree-fern stem. In the north-east, on Vao, a sparrowhawk with spread wings would be carved out of a tree root. Formerly, a new men's house would only acquire real prestige after ancestral skulls and pigs' jawbones had been placed in the rear part.

When the yams are ready to harvest, the people of southern Pentecost build a tall tower out of logs tied together by vines and attached solidly to neighbouring tree trunks. The structure has a roughly square section 3.5 metres along each side and is up to 25 metres tall. Platforms are built at about fifteen different levels, representing the parts of the human body that the tower suggests (Muller 1971:227). The men climb up to the platforms with vines firmly tied around their ankles. They attach the other end of the vines to the platform, and throw themselves headfirst into the void until the fully stretched vines break their fall. They are then feted by the whole village. This 'Pentecost Jump' is connected to a local myth about the fertility of the yams.

The boldness of this ephemeral architecture recalls the technical prowess of both the Kanaks of New Caledonia in building their great huts (Boulay 1990), and the Papuans in the construction of their great ceremonial houses (Coiffier 1982; Hauser-Schaublin 1989).

The Shepherd Islands

The spatial organisation of housing reflects the local social organisation, based on the ownership of political and land-holding titles (Bonnemaison, in this volume). Individuals thus find themselves grouped, according to the extent of their rights, under the authority of chiefs who possess the biggest share of those rights (Espirat et al. 1973, and cf. Bonnemaison, this volume).

A village may consist of several groups, each with its own men's house (*varea* or *gamali*) used as an official house for a chief and his male dignitaries. These houses are distinguished by their size, larger than family houses, *na suma*. There used to be three types: the *na gamali na toka*, supported only by side pillars; the *na gamali na mangui*, with a ridgepole resting on a row of central pillars; and the *na gamali na mangui raru*, with two rows of central pillars forming a portico (Hébert 1963-1965a). A bird with outstretched wings, carved out of wood and painted, was placed at the end of the ridgepole above the thatch, symbolising the spirit of the chief watching over the village. Unlike dwelling houses, the opening on the leeward side was much wider, and could sometimes occupy half the perimeter of the building. Formerly, sets of big slit-gongs stood on the dancing ground next to each *varea*.

The design of these houses, sometimes called 'hurricane houses', is one of the most original forms of Pacific Islands architecture, principally for their remarkable adaptation to climatic extremes of wind, rain and heat. They are built on an elliptic plan and have an ogival shape, like that of an overturned canoe. In fact, they consist only of a roof placed directly on the ground, which does offer less resistance to the force of the most violent cyclones. This shape is obtained by sinking posts into the ground opposite each other, then bending them and crossing the ends to hold up the ridgepole. Similar sorts of architecture were formerly widespread in other islands to the south (Efate, Tanna (fig. 259), Aneityum, and Futuna). Big men's houses do not exist on Tanna, where the men meet to drink kava in the evening on the dancing ground itself (called *y imwayim*; Guiart 1956c; Bonnemaison 1986b, 1986c). Traditional low dwelling houses of the 'anti-hurricane' type (figs 260-263) are, however, built here along the same lines as those in the Shepherds.

A new communal building is put up when a new chief is named or when a new village is established. From southern Melanesia to Polynesia, each village has its specialised carpenters (*na mataesau*) who know the building techniques. First the ground is cleared and levelled, then tree trunks are dragged to the construction site by the whole village, singing ritual songs. There is a correlation between the technical function of the various elements of the building and the social rank of the individuals responsible for preparing and putting those elements in place. The most important men supply and put up the main pillars, while less important components are prepared and assembled by the others. 'Vassals' of lesser importance look after building the roof, but it is the chief who supplies the ridgepole.

Fig. 257
Posts with faces of ancestor spirits, used to support the hawk carving and the roofs of small ceremonial houses to shelter grade pigs. Atchin Island, north-east Malakula
Paris, Musée national des Arts d'Afrique et d'Océanie.

Fig. 258
Ponarat (p'naret). Fern-tree sculpture representing the face of the founder of the *nakamal* in the old village of Tenmaru. Drawing by Evelyn Cheesman, 1929.
Big Nambas, north-west Malakula.

The women help prepare certain materials, and meals for the workers. In the island of Erromango the women also used to have their own meeting houses, equal in size to those of the men (Aubert de la Rüe 1945:126).

Many species of plant are used in the construction of the big meeting houses: pandanus for the main pillars, *Terminalia* sp. for lintels, breadfruit for ridgepoles, areca-palm slats for the roof frame. The thatch is made of tall reeds, and the ridge of very close weaving.

As in many parts of Oceania, these big meeting houses mark the unity of the community and the power of its dignitaries. They can attain a great size, more than 25 metres in length, 10 metres in width and sometimes more than 5 metres in height.

Prospects

Vanuatu's economic development since independence in 1980 has enabled new settlement sites to

Fig. 259
Family cyclone-house, photographed by Speiser in 1912.
Tanna.

224 ▼ THE ART OF POWER

Fig. 260

Fig. 261

Fig. 262

Fig. 263

Fig. 260
Traditional house. Shepherd Islands.

Fig. 261
Low traditional house under construction. Tanna.

Fig. 262
Reed roof structure. Tanna.

Fig. 263
Family dwelling. Whitesands, Tanna.

be opened up and sometimes caused old villages to move. Changes in ways of thinking and ways of life have led to rapid changes in styles of building and choice of materials. The use of corrugated iron and concrete, however, has not always brought the expected comfort to ordinary people's housing, nor are the new materials always very beautiful. Perhaps the recent development of tourism in the region will give new life to Vanuatu's traditional architecture.

Plates and bowls from northern and central Vanuatu

Kirk W. Huffman

From Efate northwards through Vanuatu, wooden plates and dishes of many forms were, and in some areas still are, produced and used in stages of the preparation and eating of various types of puddings and vegetable-leaf foods. Large elongated troughs, sometimes from 3 to 5 metres in length, were at one time found on, for example, Nguna and Leleppa and used for communal feasts. The commonest form of wooden dish or bowl in the Tongoa-Shepherds-north Efate region is an ovoid type with pointed ends and finial designs that are a conventionalised representation of a turtle: some of these can be quite small, with sizes ranging to nearly 2 metres in length. A few carvers in the Shepherds region retain the knowledge of the carving of a particular style of oblong wooden dish, said to be reserved for human meat, that has carved representations, on either end of the dish, of the vines used to tie the victim's wrists and ankles.

On Ambrym today, one finds large oblong or round wooden plates, sometimes with short legs or 'feet', used for food preparation. These plates, often for the beating and preparation of breadfruit, taro, and so on, could sometimes possess beautifully carved undersides (see one such example from west Ambrym in Guiart 1963a:240, fig. 220). Large round wooden dishes, called *siye* in north Ambrym, were and are of similar use, and intricately carved undersides could indicate that they are *siye kon* ('plate tabu'), for use by those men of rank in the *maghe* (male graded system) there. Besides food use, large wooden *siye* can also be used as a form of musical instrument, as in the north Ambrym *urundengdeng* dance (for example, during *maghe* rituals). For this, a hole is dug in the dancing ground (*ranhara*), which is covered with the wooden *siye* plate, the latter is then in turn lightly covered with earth. This resonator is then pounded with wooden or bamboo poles to provide the rhythm for the *urundengdeng* dance. In north Ambrym, when the plate is used in this way it is known as *si bepwe*

('plate sleeps' or 'lies down'). Use of such wooden 'sound platforms' is also known from south-east Malakula, but is much more common in the areas of Santo-Malo (figs 264-267) and the Banks Islands (see fig. 188 in Crowe, this volume, showing Speiser photo (F)Vb 1986, as in Speiser 1991, pl. 105, no. 5, showing Ureparapara men pounding a sounding board).

Flattish rectangular or ovoid 'legged' plates of lightwood are found in Ambrym (for example, Speiser collection, Vb 4318, l. 48 cm, as in Speiser 1991, pl. 25, no. 2) and also in southern Pentecost. The similar plate (Basel Vb 4321, l. 75 cm) collected by Speiser (1991, pl. 25, no. 3; fig. 268, this volume) in 1911, and which he says is from 'northern Pentecost', was probably collected in southern Pentecost, as his collecting trip at that time took him only from Banmatmat in south-south-west Pentecost, on a roundabout route as far north as Bwatnapne (on the northern fringes of the Apma-speaking area) and back. Such 'table plates' are still in use in southern Pentecost, particularly in the non-missionised areas of Bunlap, Lobwe, Pohodur and Sankar in the south-east. Here a man will sit with the plate lengthwise in front of him at waist level, pounding or scraping breadfruit (or taro) so that it covers the plate in a flat layer. Coconut milk, heated in a small, deep wooden bowl or a larger coconut shell, *belaül nawat* ('coconut shell stone'), by putting a hot stone into the fluid, is then poured over the pudding. This pudding is scooped into green bamboo tubes for cooking. Other round, thick and deep, small wooden bowls (usually around 25 to 35 centimetres wide) from southern Pentecost may be confused with food bowls, but are actually canoe bailers, *minmin* ('drink drink'), and as such usually have an interior wooden handle.

Wooden ovoid or rectangular plates, some in the form of a conventionalised turtle, some with conventionalised pig's-tusk finials (see Speiser 1991, pl. 25, no. 1, Vb 4317, from Vao) were found throughout the Small Islands off north-

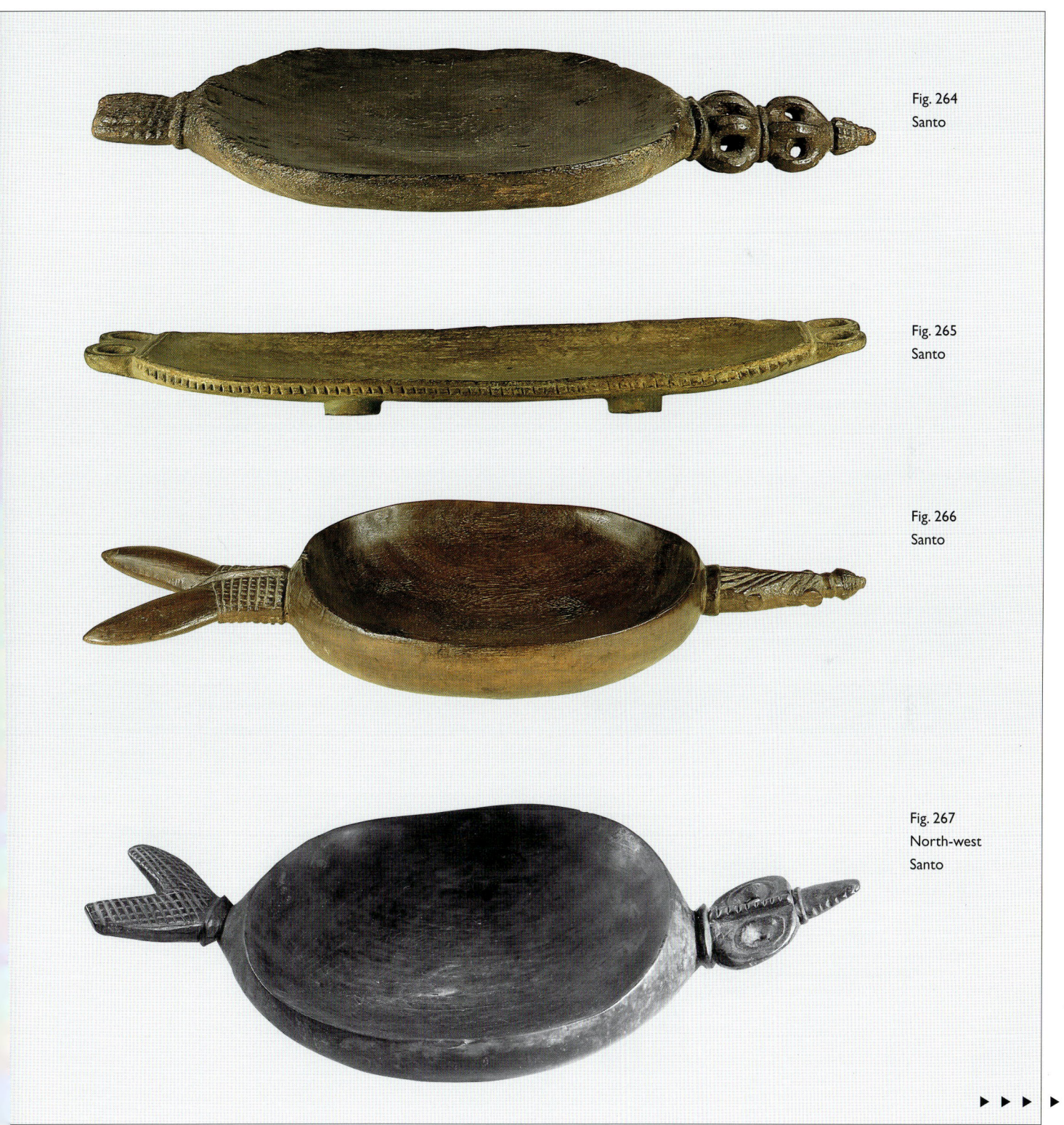

Fig. 264
Santo

Fig. 265
Santo

Fig. 266
Santo

Fig. 267
North-west
Santo

PLATES AND BOWLS FROM NORTHERN AND CENTRAL VANUATU

east Malakula. On Vao these are called *röv,* on Atchin *röw* (but also *röv*), and on Wala *row*. Since the late 1960s, there has been a resurgence of the carving of superbly finished wooden plates, particularly on Vao. Some of these have recently taken the form of the early stone kava 'bowls' (based on the form of an intersex pig), known on Vao as *navat ma malokh mbo narav,* and on Atchin as *ni wat na malo buha ratsin*. In the Big Nambas area of north-west Malakula, wooden kava 'troughs', in the form of a small, sharply keeled canoe with pointed truncated ends, were originally used, and called *nawak na maleh* ('the canoe for the kava'), but these have long since disappeared, to be replaced by the shaped palm spathe (*nas'r'uh*). This reference, among the Big Nambas who traditionally had no canoes but had rafts for short voyages, to a link in shape between canoe and plate is of great interest.

Wooden pudding plates (singular, *rova*) from Malo were of many and varied forms – those for household use often in the conventionalised form of a turtle, *rova avua,* with protruding 'flippers', or slightly more intricate forms for use by men of varying status in the men's house, *rombu*. Dentate patterns (*gundugundu*) around the edges of these plates (as in Basel collection, Vb 4315, l. 53 cm; see Speiser 1991, pl. 24, no. 12) emphasised the importance of the food. The headed, wooden, 'legged' plate (fig. 270; Basel collection, Vb 4323, l. 72 cm), collected by Speiser on Ambae, is very much of the Malo style, linked to the ranking system, and it may therefore be from a culturally related area of Ambae or from Malo, although the Malo plates tended to have a longer neck, *hali*, for the face, *naho*. On Malo, the first food from the plate was placed in the mouth of the spirit face (fig. 269; Malo plate from MAAO, Cat. 63.8.2).

Some of the largest plates for the pudding called *nalot* in Bislama are found in various areas of Santo, even in the interior, and are still widely used. Groups of men will squat around the large plates pounding the scraped taro, breadfruit, banana, or whatever the *nalot* pudding is to be made from. At Wusi, on the west coast of Santo, such plates are called *ropa* (singular); the most highly decorated plates come from north-west Santo around the Cape Cumberland peninsula. One such beautiful example is that collected by Speiser in the latter area in 1910 (fig. 271; Basel, Vb 4309, l. 8 cm), with the bulbous dentate carvings typical of the area (as in the men's house posts, collected by Speiser near Talamako; Basel, Vb 4743). I do not know what this decoration represents: a friend from Nguna, looking at a photograph of a similar plate, exclaimed '*nawa ni naparou*' ('fruit of the pandanus') – there are slightly similar decorations on the traditional Ngunese fighting club (*nap'we*) of the same name – but then north-west

Fig. 268 South Pentecost

Fig. 269 Malo

228 ▼ THE ART OF POWER

Fig. 270a, b, c
Ambae

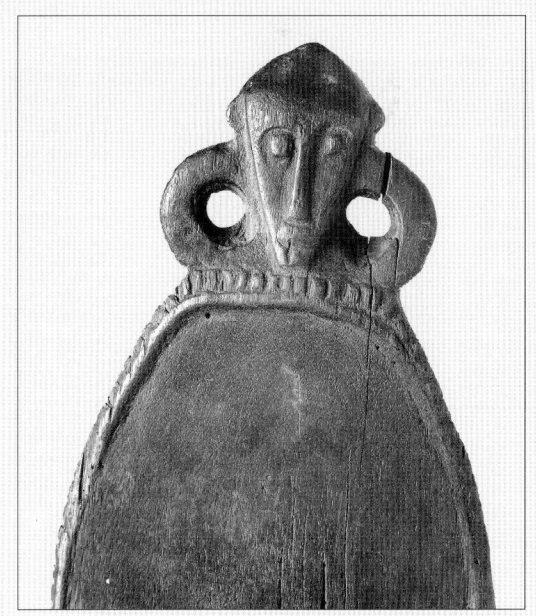

Santo is a different world with different traditions. The curved projections are obviously pigs' tusks, symbolic of rank, but also useful for hanging the plate in the *anali* (men's house) when not in use (cf. Speiser photograph of a large wooden plate hanging inside a men's house on Vanua Lava, (F)Vb 1952; Speiser 1991, pl. 18, no. 5). The dentate pattern on the plate's handle, probably symbolic in nature, and also found on some of the Santo *nalot* pounders, would equally serve the practical purpose of enabling a better hand-grip, because *nalot* preparation is sticky work.

Large, round, flat *nalot* plates are found throughout the Banks Islands (figs 272, 273; see Basel Vb 4332, 1.6 cm, without legs, from Gaua). On Mota these are called *tapia,* on Mota Lava *tambe* (also *t'm'be),* and *tambi* on Vanua Lava. Some are so large that they could have ten or so people working the *nalot* on them before it is cut off in portions, wrapped in leaves and cooked. Associated heavy wooden ladles, called *bwet'koi* on Mota Lava, are sometimes confused by museum curators overseas with 'kava beakers',

PLATES AND BOWLS FROM NORTHERN AND CENTRAL VANUATU ▼ 229

Fig. 271a, b
Santo

but are coconut-milk containers in which hot stones (put in first) heat the coconut milk to be poured on the *nalot* spread on the plate. Larger, deeper, Banks Islands bowls (as Vb 4337, from Gaua; cf. Speiser 1991, pl. 26, no. 1, l. 58 cm, and Vb 4335 from Ureparapara, pl. 26, no. 6, l. 7 cm) could be used as eating dishes or for heating (with hot stones) larger volumes of liquid: such bowls are called *wumeto* on Mota Lava.

The large stone bowls from south-eastern Gaua (cf. Speiser photograph (F)Vb 1911, as in Speiser 1991, pl. 18, no. 4), called *nu'um* by the present-day population of the area, most of whom are originally from Mere Lava, were mostly ritual in nature. In rites associated with the culture hero Qat, some (not all) were used as mirrors to assist facial painting by filling them with water: some colours or types of face-painting do not reflect well if ordinary water was used, so in certain cases fine, white fire-ash could be sprinkled lightly on its surface to improve the reflection. The function of most of these stone bowls was possibly different from the shallow oval stone bowls from the Big Bay area in north Santo, of similar size to wooden *nalot* plates and probably for the same purpose – they were seemingly in use at the time of de Quirós's 1606 visit (examples exist in the Australian Museum collections, E 23577 and E 23578). The slightly deeper stone dish collected by Speiser in 1910 (Vb 4245; cf. Speiser 1991, pl. 26, no. 8, l. 48 cm) from a nearby area may, as he says, have been for 'kava preparation'.

Many areas of Vanuatu used and still use large leaves as bases for food preparation and eating. Some areas also had or have intricate plaited or woven dishes made from liana or pandanus, often coexisting with wooden plates, used by other people or for other purposes (for example, rituals) within the same local culture – an example is the diamond-shaped woven pandanus plate, *parovi*, for wedding *laplap* in south-eastern Malo. Of course, metal food-preparation pots and pans of foreign manufacturers are widespread throughout most areas of Vanuatu today – like the thousands of aluminium and steel trays, plates and food utensils dispersed from US bases on Santo and Efate towards the end of World War II. But these do not have the same ritual significance as the traditional ones and can never fully take their place. Thus it is important for ni-Vanuatu to recognise that their traditional plates, dishes and bowls, of whatever form or material, are also an important part of their identity and heritage to be preserved, promoted and developed. Organisations and institutions overseas wishing to assist in this may consider supplying the Vanuatu Cultural Centre with stocks of metal carving adze-type blades, as most carving was originally done with stone or shell adzes of many shapes and sizes, shell chisels (for example, the Mota *tive*), sharks' teeth, and so on. Nineteenth-century hoop-iron from barrels was immediately adapted into adze-blades for carving (as were metals from crashed World War II aircraft). Some of these still exist, and are used, but are almost worn out. Such adze-type blades are also essential for aspects of canoe and slit-drum carving and produce the traditional-style effects that other modern tools cannot give. Specialist manufacturers of such metal blades still exist in Australia, New Zealand, the UK, France, and parts of Asia. Distributing such blades to the outer islands through the Cultural Centre's fieldworkers network would give a great boost to carvers throughout the country.

I dedicate this superficial survey to the plate carvers of central Vanuatu, especially to Joseph Taripoaliu of Tongoa, and Sepa Andrew of Buninga, and to the peoples of north-western Santo, especially the boomerang (*tio'h*)-throwing peoples around the area of Nogugu, in the hope that they will continue and revive their styles of dishes. I write this also for the memory of two dear departed friends, the famous carver Chief Willy Taso of Wuro, west Ambrym, who died in 1985, and Chief Marsden Rongo of Mere Lava, who died in tragic circumstances during Cyclone Uma in 1987.

Fig. 272
Gaua, Banks Islands

Fig. 273a, b
Gaua, Banks Islands

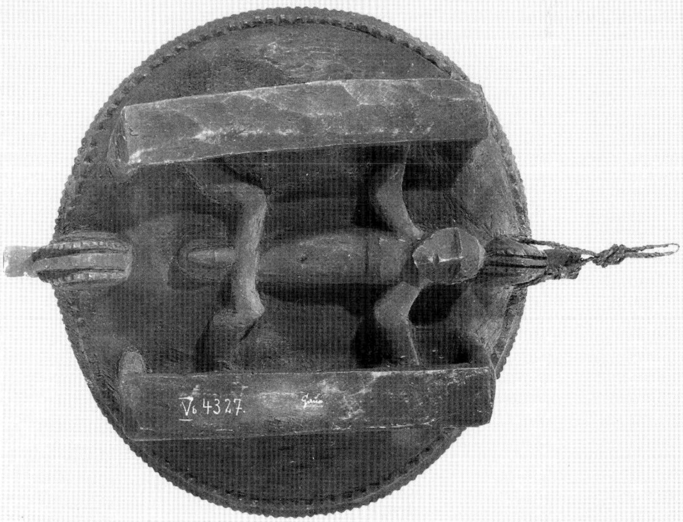

Wooden *nalot* pounders

Kirk W. Huffman

From northern Pentecost westwards to Santo, Ambae, Maewo, and through the Banks and Torres, a form of staple diet, now generally recognised under the Bislamised term *nalot*, is widespread, especially in parts of Santo and the Banks and Torres. *Nalot* is a pounded cooked pudding, mixed with coconut milk, which can be of taro, yam, banana, manioc, or so on, or particularly breadfruit in the latter areas. The essence of *nalot* is that it is cooked and pounded in preparation, not a grated or scraped staple, as in the earth-oven cooked *laplap* (Bislama). Wooden pounders found in museum collections overseas are usually from areas of Santo, and the Banks (figs 274, 275, 282) and Torres (fig. 283), each area having a particular style or series of styles. Not all *nalot* pounders, though, are or were of wood, and although throughout most of Vanuatu food staple preparation is usually a female activity, *nalot* pounding is normally essentially – though not always – a male activity. This helps explain much of the artistic elaboration of many of the pounder styles, and the often associated wooden plates upon which the *nalot* can be pounded. Especially in the Banks and Torres islands, the carvings on the upper end can be linked with material representations of spiritual aspects of associations with men's secret societies, and status in the local graded systems (figs 277-283). The Santo pounders (figs 284, 285) tend to be thicker and heavier than the lighter, finer examples from further north. A feature seemingly restricted to certain Santo examples, a type of carved, stippled, pineapple-like (to European eyes) filial (fig. 285), or middle (lower hand-grip area) band, or similar style (fig. 284), is also found on associated plates (see p. 228, this volume) and on the powerful carved men's house-post portions collected by Speiser near Talamaco in north-west Santo (see p. 222, fig. 252, this volume). This decoration style, seemingly originally restricted to north-west and north Santo, may have deep spiritual connotations of which we are as yet unaware. Other fruits of traditional use – for example, breadfruit and pandanus – could lend themselves to similar artistic depictions, but this is not necessarily to say that this design even represents a fruit. Speiser hinted that he thought the design might be related to turtles, but then again the stylistic conventions in Vanuatu are of such a complexity and depth that often a design will have many levels of meaning, completely undecipherable to an outsider, or even levels of which a member of that culture is unaware.

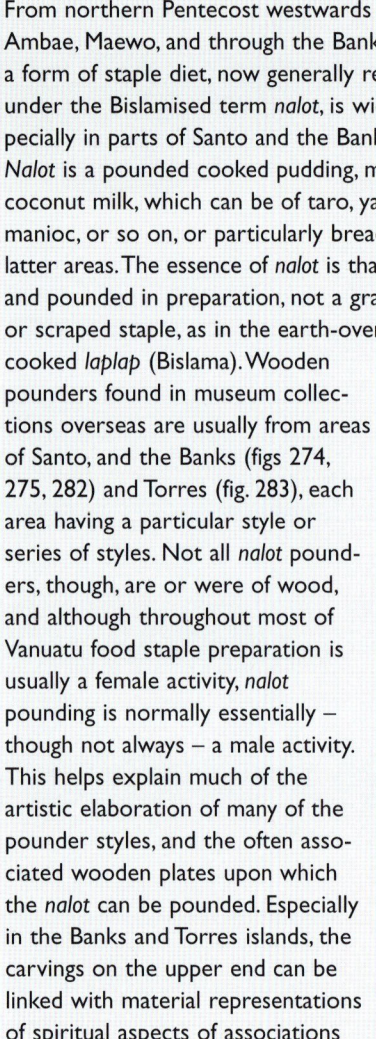

Fig. 274a Banks Islands   Fig. 274b Banks Islands   Fig. 275 Banks Islands

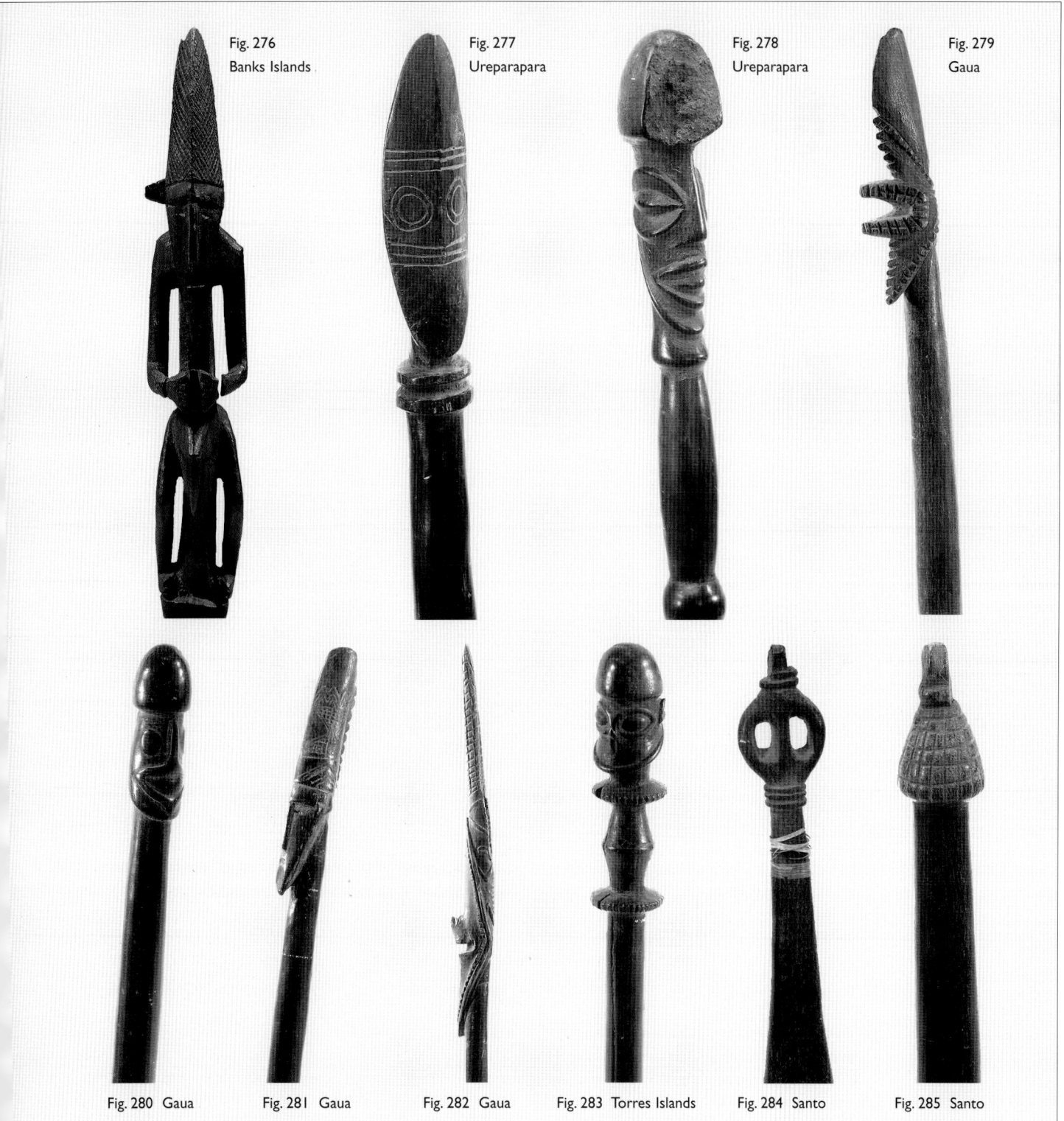

Fig. 276 Banks Islands
Fig. 277 Ureparapara
Fig. 278 Ureparapara
Fig. 279 Gaua
Fig. 280 Gaua
Fig. 281 Gaua
Fig. 282 Gaua
Fig. 283 Torres Islands
Fig. 284 Santo
Fig. 285 Santo

WOODEN *NALOT* POUNDERS ▼ 233

Masked Faces from the Country of the Dead

Bernard Vienne

1. This is a revised version of my article 'Les masques tamate des îles Banks', published in 1983. On the concept of *tamate* in the Banks Islands, cf. Codrington 1891; Codrington and Palmer 1896; Rivers 1914; Vienne 1984.

On my way home I met a wild and grotesque-looking party of men; they belonged to a tamate *society, and they had been to pull a house to pieces in order to compel the owner, or his son perhaps, to join them. They were adorned with hibiscus flowers and croton leaves, their faces smudged with charcoal, and a leaf in the mouth, each carrying a stick. Two or three of these had on a* tamate, *a hat and mask, with a long fringe of leaves reaching down to the heels.* (Rev. J. Palmer's journals, Island Voyage, 1877)

In the Banks Islands, there are many masks called *tamate*. *Tamate* (literally *ta*: belong to, *mate*: death) is the generic term for the 'ancestral dead', or in other words, the spirits of those who were once men and who usually dwell in the *panoi*, the underworld. The term is applied equally to the masks, the dancers who wear them, and by extension to the men's ceremonial societies formed, de facto, by all those who have acquired the right to wear the same mask.¹ In Vanuatu, masks are not found only in the Banks Islands or only in this one culture. Under different names and in various forms, they are found throughout the northern part of the group, associated with the institutional complex of the graded society (cf. Suas 1921; Ivens 1931; Deacon 1934b; Webb 1937; Layard 1942; Guiart 1951; Allen 1967; Rodman 1973; Vienne 1984).

The masks are worn exclusively by men on certain ritual or ceremonial occasions. From the point of view of cultural technology, it may seem incorrect to use the word mask here. It refers to the mask itself, which hides the face and thus the identity of the wearer, and is generally worn with a cloak of leaves which covers the body. It also refers to the headdress or headgear which leaves the face largely uncovered. In the cultural tradition of the Banks Islands, symbolic face-painting topped by a headdress also seems to be included in the mask category. Presented collectively, some of the *tamate* masks and headdresses symbolised the 'breaking into the world of the living of the *panoi*, the world of the dead' (Guiart 1983), this being the essential point.

Tamate

The separation caused by an individual death, and echoed by funeral rites, is overcome in the now collective rather than individual dialogue which the group establishes with its ancestors through its *tamate* dancers. It is symptomatic that the mask bears no identity and is named after any of the plastic elements which go into its making (or according to its symbolism); it represents neither a particular ancestor nor a mythic hero, nor is it attached to a local group. Forms, names and structures are forever evolving, as they are transmitted through the extended and complex exchange networks. Ownership changes hands according to the 'copyright' principle: an individual or a group that holds recognised rights to a rite, a form, or an object can transfer them to others in exchange for pigs, mats or money. The principle is that you must pay whoever paid before you.

Tamate dancers are supposed, in the eyes of women and the uninitiated at least, to embody the periodic return of the 'ancestral dead' and their actual presence among the living. What is important then is the 'symbolic efficacy' (Lèvi-Strauss) of the mask, reactivated by a dancer who has undergone the initiation rites. If the ancestors reincarnate themselves in the *tamate* dancers for the duration of a ceremony, it is through the mediation of the object and its aesthetic. This embodiment confers on the masks their power, their *mana*, and for it to take place, everyone must play his part, which explains the importance of the secrecy surrounding the making of the masks, their brief use and their destruction once the ceremony is over. The initiation ritual echoes these representations. In a paraphrase of the funeral rites, it symbolises the individual's social death, and his rebirth as a *tamate* spirit.

It is to a woman (Mota version) or to young children left alone in the village (Motalava version) that the origin of masks in general and of the institutions connected with them is attributed. They were given by a *vui* spirit, and then stolen by the men who, later, forbade women and the uninitiated to use them (cf. Codrington 1891; Rivers 1914). The particular origin of each mask, however, is not always recorded by tradition, because the flexibility of the system allows individuals, under certain conditions, to create new *tamate*. According to the prestige attributed to them or to their passing popularity, some *tamate* will extend their reputation by word of mouth, or from one person to the next, sometimes even beyond their original cultural area, while others will only survive at the local level or may even disappear.

The right to wear a particular mask, as well as the costume, body decorations, ornaments and emblems associated with it, is acquired by individuals at any time in their lives. In the Banks Islands, this right is principally obtained in exchange for shell money, *som*. Elsewhere in the archipelago, tusked pigs are used as 'money'. For important masks, initiation is accompanied by various prohibitions and obligations, such as the ban on going outside the boundaries of a certain area, or on washing, or the obligation to prepare food and clean a place. There are also some tests and ordeals, which do not include bodily mutilation.

The process of acquiring and using the mask is more coherent, more complex, and more varied than it at first appears. For the most prestigious of them, such as the *tamate liwoa*, *tamate qat*, and *tamate viov*, it depends on an initiation ceremony involving not only money, but also gifts of food and pigs, collective feasting, some teaching, tests and seclusion for varying lengths of time. On the other hand, some other *tamate* do not even require a simple headdress to be made. Their acquisition is symbolised only by a particular decoration on the dancer's body, the addition to an existing mask of a specific decorative motif, its own special emblem or ornament. They are then acquired without ceremony, by simple payment. This is the case, for example, of the *tamate tawene av* (of the *tamate matawonowono* group), the emblem of which is a firebrand held in the hand during night dances, and which allows the wearing of a body decoration symbolising fire. These differences in the importance and complexity of rites for the acquisition of the right to wear a mask have, more than anything else, to do with the segmentary nature of the underlying structure of the *tamate* as a whole, called, in the Banks Islands, *wangarai tamate* or 'branched *tamate*', and which is compared with a piece of tree coral.

Ritual initiation or simple acquisition of a mask are in no way obligatory. They may take place at any age and be carried out individually or collectively. All those who have acquired the right to wear the same mask are under more or less strict obligations of solidarity. 'Initiates' of the same mask form an

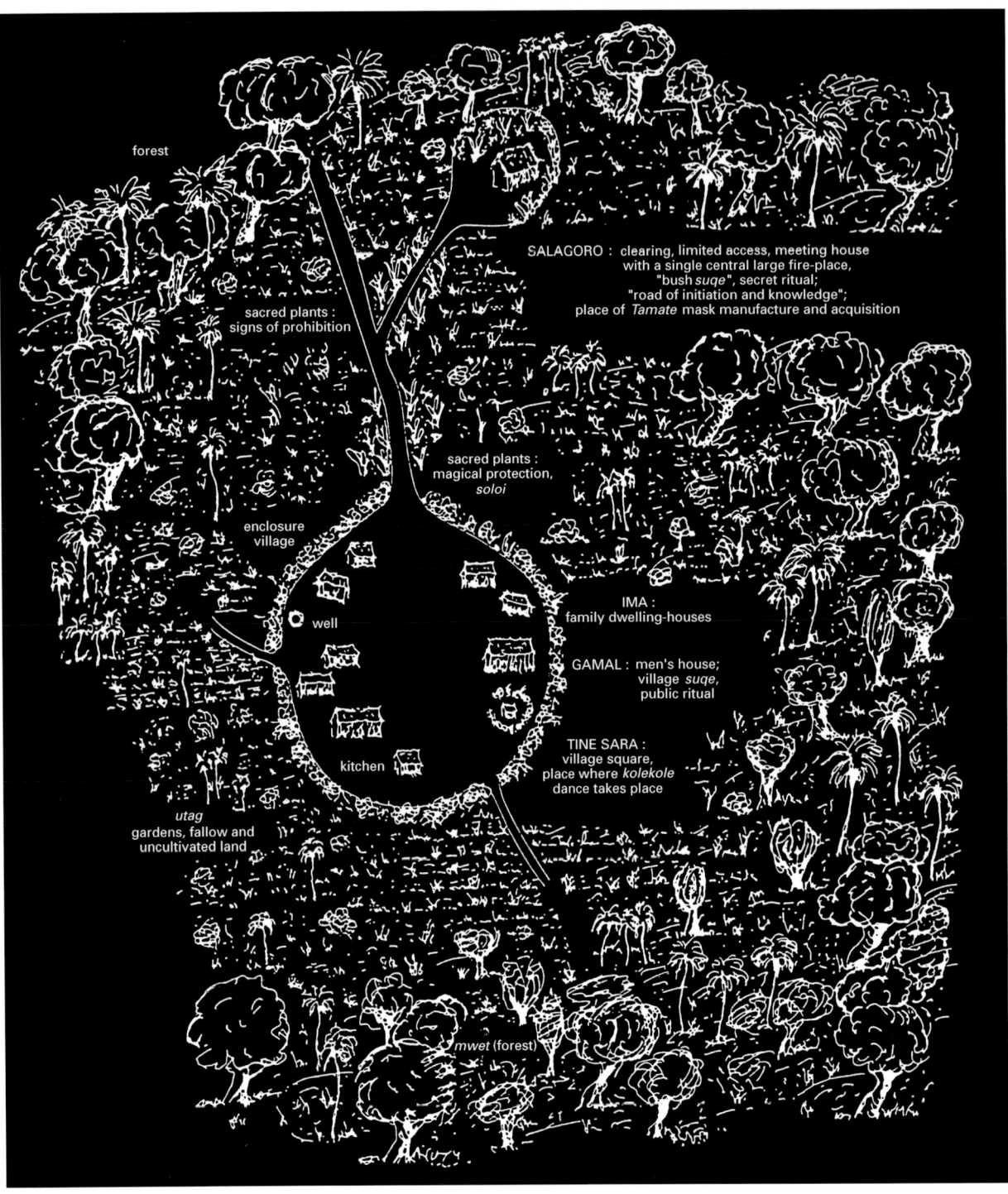

Fig. 286 Sketch of village social organisation.

interest group, a sort of informal association with a ritual and ceremonial role, also known as a *tamate*. Described by early authors (Rivers 1914) as 'secret *tamate* societies', these ceremonial associations of masked men represent the community of 'ancestral dead', custodians of the 'path of initiation', in whose honour grade-takings continue to be held. In Banks culture, their presence and permanence safeguard the foundations of social order. Codrington (1891) relates how the mask was used to make public and enforceable decisions negotiated to restore social order after a period of disturbance. The most important *tamate* societies also ensure the protection of property against theft. To do this, the *tamate* have their own tabu marks, *soloi*, whose effectiveness is guaranteed by the community of members. It is their duty also to ensure, by means of rituals, the legitimacy and worth of notables and men of power of various kinds. The *tamate* are thus an essential facet of the institutional arrangements which underpin the social order. Thus sketched briefly, the institutional pattern rests, on the one hand, on the principle of hierarchy from which public law and reciprocal obligations flow, and on the other hand, on individual power marked by wealth, strength and skill, renown and prestige. These marks of power and the prerogatives that go with it are not passed on, but are 'earned' individually throughout life by means of strategies which place everyone potentially in competition with everyone else.

Suqe, salagoro and kolekole

Melanesians like to present their institutions as being independent of each other and subject only to logic. Those institutions are supposed to be first and foremost systems of ceremonial exchange, finding in themselves their justification and ultimate purpose. The same goes for the *suqe*, the *salagoro* and the *kolekole* of the Banks Islands (see fig. 286), but in reality these three essential institutions make up a single structured system.

The central element of this institutional arrangement is indeed the grade hierarchy of the *suqe*, the 'village *suqe*' as it is called, physically represented by the *gamal*, the men's communal house. The other elements are the *salagoro*, which is seen, by opposition, as the 'bush *suqe*', represented by a fenced space forbidden to non-initiates, and the *kolekole*, a true cycle of collective festivals, whose distinctive space is the *tinesara*, the dancing ground. Generally speaking, statues stand in relation to the *suqe* grade hierarchy (fig. 287), masks to the *salagoro*, and dancing to the *kolekole*, although this is a rather arbitrary distribution, as each important moment in ceremonial life brings all three institutions inextricably into play.

This set of complementary institutions is presented as the 'path', traced by the community of ancestors, which a man must follow during his life. To

Fig. 287a, b
Statue of one of the highest grades of *suqe*. Front and profile. Gaua, Banks Islands. Basel, Museum für Völkerkunde.

Series of incised bamboo and cane ornaments from the Torres and Banks islands, Ambae and Maewo

Kirk W. Huffman

Fig. 288: Man from the island of Loh in the Torres group, wearing incised bamboo/cane ornament in right ear. Detail of field photograph by J.W. Beattie, 1906.

Worn through pierced earlobes, these small (those pictured vary in length from 11 to 29 centimetres), thin (normally less than 1 centimetre in diameter), beautifully incised ornaments are no longer seen in northern Vanuatu, their widespread use having largely disappeared by the end of the 19th century with conversion to Christianity in the Anglican mission areas. Designs can represent aspects of the natural, material and spiritual worlds; for example, sea life, fish scales, plant life, woven-cane garden fences, spirit and headdress figures, and sun aspects, to mention but a small section of the vast range. Many combine several designs. It is important to note that such materials could be worn by men or women or both, depending on status, design and occasion. According to Speiser, figure 309 was of a style that could be worn by men and women on Maewo; figures 307 and 308 were, he says, worn by women in the Torres. Other types and designs could be restricted to men. Although they are not illustrated here, it is possible that such ornaments may have existed also in the Raga-speaking area of northern Pentecost.

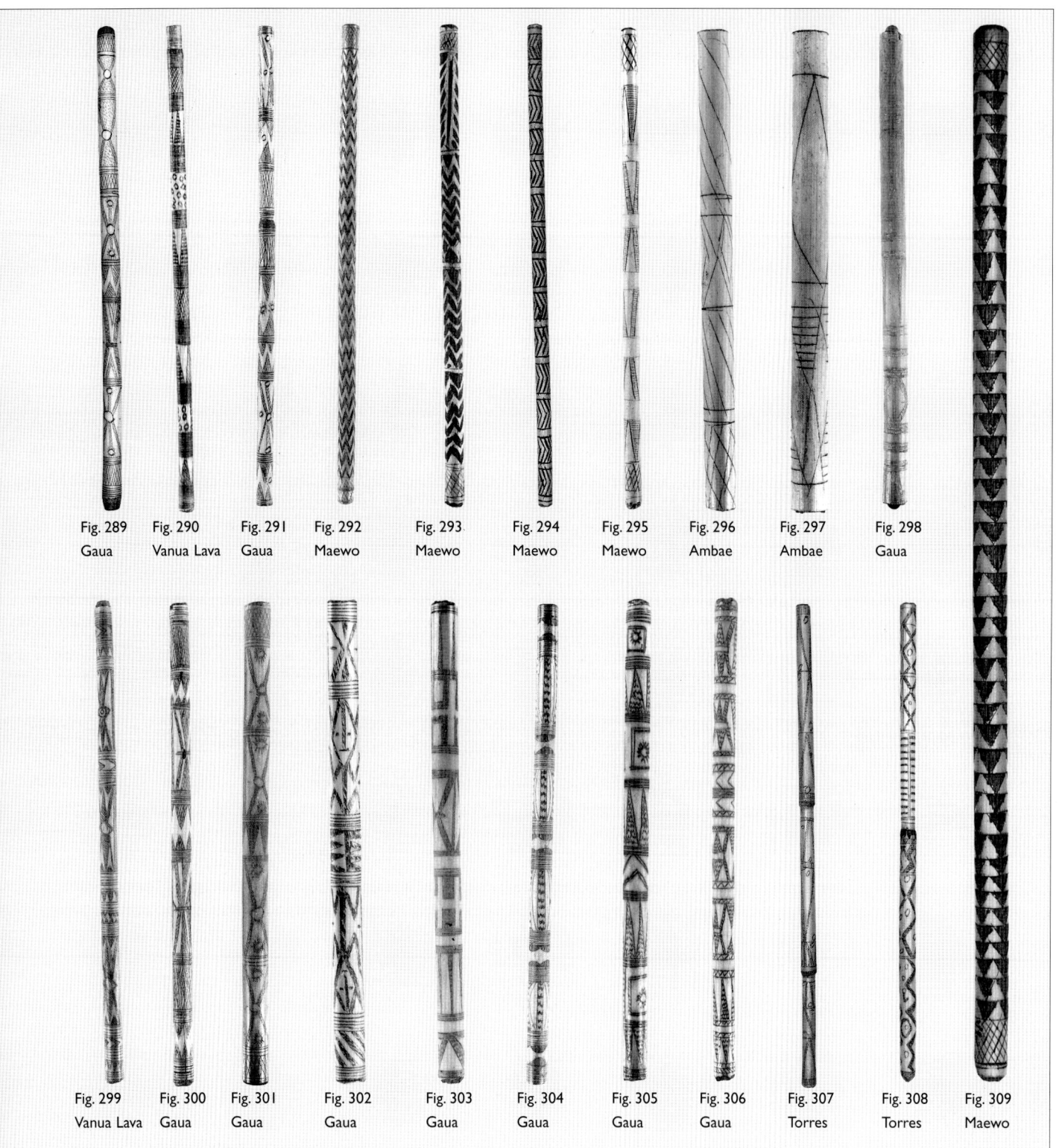

| Fig. 289 | Fig. 290 | Fig. 291 | Fig. 292 | Fig. 293 | Fig. 294 | Fig. 295 | Fig. 296 | Fig. 297 | Fig. 298 |
| Gaua | Vanua Lava | Gaua | Maewo | Maewo | Maewo | Maewo | Ambae | Ambae | Gaua |

| Fig. 299 | Fig. 300 | Fig. 301 | Fig. 302 | Fig. 303 | Fig. 304 | Fig. 305 | Fig. 306 | Fig. 307 | Fig. 308 | Fig. 309 |
| Vanua Lava | Gaua | Gaua | Gaua | Gaua | Gaua | Gaua | Gaua | Torres | Torres | Maewo |

INCISED BAMBOO AND CANE ORNAMENTS ▼ 239

follow the path, 'proper behaviour' comes down to 'paying his debt' to the ancestors, but also to his social partners. Without going so far as to say the place filled by each man in this system prefigures the one he will occupy in the reverse world of the dead, this ethical relation to the ancestors is fundamental: the world of the dead is only described as 'pleasant' insofar as moral conformity with the ancestors is respected in the code of conduct.

The *suqe* may be described as a hierarchy of individual statuses in the form of a sequential scale; access to a grade and a title involves first holding the grade and title which precedes them. Each grade is symbolised by the possession of a statue carved from tree fern (or an equivalent emblem), and special privileges go with it: a man's own space is set aside for him in the *gamal*, and he has the right to wear special body ornaments and decorations. It also confers rights of precedence at meetings, in speech-making, dances, and ceremonial distributions of food, money and pigs. Each grade-taking is the occasion for a public ritual which includes a series of monetary distributions, gifts of food and the slaughter or transfer of a number of pigs. Its legitimacy stems from its public nature, and on this occasion a meal prepared by the holders of the title, and offered to the new grade-taker, is shared in the *gamal*. The change in social status, thus made known to all, is marked by a period of seclusion in the *gamal*, the end of which is signalled by a ceremonial bath, a period during which the new grade-holder is supported entirely by the community. This period of seclusion echoes mortuary rites.

Rising grade by grade up through the *suqe* follows the principle according to which one pays those who have paid before oneself. The first grade-taking may be at any age and often takes place with a kinsman as intermediary during early childhood. For a male child, it embodies passage from the world of women to the world of men. Holding a rank in one's village also gives one a rank in other villages; the grade hierarchy creates, in effect, a social stratification of individuals on the widest geographical scale, that of the whole of the Banks Islands. It is a structure of sociopolitical integration which finds its culminating expression in community reference to a single value system and a single code of conduct.

The 'village *suqe*' is matched by the 'bush *suqe*', the *salagoro*; the public ritual by a secret ritual; the men's communal house by the private enclosure of the *salagoro*, protected by tabus. The *salagoro* takes the form of a clearing, sometimes situated on the seashore; access to it is protected by tabu signs, and a meeting house stands there with a single central fireplace. There, the dancers meet and prepare the *kolekole*; it is the place of seclusion of each new initiate; everything necessary for the making of masks and body decorations is kept there, and there the masks are burnt when the dancing is over.

The *salagoro* may be permanent or temporary; in fact, any place protected by tabus where the *tamate* meet to make their masks, prepare their dances, carry out an initiation, or simply share a meal or spend time together, is a *salagoro*.

The *salagoro* is the preferred institutional framework for acquiring the various *tamate* masks and the dance costumes used in *kolekole* and grade-takings.

They can be described in general, and this is the primary sense that informers give to the institution, as a secret initiatory ritual complex, as opposed to the public hierarchy of the *suqe* grades. Although the link was long suspected, people have generally only seen them as juxtaposed institutions. The functional interpretation of *salagoro* rites, however, is part of the same logic as that of the *suqe* grade hierarchy, of which the *salagoro* is of necessity the complementary mirror image.

The *salagoro*, 'path of initiation, of knowledge', is associated in various ways with the *suqe*, 'path of social peace'. At the normative level, initiations into the *tamate* of the *salagoro* form a parallel series to those of the *suqe* grades, and one cannot progress along the path of the grade hierarchy without a concomitant progression in the *salagoro*. In the ceremonial of the higher grade-takings, the *tamate*, partners in the ritual, play an essential role of legitimisation by representing the ancestors. At the level of values, the *salagoro* is, like the *suqe*, a hierarchy, though one which is not an outgrowth of rank, but of the power and prestige which come with the individual accumulation of the most sought-after *tamate* masks. A loose ritual association, the *salagoro* also transcends the cleavages due to locality and kinship, and helps to widen and maintain communication between individuals from communities which are outsiders to each other. The privileges of the *tamate*, which even include ritual depredations, bear witness to the power attributed to them. In the *suqe*, the supremacy of the individual, his prestige and success, are affirmed; in the *salagoro*, the primacy of the community is foremost: individual behaviour must conform with the ancestral order. While the *gamal*, ultimately, is the place where the village group manifests itself as the political community of the living, the *salagoro* enclosure symbolises the presence of the ancestors, and continuity between the dead and the living.

The power conferred on the individual by his place in the *suqe* and the *salagoro* is only made legitimate by public demonstration of his prestige and wealth. That demonstration is the object of the *kolekole*, which are collective manifestations for the benefit of an individual, man or woman. Each grade-taking and each important *salagoro* initiation normally give rise to a *kolekole*. This consists essentially of dances which conclude with a large distribution of wealth (money, pigs, food) which the individual has accumulated, the display brought to the ceremony being the measure of the personal prestige of the giver. *Kolekole* are thus partly necessary and partly voluntary, because they can be done for nothing and made larger or smaller in scale according to the renown one expects to get from them.

A *kolekole* can be given for one's own benefit or for a third person, a kinsman or 'client', whose status is enhanced just as the prestige of the provider is magnified. In this way, for example, a man may pass on his social rank to his wife by having her acquire house, tattoos, necklaces, bracelets and ornaments.

For a *kolekole* to be prestigious, the wealth and power of the giver must be considerable. The success of a *kolekole* depends therefore on the number and quality of participants and the scale of the ceremony as measured by the number and magnificence of the dances and distributions of goods. The organisation of a *kolekole* is left to the judgement of its sponsor. Getting everyone to participate, assessing what should be distributed, rewarding the dancers and those who have composed the songs – everything is a matter for judicious negotiation, often a long time in advance. Everyone, in fact, expects to get some personal benefit out of it. Knowledge of songs and dances, the *tamate* masks, the decorations, everything that makes it possible to take an active part in *kolekoles* is acquired in the context of the *salagoro*.

Fig. 310
Tamate dancer, photographed in 1970. Lotawan village, Mota, Banks Islands.

Classification of *tamate*

W.H. Rivers described more than sixty *tamate* on Mota in 1914. In 1970 (figs 310-313), my informers[2] gave the same number for that island, and their information largely corroborated that of Rivers, except on one essential point, the classification of *tamate* and their association with various *salagoro*.

The distinction between initiates and non-initiates, which symbolically intersects with the opposition of the sexes, defines a first category of *tamate*, the *tamate matawonowono*, or '*tamate* with their eyes still closed'.[3] By acquiring them, those who are not yet initiated either into the *suqe* or into the *salagoro* can nevertheless participate, at their own level,

2. My information on this point comes more particularly from the village of Lotawan.

3. This name makes implicit allusion to a very widespread practice: in a first confrontation, with closed eyes and guided by someone with knowledge of them, one discovers certain sites and certain places, certain objects ...

Fig. 311
Tamate dancer in full costume, photographed in 1970.
Lotawan village, Mota, Banks Islands.

Fig. 312
Presentation of a *tamate liwoa* mask during a *kole-kole*, photographed in 1970.
Lotawan village, Mota, Banks Islands.

Fig. 313
Decoration variations in a group of *tamate viov* masks, photographed in 1970.
Lotawan village, Mota, Banks Islands.

in the *kolekole*. One might describe them as the '*kolekole tamate*' who stay on the outer edges of the dancing ground to which they have access only with certain reservations: they 'stand at the door' of the ceremonial space.

Although they have their own emblem or effigy (cf. descriptions published by Rivers 1914), it is rare for these *tamate* to share in the making of a specific mask. They can generally be acquired for a small handful of money without any particular ceremonial, at any age: a father will get one for a son who can not yet walk. Certain *tamate* of this group have only a derisory value, they are 'joke *tamate*'; nevertheless, the insignia which represent them are used at some *kolekole* dances and are often associated with the emblems of more prestigious *tamate*: in this way the dancer is demonstrating both his rank in the *salagoro* and the legitimacy of the course he has chosen. The *tamate* of this group often form part of a very localised village or district tradition.

The '*tamate* with their eyes still closed' seem to permit a physical presence at the ritual level of the community of women and non-initiates, as opposed to the hierarchy of men who belong to the *suqe* and the *salagoro*. These *tamate* are generally acquired outside any ceremonial context and are not an occasion for any true initiation. For some of them, however, a particular rite is mentioned, but there is no test, no revelation, no secret, no seclusion. Nor do the tabus relating to space, movement and noise apply, as they usually do on such occasions, to women and the uninitiated.

The internal organisation of '*tamate* with their eyes still closed' is analogous with that of the initiates' *tamate*. One finds the same division between air and water *tamate* (one represented by birds, the other by fish), and day and night *tamate*, linked respectively to daytime and night-time dances. The same characters and roles are staged: the couple of demiurges, *qat* and *marawa*, here stripped of all their importance, derided and satirised; the land snake, no longer a water snake, who lives near waterholes; and finally fire, by which the masks will be destroyed at the end of the dances. Those whose role it is to pursue and beat women and non-initiates indulge in all sorts of extortions. These *tamate* of no importance are also 'commanded' by a more prestigious *tamate* than the others, *tamate mweretang*, for which initiation is individual and the occasion for learning a particular beat.

The second category is the *tamate talo salagoro* (or *tamate salagoro*), the *tamate* of the *salagoro* (fig. 314). More than half the *tamate* mentioned belong to this group, whose origin lies in the distinction between the *suqe* and *salagoro* institutions. These *tamate* can only be acquired by men who have already been initiated into the grade hierarchy; on the other hand, one can only progress beyond a certain point in the *suqe* after one has been initiated into the first *tamate* of the *salagoro*. This last is called *tamate liwoa*, and its mask, with that of the *tamate qat* and the *tamate viov*, is one of the most prestigious in the Banks Islands. A dance, a song, numerous insignia and plant emblems go with it; it 'commands' the whole of the group of *salagoro tamate*, acquired only after initiation into *tamate liwoa*. Among the many *tamate* of this prestigious group, the most notable are *tamate omwai* (or *mwaitur*), who carry a carved dance stick in the shape of a snake and advance at the head of the masked dancers, playing the role of 'ballet master',[4] at *kolekole*, and the *tamate wis*, *tamate saka*, *tamate qatwasawasa*, and *tamate sesekor*, responsible for chasing and beating the women and children and indulging in all sorts of ritual depredations at high-ranking grade-takings. Finally, *tamate memegil*, *tamate lakatapas*, and *tamate wewe* are the masters of the most prestigious collective *kolekole* dances of the group.

The third category is the *tamate talo nin* (or *tamate salagoro nin*), the '*tamate* of the enclosure',[5] which are the *suqe tamate*, the masks of the grade hierarchy. Their *salagoro* is a temporary enclosure around the men's communal house or at the edge of the dancing ground. That they have no permanent *salagoro* distinguishes them from the preceding group and gives them the name of *tamate talo maea*, the '*tamate* of empty space'.[6] To claim the right to acquire the *tamate* of this group, one must have been initiated into the *suqe* grade hierarchy.

This '*tamate* of the enclosure' group is itself divided into two subgroups, corresponding to the distinction between *suqe* and *salagoro*. The *tamate* attached to the *tamate viov*, initiation into which is individual, are the 'masks of the *salagoro*'.

The *tamate qat* dance is the most famous and prestigious of the Banks Islands. Its only rhythm

4. Sometimes the origin of masks is attributed to these *tamate*; cf. Vienne 1979.

5. This category corresponds to Rivers' *tamate talo maea*.

6. On the nature of different spaces and on the concept of *mana*, cf. Codrington 1891; Vienne 1979, 1984.

Fig. 314, 315
Salagoro dancers during a *kolekole*, photographed in 1970.
Lotawan village, Mota, Banks Islands.

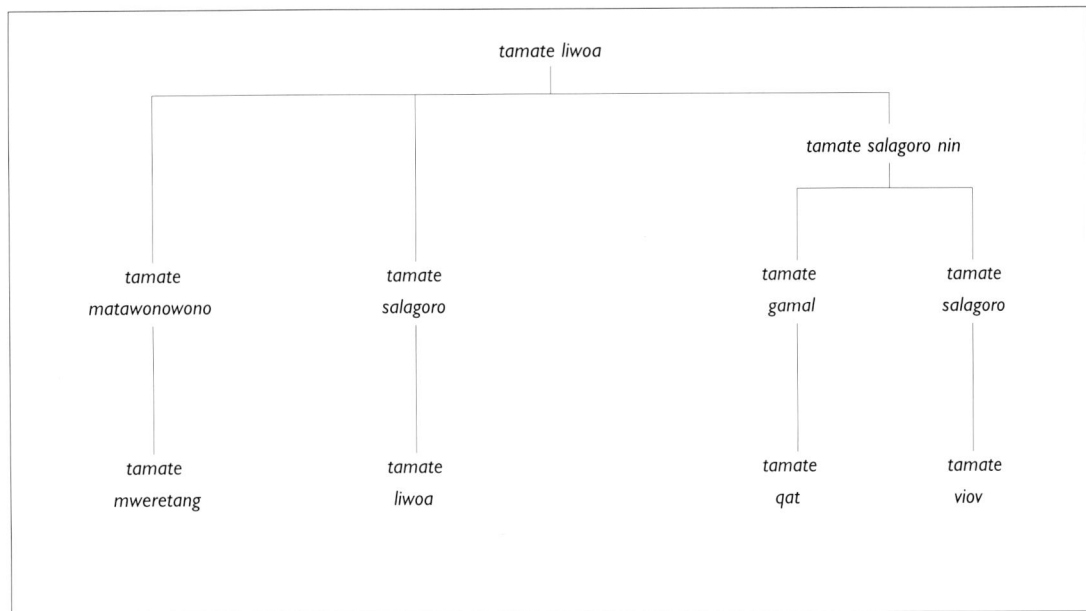

Fig. 316 Classification of *tamate*.

7. Cf. Codrington 1891: 'Any one might start a new society, and gather round him his co-founders, taking any object that might strike their fancy as the ground and symbol of their association. A visitor to Norfolk Island having seen there a bird that was strange to him, established on his return to Mota a society called "the Norfolk Island Bird". Some such new foundations will succeed and flourish, some will fail.'

comes from the drumming of the dancers' feet on the beaten earth; the rattles and bunches of dried seeds attached to their ankles shake together. The execution of this dance must be perfect, on pain of punishment, which means each group of initiates has a long apprenticeship to go through. It is a public dance, executed in broad daylight, for the benefit of the whole assembled community (fig. 315).

Initiation into *tamate viov* is recognised as the most important and costly of all. The symbolism of the *tamate viov* group makes an implicit reference to the *panoi*, the world of the dead where the *tamate* habitually reside and which is conceived of as a reverse image of the familiar world of the living. These are also the *tamate* of secrecy, of occult power, which arouse awe and fear in people.

If we consider that the *tamate liwoa* is the father of all the *tamate*, figure 316, above, may show how the *tamate* of Mota in particular, and of the Banks Islands in general, are classified.

This representation should, in fact, be qualified, because the model is far from being as rigorous as this. Flexibility is a constant characteristic of Banks Islands culture, which always reserves an essential place for individual innovation, for divergencies of interpretation and codification.[7] For example, variations on a given theme, the incorporation of foreign elements into a pattern, the workmanship and aesthetic feeling are all factors which can increase the value of a mask, its power, its *mana*. Thus the importance of such and such a *tamate* varies considerably from one place to another and is not unaffected by passing fads. What is more, *tamate* can be born and die; some have only a fleeting existence, others can disappear over a longer period of time and reappear on occasion, which can lead to shifts even in the classification itself.

All the masks, insignia and ornaments mentioned are made by paid specialists, in the enclosed space of the *salagoro*. Anything to do with their making is secret and is handed down, in exchange for payment, from one individual to another, often outside kinship networks. The masks, made on request for a given ceremony, are fashioned around a framework of split bamboo, pandanus root or dried vine, covered with the vegetable material enveloping coconut trunks, with *varu* (*Hibiscus tiliaceus*), *mwake* (*Inocarpus edulis*), or *patau* (*Artocarpus altilis*) leaves, or leaves from other species of plant; they are then coated with a lacquer based on *patau* or *ngai* (*Canarium* sp.) sap mixed with various vegetable or mineral pigments. They are often surmounted by an effigy of the *tamate*'s symbol (bird, fish, crustacean, natural being, and so on), and they are ornamented with decorative motifs referring to the *tamate* which commands the group to which the mask belongs. The arrangement of motifs may vary on the same mask according to the system of symbols favoured by the maker or his client. The symbolism of masks may be anthropomorphic (representations of a face, with its various elements: eyes, teeth, hair, and so on), cosmographic (stars, rays of the sun, rain, ocean, appearance of the sea at sunrise or sunset, fire, and so on), or zoomorphic. Each mask also has its corresponding plant symbol, often a variety of croton or hibiscus, but also the leaves and flowers of various decorative or other species.

To be recognised as a 'big man', a 'chief', a *tavusmwele*, one must have been initiated at least into the four big *tamate* which 'command' each of the groups: *tamate mweretang, tamate liwoa, tamate qat, tamate viov*. One could no doubt go further and show that the 'initiatory cycle' of the *salagoro* – just like that of the *suqe* grade hierarchy – calls in turn on the essential qualities required to become a man of power: mastery of word and gesture (*tamate mweretang*), success and knowledge (*tamate liwoa*), behaviour in accordance with the moral and social order (*tamate qat*), and demonstration of strength, prestige and wealth (*tamate viov*).

These institutions, while they provide us with a better understanding of what is represented by the mask in Banks Islands culture, now no longer have the importance they used to. The mask, today, is limited more and more to events staged solely for the benefit of tourists. But as long as awareness of cultural identity persists, the traditional object, even with its veil stripped away, preserves its specific value, its symbolism and its aesthetic, thus perpetuating the presence of the masked face of the *tamate* of the land of the dead.

'Su tuh netan'monbwei:[1] we write on the ground': Sand-drawings and their Associations in Northern Vanuatu

Kirk W. Huffman

Generations from now, archaeologists may by accident periodically come across small collections of round stones, 4 to 5 centimetres in diameter, incised with complex geometrical and curvilinear designs, on one of the islands in northern Vanuatu.[2] Expatriate archaeologists, if unfamiliar with the traditional cultures or the ethnographic literature, would be extremely puzzled and might try and develop elaborate theories, or minimise their importance. If the future archaeologists are ni-Vanuatu, and if they have retained aspects of their cultural traditions, they will be extremely gratified to know they have discovered the private collections of the 'memory-holding' stones belonging to particular high-ranking or sacred men. Some of the incised designs on the stones are the only permanent form of representation of one of northern Vanuatu's most beautiful and complex artistic traditions, more properly called 'ground writing', but commonly known to scholars as 'sand-drawing'. Despite misgivings, I will use the term sand-drawing, because it is widely known overseas and has become acceptable in Bislama in Vanuatu – at least in the capital, Port Vila – in the form *sandroa* or *sandroing*.

From the north-western part of the island of Epi, northwards through the northern-central islands, on through the Banks and Torres and into the south-east Solomons, there existed, and still exists in some areas, the tradition of executing, with the index finger of the right hand, a myriad of ritual designs, or 'writings', of varying complexity on the ground or, if on the coast, on the beach. These can range anywhere from simple messages drawn on the earth outside someone's house, meaning, for example, 'I came to visit you but you were not here', to more complex configurations. Such types of sand-drawing, for communication, are called, for example, *matamata* in the Tinjivo language/dialect spoken today in south-east Malo. Styles of these communication, or message, writings were usually restricted to one language or cultural area, and although related to those used in neighbouring cultures, were usually different from island to island. They were possibly examples of a potential written language in process of development.

The type of sand-drawing for which Vanuatu is best known, internally and overseas, is, however, the often incredibly complex continuous-line geometrical, labyrinthine or maze-like drawings which seem to have reached their 'highest' development in north-central Vanuatu. In west Ambrym these are known generally as *tuh netan* (*tu netan* in north Ambrym), '*tan*' meaning 'ground'. In Raga language of north Pentecost, they are called *uliuli*. On

1. As from the dialect spoken in the westernmost tip of west Ambrym. This short article is written in memory of my dear friends Maëlib (Gülgül Vetu) of Lolibulo, Chief Willy Taso of Fonah and Wuro and Chief Gaston Batick of Sesivi, all in west Ambrym and all now dead – and is dedicated to young Kailabnalit of the Mbotkote-speaking area in south-central Malakula in the hope that when he grows up he will have learnt the *naites* of his people.

2. The author refrains from divulging the name of this island, to protect the still-existing 'private collections' hold by elderly sacred and wise men from the rare visit of (often sympathetic but often

Fig. 317
Jacques Gédéon, from Paama, tracing the sand-drawing *timaëh keilu*, the twins.

unscrupulous) expatriate 'art dealers'. Other islands may produce slightly larger and less well-produced versions of aspects of these incised stones, but they serve a different purpose.

3. Henri donated in 1983 to the Vanuatu Cultural Centre copies of many of these designs, plus a video cassette of Albert Tobül of north Ambrym drawing six different *tu netan*. Also in the Cultural Centre's National Film Collections are my 1981 8-millimetre films The most beautiful film sequence of sand-drawing to date is that done by Film Australia in 1985 (as part of the '*Blong Save Hu Nao Yumi*' Malakula Arts Festival Film).

4. One of the sadder effects of the spread of mission influence in Vanuatu is that in some (though not all) areas, one of its effects has seemingly been to much more effectively destroy the more sacred aspects of women's ritual life than that of the men. But then, as a man, I can not delve deeply into the more tabu elements of women's ritual – that is only for women.

Vao, in north-east Malakula, the act of sand-drawing is known as *ghir*, and the design made can be called *wör*, although the latter term also covers such designs as ritual tattoos and keloids. Around Larevet, on the western 'neck of the dog' of Malakula, they are known as *rolu*. In the Ninde-speaking Mewun area of South West Bay, Malakula, they are known as *nana*, as *nitüs* in the neighbouring Nahati-speaking Wilemp area, and *nitüs na'ana* in the Nahava-speaking Seniang area just to the south. The Mbotkote-speakers in the mountainous southern interior call them *watatés*, or, more commonly, *naites*. These are just samples; each language will have its own general term, and of course each particular design (and there are hundreds of them) will have a particular name, or a series of names, depending on which level the drawing is being made or used.

Basically, we owe the now generally accepted term sand-drawing to Bernard Deacon, who, by the time of his tragic death in South West Bay in 1927, had collected 118 different designs from Malakula, Ambrym and Ambae. John Layard, who began collecting different designs in north-east Malakula in 1915, was still considering the publication of a special study of more than 100 different designs at the time of his death in 1974. Layard preferred the use of the term 'sand-tracings'. Amazingly, Felix Speiser, in his two years of Vanuatu peregrinations between 1910 and 1912, collected no examples ('These are rarely encountered. Those that are seen are the usual drawings of sailing ships.' Speiser 1991:394); never staying long enough in one place to gain the confidence of ni-Vanuatu, he sadly missed one of the country's great riches. Between 1978 and 1983, Henri Tailhade, art teacher at the Vanuatu National Institute of Technology at the Lycée Antoine de Bougainville in Port Vila, collected more than 180 different designs from students at the Lycée and during his travels in the northern islands.[3]

It seems to be widely assumed (at least by men) in Vanuatu – and overseas – today, that only men do sand-drawings (fig. 317). This was not always the case, and in some instances may still not be so. It is said that women in south Santo used to draw, but as this area was largely depopulated by the beginning of this century it is now probably too late to collect any information. There are stories of women in the Banks Islands doing such drawings and men taking these drawings for part of their *tamate* regalia, thus 'copyrighting' them and prohibiting their further use by women. It is quite probable that women on Ambae, Maewo and north Pentecost[4] had sand-drawings on their own for women's rituals, and there are indications that such drawings were used in part of the higher-rank rituals for the now long-defunct *yemarkon*, the women's graded society in the Meltung'n area of west-south-west Ambrym. It is true, however, that sand-drawing is now (almost) exclusively a male activity, with the rights to certain designs being passed down from father to son and nephew, or 'sold' to neighbouring individuals and even other islands. Because the designs have become part of the copyright system extant in north-central Vanuatu, one thus finds similar designs, with minor variations – for example, the turtle being one of the most popular ones – cropping up in many different areas under different names.

For the process of sand-drawing, one needs a flat, compact beach area, or, if in the bush, a flat area of compact dark soil or volcanic ash. In the latter cases, a thin covering of white fire-ash will make the resulting design much clearer. Once ready, the 'drawer' then marks out a line grid – on which the design will be 'founded' – starting with the vertical lines (from left to right) and then the horizontal lines (from top to bottom). Each design has a particular starting and finishing point, and the drawer's right index finger should ideally complete the design between these two without leaving the ground – except, of course, in those designs that require dots (as the eyes of the dead man in fig. 323). Depending on the status of the design – public, sacred, or so on – the drawer may be surrounded by a group of children, or adults, telling the tale and singing the songs (if they exist) of the design as he goes along. Once finished, the drawing is usually wiped away.

Sand-drawings do not exist in a cultural vacuum: they are done for many reasons at many different times, and can sometimes have different levels of meaning depending on the context in which they are done. Some are just for children's 'play'; others, 'free' in one context as a message design, can also be sacred and an essential element in the passage of one's spirit to the world of the dead in another (see below). Some reflect stories of the animal (fig. 318) and natural world, others humorous or risqué human affairs.[5] Some depict material objects – fighting or dance clubs, canoes (fig. 319), bows and arrows. Others depict aspects of the spirit world, or historical events. Many are also linked to other

Fig. 318
Jellyfish sand-drawing *aë katiat*, by Jacques Gédéon.

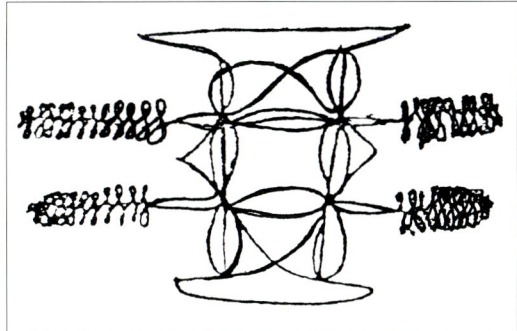

Fig. 319
Sand-drawing of a double-hulled canoe, *rue rue*.

5. One day in October 1978 I showed old Maëlib of Lolibulo, west Ambrym, Jean Guiart's sand-drawing photograph – Guiart 1963a:117, fig. 87. Maëlib said, 'That one is called *Long'o'pwerr*' (*lap-lap* taro) and then chuckled: the story of the drawing is of a woman, her hands dirty from making taro *laplap*, having intercourse and having to hold her hands clasped above her head so as not to leave tell-tale marks on the man's body. The story is based on an actual incident, and the 'inventor' of this widely resold design, Maru of Wo'h in north Ambrym, would have known the names of the individuals involved, but this information would probably not be passed on during the 'copyright reselling process'.

6. For insights into the world of north Pentecost *uliuli*, I am grateful to Chief Silas Nari Leo Bule of Lobultamata, and for the *rue rue* my thanks go to *olfala* Harper Lini of Agatoa, and especially to Richard Leona of Loltong. Harper Lini, wise in the ways of *kastom* since his youth, is the (now very elderly) father of Father Walter Hayde Lini, the first prime minister of Vanuatu.

7. Pers. comm. to author, 1974. In 1915, Layard also went on one of the Atchin initiation voyages to south-west Ambae.

Fig. 320
Myzomela cardinalis (cardinal honeyeater) sand-drawing.

activities – string figures, games, songs, messages, flute or drum rhythms, dance patterns, tattoo and mat designs, body paint and mask designs, mythical heroes, specific geographical features, spirit travel and the world of ancestral spirits, membership of secret societies, and so on. Some can even combine almost all of these aspects at the same time meaning different things or levels, depending on who is watching or participating and at what time. Knowledge of some may be absolutely essential for life after death.

Four figures have been chosen as examples to illustrate various aspects, and a fifth will be described but not illustrated (for ritual reasons). Reasons for choosing some of these are the light they may throw on interconnections and also an attempt to avoid many of the types and much of the information usually covered in previously published material. Layard and Deacon already cover much material.

Figure 319 is a *uliuli* from the Raga-speaking area of north Pentecost, and is entitled *rue rue* – 'double-hulled canoe' (see Huffman, 'Trading, Cultural Exchange and Copyright', p. 184, this volume).⁶ This figure is taken from Haddon (1934: 144, fig. 2), and was one of many drawings originally provided by the (then young) Harper Lini to Miss Hardacre, who was an Anglican missionary based at Laone, and who collected (on paper) Raga *uliuli* for Raymond Firth and A.C. Haddon. Haddon had an English draughtsman redraw the figure (Haddon 1934:145), but the latter made mistakes in the redrawing, so it is preferable to use the original (paper) drawing; this is often a problem when one uses a 'modern' artist to professionally copy a traditional sand-drawing. Not knowing the meaning and significance of often minute features, the copier can make mistakes that sometimes leave out or change essential elements. This *rue rue* drawing is important in that it is one of the only surviving depictions of the early double-hulled trading and voyaging canoes that once existed in northern Vanuatu. In Vao, the language term for them, *nuwak gheru*, still exists, but no depictions. No early European 'visitors' to Vanuatu reported ever seeing any of these canoes, but they definitely existed, and voyaged and traded over great distances. The *rue rue* illustrated here is originally linked to a now-disappeared stone feature near the north Pentecost shore, and the canoe's two owners, Vulamwel and Rurudenga.

Figure 320 is a rare rectangular sand-drawing from Ambae, collected originally by Bernard Deacon in 1926-27, and copied for this article from Layard (1942:656, fig. 62; he copied it from the redrawn version in Deacon 1934a:172, fig. 78). The letters A and B show, respectively, the starting and finishing points. This drawing represents the nest (the lozenge in the centre) of the cardinal honeyeater (*Myzomela cardinalis*), the *redhed*, a small black bird with a red, hooked bill. It is not known what area the original of this drawing is from on Ambae: Deacon picked up much of his non-Malakula material from islanders in the prison or Condominium Police Force in Port Vila (while waiting to go to Malakula), and from plantation workers from other islands working on Malakula. It seems likely, though, that rectangular sand-drawings of this type (there were also many other types on Ambae) were possibly widespread in the Lolokaro area of south-west Ambae, which had strong cultural and ritual links with north-east Malakula (see Huffman, this volume). By the time of Layard's 1914-15 stay in the latter area, it seemed to him⁷ that *certain* of north-east Malakulan 'rectangular linear' dances of

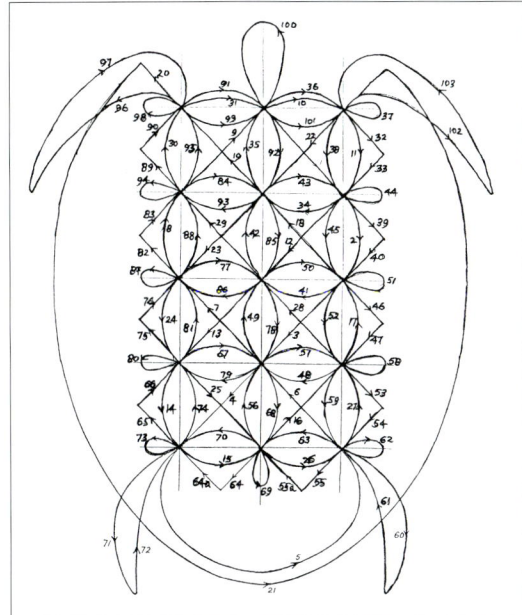

Fig. 321 Sea turtle sand-drawing.

Fig. 322 Turtle sand-drawing, *ahü*, by Jacques Gédéon.

the *naleng* type were following linear patterns portrayed in the Ambae rectangular sand-drawings. It is also interesting to note that a type of curvilinear *narel* dance still done on Wala, north-east Malakula, if seen from above, follows the lines and movements of a human birth, and can be related to a Malakulan sand-drawing representing that. Regarding the designs of some of the many Ambae rectangular sand-drawings, there may be links and parallels to some Ambae mat designs and tattoos (the *bulu* or *tatai*) of Ambae *bure*[8] (high-ranking tattooed women).

The geometrically redrawn (with the linear order of the drawing lines numbered) Ambrym sand-drawing of the sea turtle in figure 321,[9] taken from Deacon (1934a:154, fig. 20), and its many variants throughout Ambrym and Malakula, is today one of Vanuatu's most widely known, popular and 'publicised' styles (see fig. 322). Deacon calls the drawing *hi*, which indicates he must have obtained the original from a south-east Ambrym man. In north Ambrym, this *tu netan* is known as *viu*, and in the western point of Ambrym as *viuvi'o*. In the Ninde, Nahava and Naha'ai-speaking areas of south-west Malakula it is known as (general term for sand-drawing followed by) *nambá*. Aside from the beauty and symmetry of its design, it also has connotations with bows, musical bows, power over the waves and the white man.

Figure 323 is a geometrically redrawn and line-numbered funerary sand-drawing originally from Uripiv Island, north-east Malakula. Deacon (1934a: 167, fig. 60) calls it *nitangian Uripiv* ('The mourning of Uripiv'). Although it is possible that the original drawing was collected in the district of Lagalag, stretching across the southern part of the 'neck' of Malakula, its title definitely indicates Uripiv as its origin. It represents a dead male body surrounded by six mourners (two on either side, and one each at the head and feet).[10]

Not illustrated to respect traditional tabus, the fifth figure is called *naites sombunderre* ('The writing "You wait"') from the Mbotkote-speaking area in the interior of southern Malakula.[11] The rich cultures of the Mbotkote and 'Nabwol'-speaking peoples from the interior mountains of southern Malakula have a wide variety of geometric continuous-line drawings of numerous types and styles (under the general term *naites*), but the nearest sandy beach is at least a day's walk away, so in this area one must definitely talk about 'ground writing'

8. Although sand-drawings are not mentioned in the text, see Kanegai 1994.

9. Possibly the hawk's bill turtle (*Eretmochelys imbricata*).

10. I include this Uripiv figure particularly to try to interest the Uripiv people. They are the inheritors of a rich and complex culture, but since the death of *olfala* Veremato, there are only a few old knowledgeable men and women to draw upon as 'cultural resources', and there is a lack of early information in the published ethnographic literature. I include it also as it deals with death, thus bringing us close to the ultimate, highest and most critical aspects of some of northern Vanuatu's sand-drawings: the essential key to entry (in some areas) to the world of the dead.

11. For insights into the world of Watetés and Naites in south-central Malakula, I am grateful to Metaknambymb of Lendaboë, Komanlüver Sinmürmindrik of Komanliveur, the late Komanlyk of Imorao, and especially to Komanlyklawan of Bailit. Thanks also to Taso Ataor.

12. So, as one can see, some early missionaries had a particularly difficult and confusing time in areas of north-east Malakula.

Fig. 323
Sand-drawing representing 'the mourning of Uripiv'.

or 'ground drawing'. Deacon (1934a, 1934b) and Layard (1942) have written at length about the absolute necessity for men from various areas of south-west Malakula to learn a particular sand-drawing of the type known as *nahal* ('the path; in Vao *na-hal*, in Atchin *nisel*) as their safe pass-key to the world of the ancestral spirits after death. For many of the different cultures of the South West Bay, Malakula, the Home of the Dead lies somewhere in the region of a sacred rock (called many different names; there are differing versions of the myth) in the sea, not far from the present-day village of Wintua. Varying according to the myth version, somewhere along the way the female devouring spirit (known as *temes savsap* in Nahava language) lies in wait for the spirit of the dead man – before her she has drawn the sand-drawing, *nahal*, and has rubbed out half of it, or the middle (depending on myth version). Upon coming up to the *nahal* drawing, the spirit of the dead man must recomplete the drawing, otherwise the female spirit will eat him and he will never pass through to dance with his ancestors. Similarly, spirits of dead men from Vao, Atchin and Wala, in north-east Malakula, must follow various spirit paths southwards along the mainland (depending on myth version) to eventually try to cross to Ambrym to live with the other ancestral spirits in the volcano there (called Bot Gharambi – 'head, source of fire' – on Vao). At differing points along the way, according to myth version, the Devouring Spirit lies in wait to try to stop them: for the Vao people, this spirit is Lehevhev, neither male nor female, yet both; for Atchin and Wala people, the spirit is Lesawsaw, definitely female. Again, the Devouring Spirit draws (the relevant version of) 'the path' sand-drawing, rubbing out part of it; if the spirit of the dead man cannot recomplete the drawing when he comes upon it, his spirit is eaten and he never reaches the 'heavenly eternal fire'.[12]

The Mbotkote and 'Nabwol' peoples from south-central Malakula have another variant of this spirit voyage. All males from this area must learn *naites sombunderre* 'ground writing'. It is also useful during life as a 'communication writing' – if you go to visit someone and they are not home, you draw it on the ground near their house. It is a command: 'You wait.' You can wander off to hunt wild pigs or whatever, coming back later with the knowledge that if the person you wanted to see has come during your absence, they will be waiting. The concept spills over into coded drum rhythms. If you want to go to see someone, you can beat out the *tuktukai* 'attention-commanding' rhythm on your slit-drums. When the slit-drums of the area you want to contact (everyone knows the sound, style and positioning of the drums scattered throughout the mountains) give the *indamó* ('All right'; that is, 'Waiting for your message') reply, you then beat out the rhythm *naisembundao* ('You wait where you are (I am coming)'), likened to the sound form of *naites sombunderre*. So one has plenty of opportunities to practice all aspects of this essential *naites* during one's life.

One hundred days after your death, when your family and colleagues have finished your *nemasien* rituals, your spirit can begin its travels to the world of the dead – but there are two worlds: Lowüren-

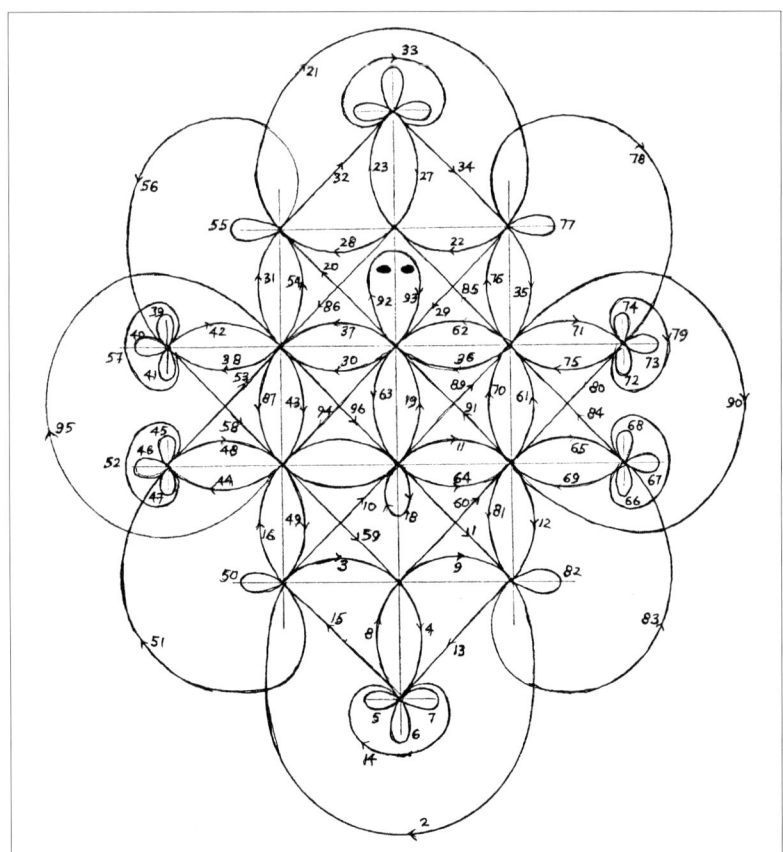

serr, the good sky, or cloud, world, where life is easy and night never falls; and (Ne)Gerowonbi/Garowanbie, the 'place of pain and fire', the 'bad' spirit world down below at a specific spot on the coast or in the sea. Along your spirit path lurks – at a specific place – the (definitely male) spirit Kambilek/Ambilenk who has drawn a partially incomplete *naites sombunderre* on the path. When your spirit arrives, Kambilek checks you to see if your ears and nose have been pierced – if not, he pierces them in a painful and particularly embarrassing way. Your spirit then has to complete the *naites:* if you can do it, you pass on the 'good path' to Lowürenserr; if you can not do it, Kambilek 'hooks' your spirit with the sacred form of the pig-killing club and throws you onto the 'bad path' leading to Gerowonbi.[13]

I write this short, incomplete paper about sand-drawings[14] in the hope that it will help to stimulate ni-Vanuatu interest and pride in one of the country's most fascinating and complex, enjoyable, meaningful and 'artistic' ritual activities, of a form and beauty that can be admired around the world. I do, though, make a plea to young ni-Vanuatu to not overly place their confidence in the white man's way of trying to reproduce these figures in a 'geometrically perfect' way with modern instruments: these hundreds of beautiful 'drawings' are a form of language, and 'modernisation' will stunt their normal growth and flow – and sometimes make them incorrect. I also fervently hope that the sand-drawings of one particular style or island should not take over and become the 'official' or 'national' style – many islands have unique series and styles, and these should all be revived and permitted to survive and develop. They are an important part of Vanuatu's rich cultural identity.

Sketches used in this paper were reproduced with the permission of the Royal Anthropological Institute of Great Britain and Ireland. Exact references can be found in the text.

13. Gerowonbi *is* so horrific there may not even be any pigs there. In Lowüreserr, however, above the clouds, the spirits of all the pigs you have killed ritually during your life are waiting there to greet you: it is literally, 'Pig Heaven'.

14. Readers will note that the figure illustrations that I have used were already published more than sixty years ago, and that I do not provide an illustration of the last figure that I talk about in detail. There are particular reasons for this, involving concepts of respect, copyright and tabu.

Mastering the Arts: An Examination of the Context of the Production of Art in Vanuatu

Mary Patterson

No-one taking a stroll around the capital of Vanuatu could fail to notice the prominence of a certain kind of carved wooden slit-drum, mostly monumental and all of a certain style that identifies them immediately as coming from the island of Ambrym. The evolution of this musical instrument and means of communication into a national icon represented outside national institutions, on postage stamps, as a newspaper logo, on hotel brochures and theatre advertisements (fig. 324), and as the base over which the national flag is draped on Independence Day, has come about undoubtedly because it is durable, imposing and appealing to the aesthetic sense of a wide range of people. The fact that hardwood replicas of these drums, scaled down to fit into the average suitcase, are now available in every shop and hotel lobby, while no fine mat of the kind given in mortuary and other kinship ceremonies has been produced in Ambrym since late last century, is a reflection of the kind of processes in operation in Vanuatu before contact with Europeans, but nevertheless accelerated by the transformation of 'artifact' to 'art' and by the demands of a global tourist market and the needs of local producers.

There is a certain irony in the prominence of Ambrym craftsmen in the production of sculpture for the fine-art and the tourist markets, because many of the rituals represented by carved objects in Ambrym have their provenance in other neighbouring islands. The particular genius of the Ambrymese sculptors has been to somehow refine and yet creatively redefine the designs that are not unique to the island into a recognisable and unique style. To place this cultural elaboration in context, we need, on the one hand, to look at the situation that has informed the collection of such items and their exhibition, and, on the other hand, at the much longer history of interaction between groups of settlers in this area of Vanuatu.

Ambrym lies in the north-central region of the archipelago, and is a beautiful, mountainous island, well-known for the active volcanoes at the centre of its roughly triangular land mass that have periodically disrupted the lives of the people and at times made large areas of the island uninhabitable. Perhaps because of this not infrequent need to find a safe haven, Ambrymese have been particularly keen to cultivate their near neighbours in Malakula, south Pentecost and Epi, with all of whom established trading links and even occasional intermarriage occurred in the period before the middle of the last century, when contacts with European recruiters and missionaries began to be made. It is, I think, this outward-looking attitude that accounts for the large numbers of Ambrymese recruits in the early days of the labour trade, and for the eagerness of Ambrymese to engage in cultural commerce with the people of the nearby islands. New rituals were being acquired in the north and the west at what seems like an increasing rate until the devastating volcanic eruption of 1913 displaced a large section of the population of west Ambrym, hastening the abandonment in that area of most of the rituals that had been disseminated to the north and south-east of the island after their acquisition from Malakula. We know that this trade in intellectual property, principally in the purchase of the rights to perform the rituals of status acquisition, called in Ambrym *mage* (figs 325, 326), and the most secret rites of *luan* and *bato* (represented, for example, by sculpted and painted tree-fern statues, and by some of the masks and figurines (fig. 7) from the British Museum), was relatively recent, because their provenance in Malakula is generally known and undisputed for most of the *mage* grades and for the secret rites. (For an account of *mage*, *luan* and *bato* in north Ambrym see Patterson 1981 and Guiart 1951, respectively; for comparison of *luan* with the *nalawan* of Malakula, see Deacon 1934b, chapter 13).

While performances of the rites of the *luan* and *bato*, which have a long seclusion period for the candidates and an association with the acquisition of knowledge about sorcery (in north Ambrym called *abio*), have not been performed since the 1940s, other rites involving the secret construction of masks and costumes revealed in a public dance have been performed continuously in north Ambrym since they were originally purchased from Malakula by west Ambrymese. The right to these *rom* (figs 327, 328, 329), as they are called in the north – that is, the right to the knowledge necessary to construct one of the multiplicity of intricately designed masks or headpieces and costumes, and to perform the figure dance that precedes the payment for every activity and material aspect of the particular *rom* – consists of pigs, fowl, and, for some time now, also money.[1] The most important right, other than to wear the costume and insignia, of course, is that of resale. *Rom* are extremely popular in north Ambrym because, unlike the somewhat similar *ngulong*, which has a conical hat with a mask in front but no cloak, the costumes are kept until they disintegrate,

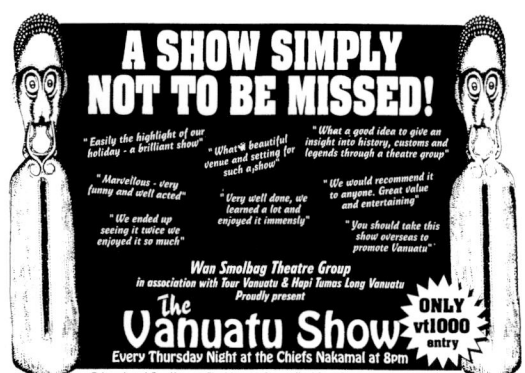

Fig. 324
Announcement inviting tourists to the show put on by the Wan Smol Bag Theatre Group, Port Vila

allowing the candidates to put them on whenever they feel like creating a bit of havoc in the village by chasing the women and children.

Some *rom*, like *rom bako* (the shark), may only be bought by men above a certain rank in the *mage*, and the purchase may take place at the same time as the acquisition of rank. The *ngulong* headdresses, however, are destroyed straight after they are revealed in the dance and paid for, which undoubtedly accounts for their absence from major collections. The *ngulong* headdress, with its 'beard' of fowl's feathers or cycad leaves, most resembles the Malakulan mask from the Speiser collection (cf. fig. 5). This mask appears to have lost its upper and lower feathers or leaves, however. The *ngulong* dance is performed by candidates wearing rattle anklets but no cloaks; they all carry a ceremonial club, a *womdal*, which is usually worn slung over the shoulder by a plaited rope loop, but in this case the club is inverted and held in both hands. It also seems likely that different varieties of *rom* have been created in west and north Ambrym, because I was told on a number of occasions that certain kinds originated in a particular region and that the west Ambrym varieties are 'stronger' than those of the north.

Although all of the male 'secret societies' in Ambrym, including those with long seclusion periods, greater secrecy and higher prices, as well as those considered less 'strong', like *rom* and *ngulong*, have the same basic structure and are clearly elaborations or redefinitions of the Malakulan *nalawan* rites, from which they probably originate; there is no dogma of compulsion in their acquisition, nor is there any fixed hierarchy governing the order in

1. The *rom* candidate purchases a costume consisting of a banana-leaf cloak called *rablat*, a set of rattle anklets (*wongbal*), and a wicker 'arm' with a rattle of seed pods at the end (*wiran rom*), with which to strike at anyone in his path.

2. Any man who wishes to avoid participating in the purchase of *bato* or *luan* must make sure that he stays out of the way of the candidates; should they see him they will coerce him into joining them.

Fig. 325
Mage ne sagran grade monument, collected by Guiart.
Fanla, north Ambrym.
Paris, Musée national des Arts d'Afrique et d'Océanie.

Fig. 326
Mage lon bul grade monument collected by Guiart in 1963 from Mage Korkor, who painted it.
Weha, north Ambrym.
Paris, Musée national des Arts d'Afrique et d'Océanie.

which they may be purchased.[2] The only restrictions relate to those 'societies', for want of a better word, which only grant admittance to men who have achieved a certain rank in the *mage*.

If the Ambrymese were eager for imported novelty, they also had some extremely important rituals of their own that were seen as conferring more power on those who participated in them than any of the 'foreign', recently acquired ritual complexes. These rituals, which I have described in detail elsewhere (Patterson 1981), involve the sacrifice and payment of tusked boars to certain categories of kin. Their performance, particularly the ones that conferred the greatest prestige and power, the *tobuan*, *berang yan yan*, *fenbi* and *serebuan*, throws into sharp relief the important structural elements of the system of kinship and marriage and its acknowledged function, which is to ensure the continuity of the flow of life, and the physical and spiritual integrity of the living and the dead. The religious elements of these rites, as opposed to the predominantly secular character of the *mage* and secret society rites, were not incorporated into the importations in any significant ways.

With the exception of the highest ranks of the *mage*, women were generally excluded from the rituals that were not of local origin; women's participation, however, was central to the performance of those rites mentioned above that were said to be indigenous to Ambrym. All of these rites involved the payment and prominent use of those items made by women, the red mats and fine mats that in recent times have been imported from Pentecost and have not been manufactured in the north, or indeed anywhere else in the island since late last century.

The decline in the making of fine ceremonial mats – of which there were apparently three main kinds: a white mat possibly fringed with yellow feathers (*kakau wan*); the long, narrow, deeply fringed and partly red-dyed 'money' mats (*tewen*); and the red-dyed wider mats (*hobati frifri*), the manufacture of which was kept hidden from men – must have begun long before this time, though. Speiser claimed fine mats were no longer made in Ambrym (though he describes the *tewen* variety), and that the art of dyeing was no longer practised (Speiser 1991:239).

Both kinds of red mat featured in various kinship presentations; the larger red mats were brought by

Fig. 327

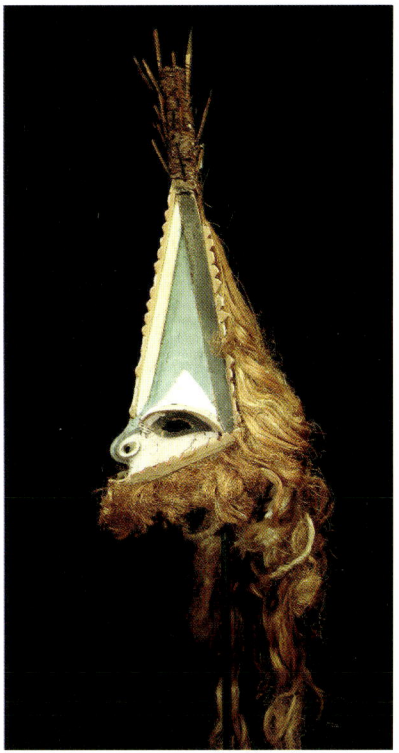
Fig. 328

Fig. 329

female kin after a death to wrap the corpse in, and they also formed a significant part of the mortuary payments. Blankets have for some time largely replaced red mats, which have also been imported from Pentecost in place of those locally made.

Because the *fenbi* and *berang yanyan* rituals were last performed sometime in the 1930s or early 1940s, and also because they were only performed by extremely high-ranking men, of whom there very few, there are no examples of the tree-fern statues, or *berang*, or of the headdress called *lilian* worn by the initiator, in any public collections I know of. I was shown, and photographed, the beaded garters (*akorbu*; cf. fig. 221) worn below the knee, which were also acquired by the man who was the last initiator of these rites in North Ambrym, but his son no longer has them in his possession. The carving of the *berang* is said to be the same as that for the grade *mage ne im gatlam* ('*mage* of the big house'), except it has no arms and is differently decorated.

The ethnologist Rivers (1914), in his attempt to reconstruct the history of Melanesia as the progressive diffusion of cultures carried by various waves of immigrants into the area, saw Ambrym culture as representative of an earlier period in this history, only relatively recently influenced by later arrivals. According to Rivers, this history is particularly evident in the artistic production of the peoples of northern Vanuatu. He argued that the 'kava people' brought with them the kava plant, the cult of the dead, secret societies and the patrilineal system, and that their art was based on the representation of the human body in sculpture and drawing, whereas the more 'archaic' peoples who were already in the islands, the 'dual people', as Rivers called them because of their division of society into two intermarrying categories, managed to influence this art towards abstraction, or what he refers to as 'conventionalisation'. He also saw their use of abstract geometric design as a means adopted by the kava people of representing their secret society sculptures in a way that concealed their nature from the 'dual

Fig. 327
Rom mask, collected by Speiser between 1910 and 1912.
Ambrym.
Basel, Museum für Völkerkunde.

Fig. 328
Rom mask, collected by Speiser between 1910 and 1912.
Ambrym.
Basel, Museum für Völkerkunde.

Fig. 329
Rom mask, 1992.
Ambrym.

Fig. 330
Dancing ground, photographed by
Speiser between 1910 and 1912.
Dip Point, west Ambrym.

Fig. 331
Dancing ground, photographed by
Speiser between 1910 and 1912.
South Malakula.

people'. We have no way of knowing whether the tree-fern statues of the indigenous rites in north Ambrym were always carved in human form or whether this was a result of the influence of the 'kava people', but because Ambrym is one of the very few islands in the archipelago in which kava was not traditionally used, and because Rivers thought that the 'kava people' avoided volcanic islands, this seems highly unlikely. We do know that the large slit-drums of Ambrym take a more recognisably human form than those of most of Malakula, which are represented in a more abstract fashion. We also know that in Ambrym, as elsewhere, the geometric designs that adorn most of the utilitarian bamboo items, like breadfruit paddles and combs and the beautifully decorated flutes, have multiple referents and are also the same as, or combinations of, those symbols used by men of high rank as insignia of their grade.

The lozenge, a dominant motif in Vanuatu ritual art (fig. 220), is seen repeated in almost all of the decorative art applied in the manufacture of ritual and utilitarian objects in Ambrym. This shape may, in some contexts, symbolise the *nana*, or face, the body of the figure with spread, flexed legs, and flexed arms resting elbows on knees that is typically associated with *bato* and *luan* figures, and, when drawn as two opposed but not quite joined chevrons, may represent two pig's jaws. As a symbol marked on trees, and so on, it represents the rank *lokbaro*, or, with the addition of three dots in the position of eyes and mouth, the rank of *mal*. The chevron alone represents the hawk or a pig's jaw, and is the insignia of rank of the grades *neim gatlam* and *meleun kakare;* the chevron beneath a lozenge signifies the grade *meleun gatlam*. The spiral signifies the boar's tusk. All of these motifs appear on carved human representations, as well as being repeated in abstract patterns on the items mentioned previously.

The way in which a particular style of art may evolve in an area is amply illustrated by the Ambrym slit-drums, and demonstrates quite well the opposite of Rivers' assumption that particular practices, items of material culture and styles of representation need major or minor waves of immigrants to disseminate throughout an area, displacing, transforming and mingling with what already exists. Because

Fig. 332
Dancing ground. Watercolour by AB.M., 1875. Port-Sandwich, southeast Malakula.

of their aesthetic appeal and their monumental character, together with the focal position they occupied in social life in all the societies where they are found, Malakulan and Ambrym slit drums were collected from the late 19th century on, and were extensively photographed (fig. 330), as well as being the subject of some drawings and paintings. We can see from these sources some interesting developments in the style and elaboration of the sculpture, some of which undoubtedly relates to the introduction of metal tools, which enabled a certain refinement of some elements of the designs.

In all of northern Malakula, and much of the centre and south, slit-drums are carved with a truncated top and squat stylised face in low relief. They frequently have two holes in the top section, through which the vines were put when they were hauled into place; these features we would now see as the 'Malakulan' style, which is quite different from the slit-drums now identified as quintessentially Ambrymese.

In a photograph taken by Felix Speiser during his expedition of 1910 to 1912 (fig. 331), however, in an unspecified location in southern Malakula, a man stands among three slit-drums (Speiser 1991, pl. 100, no. 4). At the rear, the shortest has the 'typical' Malakulan style with cropped head and squat face, except that the eyes are large round discs and there is above the slit a curved line for a mouth, which, in the north of the island is usually represented by the slit itself. To the left of the picture, on the man's right, is a slightly larger drum with a more ovoid face and a greater, though still relatively small crown above the face. There is a row of crudely worked 'toothing' around the edge of the face. The third and tallest drum has a much more elongated face in what we would now consider the 'Ambrym' style, with a quite large crest, the brow and eyes carved in deeper relief than the other two, disc-shaped eyes, a mouth, and two small hands on either side above the slit. There are two rows of 'toothing', representing hair, above the face. These are all features common to the modern drums seen around Vila and carved by contemporary Ambrymese sculptors who have the copyright to carve them. I think we may assume that these drums were photographed in the

Fig. 333
Three slit-drums from west Ambrym: Fanla, Metamli and, at centre back, from Craig Cove, carved by Tokor in 1951, and a slit-drum from Matanvat, north Malakula.
Paris, Musée national des Arts d'Afrique et d'Océanie.

Fig. 334
Slit-drum used by a ni-Vanuatu in 'modern dress'; photographed by Lamb, before 1905.
West Ambrym.

region of Port Sandwich, the area which was the disseminator of local culture to the people of Ambrym. A confirmation of this assumption comes from an early watercolour in the collection of the Alexander Turnbull Library in Wellington, New Zealand, signed by an unknown artist with the initials 'B.M.' He or she has written 'Sandwich Harbour, Mallicolo. New Hebrides July 1875' (fig. 332). The painting depicts a scene in a ceremonial ground. To the right of the picture is a group of four drums, two large and one small, all with faces and hands, and one smaller one that appears to be plainly carved to a cone shape. The carving on the large drums does not appear elaborate; they taper gradually to a rounded point, and all three have small arms with hands above the slit.[3] Three small slit-drums acquired by the Bishop Museum in Hawai'i in 1898 are also of interest in this context. Unfortunately, like many museum pieces collected in this period they have virtually no documentation, the provenance of one (though we do not know which one) being entirely absent. Two of the drums are catalogued as having been collected in Malakula, and obtained from a W. Truss with 'other artifacts' for the sum of £50. None of them is particularly well-crafted, and all three are roughly cut off at the top. The most stylistically 'Ambrymese' one has a more rounded 'head' and rough-cut toothing around the face. The other two have traces of black paint on the face, not commonly found on Ambrym drums, and noses more tear shaped than the typical 'Ambrym' drums. Nevertheless, the general impression is much closer to 'Ambrym' than 'Malakula'. The interesting question here is whether the Ambrym style evolved out of the influence of the Malakulan graded-society tree-fern sculpture in the south-east on the northern Malakulan slit-drum, being then exported to Ambrym, where it was further redefined and elaborated on by the addition of faces and variations in the details of eyes, painting and so on (fig. 333). Alternatively, the Ambrym slit-drum designs may well have been part of the return currency exchanged for the acquisition of new rituals from the Port Sandwich area. This might explain why some of the slit-drums I have discussed appear so poorly carved, even taking into account that they might not have been worked with steel or iron tools. Carvers skilled in working the softer tree fern might well have experienced difficulty in rendering the Ambrym designs in wood. The stylistic similarity in the carving of 'magic' stones, like those in this exhibition, which were undoubtedly, given Ambrym's reputation for magic and sorcery, also export items, perhaps also supports this latter view of an Ambrym origin for the drum designs. In west Ambrym, the proliferation of design features, particularly in the elaborate carving of one face above another (fig. 334), has had a resurgence in the last decade or so, with many of the drums in Vila emanating from this area. In the north, there seems to be a greater conservatism in style, though in the past there was a considerable variation in design features, particularly in the shape or even absence of the eyes. Tofor, of Fanla village in the north, however, has a small, somewhat functionally inadequate-looking drum that has more faces on its upper part than any I have ever seen (fig. 336).

The popularity of Ambrym sculpture abroad has enabled the carver's skill to be retained and encouraged (though not drum-playing skills to the

Fig. 335
Dancing ground, photographed in July 1992.
Fanla, north Ambrym.

Fig. 336
Tofor slit-drum, heavily decorated style, photographed in July 1992.
Fanla, north Ambrym.

3. The copyright for this detail (that is, arms and hands) in north Ambrym is owned by some of the men of Fanla village, who acquired it a couple of generations ago from a west Ambrymese who brought it with him when he settled in the north.

same degree, something lamented by the older generation) while the continuing popularity of rituals like *rom* has ensured that the arts of mask making, figure dancing and the composition of love-magic songs are kept alive. That this renaissance of artistic production in Ambrym is male dominated is an unfortunate consequence of the exclusion of women from the acquisition of these most popular rituals, except as spectators and accompanying dancers, and the series of historical events that brought about the demise of mat-making skills.

If, in focusing on artifacts removed from their cultural setting, we run the risk of losing an important means of 'reading' their significance, we can perhaps be encouraged by the reminder that, as we have seen in the case of Ambrym, cultural fluidity and transformation is the norm, not the exception, and that creativity lies within the heart of tradition.

Chapter V
Towards a history of the visual record

European Perceptions of the Arts of Vanuatu: Engendering Colonial Interests

Margaret Jolly

The category 'art', highly problematic even in exclusively European contexts, is still more contested in those situations of translation and cross-cultural interpretation where outsiders look at and collect the art of others. In the indigenous languages of Vanuatu, there is no category which might generically be translated as 'art' (see Tryon and Huffman, this volume), and ni-Vanuatu probably employ different criteria of aesthetics or efficacy to those familiar to Europeans (see Thomas 1995). Most of the objects or events which Europeans classify as art are already detached from their practical or ritual uses, in the process of being collected and held in museums or galleries.

Apart from the difficulty of segregating a class of art objects, there is also the problem that some of the most stunning creations of ni-Vanuatu art are ephemeral. At the furthest extreme are the intricate sand-drawings of Malakula or the body tattoos of Ambae. But many other creations are vulnerable to the effects of time and decomposition – the ochres applied to the face of a slit-gong or a mask, the pandanus and banana fibres from which mats, penis sheaths and skirts are fashioned, the fragile tissues of spiders' web and tree fern, and even the wood of platters, weapons and slit-gongs. Even in the best-controlled environments, processes of deterioration, desiccation and rotting are patent.[1]

Such questions of use and impermanence intersect with the gendering of art. By this I refer to the gender of the creators, and to how the objects themselves are perceived – as masculine or feminine. In Vanuatu, as in much of the Pacific, women are the creators of plaited, woven or beaten fibrous forms[2] – baskets, mats, grass skirts, penis sheaths and tapa – and men are the makers of sculpted wooden, stone or ivory objects, plastic and painted forms (see Keller 1988; Bolton and Tarisesei 1992; Bolton 1993 and this volume; Teilhet 1983). There is clearly an indigenous distinction between women's and men's artistic creations. But European collecting and curatorial practices have tended to reinscribe this in terms of the distinction between art and craft – men's sculpted forms, be they slit-gongs, masks, effigies or weapons, are more often assimilated to the category of art, while pandanus baskets and mats or tapa cloths are classified more often as craft than art (cf. Teilhet 1983:46).

To illustrate such persisting difficulties, I now consider a range of European perceptions and responses. These are not only of historical importance, but have contemporary effects. The aesthetic adjudications of Europeans, be they museum

---

1. Perhaps the only indigenous art materials which robustly resist the weathering of time are the ivory of the pigs' tusks or the shells of various sea creatures.

2. Women are also the makers of pots in Santo, and presumably in the past on a number of other islands in the archipelago (see Speiser 1991:230-233; and Galipaud, this volume). They are also, since the introduction of imported cloth, expert seamstresses. I do not have time to discuss either of these arts here. Teilhet (1983) suggests that throughout Melanesia and Polynesia it is men who dominate the hieratic visual arts because of their exclusive rights to use certain materials (wood, stone,

A brief history of Vanuatu collections in France

Sylviane Jacquemin

Fig. 337 Detail of a fine tapa cloth with decorated and feathered border, collected by Lieutenant Pineau in the 1880s, and donated to the Louvre Museum in 1890.

In 1798, when de Bougainville made landfall in what is now Vanuatu, he named the islands the New Cyclades, a misleading reference to the Aegean archipelago, because, paradoxically, he found the land and the society harsh and inhospitable. In 1774, Cook was more noncommittal and called the islands the New Hebrides, after the islands off the north-west coast of Scotland. So the history of Vanuatu is also part of the history of France and the United Kingdom and of their sometimes uneasy relationship.

Vanuatu's destiny was also linked to that of New Caledonia, which became a French colony in 1853. The Compagnie calédonienne des Nouvelles Hébrides was founded in 1882 with the aim of annexing the archipelago by purchasing land from the English settlers. The purchases had been completed by 1885, but then in 1887 the Anglo-French Condominium was set up. In 1980 the country finally gained independence as the Republic of Vanuatu. These political events were to influence the way people looked at and appreciated the art of Vanuatu.

It is interesting to see the close relationship between French collections from Vanuatu and those from New Caledonia: a certain similarity in the colonial histories of these neighbouring countries, in the collectors' personalities, and in the kinds of objects collected; and the same relative indifference to the societies that produced them, and to their forms of artistic expression. Museums' reserve collections provide a clear illustration of this state of affairs: artifacts from Vanuatu and New Caledonia are stored together, they were usually brought back by the same donor, and that donor's identity is generally unknown and his ethnographic knowledge lost.

It is true that Vanuatu produced objects whose characteristics determined whether or not they would be collected. Among the country's various art objects, largely hidden away from European eyes, were monumental figures, easily broken and thus difficult to transport. Rare indeed are the standing slit-gongs, the grade monuments, the funerary figures, the ceremonial headdresses in our museums. What we do find are a profusion of weapons – clubs, bludgeons, arrows, fishing spears – brought back in great quantities, and now taking up storage space. It should be pointed out, however, that Vanuatu is particularly rich and prolific in this area.

What was collected also depended largely on who the collector was. Military men, naval officers, businessmen and priests were the principal collectors. The lack of interest in Vanuatu, evident from the absence of scientific expeditions in the 19th and early 20th centuries, provides a further explanation of the gaps in French collections. This is so much the case that any object other than a weapon becomes something extraordinary and precious. It is astonishing that we have no information about the spectacular statues from the Banks Islands in the Aquitaine Museum in Bordeaux.

The soldiers' and naval officers' professional bent led them overwhelmingly to bring back weapons. Their activities did not generally make them attentive observers of the society with which they were rubbing shoulders. Admiral Huguet at Boulogne-sur-Mer, and Admiral Gourdon at Pithiviers are perfect examples, though Palma Gourdon did bring back some remarkable headdresses, in addition to an impressive collection of weapons.

There are similar exceptions to the rule in other museums, such as Dunkirk, Langres (with a collection whose origin must be very old), Lille and others, where one finds platters, mats, ceremonial ornaments, and so on, all jumbled together. But these objects are few and not generally recorded in the museum's inventory, which means that the donor has not been identified and the date of the gift is unknown.

The story of Lieutenant of Marines Pineau runs counter to the majority in this respect, and is worth mentioning. Pineau went to Vanuatu in the 1880s, though, curiously, his military file does not mention the posting. He showed a real interest in the society. As well as making a large collection of artifacts, he co-wrote articles with Dr Hagen, an army doctor who was responsible for overseeing the recruitment of native labour in Vanuatu and the Solomon Islands. Pineau donated his collection to two different museums, the Louvre's Musée de marine et d'ethnographie (whose holdings went to the Musée de Saint-Germain-en-Laye at the end of the 19th century and to the Musée des arts d'Afrique et d'Océanie in 1991), and the new Musée d'ethnographie du Trocadéro, which received a series of 174 objects in 1890.

Rather strangely, traders and businessmen also contributed to the collection which was to form the nucleus of the Trocadéro museum's Vanuatu holdings. Higginson, founder of the Le Nickel company in New Caledonia, the Compagnie calédonienne des Nouvelles-Hébrides in 1882 and the Société française des Nouvelles-Hébrides in 1884, kept the museum comfortably supplied. Higginson was, in fact, under an obligation to do so, in exchange for the considerable financial advantages the French government had given the Compagnie des Nouvelles-Hébrides.

The Le Mescam collection was soon added to these already considerable holdings. Louis Le Mescam set out for New Caledonia in 1873, where he was to build the first blast furnaces at Pointe Chaleix. In 1891 he became the United States' commercial agent and acted as consul. His many travels enabled him to acquire a large collection from New Caledonia and the New Hebrides. This collection originally went to the Havre Museum, and was the subject of a publication by Gustave Lennier, the museum's curator; later, in 1889, most of it passed to the Trocadéro museum.

The colonial exhibition of 1931 did not attach any great value to Vanuatu's art, and its people were presented to the public as 'man-eaters'. The collection destined to decorate the colonial pavilions was, however, to form the nucleus of the holdings of the Musée des colonies at the Porte Dorée. Again there was a striking lack of information about, and interest in, a series of objects from the collection of a certain Mr Austin, a resident of Port Vila, about which we have no other indication as to their provenance, though it includes some important pieces: ceremonial headdresses, animal figures, platters, pottery and funerary figures – the latter recorded in the museum's inventory as mummies.

It was not until the founding of the Musée d'art d'Afrique et d'Océanie (formerly the Musée des colonies and later the Musée de la France d'Outre-mer) that a proper acquisitions policy took shape. Jean Guiart, in charge of the Oceania section, undertook field trips in 1963 and added considerably to the museum's holdings, most notably with a large number of slit-gongs and grade monuments.

Quite recently, in 1991, a purchasing expedition organised through the Réunion des Musées Nationaux acquired a set of ceremonial headdresses for the Musée d'arts d'Afrique et d'Océanie in Paris. At last – a sign of willingness to give the art and culture of Vanuatu the attention they deserve.

Reference materials used in the preparation of this paper include: Hagen and Pineau 1889; Jacquemin 1991; Lennier 1896; the acquisitions register of the Musée d'Ethnographie du Trocadéro oceanic collections, Le Havre (a publication of the *Le Havre* newspaper); and the register of objects given to the permanent Colonial Museum by the administration of New Caledonia in 1931 (archives of the Musée National des Arts d'Afrique et d'Océanie).

curators, art collectors or tourists, can still exert a strong influence not only in New York or Basel, but on creative and curatorial practices in Vanuatu itself. I will deal primarily with the visual arts and consider successively the representations of 18th-century explorers,[3] 19th-century missionaries and 20th-century ethnologists and anthropologists. The colonial interests of these viewers structured their response to the arts of Vanuatu – seen successively as signs of a state of savagery by Enlightenment scientists, as evil incarnations of heathen religiosity by Christian missionaries, and as signs of cultural diffusion and/or colonially induced degeneration by ethnologists and anthropologists. This all sounds very denigrating. There were also celebrations. But negative and positive views were equally saturated by a colonial interest.

'As few Arts as most I have seen': The 'enlightened' views of de Bougainville, Cook and the Forsters

De Bougainville's contact with ni-Vanuatu in 1768 was fleeting and restricted to Ambae. He had little to say about indigenous art, and what he did say was the usual mixture of ignorance and prejudice. But even from these very brief encounters, an attitude to indigenous arts emerges. The creations which most engage his attention are weapons – the bows and arrows, clubs and spears made and used by men. He mentions the ironwood sabres (spears) of Ambae, and describes in some detail the form of their reed arrows and barbed points (Bougainville 1772:291). The fact that men were habitually bearing arms he takes to be a sign of perpetual internecine war, which he claims made their lives 'very wretched' (ibid.:292).[4] Whereas men are negatively portrayed as preoccupied with the martial arts, women's art occasions a celebration. He thought the cloths of Ambae (and especially mats used by women to carry children on their backs) had 'very pretty drawings made with a fine crimson colour' (ibid.:291). This is perhaps the only positive evaluation which de Bougainville offers of ni-Vanuatu arts – his depictions exemplify his prejudicial view that people and material and cultural creations were 'savage'.

Cook's explorations of Vanuatu in 1774, on his second voyage in the Pacific, were longer and entailed more intensive contact with people on the

Fig. 338 Carved spearhead, twin. Big Nambas, north-west Malakula. Paris, Musée national des Arts d'Afrique et d'Océanie.

islands of Malakula, Erromango and Tanna. But the prevailing view of ni-Vanuatu arts echoes that of de Bougainville – they are signs of savagery. Again the objects which most engage the captain's attention are men's weapons (figs 338, 339, 340) and women's mats, but there is also some mention of canoes, houses and forms of bodily ornamentation. Most of Cook's remarks concern the debatable efficacy of poison-tipped arrows and the curiosity of men's bodily costume and ornamentation[5] – bracelets of shell and pigs' tusks, nose jewellery and tortoise-shell earrings (Beaglehole 1961:464-465). The face painting of men and women he adjudges ugly (ibid.:464). He considers Malakulan canoes 'ill built' (ibid.:465), describes Tannese houses as 'mean and small hovels' and the pandanus mats made by women 'a Course kind of Matting' (ibid.:506). In summary, he proclaims, 'these people seem to have as few Arts as most I have seen' (ibid.:506).

ivory) or tools (adzes), and especially because they usually have the exclusive right to represent the human form or anthropomorphic figures. This also seems to hold true for Vanuatu, with the exception of those places where women are responsible for dyeing such forms onto mats. In south Pentecost, men perform this part of the process of dyeing stencilled patterns, while on other islands such as Ambae, women do all the work of making mats – collecting, treating and bleaching the pandanus, plaiting and/or weaving, and dyeing (see Keller 1988; Bolton 1993; Bolton and Taresesei 1992; Bolton, this volume; Walter, this volume).

3. Of course the 18th-century exploratory voyages of Cook and de Bougainville were not the first. They were preceded by de Quirós in 1606 (see Jolly 1992a), who visited the Banks and Santo. But the accounts of this voyage contain little reference to indigenous arts, so I do not consider it here; see, however, Bonnemaison (1986a).

4. That this 'first contact' with Europeans might have occasioned legitimate alarm is not acknowledged, nor does the fact that the French were also heavily

armed and freely used their muskets (Bougainville 1772:292, 295-60) condemn them to a similar state of savagery.

5. For more detailed accounts of this, see Jolly 1992a.

6. Their views were contemporaneous with the theories of the French and Scottish Englightenments, but although these employed a theory of stages, they were significantly different to later evolutionary theories. The Forsters' schemes were not rigidly evolutionary, partly because they were less confident of European superiority (see Jolly 1992a), and partly because they deployed a contending classification based on a theory of geographical determinism (see Thomas 1996).

7. Forster senior says little about Vanuatu in his chapter appraising Pacific arts and sciences (Forster 1778: 435-532). This is primarily a detailed discussion of Tahiti.

8. Georg Forster observed that because casuarina was scarce on Tanna, most clubs came from Erromango (1968:519). He also noted: 'Their bows are strong, elastic and nicely polished; their arrows very well wrought; and those which we supposed to be

Fig. 339
Carved spearhead. The support for the spear tip is missing.
Big Nambas, north-west Malakula.
Geneva, Musée d'Ethnographie.

Fig. 340
Carved spearhead, with human-bone tip.
Big Nambas, north-west Malakula.
Paris, Musée de l'Homme.

A rather more detailed appraisal of ni-Vanuatu arts from the second voyage emerges from the narrative of Georg Forster (G. Forster 1968), son of the German scientist Johann Reinhold Forster, both of whose recorded observations of Pacific peoples on this voyage were crucial in the emergence of later evolutionary theories of human society.[6] In such a grand schema ni-Vanuatu did not fare too well being cast as less advanced than those inhabiting islands further east. This adjudication was based on a racial hierarchy, indexed by the position of women (Jolly n.d.a.) but also by material culture and art works. In his huge comparative work, Johann Forster (1778:439) propounds his view that:

> ... though the more Western isles have the same advantage of a happy climate, are far from being barren, and the numbers of the people by no means inconsiderable; yet they are less improved, have fewer arts and improvements.[7]

Georg Forster elaborates on this general principle in relation to material culture and art. Like Cook, he was preoccupied with the character of men's weapons and gives endless descriptions of bows, arrows, spears (fig. 341) and clubs (1777:459-60), which he often applauds for their refinement – the polish of their casuarina clubs[8] or the deep mahogany of their bows. He concludes that 'much more care and ingenuity have been bestowed on this part of their manufactures than upon any other' (ibid.). This is a rather back-handed compliment, because their very dedication to the arts of warfare is testament to savagery.

Georg also disparages Malakulan canoes as small, of 'indifferent workmanship' and 'without ornament' (ibid.:463). The comparison was as always with the islands further east (ibid.:537):

> It seems the fabrick of a boat is so tedious an enterprize to people who are in a continual state of

warfare, that they cannot spend much time in polishing their timbers, and giving them that perfection and elegance, which is conspicuous in the manufactures of the Friendly Islands.

Apropos the construction of Malakulan houses, he states that 'we have no great reason to admire their skill in the arts' (ibid.:469), while Tannese houses he judged to be 'mere sheds, which barely cover them from the inclemency of the weather' (ibid.:540).

All observers on this voyage testify to the difference between the bodily ornamentation of men and women. Body painting with ochres, turmeric or lime is uniformly deplored as yielding a filthy or greasy appearance (for example, G. Forster 1968: 462). The scanty attire of men and women is consistently castigated, and especially the facts that *nambas* (penis sheaths) covered the penis but left the testicles exposed, and bark belts were laced so tightly around men's waists as to disfigure them (see Jolly 1992a:337-338). Georg Forster speculates whether this 'absurd ligature' was to stave off hunger and whether dress in such a climate was indeed an article of luxury and not a necessity. Perhaps at 'Mallicollo they have not yet attained that degree of opulence which could have suggested the invention of garments' (ibid.:468).

Much was made of the difference between men and women in the jewellery and finery they wore. This was especially pronounced on Malakula, where men wore tortoiseshell earrings, shell armbands and necklaces, and nose jewels of nephrite or alabaster, while women were comparatively unadorned. From this he draws a broad conclusion: 'Wherever that is the case, the sex is commonly oppressed, despised, and in a deplorable situation' (G. Forster 1968: 462).

Women on Tanna were seen to have rather more finery, but here too men were more heavily adorned with body painting and cicatrisation,[9] shells and stones, and elaborate hairdos (figs 342, 343; ibid.: 493, and Jolly 1992a:336-7). And again he related this to the fact that women appeared to be 'drudges and beasts of burden', that 'they were not held in any esteem by the men' (G. Forster 1968:520), and that generally they looked 'gloomy and melancholy' (ibid.:499).

Fig. 341
Carved spear point, collected by Guiart in 1966. Ambae.
Paris, Musée national des Arts d'Afrique et d'Océanie.

poisoned were very neatly ornamented' (ibid.:470).

9. Tannese women wore tortoiseshell earrings and shell necklaces, and some older women wore bonnets of plantain leaves or pandanus matting. See, for example, the engraved portrait *Woman of the Island of Tanna*, derived from Hodges (reproduced as pl. 4, Jolly 1992a:352). Cicatrisation was often compared to tattooing, and seen as the form of puncturing practised by people with darker skins.

Fig. 342, 343
Woman and man of Tanna. Engraving by William Hodges, 1774, after Cook, *Atlas*, Second Voyage.

Fig. 342

Fig. 343

Only the culinary and musical arts of Vanuatu elude this generalised portrait of 'savagery'. Georg Forster delights in the puddings made of bananas, taro, coconuts and okra leaves, offered him by women. And although the only musical instruments he saw on Tanna were drums and panpipes (cf. Crowe, this volume), he thought their songs more harmonious and their lyrics more metrical than those of other Pacific islands. Not only did Tannese songs have a more 'considerable compass of notes' than those of Tahiti or Tonga, but a 'serious turn distinguished it very remarkably from the softer effeminate music of those islands' (G. Forster 1968: 517). That ni-Vanuatu music was in 'greater perfection than any in the South Sea' was not in Georg's view inconsequential, for 'a predilection for harmonious sounds implies great sensibility, and must prepare the way for civilization' (ibid.:540). 'Civilization' meant population growth, economic and political development, increased commerce and the dissemination of knowledge. Nineteenth-century missionaries also valued these European attributes, but saw them as intrinsically connected to Christianity.

'Christian light in Heathen darkness': the missionary aesthetics of Paton and Robertson

Whereas the representations of 18th-century explorers combined the will to know with the anticipation and legitimation of future colonial control and settlement, the views of missionaries are indissolubly linked to their continuing presence in the place and their project of conversion. The arts of Vanuatu could also denote savagery for them, but more crucially they were marks of heathen darkness to be vanquished by the victorious 'bringing of the light' of Christianity. Those works most crucial to the rites of ancestral religion were attacked as works of the devil or idolatrous representations of heathen gods. To become Christian might entail the destruction of such art works, or else their removal to the security of a mission museum or an overseas collection. But in missionary representations, this attack on the works of the devil vied with an aesthetic response to their beauty, or a positive evaluation of them as manifestations of indigenous industry or talent (see Thomas 1992).

Moreover, because the main objects which were

the subject of missionary attacks were those made by men – gongs, masks, effigies and weapons – this led to a gendered asymmetry in the art objects that survived in mission communities. The sculpted wooden forms created by men were more often burnt or dispatched (being more obviously related to war or ancestral religion), while the plaited or beaten cloth made by women persisted. Though the indigenous attire of mats, grass skirts and penis sheaths was outlawed, and cloth became a crucial sign of the Christian convert, women's new industry of sewing developed alongside those older, seemingly more benign women's arts of plaiting, weaving, beating and colouring of fibres.

I will here consider only the Presbyterian effort in the southern islands in the mid- to late 19th century, focusing on the sojourns of John and Margaret Whitecross Paton on Aniwa, and Frederick Robertson on Erromango. They are significantly different – the Patons manifest a far less appreciative attitude to indigenous arts. They are preoccupied with the arts of the body – the passage from heathenism to Christianity necessitates a transformation from nakedness to Christian costume. Thus John Paton (1889:281) depicts the corporeal conversion of the recalcitrant heathen chief Nasi[10] in these terms:

> He took the ugly paint patches from his face; he cut off his long Heathen hair; he went to the sea and bathed, washing himself clean; and then he came to the Christians and dressed himself in a shirt and a kilt.

Beneath the covering of cloth, the more permanent stigmata of the heathen past might remain. Thus John Paton describes how the form of a snake or a lizard cut deep into the flesh of men's arms was seen by converted women and children as the marks of *teapolo*, or the devil. Christian men were keen to render these 'visible horrors' of scarification invisible by shielding them from public view (1889:159).

Paton constantly describes the indigenous attire of the Aniwans as hideous and savage. His description of the crowds which assembled for the 'last heathen dance' in November 1867 on Aniwa is typical: 'Men, women and children poured past us, painted, decorated with feathers and dressed in their wildest form, though almost entirely nude as regards the clothing of civilization' (ibid.: 162).[11] Margaret Whitecross Paton's comments on this dance feast are rather more enthusiastic. Although she too laments their 'wild and fantastic appearance', the thumping of feet and the 'horrid yells', she is more complimentary about male and female costume. She depicts the women, painted and decorated with leaves, as like 'moving shrubs', and the men as being adorned with shells and other ornaments and on top of their hair 'long waving plumes' (1896:41). Elsewhere (ibid.:370) she prevaricates – it is

> ... sickening to see so many of them coming about with nothing but paint stuck all about over their bodies! The dark colour of their skin softens off the effect a very little though; and there really is a look of free independence and dignity about them as they stalk along so erectly.[12]

Her husband rarely credited such dignity to the heathen body. As well as the centrality of body arts in the aesthetics of conversion, heathens were enjoined to rid themselves of their 'idols', the sculptures men created from wood or stone. The process of conversion gathered speed on Aniwa in the late 1860s, notably after the conversion of the chief Namakei and subsequent to Paton's sinking of a well – which miraculously flowed with 'Jehovah's rain' from the ground, not the sky. And from this time onwards, Paton (1889:192) reports the destruction of many sculpted forms:

> That very afternoon, the old Chief and several of his people bought their idols and cast them down at my feet beside the door of our house. Oh, the intense excitement of the weeks that followed! Company after company came to the spot, loaded with their gods of wood and stone, and piled them up in heaps, mid the tears and sobs of some, and the shoutings of others, in which was heard the oft-repeated word 'Jehovah! Jehovah!' What could be burned we cast into the flames; others we buried in pits twelve or fifteen feet deep; and some few, more likely than the rest to feed or awaken superstition, we sank far out into the deep sea. Let no Heathen ever gaze on them again!

Some recalcitrants tried to sell their idols, but this trade was spurned. Some attempted to secrete them, but were exposed by a 'detective committee' composed of Sacred Men (indigenous priests) who had given themselves to God (ibid.:193). Ironically, given the Christian message of peace, weapons of war

---

10. Nasi was Tannese but lived on Aniwa.

11. Paradoxically, this dance was held to honour the mission's work; that is, the completion of the burning of a kiln for lime used in building and decorating the mission houses. The locals seem to have been shocked that Paton did not appreciate this dramatic performance. Along with Aneityemese and local converts present, he expressed shock and horror that heathen gods were summoned up in the presence of the Saviour. I should note that Speiser misreads Paton as to the gendered pattern of this dance. He quotes him as saying that men danced with women and women with men and, on the basis of this misreading, suggests this was probably the only reported instance of mixed dancing in the group (1991:383). In fact, the original reads: 'They danced in inner and outer circles, men with men and women with women' (1889:162).

12. In the writings of Margaret Whitecross Paton, and of her husband John, there is also caustic comment on how European-style clothes are worn inappropriately – for example, women in men's clothes and vice versa, or using trousers as a shawl, or so

Fig. 344
Tattooed woman. Drawing, executed in 1879, from Mikloucho-Maclay 1950-1954, vol 5.

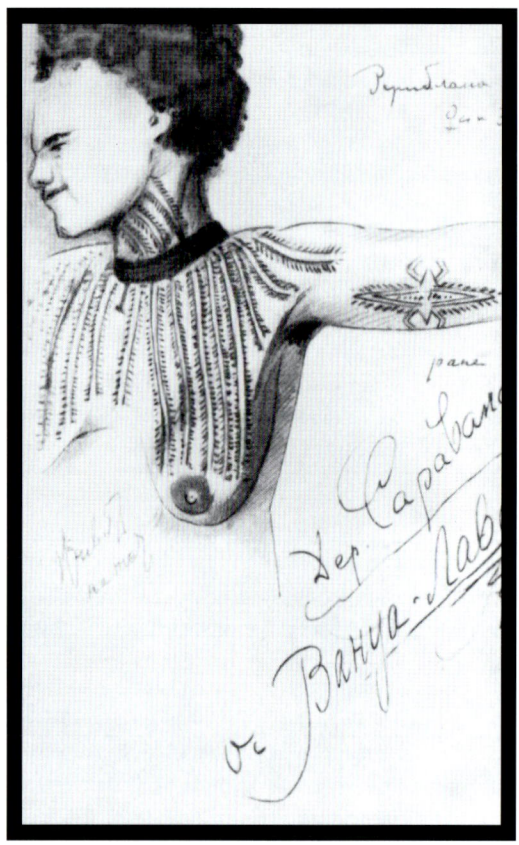

on (for example, J. Paton 1889:169-170, M.W. Paton 1896:36-37). She seems particularly plagued by the 'risibles' (that is, convulsive laughter) at church as she witnesses Sunday costume. This disturbingly harsh satire deserves separate treatment.

13. Lawson reports that Robertson was even more tolerant of firearms being used by his mission supporters, some of whom had veritable armouries (1990:136).

Fig. 345
Contemporary tattooed woman.
Ra Island, Banks Islands.

continued to be made and used by men. Paton reports that for some time men came armed to church, and that he was frequently accompanied by Christians wielding tomahawks or spears to protect him from the 'heathen party' (ibid.:154, 189).[13]

Robertson no doubt responded to Vanuatu arts with greater appreciation than either of the Patons. He is especially interesting because he was also a great collector of ni-Vanuatu art,[14] much of which is now in a museum in Canada. In his writing, there is a pronounced tension between aesthetic appreciation and missionary denigration, a tension most pronounced when he is talking about women's bodily decorations, costume and especially tattooing (figs 344, 345). After describing the way in which the operation was performed, he suggests (Robertson 1903:368) that:

> The tattooing when well done is not at all unsightly; some of the leaves are finely formed, and their dark, blackened veins show out well against the dull brown of the woman's cheek. But it is a barbaric feature of heathenism, and as such we have discountenanced it very strongly. We approve of the natives keeping up their old customs when these are innocent and good ones; but as so many of them are connected with their superstitious and cruel rites this is not often possible.

Less connected to superstition and cruelty, apparently, were women's arts of tapa making (according to Robertson, *nemas-itse* in Erromangan). Robertson has a loving description of how women made it – how the bark is stripped, the bundles beaten and joined up, and designs drawn representing the crescent moon, palm leaves, birds, fish, lizards, flying foxes, and occasionally human beings. He records one lady artist who 'moved with the times' by drawing men on horseback on her tapa (ibid.:369). Then follows a lengthy discussion of how tapa was used to carry babies, and as a shawl across a woman's shoulders. There is an equally detailed description of how women made their pandanus skirts (fig. 346). Whereas other mission texts have 'before and after' shots of women in heathen and Christian costume (for example, Gunn 1924, opposite p. 127), as well as photos of clothed converts (Robertson 1903, plates opposite pp. 74, 344), Robertson also reproduces a splendid photograph captioned 'An Erromangan belle in heathen dress' (ibid., plate opposite

p. 231). The text further qualifies the aesthetic improvements of Christian conversion. We are told (ibid.:367) that:

> An Erromangan woman in full heathen costume is a picturesque sight – the long trailing skirts helping to make her look tall and graceful, and from their custom of carrying all burdens, even very heavy ones on their heads, our women have exceptionally straight figures and well poised heads.

So even the carrying of heavy loads, a constant trope in missionary criticism of women's indigenous position, is here aestheticised (see also ibid.:370; Jolly 1991b).

It has to be admitted that Robertson still insisted that women wear European cloth dresses to church (Lawson 1990:134), and that he is not nearly so complimentary about the indigenous attire of men. The artifacts which men made are rather more generously described. Robertson gives detailed accounts of the form of the different varieties of clubs, bows and arrows, battleaxes and spears, and notes how difficult these must have been to sculpt when only stone tools and pigs' tusks were used. Despite his intense curatorial interest and his compliments on the 'neatness and perfection' or the high polish on these weapons, Robertson's very presence of course helped to render this a dying art. Missionary campaigns against war, together with the coercive interventions of the metropolitan powers, were crucial in pacifying the peoples of the southern islands. And as war became increasingly relegated to the past, to the time of darkness, Robertson continued to collect men's weapons and dispatch then back to Nova Scotia.[15]

Significantly, although he, like other Presbyterian missionaries, promoted more European styles of housing, he also thought the 'turned turtle' shape of old-style huts, though less healthy and cool than the new, looked beautiful covered with woven reeds. And the large *siman lo* – the communal cooking and eating house for young unmarried males, still built in the old way without walls – was, he thought, 'very rustic and picturesque' (ibid.:374). But the missionary aesthetic triumphs with the observation that Erromangan houses, though pretty at first, are quickly rendered filthy by habitation, and that disorder prevails within, 'clothing, children, adults, knives, guns, axes, food and ash-piles all mixed up together' (ibid.). But we are reassured that Christian Erromangans were starting to do better – building larger and roomier houses, with doors and verandahs, floors covered with mats, raised seats around the wall, everything 'neat and tidy' (ibid.: 375). Beauty, order and cleanliness thus converge in the notion of a good Christian house, even if there is a lingering lament for the beautiful body of the heathen woman in indigenous attire.

'He made ethnology a science':[16] the 20th-century ethnology of Speiser and Layard

I now turn to the early-20th century observations of the ethnologists Speiser and Layard, whose project was not cultural conversion but conservation. Although they aspired to a distinctive project of intensively documenting and understanding the indigenous cultures of Vanuatu in a disinterested and scientific way, their representations, like those of

14. See Barbara Lawson's thesis (1990) and subsequent book (1994) about his collection held in the Redpath Museum of Montreal, Canada.

15. There are a number of these in this collection (see Lawson 1990). By contrast with his comments on clubs, and bows and arrows, Robertson thought Erromangan spears and canoes very rude and poorly worked (1902:373-374).

16. This was allegedly what the ethnologist W.H. Rivers wanted inscribed on

Fig. 346
Woman with long, decorated skirts. Photographed by E. Aubert de la Rüe, 1935. Erromango.

his tombstone. It appears as Layards' dedication to his *Stone Men of Malekula* (1942).

17. An earlier account in English was published by Mills and Boon (Speiser 1913). Speiser describes the earlier work as a 'popular travel book', and admits that it contained some peremptory observations, contradicted by the later scholarly tome. Of the latter he proclaimed: '[T]he material contained in this work is authoritative' (Speiser 1991:1). The translation of this work into English was at the request of the government of the independent Republic of Vanuatu.

18. Or should I say male creativity – see my later comments.

19. This thesis was basic to his several attempts to chart the cultural history of Melanesia in several papers subsequent to this volume.

20. By this, Speiser refers to the use of human skulls in ritual practices in Malakula, Ambrym and the Banks (Speiser 1991:319-320). He recognised that the head was everywhere thought to be sacred and the seat of life, but that in certain places this extended to the sacralisation of the skulls, especially those of

explorers and missionaries, were also structured by colonial interests, albeit different ones. Their views represented their concern to zealously document and compile cultural materials from a people who were seen to be 'dying out' or degenerating as a result of colonial contact, and to claim the authoritative right as professional anthropologists to interpret these for a European audience. This particular colonial interest structures the extensive ethnographic corpus of Felix Speiser and John Layard – in their writings on economy and kinship, myth and ritual, but also in their views of art. Although these authors diverged considerably in their theories of culture and art, they both used the language of diffusion and of degeneration.

First, let me consider Felix Speiser, who was in Vanuatu from 1910 to 1912 although his major work was not published in German till 1923[17] and in English till 1991. I refer primarily to the latter, and to a later article on art (Speiser 1929). Speiser's tone is at once obvious in his general appraisal of the visual arts (1991:386):

[T]oday these are completely degenerate and no good works are being produced. Nor is this surprising since, clearly, a healthy art can flourish only on the soil of a healthy culture, and as culture in the islands is no longer healthy, art must perforce degenerate too.

The language of cultural degeneration saturates Speiser's ethnography (see Jolly n.d.b., n.d.c.). The morbidity of ni-Vanuatu culture is in large measure ascribed to the effects of colonialism. Epidemic disease, depopulation, indentured labour and missionary work were all perceived by Speiser to compromise the robustness of ni-Vanuatu, physically and morally. But his idea of degeneration also informs his view of indigenous differences between the cultures and arts of various regions. South Malakula is often exempted from his general appraisal, and it is clear from his comments in the text and from the preponderance of artistic materials he collected from there (many still in the Basel Museum) that he thought creativity was in a healthier state in that region.[18]

In his concluding comments to the English translation of this work, Christian Kaufmann notes (Speiser 1991:412-413) that Speiser subsequently developed a more general theory of artistic creativity and its intrinsic relation to religion. He postulated that

the first aesthetic forms were more representational of human and animal forms, and more directly linked to use (for example, the image of one kind of bird on a particular arrow which it was designed to kill). In the process of duplication, generational transmission and diffusion, forms became more abstract and divorced from the original religious source of imagery. Renewed creativity depended upon the rediscovery of new religious meanings. He thus adjudged some regions robust and others degenerate (1923).[19]

Thus the arts of Santo and the southern islands are seen as inferior to or derivative of other islands. Pentecost, Ambae and Maewo are seen as marginally better, with south Pentecost receiving praise for its fine masks and very beautifully coloured mats, Ambae for its mats, wooden dishes and tattooing, and Maewo for its incised ear ornaments. But the islands which he sees as richest in art were the Banks Islands, Ambrym and Malakula. In the Banks, he appreciated the tree-fern statues, house posts, board painting, tattooing, carved dishes, knives and pestles, and plaited mats and belts. 'Even the patterns on the women's belts are rather pretty' (Speiser 1991: 387). Ambrym is, as always, celebrated for its sculpted and painted slit-gongs.

But it is Malakula, and especially south Malakula, which he finds most rich and robust, and this, he argues, is because of their 'skull cult'[20] and the greater maturity of animistic religion there. He claims that 'nothing stimulates pictorial art so much as religious ideas' (ibid.:387). Leaving aside the problematic character of this theory of representation and of art history, Speiser's aesthetic adjudications are patently gendered. His stated preferences are not only for the arts of south Malakula, but more particularly for those pictorial forms which men are exclusively authorised to create, in the context of ancestral cults and funerary rites. Interestingly, the items reproduced in colour in the 1991 translated edition of this volume are primarily masks, effigies, house posts, and board paintings. They are overwhelmingly from Malakula with a few from Ambrym and the Banks. They are, with a singular exception, creations by men – with only one example of women's art reproduced in colour – one of those 'beautifully coloured red mats', which bears the caption 'Money mat (detail), northern Pentecost'.[21]

Fig. 347
Undyed mat, with very finely woven patterns, collected by Speiser between 1910 and 1912. Maewo. Basel, Museum für Volkerkunde.

high-ranking men. In some of the *rambaramp* figures of south Malakula, skulls are used as the basis for clay modelling of an effigy of the dead.

21. How far this selection is representative of Speiser's collection held in the Basel Museum is unclear, since in the text, as in the original drawings and black-and-white photographs, women's art was equally well-documented as part of Speiser's encyclopaedic array of bodies, houses, canoes and diverse material cultural forms. I also appreciate that this selection may have been one of practical necessity.

Although Speiser faithfully documents the different styles of plaiting, weaving and dyeing mats (fig. 347), baskets and sheaths, the ways of beating and painting on tapa, and the different forms of fashioning pots and decorating them (ibid.: 230-241, pls 63-78), they are typically described using the language which appraises the finesse of the technique or the surface prettiness of pattern (see above on the belts of Banks Islands) rather than one which affirms their deep spiritual beauty (cf. Bolton and Walter, this volume).

Despite his very different theoretical predispositions, Layard shared Speiser's view of Vanuatu arts in two significant ways. His fieldwork on Vao yields a Malakulan perspective on Vanuatu, and he concentrates on the spiritual life of men. I have elsewhere argued that his psychoanalytic theory of pig sacrifice and ancestral religion in general assumes not only the identification of men with pigs, but the identification of the reader with the spiritual plight of an indigenous male ego (Jolly 1991a). This argument I will now further develop in considering the way in which Layard talks of the arts of the Small Islands.

First let me quote a significant observation by Layard (1943:648):

Among a people whose artistic sense is expressed primarily not in the plastic arts but in dramatic performances and in the elaboration of ritual, one element of

Fig. 348
Contemporary woman. Tanna.

22 I cannot expound this here, but it has been well-summarised by Allen (1981, 1988).

culture that easily escapes the casual observer is that of the ingenious designs drawn by the natives in the sand or in the fine volcanic dust that covers the floor of the dancing-grounds.

As we might expect then, in writing about artistic expression in the Small Islands of Vao and Atchin, Layard focuses on ritual and sand tracings (cf. Lindstrom, this volume). There is no doubt that he found the dramatic performances of initiatory rites, grade-taking ceremonies and funerals very moving. For him they stirred the deepest emotions. But he posits that although the average European may be 'moved beyond words by the intense, almost ecstatic feelings they arouse' (Layard 1943:336), most would never comprehend their deep spiritual significance without the help of the scientific ethnologist. More accessible were the 'figure-dances' and mumming plays, *na-leng*, which are 'more easy for the white man to appreciate' (ibid.).

Layard (ibid.:270-454, 473-528) offers very rich interpretations of all these ritual dramas – the meanings of various dance movements, the sense of songs which accompany them, the different messages encoded in the rhythms of slit-gongs, and the spiritual import of the variety of wooden and stone sculpted forms and the bodily decorations which are an inherent part of such performances. His dedicated exegeses and his comparative scope (in situating Vao within the congeries of northern Vanuatu cultures) remain unrivalled by anthropologists to the present.

The same applies to his analyses of sand tracings (ibid.:649-683). He is thrilled by the mnemonic and geometric virtuosity of these tracings. But he is also at pains to explain them – not just in terms of their indigenous glosses as 'a kind of yam' or 'five clubs' or 'flying foxes hanging on a breadfruit tree', but in terms of his own theories of ancestral religion. This had diffusionist and psychoanalytic sources,[22] but the aesthetic decoding which he offers relies on the identification of the viewer with the male Malakulan on his spiritual journey. Although we are told by Deacon for Seniang that sand tracings were the creation of the female guardian ghost (ibid.:650-651), or by Godefroy that on Vao, as on Santo, women formerly drew them (ibid.:653), they were clearly a male creative preserve during Layard's sojourn on Vao in 1915. Layard classifies the different forms of the sand tracings as representing either the labyrinth, the path to the land of the dead and spiritual rebirth, or the body of the female guardian ghost. The risky and dangerous act of negotiating the labyrinth is always imagined as traversed by a man, and it is always a woman who guards the entry through the cave into the land of the dead, threatening to devour him if he cannot remember the maze.

Thus we can see the main focus of Layard's attention, as for Speiser, was on those artistic works made by men and with deep spiritual significance. Unlike Speiser, Layard does not even describe women's artistic endeavours. On Vao (although probably to a lesser extent than on Ambae and Pentecost), this was the plaiting of pandanus. Although Layard uses mats to distinguish the different cultural regions of Vanuatu, and at several places alludes to the central significance of the valued 'money mats' in the rites of birth, of death, and of the initiatory pilgrimage to

Ambae, there is never a similarly dedicated consideration of how these beautiful and valuable objects are made, or what the various dyed patterns on these mats might represent. Layard acknowledges the difficulties which he had in relating to women (1942:45), and clearly the sex segregation of ni-Vanuatu society was here once again compounded by the androcentricity of anthropology to render women invisible or marginal. But whereas Layard at least admits the fact of women's separate and sometimes secret religious and ritual life, the artistic dimension of this was never brought into view.

Engendering the arts in post-colonial Vanuatu

It has only been with the last generation of anthropologists that women's arts in Vanuatu have claimed an equivalent attention in European eyes. With some exceptions, like Speiser and Robertson, there has until recently been little written on how fibres were bleached and made pliable, how they were plaited in different designs and how the beautiful hues of red, yellow or blue-black were applied. Not only was there little technical information, but the aesthetic criteria women employed, and the religious meanings they embodied in such work, were ignored. European representations persistently stopped with the observation that their surface patterns were refined or pretty. With the recent work of Walter (this volume), Saint Pierre and Wellington (1985), Keller (1988), Bolton (1993; this volume), and Bolton and Tarisesei (1992), it has become abundantly clear that the patterns women create with fibrous forms can have an equally complex and rich set of meanings – meanings which in many cases reflect women's perspective on ancestral religion. This reclamation of women's creative work as their *kastom*, in the work of the Women's Culture Project of the Vanuatu Cultural Centre, is a crucial context for this in the present. In film and texts we have a vivid demonstration of how, on the island of Ambae, women have been moved to revive and revalue this art form. In the words of one Ambae woman, '*Bifo yumi ting se samting nating*', with the clear implication that now they are something of value. It is hard to say how far the past devaluation of women's art and *kastom* was a characteristic of indigenous aesthetic configurations, and how far the result of the uneven effects of colonial influences on the different art forms of men and women. Although women's creative forms were celebrated (fig. 348), thought to be refined or pretty, they were often considered less definitive of indigenous culture than men's creations. Whether the latter were denigrated as signs of savagery, the works of the devil, or the hallmarks of cultural degeneracy or health, they were typically given more attention by Europeans.

Perhaps the history of these colonial perceptions is increasingly irrelevant to the consciousness of ni-Vanuatu creating and performing their arts in villages and towns. Perhaps only the views of missionaries had much impact at the local level. But as ni-Vanuatu artworks enter the global commodity market and are relocated in galleries and museums, and as tourists increasingly attempt to purchase local arts, such colonial classifications can still be burdensome. This is not a subject I can pursue here. Intrinsic to this process has been a tendency for outsiders to classify men's creations as art, and women's creations as craft. This tendency has, of course, been observed for European art forms and in how the classifications and adjudications of the gallery and the museum have interacted with Aboriginal and Maori arts. I hope that future exhibitions (such as that held in Port Vila, Nouméa, Basel and Paris between 1996 and 1998) will represent both the male and the female creative imagination in their displays of the arts of Vanuatu. This will be crucial in undoing the colonial engendering inherent in past European representations of the arts of ni-Vanuatu, so that they do not persist too long into the post-colonial present.

History of Audiovisual Documents: Earliest 'European' Paintings, Photographs, Films and Recordings of Vanuatu

Kirk W. Huffman

1. Financial assistance for this has come mainly from the Australian Government's South Pacific Cultures Fund.

2. British Museum, Add. MS 15743.3, reproduced in Beaglehole 1961, opp. p. 468.

3. Thanks to Dr L.A. Lindstrom for assistance on the written form of these names, which could also be spelt Nagi and Uapo according to John Lynch's Tannese orthography.

4. Unpublished journal and watercolours in the Alexander Turnbull Library, Wellington, New Zealand.

Since 1977, the Vanuatu Cultural Centre has made a major attempt to obtain copies of early audiovisual material related to Vanuatu, and has built up an extensive collection of more than 2000 early photographs (up to the 1920s), and copies of early paintings, films and recordings from all over the world. The search for material continues.[1]

Paintings

The earliest European depictions of Vanuatu were done during Pedro Fernández de Quirós' short (and disastrous) visit to Big Bay, Santo, in 1606. Two watercolour illustrations survive: *Chart of the Bay of San Felipe y Santiago* (fig. 349) and *Natives of the Bay of San Felipe y Santiago* (fig. 350), both probably painted by Don Diego de Prado y Tovar, unofficial cartographer to the voyage (Kelly 1966, pls IV and V). The male costumes depicted in the latter painting would still be recognisable today in some areas of interior Santo, as would be the curved clubs held by the two men on the right of the painting. Memories of de Quirós's visit may survive today in the stories of the destructive white spirit *son hapuara* (*hapuara*, north wind), told today by the last surviving Big Bay peoples, brought out of the area in 1906 and resettled in eastern Santo.

Louis Antoine de Bougainville's 1768 visit produced watercolour island charts and profiles, but no depictions of the inhabitants.

The artist William Hodges, of Captain Cook's 1774 voyage, produced the first drawings and paintings of real ethnographic value. Hodges' illustrations were quite accurate, within limits, and keeping in mind the conventions of the time. His wash drawing *View of Malekula, New Hebrides* (fig. 351),[2] a view of Port Sandwich, south-east Malakula, has, in the foreground, an outrigger canoe of north-east Malakulan type, with stylised bird-figure prow. The bow held by the man in the right of the canoe is also not the (then) normal ogee-shaped Port Sandwich style. Unbeknown to Cook's men, there are indications that there was a trading canoe, possibly from Wala, in the Port Sandwich area at the time. This leads to interesting speculations: no dogs existed on Malakula at the time, and Cook's men left, in trading, a pair of dogs in Port Sandwich. With Port Sandwich's cultural links to south and south-west Malakula, this may link up with use of dog effigies in the Nahava-speaking Nimbe'ei society rituals and stories that the cultural hero(es) Hambat in Lambumbu had dogs – although the 'dog connection' could also have reached Lambumbu along cultural links between Wala-Lawor-Botwalim, across the neck of the island to Lambumbu. There are also stories of dog rituals from parts of Ambrym, which had close cultural links with Port Sandwich.

The island of Tanna has retained many stories of Cook's visit. Hodges's sketches of a *Woman and Man* from Tanna (figs 342, 343) were identified in the 1980s by elderly Port Resolution men as being of a couple called Nangi (the woman) and Wabo (the man),[3] because they were the only 'couple' to sit for Cook's *man blong droa*. Hodges's separate *Man from Tanna* (with face painting; as reproduced in Kaeppler 1978:247, fig. 536) made the same Tannese think of their culture hero Kasiken, who controlled contact and exchange routes with the exterior.

P.D. Vigors[4] was a young botanist on the 1850 voyage of Captain Erskine's HMS *Havannah*. Six watercolours painted during this voyage are of ethnographic value for Vanuatu. His paintings of an Erromango 'chiefs house' and a yam-storage tower have been respectively identified as a *simanlo* men's sacred hut and a *nevsem* tower (fig. 352) for *nehekar* rituals, both at Bonkil, Erromango. Paintings of slit-drums, a village scene, and the first European drawing (we think) of south Malakulan mortuary effigies (fig. 353) were made in the Port Sandwich area. He

Fig. 349
Chart of the Bay of St Philip and St James (Big Bay, Santo). Watercolour by Don Diego de Prado y Tovar in 1606. Archivo General de Simancas: Mapas, Planos y Dibujos, VIII, 82. (From Kelly 1966, vol. I, pl. IV).

Fig. 350
Natives of the Bay of St Philip and St James (Big Bay, Santo). Watercolour by Diego de Prado y Tovar in 1606. Archivo General de Simancas: Mapas, Planos y Dibujos, VIII, 81. (From Kelly 1966, vol. I, pl. V)

Fig. 351
View of Malekula, New Hebrides (Port Sandwich, south-east Malakula). Wash drawing by William Hodges in 1774.

Fig. 352
Nevsem tower for clan alliances (*nehekar*) and funerary rituals. Drawing by P.D. Vigors in 1850. Pongkil Bay, Erromango. Wellington, Alexander Turnbull Library.

also left us a unique document on female dress on Efate (fig. 354).

Another watercolour artist known only by the initials 'B.M.'[5] accompanied Commodore James Goodenough on his tragic second 1875 voyage. Of eight 'portraits' from central and north-central Vanuatu, the most important is that of the Efate chief wearing the chiefly shell chest-ornament, a style that goes back at least to the 13th century AD (fig. 355). Slit-drums and grade figures (fig. 356) from south-east Malakula, and grade figures from west Ambrym (fig. 357) figure in three important paintings, as do slit-drums from Nguna in one (fig. 378).

The famous Russian explorer Mikloucho-Maclay spent two months in Vanuatu in 1879, producing many detailed drawings of ni-Vanuatu and local life on Efate, Tongoa, Emaè and Epi. His drawings of Tongoa tattoos/scarifications are of particular importance (figs 73 and 344).

One of the most outstanding paintings ever produced of Vanuatu is English artist Charles Gordon Fraser's vast oil work *Cannibal Feast on the Island of Tanna*, painted in 1891. It was rediscovered only in the 1980s, but attention to detail was so fine that the Vanuatu Cultural Centre was able to identify the ritual portrayed as having taken place in the Yanekahi area of south-east Tanna, near the volcano.

English artist and ethnographer Norman Hardy toured Vanuatu and the Solomons in 1895, producing many accurate and detailed watercolours of great ethnographic value (for examples, see Elkington and Hardy 1907). Unfortunately his large collection was dispersed after his untimely death in 1914. His most important published paintings are *A Village in Santo* (showing house styles and pottery); *Chiefs House, Ambrym*; *The M'aki Ground and Jaws of the Sacred Pigs* (from one of the Small Islands off north-east Malakula); *Old War Canoes near Malekula* (showing some of the giant old trading canoes of north-east Malakula); *A memorial Effigy, Malekula* (a *rambaramp* figure from south Malakula); *Drum Grove at Mele* (this was so accurate that the Vanuatu Cultural Centre was able to identify, in the 1970s, the site where this slit-drum orchestra stood on the mainland of Efate, opposite Imere Tenuku (Mele Island), south-west Efate); *The stone 'Demits'* (north-east Malakula); and *A sacred man, Aoba* (Ambae; fig. 358).

Early photographs – until the end of the glass-plate camera era

The first photograph taken in Vanuatu is that of a 'Mission convert' on Aneityum in 1853 by Wilson,[6] who was an artist on HMS *Herald* on her visit in October-November 1853. Quite a few early unidentified or 'unlocalised' photographs of ni-Vanuatu are spread throughout museum, university, geographical, medical, or marine or naval institutions in Europe, Australia, New Zealand and the USA, many taken on exploration or cartographic voyages in the 1860s, 1870s and 1880s. They are usually unidentified as to origin, photographer or date, and are often mixed in with other photographs from the south-west Pacific, or mislabelled 'Solomons', 'Fiji', or suchlike. Not until the 1880s does one begin to come across identifiable photographers (besides earlier and contemporary photographic studios in Nouméa) who produced photographic collections of Vanuatu subjects. One of the earliest and most notable of these was French military doctor Felix Gaillard, who toured Vanuatu from 1886 to 1888 with a French military force that attempted to occupy strategic locations in the islands (particularly on Efate and south-east Malakula). He photographed aspects of traditional life on Efate (fig. 359), the Shepherd Islands, Ambrym and Malakula; his photographs are

5. Unpublished watercolours, as in note 4. The monogram reads correctly 'A.B.M.', and may stand for Adam B. Messer (pers. comm., Maria Minson, Curator for Drawings and Prints, Alexander Turnbull Library, Wellington, NZ, November 1995).

6. Mitchell Library, Sydney.

Fig. 353
The first European representation of the famous south Malakulan funerary effigies. Two of these with overmodelled skulls are seen inside a *nakamal*. Another style is seen on a post. Sketch by P.D. Vigors in 1850. Wellington, Alexander Turnbull Library.

Fig. 354
Two south Efate women in traditional costume. The 'tails' are of woven and dyed pandanus. Sketch by P.D. Vigors in 1850.
Wellington, Alexander Turnbull Library.

7. Examples of Gaillard's photos can be found in the Photothèque of the Musée de l'Homme, Paris, and the National Library in Canberra.

8. Fonbonne collection, Mitchell Library, Sydney.

9. Many are held in the Mitchell Library, Sydney.

10. Lindt photos can be found in the J.A. Ferguson collection at the National Library of Australia, Canberra; the Museum of Victoria, Melbourne; and the Royal Geographical Society, London.

Fig. 355
Portrait of an Efate chief wearing nose discs, the symbol of chieftainship on his chest, and beaded armbands on both arms. He is dressed in barkcloth and a woven belt. Watercolour by A.B.M. in 1875.
Wellington, Alexander Turnbull Library.

of good quality, and his best ones are from the Port Sandwich area, where the French set up a short-lived fort.[7] Another French photographer, P. Fonbonne, was at least working on coastal areas of Malakula and Ambrym around 1887, though there seems to be some indication that he may also have been taking pictures much earlier.[8]

From 1879 to 1892, the lay preacher (later Reverend) James Lawrie was based on Aneityum. From the Free Church of Scotland, he was not accorded much status by the other Presbyterian missionaries in the archipelago because he came out as a layman, but he certainly produced the best early photographic record of them all. Several hundred of his photographs remain, taken on Aneityum, Futuna, Aniwa and Tanna.[9] Ethnographically the most important are those from Futuna and Tanna, although several excellent ones from a Malakulan visit exist.

Dr William Gunn, the Presbyterian mission doctor on Futuna (fig. 360) and Aneityum from 1883 to 1917, was not as prolific a photographer as Lawrie, but the quality of his photographs – ranging from the southern isles to Uripiv, Malo and Santo – is slighty better.

Early French Catholic missionaries certainly produced much photographic material, but the present writer prefers to leave information about them for a hoped-for future publication by Reverend Père Paul Monnier, historian of the Catholic Church in Vanuatu, who by 1992 had already produced fifteen volumes of the Church history.

The first professional photographer to visit Vanuatu was probably giant, German-born, Melbourne-based photographer John William Lindt, in Vanuatu in 1889 (Tanna) and 1890 (Santo, Ambrym, Malakula and Epi (fig. 361)). Of great ethnographical and historical importance, his photographs document not only traditional costume and life, but 'recruiting' activities. His south Santo photographs caught traditional life there before the height of depopulation decimated the people of the area.[10]

Commodore H. Boyle Somerville, of HMS *Dart*, was on hydrographic survey work in the islands in 1890 and 1891. Most of his excellent photographs, particularly those from Uripiv and Port Sandwich, remain unpublished (Somerville 1928).

In 1895, the Austro-Hungarian Count Rodolphe Festetics de Tolna – on his honeymoon yacht – voy-

Fig. 356
Tree-fern grade figures surrounded by their ritual paraphernalia near a *nakamal* in the Port Sandwich area. The ceremony appears to have taken place shortly before the artist's visit. Watercolour by A.B.M. in 1875. South-east Malakula. Wellington, Alexander Turnbull Library.

11. Collection in National Library, Canberra, Australia.

12. For information regarding the relationship between Speiser and Lewis, the dates of Lewis's visit and extent of his collections, the author is indebted to Dr Phillip Lewis (pers. comm., 23 April 1993).

aged and photographed his way along Aneityum, Tanna, Efate, Epi, Ambrym, Pentecost, Ambae and Santo. Some of the published photographs (Festetics de Tolna 1903) are slightly retouched, but are important material. The originals are in Budapest, according to Dr Judit Antoni (pers. comm., 31 March 1995).

In 1906 the Hobart, Tasmania, photographer J.W. Beattie was employed by the Anglican mission to tour 'their' areas of Vanuatu on the *Southern Cross*. Beattie produced several hundred photographs, which are of great value because they are from the northern islands, little-photographed previously – Ambae, Maewo, north Pentecost, the Banks and Torres – scenes of traditional and mission life,[11] with an emphasis on the latter.

Some most interesting photographs sometimes appear in postcard series from the beginning of the 20th century. The photographer often remains unknown, and the captions contain numerous errors (figs 362, 363).

Interestingly, the two greatest early photographic collections of ethnographic importance were both made around the same time by two different museum ethnographers collecting for their respective museums. The Swiss ethnologist Felix Speiser, from the Museum für Völkerkunde, Basel, was in the archipelago from May 1910 to July 1912. The American ethnologist Albert B. Lewis, from the Field Museum of Natural History in Chicago (on the 1909-1913 J.N. Field South Pacific Expedition) was in Vanuatu from April to July 1911. Their paths crossed: relationships were friendly and cooperative, and Speiser assisted Lewis to collect certain items (Speiser 1991; see also Lewis 1932).[12] Speiser travelled more widely: Santo, Malakula, Maewo, the

Fig. 357 Tree-fern figures in ritual stance. Watercolour by A.B.M. in 1875. West Ambrym. Wellington, Alexander Turnbull Library.

Fig. 358 Man of high grade wearing tasselled white high-status mat. Watercolour by Norman Hardy in 1895. Ambae.

Fig. 359 Slit-drum orchestra on Efate mainland opposite Imere Tenuku (Mele Island). Photograph by Felix Gaillard in 1887.

Banks group, Epi, Ambrym, Paama, Malo, Pentecost, Ambae and Tanna (roughly in that order, but often returning to different areas of previously visited islands). Lewis tended to concentrate on northern-central Vanuatu, particularly Malakula and the surrounding islands. Both amassed vast photographic and ethnographic collections (Speiser 1600 photographs and 1826 artifacts; Lewis 160 photographs and 1200 artifacts). Their detailed and systematic photographic and ethnographic collections form two of the greatest treasure-troves of Vanuatu material in the world today.

The Cambridge anthropologist John Layard spent eighteen months on Malakula in 1914-1915, based on the small island of Atchin (fig. 364). He worked widely throughout the Small Islands, and spent an intensive week in the Nahava-speaking area of south-west Malakula in May 1915. Layard took 358 photographs, most of which have never been published. He was still working on his vast collection of material at the time of his death in 1974, and his monumental *Stone Men of Malekula* (1942), mainly about Vao, was planned as the first of a four-volume series (Layard 1928, 1942).[13]

American commercial photographer and film-maker Martin Johnson (and wife Osa) arrived to work on Malakula in 1917, returning to Malakula and Santo in 1919. Their absolutely superb-quality photographs (about 1000), distributed widely in books (for example, M. Johnson 1922; O. Johnson 1940, 1945; see also Imperato 1992), magazines and as postcards, reached a vast audience. Although many of their photographs are of great anthropological value, some are staged, or 'do not exactly represent the ethnographic truth', to say the least. The Vanuatu Cultural Centre has done much work on identification of Johnson's photographs.

By the 1920s the introduction of the Kodak Brownie camera and celluloid film brought to an end the rule of the large glass-plate negative camera. An era had ended.[14]

Earliest films: the first movies

Martin Johnson shot more than 25 000 feet (7600 metres) of film footage on Malakula and Santo in 1917 and 1919. In 1917, he filmed in Vao and on mainland north-west Malakula around Matanvat, and up at At'nmarao (Tenmaru) in the Big Nambas area. Returning in 1919, he filmed again on Vao, some on Atchin, and for a week in At'nmarao, with the avid assistance of chief Nihrapat (fig. 365). He filmed later in south-west Malakula, Tomman and Port Sandwich, finally filming inland in south Santo, opposite Tangoa Island. With his 1917 Vanuatu and Solomons footage, he had produced a film entitled *Cannibals of the South Seas*. Combining this with his 1919 footage, he travelled widely in the United States and Europe showing an expanded version of the 1917 film. Eventually most of the footage was lost or destroyed. After a search of many years, the Vanuatu Cultural Centre eventually discovered eleven minutes of the Vanuatu footage at a restricted-access military airbase in the United States in 1980. The surviving cellulose nitrate footage was copied onto 16-millimetre fine-grain positive film, and then onto video, and has been shown widely in Vanuatu since then. One Malakulan in the film, Aileh 'Ran Sabdal of Ium Lo'or, Tomman, died only in 1985;

Fig. 360 Important man, possibly one of the chiefs of the Kawiameta or Namruke moieties, with *feialu* hairstyle. Photograph by Rev. William Gunn, late 1880s. Futuna Island. Vanuatu Cultural Centre Archives.

13. Layard, with whom I worked closely during several years until his death, was possibly the first 'European' to wear a *nambas* (penis wrapper), in rituals on Atchin.

14. The recent work of David Becker, with his old, large, plate camera, in Vanuatu and New Caledonia, brings back an earlier era of quality photography.

Fig. 361 Rare ethnographic photograph from Epi. Note the mat skirt worn by the woman. Photograph by John William Lindt. London, Royal Geographic Society.

Fig. 362
Dancing ground with row of huts, with ancestor-image posts, that contained valued tusker pigs during a recent graded ritual. Early 20th-century postcard, anonymous photographer. Wala, north-east Malakula.

Fig. 363
Slit-drum orchestra in front of grade monument flanked by sacred huts for important tusker pigs from a recent ranking ritual. Early 20th-century postcard, anonymous photographer. Wala, north-east Malakula.

another survives at the time of this writing (1993), although blind and bed (mat)-ridden. The Vanuatu Cultural Centre also has nearly three hours of film shot in Vanuatu by US forces cameramen during World War II: eleven minutes in colour, the rest in black and white, now transferred on video.

The second early film shot in Vanuatu was the forty-minute *Chez les Mangeurs d'Hommes*, which had its *première* in Paris in March 1930, and was publicised as a documentary of warfare and cannibalism among the Big Nambas. Filmed from December 1927 to July 1928 by the French A.P. Antoine and R. Lugeon, it was actually shot on Atchin, north-east Malakula, with enthusiastic ni-Vanuatu from Vao, Atchin, Wala and Rano taking part in the (mostly) acting – they were paid 1 shilling a day, and there were liberal supplies of gin and wine available. Despite 'certain ethnographic inaccuracies', the resulting film (with sound added later) contains much valuable footage (for example, *naleng*, drumming, canoe footage, art, material culture, and so on); the photography, editing and synchronisation are excellent. It is a production *à la* Hollywood. The Vanuatu Cultural Centre managed to obtain what may be the only complete copy of the film, and have it repaired and copied onto video. Some of the Atchin 'actors' of the film were alive as late as 1982. The 'hero' of the film has been identified as Melteg Tali of Senhar village, Atchin.[15] The film is also of interest for linguists, because the soundtrack contains small sections of what are probably the first recorded examples of spoken Bislama.[16]

Earliest recordings

The first audio-recordings done in Vanuatu were by John Layard on Atchin, north-east Malakula, in 1914-1915, on wax cylinders produced on a small Edison Type 2 'standard' phonograph recorder. The cylinders were copied privately onto 78 rpm discs for Layard in 1940 by HMV.[17] The Pitt Rivers Museum, Oxford, provided the Vanuatu Cultural Centre with audiotape copies of these recordings in 1979, and the Cultural Centre produced a series of radio programs (in Bislama) centred around them. The recordings consist of twenty-six separate items, including slit-drum rhythms, drum-raising songs, coded conch-shell blowing signifying pig-tusk curvature, many song types, and 'bundle' flute playing.

As far as is known, no further audio-recordings were made in Vanuatu until the early 1940s,[18] but the Vanuatu Cultural Centre is now following up the possible existence of a series of recordings (associated with filming) from the mid-1930s.

Fig. 364
Men smoothing ceremonial yam mounds, with sprouting yams entwining canes at centre. Photography by John Layard, 1914-1915.
Atchin, north-east Malakula.
Vanuatu Cultural Centre Archives, courtesy Richard Layard.

Fig. 365
Chief Nihrapat (Nikhapat) of At'n'marao (Tenmaru). Photograph by Martin Johnson in 1917.
Big Nambas, north-west Malakula.
Vanuatu Cultural Centre Archives.

15. A book, Antoine et al. 1931, was produced, with stills from the film.

16. The Bislama conversations in *Chez les Mangeurs d'Hommes*, however, were probably post-recorded in Europe. The short, murky, 'human sacrifice' scene towards the end of the film was, of course, 'staged' back in Europe with suitably-attired actors. Aspects of the filming were later remembered with great hilarity by some of the oldest men on Atchin: in 1973, I was told, amid much laughter, that they would be willing 'to fight again and burn some more houses' for only 2 shillings a day (gin included). Melteg Tali's large wooden slit-drum is one of the prize objects of the Vanuatu Cultural Centre's Museum collections.

17. These discs are in the Pitt Rivers Museum, Oxford. Acc. nos. 1940. 12. 019-024.

18. American radio technicians working with the US forces on Efate and Santo during World War II may have recorded some material. This has not yet been followed up.

Audiovisual Documentation of Living Cultures as a Major Task for the Vanuatu Cultural Centre

Jacob Sam

One of the Vanuatu Cultural Centre's major projects is the audiovisual documentation of traditional ritual and cultural activities. The aim of this is to assist in the preservation and promotion of *kastom* and culture, and to try to ensure that as much as possible of ni-Vanuatu traditional activities is recorded for posterity. Not only are filmed major rituals such as initiation, pig-killing and grade-taking, funerary rituals, traditional marriages, clan-alliance ceremonies, seasonal agricultural rituals, and the like, but also activities such as weaving and gardening, fishing techniques, village festivals, historical events, myth re-enactments, and historical and cultural reminiscences. All these things are of great importance and interest to all ni-Vanuatu, and it is widely understood that future generations of ni-Vanuatu will be able to learn, study and benefit from this documentation project.

We all know that everything is changing rapidly in today's world, and one of the aims of this project is to help educate ni-Vanuatu about the value of their own and related cultures. Our country is very dispersed and culturally diverse, but our people can learn, through the material produced by this project, about cultures from other areas of the country, about which they may have had little knowledge before. Future generations can learn of the activities of their parents' and grandparents' generations. Before the recent arrival of new film and video techniques, recording was only in audio (reel-to-reel and cassette tapes); now, with video, we can hear and look. This is one of the reasons why many areas are reviving certain rituals not performed for many years – so that the ceremonies can be preserved for the future in audiovisual form.

The Vanuatu National Film Unit, which is part of the Cultural Centre and Museum, provides its services free of charge to communities in the outer islands to document, at their request, ritual and historical events of importance. Sponsors of the ritual, chiefs, and/or the village community involved, retain a copy of the resulting video, which they can then use as they see fit, if their area or island has video-viewing facilities. Public interest and awareness of this project has become so great that it is impossible to fulfil all requests.

Our forty-seven (1994) Cultural Centre fieldworkers spread throughout the islands concentrate, at the moment, mainly in their collecting side, on the tape-recording of oral traditions and rituals (and their photography) in their own and adjacent cultural areas. We do not at the moment have enough video equipment to distribute evenly throughout the country, although we have Cultural Centre film units based permanently in South West Bay, Malakula, and at the Malakula Cultural Centre in northeast Malakula. I hope we will eventually have more units based throughout the islands.

In 1992, we began for the first time a major long-term project on the side of women's culture, and we now have a full-time ni-Vanuatu woman on our staff to document audiovisually women's traditional activities, certain of which before we men have been unable to film because of traditional Melanesian or ni-Vanuatu tabus.

Besides recording in the field, our Film Unit has to look after the unique and irreplaceable archive of films about Vanuatu. It includes material recorded earlier this century, which has been sought out and returned to Vanuatu, as well as more than 3000 hours of footage recorded by the Cultural Centre staff and volunteers. The archive includes 8-millimetre films, Video 8 and VHS 1/2-inch video, as well as small holdings of other formats.

The National Film Unit has achieved its objective of documenting and promoting ni-Vanuatu culture through video. Copies of certain of the non-tabu films are regularly shown, with permission, to schools, village communities, and so on. They are sometimes also used at local meetings, courses or workshops, or even sometimes taken by government representatives on workshops or conferences overseas. With the recent introduction of television (founded in 1992) in Vanuatu, we hope soon to be producing regular local documentary film features for broadcast. The Cultural Centre could thus benefit from TV Vanuatu by coproducing regular programs on cultural matters by using existing films stock and by recording new materials.

Using modern audiovisual techniques and facilities, we work to document and emphasise Vanuatu's cultural richness and diversity, and to help ensure that our small island nation does not lose its unique cultural identity.

Fig. 366
The fieldworkers together for their annual assembly in front of the National Council of Chiefs' *nakamal*.
Port Vila, 1994.

The Fieldworkers of the Vanuatu Cultural Centre and their Contribution to the Audiovisual Collections

Kirk W. Huffman

Oral traditions were early on recognised to play a key role in the development of Melanesian culture. The Cultural Centre's Oral Traditions Collection Project, designed to keep that pillar to *kastom* and art alike in operative strength, was begun by Peter Crowe in 1976, with the assistance from UNESCO and the South Pacific Commission, led on by Jean-Michel Charpentier's input for six months during that year, and directed by me from 1977 to 1989, with the delightful and essential annual linguistic assistance, from 1981 to the present day, of Dr Darrell Tryon of the Australian National University (ANU) (for the input of Tryon and the ANU, see Rothwell 1988). It is the medium through which most of the recent material was collected, much of it dealing with ritual, art and material culture. The fieldworkers, the museum staff, and, of course, Jacob Sam's Film Unit staff as well, were and are involved in the collection of audiovisual cultural material. From 1980 until the present day, the Australian government's South Pacific Cultures Fund has kindly provided essential equipment and basic funding for this project, as well as funding the annual two-week Cultural Centre Fieldworkers Workshop.

In fact, the Cultural Centre in the capital is but the tip of a hidden pyramid – most of its activities are in the outer islands of Vanuatu, with living cultures. The Cultural Centre's fifty-five (1994) ni-Vanuatu male Cultural Centre fieldworkers (starting with two at the end of 1977) and ten ni-Vanuatu female Cultural Centre fieldworkers (who held their first annual meeting at the Cultural Centre in 1994, under the guidance of Jean Tarisese, Women's Culture Project Officer, Dr Lissant Bolton of the Australian Museum, advisor to and training officer of the project, and Grace Molisa) are each based in their own linguistic and cultural areas in the outer islands, and document the culture and history of their own and neighbouring areas. All are volunteers, none receive wages, and their numbers grow each year.[1]

The Oral Traditions Collection Project is, without doubt, the Pacific's most successful grassroots cultural documentation program (Atpatoun 1991, Vianney 1991; Bongmatur 1991; for an introduction to the problematic by a Melanesian historian, see Waiko 1981). It should be pointed out that the aim of this project is not to provide information, data, films, photos, transcriptions of myths and legends, and so on, for overseas institutions or researchers. The project is purely ni-Vanuatu-oriented, and is seen as one of the many ways to assist in the local preservation, promotion and development of Vanuatu's rich linguistic and cultural heritage (see Sam,

---

1. Since the setting up of a permanent Australian diplomatic presence in the capital in 1977, the Australian consul (before 1980 independence), subsequent Australian high commissioners, and their diplomatic staff have all taken a strong personal interest in this important project.

p. 290, this volume). Particular items from this project may, if permission is requested and given, be used for certain types of promotional or overseas study or display purposes, but one of the major aims is to build up a bank of *kastom* to be used by future generations of ni-Vanuatu wishing to reach their roots, and to retain and develop their own identity. As traditional ritual and artistic activities are still very much alive in many areas of Vanuatu, the Cultural Centre fieldworkers, museum staff and National Film Unit are kept extremely busy in their documentation work. The fieldworkers continue as well with a long-term project of eventually producing dictionaries of their languages, local ethnographies of their cultures, and transcriptions of selected non-tabu myths, legends and histories for potential use in the educational system. Regular radio programs are also produced (in Bislama) based upon non-tabu selections from the audio collections.

The arrival of video in Vanuatu opened up a whole new world of easy audiovisual documentation. The Cultural Centre began filming widely in video in 1984. Until then, filming was done in 8 millimetre. We have found the medium of video of great practical use in the process of cultural revival. Holders of a particular ritual will try to ensure the best performance of that ritual so as not to offend the ancestral spirits, but video now provides a modern practical means whereby that performance can be further checked. There have been at least two incidents of ritual participants being fined (in pigs) for mistakes (or unacceptable deviations) in performance, which have been picked up by the rituals' leaders when viewing their copy of the video. The urgent work is to film, not necessarily to edit or produce a version with a commentary; the latter is only sometimes necessary if the videos are to be distributed widely in Vanuatu. A video that is produced for the people of a particular linguistic group will, of course, need no commentary if it is already in their language; moreover, if it is, say, a film of a ritual the public aspects of which last three hours, ni-Vanuatu in general will want to see three hours of video. This enables them to, for example, count and verify the exchange or payment content of the ritual – how many taros, yams, kava roots, mats, pigs were exchanged; how many pigs were killed (and of what tusk curvature); and so on. Ni-Vanuatu priorities are

Fig. 367 Aviu Koli, Vanuatu Cultural Centre fieldworker from Lamen Island, Epi, and one of Vanuatu's most famous *klevas*. Died 1994. (Photo: Kirk Huffman, 1994)

different from that of an 'overseas' audience, and they know what they are looking for. Thus Vianney Atpatoun's twelve hours of video of Tain Mal of Singon's *maki-ru* ('high' *maki*) held at Norohure on Vao, north-east Malakula, in February 1986, is par for the course, as are his twenty-five hours of video coverage of the 1985 Malakula Arts Festival. Jacob Sam's twenty-eight hours of footage of the 1990 Women's Cultural Festival and twenty-two hours of the 1991 Second National Arts Festival (held on Santo) will provide future ni-Vanuatu with as complete a record as possible of these important events.[2]

The Cultural Centre's audiovisual documentary collection contains much tabu material, access to which is restricted. Certain videos can be made on the understanding that they cannot be shown to the general public, or cannot be shown to women (on the other hand, Jean Tarisese will sometimes be documenting material that cannot be shown to men). This is normal in Vanuatu. Ultimate rights to the videos of certain rituals belong to the traditional sponsors or 'copyright holders' of those rituals.

2. An important point to note about Vanuatu's arts festivals (First National Arts Festival, 1979; Pentecost Arts Festival, 1982; Malakula Arts Festival, 1985; Tomman Arts Festival, 1988; Women's Cultural Festival, 1990; and Second National Arts Festival, 1991) is that they do not take the place of traditional rituals (which continue), and that participants must still go through the traditional observances (and often payments) and tabus as if the ritual was being performed 'at home', plus the extra ritual obligations permitting one to travel to another area, and so on.

Fig. 368
Chief Daniel Nagi, Vanuatu Cultural Centre fieldworker for the Batar'nar peoples, originally from north-central Malakula. Died 1991. (Photo: Kirk Huffman, 1980)

3. The general attitude of ni-Vanuatu who are aware of the rich collections of their art and material culture held in museums overseas is one of gratitude that the institutions involved have preserved them. As so much of Vanuatu material 'art' is fragile, made only for a particular ritual, it is realised that a great amount of time, hard work (and money) has gone into the preservation of these early collections. These collections can serve ni-Vanuatu as reference points in their cultural history, and can assist them on their road to cultural continuity and revival. Sometime in the future, when Vanuatu possesses adequate resources to look after such early material, it is hoped that certain overseas institutions will be sympathetic to the repatriation of certain selected objects to assist in this important task (the Australian Museum, Sydney, has already kindly become involved in this process). Building of the first section of the future

Eventually, audiovisual documentation of present-day traditional activities in Vanuatu enables one to appreciate, too, the arts of song, music, dance, and body painting. 'Art' is not just material objects, as found in museums overseas, or in the masks and drums used in rituals: it is the whole, rich, living complex of ceremonial life. The island of Tanna, though lacking the material side, is nonetheless, with its incredibly complex and vibrant song, chant and dance cycles, one of the artistically richest islands of the country. Looking at early museum collections overseas, trudging around the islands showing copies of early photographs and films, and viewing rituals and aspects of traditional life today, one realises that, although much has disappeared, much has also survived and much more will come to life again. The early museum collections and audio-visual documents represent particular points on a time continuum of a rich, interlinked series of cultures shifting, changing and flowing, like the rest of the world. The new is the old, the old is the new.

The presence of a dark, rich patina on a valued object in an overseas museum collection[3] does not necessarily mean it is ritually more powerful than a similar object produced today for a similar ritual. Only the spirits of the ancestors can tell.

Total of collection and list of important samples

The Vanuatu Centre's audiovisual collections total approximately 2500 hours of audio tape, 2300 hours of videotape, twenty-three hours of 16-millimetre film footage, thirty hours of 8-millimetre film footage, 3000 early (up to 1950s) black-and-white photographs, and around 4000 colour slides, colour negatives and black-and-white negatives (in contact-sheet form, because there have not been enough funds to print each photograph), the latter taken since the late 1970s.[4] Copies of much of the material mentioned in my 'History of Audiovisual Documents' (p. 280, this volume) are also part of these collections. The appended list that follows, chosen from among hundreds of different items, gives an idea of some of the highlights (relating to ritual, material culture and art) of the films made by the Vanuatu Cultural Centre Film Unit, museum staff, or fieldworkers who have had filming equipment.

- Peter Crowe's work on ritual activities, graded ceremonies and kava-drinking on Ambae; 1976-1977.
- James Gwero's films of *hehe toa*, *soso bokis*, graded rituals, funerary rituals, gardening, mat work, and so on, on Ambae (particularly west Ambae); 1977-1984.
- Kaindum Baiagk Atis' (silent) films of *nalawan* and yam rituals in South West Bay, Malakula, and female tooth-evulsion rituals in interior south Malakula; 1980-1981.
- Walter Bebe's films of south Pentecost *naghol*; 1979-1982.
- Jack Keitadi's work on graded rituals and flute playing in the interior of the Apma-speaking area, central Pentecost; films on Tanna, and Aneityum reef-fishing techniques; 1984-1987.
- K.W. Huffman's films in south and south-west Malakulan *nalawan* and female grade rituals; sand-drawing, art, grade-taking, *ole* (*rom*), sacred men's-hut opening, and so on, in west and north Ambrym; *naghol* (land-dive) rituals in south

Pentecost; Small Nambas (south-central Malakula) funerary rituals held in Lendamboï, south-central Malakula, in November 1985, for Kailabnambymb, *mweleun*, who had died in July (rituals focused around the bringing of his dried and wrapped body, with the over-modelled skull of his father, out of storage to place it in the funerary lean-to on the edge of the ritual centre's dancing ground; this is probably the last time such rituals were to be held on Malakula, because by 1989 the remaining Small Nambas in the bush, except for one elderly couple, had descended coastward and converted to Christianity; there, however, they continue many of their rituals); music and ritual in *kastom* areas of Tanna, and so on; 1977-1989.

- Vianney Atpatoun's work on west-coast Santo pottery; canoe launching, slit-drum carving, initiation and grade-taking in north-east Malakula (especially Vao); Big Nambas (north-west Malakula) chiefly graded rituals; Small Nambas (south-central Malakula) post-initiation rituals and grade-taking; south Pentecost *naghol*; Malakula Arts Festival coverage; Tanna rituals, and so on; 1980 to present. Vianney was formerly head of the Malakula Cultural Centre, opened in 1991.
- Alben Reuben and James Teslo: south-west and south Malakula *nalawan* rituals; south-west, south, and south-central Malakula ('Small Nambas') initiation, marriage, grade and funerary rituals, and so on; 1986 to present.
- Jacob Sam (head of the National Film Unit): *tatalbean*, *warsangül* and *naghol* (initiation, grade and land-dive rituals), south Pentecost; *kaür*, *niel* and *nekowiar* rituals, Tanna; south-east Malakulan *luan* and *goulong* rituals; male and female grade-taking rituals and *nulowon* in the Naha'ai-speaking region of south-south-west Malakula (Tomman); mat-weaving and dying techniques (with Jean Tarisese and Lissant Bolton), Ambae; naming rituals and men's-hut opening, Tongoa, and so on; 1986 to present.
- Jean Tarisese,[5] who joined the museum of the Cultural Centre in 1992, is working on audiovisual documentation and revival of women's traditional activities, particularly weaving and dying techniques. With the National Film Unit, she has already produced several important edited video documentaries (with Bislama commentary) for showing throughout Vanuatu.
- Hardy Ligo and Sero Kuautonga's video of fire-walking and fire-jumping rituals in southern Santo bush; 1994.

new National Museum and Cultural Centre complex (on land reserved for it since 1980) began in late 1994, so that day may not be far away.

4. The audiovisual collections storeroom was destroyed by Cyclone Prema, which hit central Vanuatu on 31 March and 1 April 1993, but the collections were saved by Jacob Sam who, during the height of the cyclone, crawled to transfer the collections to the safety of his protected Film Unit office (in the same building). The collections had survived Cyclone Uma (February 1987) unscathed.

5. Her training in Vanuatu was kindly undertaken by Dr Lissant Bolton of the Australian Museum, Sydney, an institution with which the Vanuatu Cultural Centre has had extremely close links since the 1970s, formalised by the signing of a memorandum of understanding in 1995.

Fig. 369
James Gwero, the Vanuatu Cultural Centre's first and longest still-serving fieldworker. From west Ambae. With recording equipment at the second National Arts Festival, Santo, 1991. (Photo: Kirk Huffman)

Chapter VI
The passing scene

Bislama: Origins and Functions

Jean-Michel Charpentier

Linguistic Origins of the Term

The spelling Bislama used here is that which is in general use today to denote the contact language of the the Republic of Vanuatu. This spelling is, in fact, recent, its appearance being concomitant with the birth of the republic at the beginning of the 1980s. Before this, the literature of the 19th century used a number of different spellings: bichelamar, bichlamar, bishlamar, beach-la-mar, and so on. At that time, however, the term was used to denote quite different sociolinguistic realities.

All of these terms derive from the Portuguese *bicho do mar*, 'sea animal', which designated an echinoderm also known sometimes as a sea cucumber (to which the Chinese attribute aphrodisiac qualities). This resource was first collected and sold in South-East Asia by the Portuguese (who spoke, among other things, a Portuguese creole), and its exploitation extended to the South Pacific in the middle of the 19th century. At that time, the Portuguese name for the animal was attributed to the trade jargon used between Pacific Islands fishermen and traders maintaining maritime links between the South Pacific and China; the name was also applied to all trade languages born of contact between Europeans and the indigenous populations of the South Seas.

Geographical spread

Contacts between Europeans and the indigenous people of the Pacific took place in different areas of the Pacific at the same time, so giving birth to different *lingue franche* (trade languages), all of which were English-based. European whalers were joined by American and British whalers from Australia and New Zealand. Communication between these whalers and the numerous Polynesians whom they recruited as crewmen was achieved through a jargon, later called the 'whaling jargon'. Once whale stocks in Polynesia were exhausted, the whalers pushed further and further west, as far as southern Melanesia (the Loyalty Islands, south of the former New Hebrides), bringing this jargon with them. It was in the last-named archipelago, the New Hebrides (today Vanuatu), that sandalwood was discovered as whales became rarer and rarer. This vegetal essence, highly prized by the Chinese, was the basis of intensive trading between Melanesia and China. To this was added the collection of sea cucumbers (thus it was towards 1830 that the contact languages of the Pacific took the Portuguese name *bicho do mar*, known at that time in the China Sea) (fig. 370). The whaling jargon became that of the sandalwooders, still English-based lexically, but with indigenous speakers especially those from the

Loyalties and the south of the former New Hebrides. So its vocabulary diversified and became richer. In Australia, several jargons resulted from contact between Europeans and Aborigines. None of these exchanges were sufficiently intensive, and the activities associated with them were too specialised for linguistic forms more complex than pidgin to emerge.

After 1850 the establishment of vast sugarcane and cotton plantations in Australia, especially in Queensland, created a great need for a considerable labour-force, which the Aboriginal population was unable to meet. So began the recruiting of Melanesian labour. Boats, with crews in the early days from the Loyalty Islands, plied the waters of the former New Hebrides and the Solomons recruiting labour, on a more-or-less voluntary basis, for Queensland (fig. 371). Later, this 'blackbirding', a disguised form of slavery, was replaced by proper contracts. At the end of their contracts, the Melanesians were repatriated. In Queensland, the old jargon entered into contact with that spoken by the Aborigines and became the language of the plantations. From there it was no longer limited to being a language restricted to the workplace, but came to be used in all situations. Thus its vocabulary expanded, a grammar developed, and the language evolved from being a trade jargon to a pidgin. The first recruited Melanesians, and thus the first repatriated, were the Loyalty Islanders, and it is for this reason that many scholars see there the cradle of the present-day English-based pidgin, particularly the Bislama of Vanuatu, which would be its most direct offshoot.

Recruiting involved intensive exchanges between Queensland and the whole of Melanesia, including Papua New Guinea. It was competition between the colonial powers, Germany, England and France, which upset the unity of this pidgin a little, a pidgin born in the islands, considerably enriched on Australian soil, and later repatriated throughout the different archipelagoes. The Germans had annexed New Guinea and the islands of Samoa; the English the Solomons and Papua; the French New Caledonia and the New Hebrides, the latter which they were to manage jointly with the British. When the plantation workers returned home they found themselves exposed to different European languages. The

Fig. 370
From the time of the arrival of the sandalwood traders around 1830, European knives and axe-heads were sought after by ni-Vanuatu. They used them to convert their traditional clubs into tomahawks.
Central Islands.
Nouméa, Musée territorial de Nouvelle-Calédonie.

Fig. 371
Large trading-canoe prow. Travellers in such canoes were often seized by the crews of blackbirding vessels.
Vao, north-east Malakula.
Paris, Musée de l'Homme.

Fig. 372
Cargo vessel at anchor off Erromango at the beginning of this century. The first contacts between Europeans and Melanesians took place on the shore or on the decks of boats. Early Bislama had its origins in such a trading and bartering environment.

presence of Germans in New Guinea explains how the local Tok Pisin today contains many German words. Of the three existing pidgins, the most anglicised is Pisin of the Solomon Islands, in contact only with English. In the New Hebrides (today Vanuatu), Bislama contains a significant number of French words. In New Caledonia, and more especially in the Loyalty Islands, the French monolingual education policy has caused the former pidgin spoken there to disappear. While formerly the terms bichelamar, Beach-la-mar, and so on, were a cover term for all of the Pacific contact languages, today the term Bislama covers a much more reduced area, being the principal language of the Republic of Vanuatu. What this pidgin seems to have lost geographically it has doubtless gained qualitatively; its richness and its complexity as a vehicular language bring it into the category of what specialists call an 'extended pidgin', functionally almost a creole.

The traditional functions of Vanuatu Bislama

Like all pidgin, Bislama served for a long time as a means of communication between Europeans and indigenes. As in Queensland a few decades earlier, planters, especially from Australia, settled in the former New Hebrides. They required labour, which they recruited in the country itself. Once more, indigenes from different islands, speakers of languages which were not mutually intelligible, worked and lived together in the closed world of the plantations. The only means of communication they had in common was, of course, the pidgin brought back from Queensland. This speech form became further enriched, and probably crystallised into a form close to the Bislama of today, as the structures of the local languages, all related, brought to it a great unity. At the end of the last century, most of the financially ruined Australian planters were replaced by French ones who came from New Caledonia. Thus vocabulary of French origin was added to the word-stock already in existence.

Little by little, as exchanges facilitated by colonisation intensified, pidgin lost its vertical role as a language used between masters and employees, and served as a means of communication between Melanesians themselves. In fact, at the beginning of the century (fig. 372) the New Hebrides had many languages which have today disappeared, over and above the 106 recorded in the 1970s. This multiplicity of languages made it indispensable to have a lingua franca, even more so since the indigenes were unable to learn the language of their masters as they did in New Caledonia, because there was not just one language present in the New Hebrides, but two: English and French.

This dual influence was to extend throughout the period of existence of the former Condominium of the New Hebrides (1906 to 1980). There was a dual administration, English and French. English and French missions opened schools, the former of which taught in English and the latter in French. This generalised duality only made it more indispensable to have a means of communication common to all: Melanesians, English and French. In 1980, when the Republic of Vanuatu was proclaimed, the new state presented itself as officially bilingual without a bilingual population (English-French), the Melanesian population almost always speaking several local languages.

The contemporary role of Bislama in the Republic of Vanuatu

In 1980, dividing factors played a much greater role than the possible catalysers of national unity. More than twenty different churches shared the souls of the ni-Vanuatu. One hundred and six local languages were in use among a population of 110 000 spread throughout the twelve main islands, the most distant being nearly 1000 kilometres apart. As far as education was concerned, it was either English or French, the country being divided at that time between French-speakers and English-speakers. The feeling of belonging to one of these two groups was certainly based on linguistic considerations, but corresponded above all to political preoccupations.

Even at that time, before the notion of nationalism that Bislama reinforced emerged, Bislama emerged as the only resource shared by all (fig. 373).

Feelings concerning Bislama were, however, far from united. For English-educated nationalist leaders, pidgin was the fruit of national genius, an emblem and tool which was to be called to replace the languages of the colonisers, especially French, the language of education of the 'papists' and of political competitors. For French-educated Melanesians, feelings were often less clear, a mixture of rejection (of this pidgin much too close to English) and attraction for a creation which they felt emanated from their ancestors. In fact, more than for ideological reasons, the constitution of the new state included Bislama for pragmatic reasons. In the absence of bilingual citizens in a bilingual state, Bislama was inescapable. In the preamble to the constitution, article 3, the place of honour was given to Bislama, while at the same time imposing limits due to the lack of a standard spelling for it. Bislama was declared the 'national vehicular language'; that is, a supra-ethnic language, the property of the whole population. The adjective 'vehicular' indicated that the pidgin language is used as a lingua franca by speakers who generally use other languages. In addition, it was declared an 'official' language, alongside English and French. Within this article of the Vanuatu constitution, it was also stated that the principal languages of education were English and French. Even if the possibility of teaching other languages in the future was clearly expressed, in 1980 the accent was upon the oral status of Bislama. In this constitution, Vanuatu appeared as a state with three official languages, two spoken and written (English and

Fig. 373
The masthead of the *Tam-Tam* newspaper, predecessor of the *Vanuatu Weekly Hebdomadaire*.

N° 131 SARERE 11 JUN 1983   WEEKLY   P.O. BOX 927, VILA   40 VATU

French), and one only spoken (Bislama). From a practical point of view, this amounted to authorising any ni-Vanuatu citizen to address the local administration in any one of the three official languages, and normally to be able to demand an answer in his chosen language. On the other hand, he could only write to the state administration in English or French. If he did so in Bislama, the above-mentioned administration could only reply to him legally in English or French. This was done to avoid possible confusion, given the lack of a standardised spelling in pidgin. Fifteen years after independence, the constitution has proved perfectly suitable, in linguistic terms, and the country operates largely in conformity with this judicial framework.

While it was formerly only an inter-ethnic plantation language, today there is no longer any area of life in Vanuatu where Bislama is not present. At first despised, then widely used at the end of the 1970s by the different missions, it continues to be the preferred language.

All political life takes place in Bislama: electoral campaigns during which one has to address oneself both to English-educated ni-Vanuatu and to those educated in French-language schools; and inside the Parliament, where not necessarily bilingual anglophone and francophone members have to communicate with one another.

Every ministry and administrative office brings together ni-Vanuatu trained in one or the other language of education; thus it is normal that Bislama is used there as the general language.

When the president of the republic or the ministers wish to address the whole nation, they can only do so in Bislama, a speech form understood today by nearly 99 per cent of the population. So Bislama is well and truly the national language, shared evenly by all citizens. Even if feelings cannot be quantified, it is certain that Bislama occupies a very important place in the cultural identity of every citizen of Vanuatu. To speak Bislama today is to be ni-Vanuatu. Young people born after independence, no longer, unlike their grandfathers, used to seeing Europeans speaking pidgin – because the old planters have either died or left the country, and newly arrived development-assistance workers do not remain long enough to master it – have asked me several times: '*Prom wanem yu no tekem sitizensip, yu save toktok Bislama?*' ('Why don't you take (Vanuatu) citizenship since you can speak pidgin?').

Like elsewhere, the media's aim is to address themselves to the greatest number. Thus they use Bislama, especially on national radio, where the total number of hours of broadcast in Bislama is equal to the total spent broadcasting in English and French combined. What is more, the pidgin broadcasts often take place at times when there will be the greatest listening audience.

Bislama an official spoken language and an unofficial written language

If, as we have seen, Bislama is easily the most spoken language of the three official languages, writing it has always caused problems. It is, of course, easy to bring together a committee of 'experts' and to set up an official spelling which, like all spelling systems, will only imperfectly reflect the spoken reality. This task was performed by the churches and by a group of ni-Vanuatu pidgin speakers. Thus two spelling systems coexist, which also occurs in other countries such as China and, in part, Japan, and so on.

In the different government ministries, rather than having the same text written in English or French or both, there is a great temptation to write in the language which is spoken as a personal preference, namely in Bislama. Attempts were made within the ministries of Justice and Education; they had to be abandoned since people had not learned to write pidgin at school. There were great differences in spelling, and syntax varied widely because Western concepts had to be expressed, leading to a situation in which the the greater the complexity of the subject, the more one thought more in English or French than in Bislama. This led to wrong meanings, even miscomprehensions, unacceptable in any official document. It is not, however, the spelling of Bislama which is the real problem, especially because most Melanesians, little marked mentally by European spelling systems that remain foreign to them for the most part, can very easily decipher what is written in pidgin, even when there are differences which would cause serious problems for Europeans. Europeans often look for some spelling logic or seek to recognise the etymology of the word. In

1991, during the last legislative elections, ni-Vanuatu electors easily deciphered political philosophies written on electoral posters, despite spellings and syntax varying widely according to party. For all unofficial communication, Bislama plays a considerable role, even within the government newspaper *Vanuatu Weekly Hebdomadaire*.

The only possibility that Bislama be written in a standardised way by everyone would be if it were taught in schools. Teachers in the English stream, however, are sternly opposed to it, because pidgin is constantly borrowing from English. Students would be unable to avoid interferences and would no longer master either of the two codes. It is not written Bislama which is a hindrance in schools; the problem is teaching it together with its principal lexifier language, English.

Conclusion

Bislama plays a far too omnipresent role in Vanuatu for it to be supplanted by another language in the foreseeable future. Certainly individual French-English bilingualism, more and more common in the younger generation, removes from Bislama a little of its special intermediary function between anglophones and francophones. The danger to Bislama would spring from its increasing anglicisation in urban areas, where it sees its vocabulary and characteristic structures supplanted by English norms. In town, it is often 'Bislama English' rather than Bislama that is spoken. It is this which is on the way to becoming a national English, a speech variety which would be difficult for other English-speakers suddenly encountering it for the first time to understand (due to its phonetics).

From Condominium to Republic

Jean-Marc Philibert

Margaret C. Rodman

As was first evident in the days of the sandalwood trade, starting in the southern islands in 1827, ni-Vanuatu have always been selective in their responses to the outside world and they have always sought to ensure their own survival. When demand in wood exceeded supply, they quickly raised their prices. For their part, traders found that after local needs in imported commodities were satisfied, they were forced to deal in traditional valuables such as pigs and shells, and were transformed into middlemen in a new inter-island trade system.

The labour trade between Vanuatu and New Caledonia, Fiji and Queensland, which led thousands of ni-Vanuatu abroad, started in 1863 and lasted for about fifty years. As a business venture, this labour trade required the substantial consent of all concerned. One of its results is that ni-Vanuatu saw what existed beyond their island world. Finding themselves in a multicultural milieu, they developed a contact language, Bislama, and this experience gave them a counterweight to the hegemonic worlds of tradition and Christianity back home.

Presbyterian missionaries in the late 1840s, and later the Anglican Church, established themselves in Vanuatu. The Catholic Marist priests entered the field in 1887 and were immediately confronted with opposition from the Anglicans and Presbyterians. Christianity became everywhere the main conduit for modernity. It also offered solutions to the problems confronting 19th-century ni-Vanuatu: galloping mortality as a result of epidemics, land spoliation, and economic exploitation by Europeans.

Besides the establishment of traders and missionaries, there were also planters, who tried first to cultivate cotton and, when its market collapsed in the late 1870s, turned to other crops such as bananas, coffee, cacao, and copra. But few planters were left on Efate by 1880, most having been driven away by a combination of poor markets, hurricanes, drought and malaria.

In 1878, France and Great Britain, although respectively urged by New Caledonia and the Australian colonies to declare Vanuatu a dependency, agreed to a mutual 'hands-off' policy in the archipelago. But the murder of more than twenty European settlers led to the 1886 occupation of Vanuatu by French soldiers from New Caledonia. The diplomatic imbroglio it created was resolved by the Convention of 1887 which established the Joint Naval Commission to maintain order in the archipelago. It was to be the first of many unworkable compromises that marked the colonial history of the country. The commission was not to 'interfere in disputes concerning the title of land or to dispossess of their lands any persons, natives or foreigners' (Morell 1960:204). Actually, many of the disputes between settlers and Melanesians were over land. The need to resolve them led France and Great Britain to sign the Convention of 1906. It declared the territory to be 'a region of joint influence … each of the two powers retaining jurisdiction over its subjects or citizens and neither exercising a separate control over the group' (New Hebrides Convention, Article 1).

The French and British resident commissioners in Port Vila (fig. 375) administered in common a joint budget and were extending a joint authority over ni-Vanuatu, while neither country claimed territorial sovereignty nor requested the allegiance of the population. Later, the convention allowed for the creation of a system of native administration and for the establishment of native courts.

By 1927, the European population amounted to 777 French nationals and 452 British citizens, while the indigenous population was estimated at between 40 000 and 60 000. Because ni-Vanuatu were developing their own coconut plantations, the most difficult challenge for planters was to procure a stable supply of labour, which came from north Vietnam for the French planters. The economic situation went from bad to worse in 1930, and only took an upward turn by the mid-1930s. Most of the plantations were under French control then, supported by preferential tariff rates for export. World War II was a time of prosperity for Vanuatu. By mid-1942, major American supply, aviation and hospital bases on Efate and Santo supported the war effort against the Japanese in the Solomon Islands. Altogether, half a million Allied soldiers passed through the colony. The legendary generosity of American soldiers with PX goods, their ease and friendliness with islanders, and the discovery by the latter that some of the soldiers were black like them, all made those years a time of stocktaking for many. Cargo-cult activity, such as the John Frum cult on Tanna, increased during and after the war.

Although the postwar period was an anticlimax, Vanuatu profited to some extent from the economic prosperity of the 1950s, and this was a kind of golden age for French settlers. People became

Fig. 374
Dancing ground, Nguna Island, as seen by a European. Watercolour by A.B.M., 1875.

Fig. 375
In the beginning, Port Vila was a small town inhabited by planters and Melanesians. For a long time it was only a simple trading post, strung out along the seafront. The houses and warehouses were built of wood or galvanised iron. Because there was no urban sprawl, each house had its own separate water tank. Right from its beginnings, Port Vila had charm.

increasingly involved in the cultivation of coconut palms and in cattle raising. But clearing 'dark bush' (primary forest) precipitated conflicts over land and politics. In the early 1960s, the Nagriamel movement, whose leader was Jimmy Stevens, began on Santo in opposition to the alienation of customary land, claiming the rights of the indigenous people to the dark bush. In 1971, a second strand of resistance had coalesced in the formation of the New Hebrides Cultural Association, first renamed the New Hebrides National Party and later the Vanua'aku Pati, which stood for the return of all land to the customary owners. The first political party was led by Father Walter Lini, and Anglican minister who went on to become the first prime minister of the country after independence. After boycotting the Representative Assembly in 1977, the Vanua'aku Pati gained enough concessions to participate in the interim Government of National Unity. New elections were scheduled for November 1979 and the French sought to ensure a better performance from francophone candidates, known as the Modérés. But the Vanua'aku Pati swept to victory, gaining majorities throughout the islands.

Politically, the first years after independence were ones of stability, with the Vanua'aku Pati firmly in power. But after Walter Lini suffered a stroke in 1987, he was not able to prevent the rise of rival factions within the party. In elections held in 1991, the anglophones fell from power. Maxime Carlot Korman, francophone leader of the Union of Moderate Parties (the previous Modérés) became the new prime minister.

The Felix Speiser Collection

Christian Kaufmann

The ethnography of Vanuatu owes much to Felix Speiser, the Basel anthropologist and ethnologist. His collection, made in the field and kept in Switzerland, sets the standard for all collections throughout the world, in Canada, the United States, the United Kingdom, France, Germany, and as far away as Australia, New Zealand (Aotearoa) and Hawai'i.[1]

Felix Speiser was born in 1880, and trained as a chemist, specialising in colour chemistry, at Neuchâtel in Switzerland, Göttingen and Munich in Germany, and Leeds in the United Kingdom. In 1906, while a trainee with the J.R. Geigy company in New York, he discovered an interest in ethnography, and set out alone on horseback to visit the Hopi Indians. On his return, he decided to make ethnology his profession, a decision much against his father's wishes, but which pleased his maternal uncle, Paul Sarasin, a zoologist turned prehistorian, and a cousin of Fritz Sarasin, the zoologist and anthropologist with an eye on ethnology. Felix Speiser was sent to Berlin in 1907-1908 to familiarise himself with research practice and themes at both the ethnographic museum and the university, before setting out for the New Hebrides in 1910.

On his arrival in Vila, Speiser was welcomed by the French resident commissioner, who promised him whatever help he might need and left him with a planter on the Segond Channel, on Santo, in an area almost devoid of a native population. After scouring the bush, Speiser realised this and returned to Vila, where it was the turn of the British resident commissioner, Morton King, to receive him. At that time, the authorities, or at least English-speaking scholars, missionaries and administrators, feared that the complex process of depopulation in southern Melanesia might end in the almost complete disappearance of the native population. In this context, it was for Speiser a matter of necessity to collect as much information as possible and to 'save' what remained, in the form of material culture, of the long traditions now perhaps doomed to rapid extinction. Beyond his scientific goals, he hoped, through personal and professional commitment, to reach a public sympathetic to this moral endeavour.

Speiser, a naturalist by training, at that period of his research considered himself a physical anthropologist rather than an ethnologist, so began his field studies with an analysis of the state of the population. He was also interested, however, in documenting material objects. He was always looking for typical forms in the mass of objects he observed, and, guided by his creative and artistic tendencies, he showed great discernment in his choice of artifacts bearing witness to social and religious life, which

1. The major collections are those of Robertson, at the Redpath Museum, McGill University, Montreal, Canada (Jolly, p. 266, this volume); A.B. Lewis, in Chicago; W.H. Rivers and A.B. Deacon, in Cambridge; and early acquisitions and old bequests to museums in London, Aberdeen, and Paris, as well as in Cologne, Leipzig and Stuttgart. The Museum of Victoria, in Melbourne, has, among others, the first collection of an ethnographic nature, made in Santo in 1890 by the photographer J.W. Lindt. Other collections are in Sydney and in Canberra, Brisbane, Auckland and Honolulu. A systematic study would be desirable.

Fig. 376
Felix Speiser in the interior of Santo in 1910.

2. The title of the latter was chosen by the publisher, not the author.

seemed to him essential to a systematic record. From simple cooking implements to weapons, from individual ornaments to ritual objects, he succeeded in this way in building up representative collections.

Field photography – at that time, negatives on glass plates were developed on the spot – also allowed him to record house and village architecture, social life and ceremonies. Unfortunately, his notes, that third indispensable tool of research, all seem to have disappeared.

Thanks to the paradigmatic description Speiser left of his work (1913a, 1913b[2]), we can see that his visits were arranged to coincide with the cruises of small vessels belonging to traders, plantation owners, Dr Bowie of Dip Point, Ambrym, or the British administration. He generally stayed for too short a time to be able to improve his ethnological knowledge, the exception being his visits to west Ambrym and south Malakula. By the time of his visits to the central bush area of Santo (fig. 376) and to the Banks Islands, he spoke Bislama fairly fluently.

There are some almost total gaps in the collections: there is nothing from central Malakula, except one mat and a pig-killing club, or from south-west Malakula, the Maskelyne Islands, Paame, Epi, the Shepherd Islands, Aneityum (except for a basket) of Futuna. For Erromango, the collection is incomplete. The same applies partly in the case of Tanna and, at the other end of the group, Mere Lava, Mota Lava and the Torres Islands.

As soon as he returned home, Speiser prepared to publish his records. For the files of the Museum für Völkerkunde, he made sketches to show what most of the artifacts were like. The detailed drawings of artifacts which had not been photographed and which were to appear in the book were also drawn by his own hand. He compared what he had seen with what he found in other collections, particularly those in London, le Havre and Leipzig, and with ethnographic data recorded by missionaries and administrators. In 1914, Speiser was in touch with Alfred C. Haddon and John Layard, who always showed the most friendly respect for him (Layard 1951). That same year, on the strength of the manuscript of his ethnographic monograph of the New Hebrides and the Banks Islands, he obtained his *venia legendi* from the University of Basel. From 1917 until his death in 1949, he gave courses as the first professor in Switzerland to specialise in ethnology. From 1942 until 1949 he was also director of Basel's Museum für Völkerkunde.

In Basel, in addition to the Speiser collection from the New Hebrides and the Banks Islands, there are some fifty artifacts collected by the journalist Lucas Stahelin and the Basel artist Theo Meler during their 1932-1933 South Pacific journey, as well as sixty-four pieces, including a series of pierced stones from Tanna, acquired by Speiser in 1946 from the geologist Edgar Aubert de la Rüe. Aubert de la Rüe also bequeathed or sold fifty pieces to the Geneva Ethnographic Museum, which also has in its possession the small Robert Lugeon collection of fifty-one pieces, left to the museum in 1946 by Maurice Lugeon, professor of geology at the University of Lausanne, in memory of his son Robert, who died in 1941 in Paris.

Other Vanuatu artifacts which also come from the Speiser collection are to be found in Switzerland at the Musée d'Ethnographie of the University of Zürich (seventy pieces), in the ethnography section of the History Museum in Basel (sixty), and in the Ethnography Museum of Saint-Gall (ninety-two). Zürich also has two early acquisitions of artifacts from the New Hebrides, four objects acquired in 1861 and 144 acquired in 1891.

The *Nevimbumbao* of the Picasso Museum

Philippe Peltier

On his death, Matisse left at least two women to Picasso. It is probably not by chance that these two women were connected with the world of the exotic: it is from there that modern art drew part if its strength.

The first of them was the figure of the Odalisques. Picasso, in a rare moment of recognition, acknowledged that after his death Matisse had left him his Odalisques. They appeared, in provocative poses, in the series *The Women of Algiers* (*Les Femmes d'Alger*) (Penrose 1982:467).[1]

The second one is a strange sculpture from the island of Malakula. It is not a mask, as it has often been described, but a figure constructed for use during *naluan* (if the sculpture comes from the south-west), or more probably *nalawan* (if it comes from the south of the island) ceremonies.

According to certain sources (Rubin 1984:340, note 212), the sculpture was given to Matisse by one of his friends, a ship's captain. It is unlikely that Matisse had any knowledge of the scarce information available on this type of object; a drawing of a similar piece was published by Harrison in *Savage Civilization* (1937:340), representing, according to the caption, a male 'megapod spirit', *temes malau*. This was a photograph taken by Deacon, and buried in his archives. But this is of no significance. Matisse, like Picasso, took little notice of ethnography.

On the other hand, both of them were sensitive to forms. For a long time they had been collecting 'exotica', and it was during a visit from Picasso[2] in the 1950s that Matisse gave him the *nevimbumbao* – as the figure has often been called, after a woman's name which appears in the cycle of Malakulan myths. The sculpture has, it is true, enough going for it to fascinate both painters and to occupy a place of honour in their studios.

A photograph taken in 1953 (reproduced in *Henry Matisse, A Retrospective* 1992:421) shows the *nevimbumbao* comfortably seated in a chair in the studio which Matisse had in the Regina de Cimiez hotel. There it is installed opposite the *Grande Décoration avec Masque* (*Great Decoration with Mask*), in a silent confrontation where forms from hither and yon engage one another. After the death of Matisse in 1954, his son, Pierre, transported the figure, still seated on the chair, to Picasso, who seemed to be particularly taken by the strange montage. The *nevimbumbao* was placed in the studio of his villa, California. A photograph of André Ostier, reproduced in Rubin (1984:332), shows the figure in a prominent position amid the jumble which was normal in the studios of the

1. I would like to thank Jeanne Sudour of the Picasso Museum for having found this reference.

2. Cf. the story told by Gillot [date unknown]: 247.

Fig. 377
Overmodelled female effigy, commonly called *nevimbumbao*.
South Malakula.
Paris, Musée Picasso.

Spanish painter. There she seems to be carrying on with the great dialogue between Occidental and 'Exotic' arts, a dialogue which had begun at the beginning of the century.

Transforming Representations: A Sketch of the Contemporary-Art Scene in Vanuatu

Ralph Regenvanu

There have always been a great many artists and artisans in Vanuatu. Before the more than eighty islands that make up the country were ever conceived of as a single entity, men and women of the many different cultures of these islands were creating distinctive designs, models and forms inspired by their lives and the physical, social and spiritual environment in which their lives unfolded. Many of these creations were an integral part of the rituals that attended an individual's passage through social life; many also were elaborated insignias of identity which accessed complex narratives linking people to lineage, time and place. Other creative gestures were simply the products of telling a story, passing the time, or the eternal urge to leave one's mark beyond one's lifetime. Many of these designs or forms were firmly linked in lore with their creators, and would become stylised into particular delineations that today identify different lineages, regions and islands in Vanuatu.

What is called 'art' in Vanuatu today is based on many of the same principles as these creative forms that preceded it. Indeed, contemporary art is perhaps distinguishable from these forebears only in terms of the wider range of media used, and the sources of inspiration and motivation for creative expression. Although the tradition of contemporary art in Vanuatu has its origins in the drawings and paintings of the colonial settlers and European visitors to these islands, the art scene in Vanuatu today features a prominent ni-Vanuatu as well as European presence, with the primary Western form being increasingly transformed by creations inspired by indigenous conceptions. As an expression of the individual and collective experience, contemporary art in Vanuatu is perhaps uniquely placed to provide an ongoing representation of life in a country in which the latest Western technology coexists with a living and vital Melanesian spirituality.

The earliest protagonists of the modern era in contemporary art in Vanuatu were perhaps Nicolai Michoutouchkine and Aloi Pilioko. Born in France but of Russian origin, Michoutouchkine arrived in Vanuatu in 1961 as an established artist and artifact collector, having already spent three years in the French Pacific. In his company was Pilioko (fig. 378), a Wallisian who had previously lived in Vanuatu (then known as the New Hebrides), and whose artistic talent Michoutouchkine had recognised and begun to encourage after meeting him in the gallery he opened in 1959 in Nouméa. The first exhibition of contemporary art to take place in Vanuatu was of paintings by Michoutouchkine and Pilioko, held in the Vila Cultural Centre from 26 August to

Fig. 378
Aloi Pilioko.
Mélanésie/Polynésie
(Melanesia/Polynesia).
Fabric paint on cloth.
Approximately 200 ×
100 cm.
1994.

6 September 1961. Between 1961 and 1967, the two artists travelled the Pacific region with their exhibition of paintings and artifacts, in addition to staging at least one exhibition a year in either Port Vila or Luganville (Vanuatu's second town on the island of Santo). It was during this period that they were to establish, with the help of the local communities of the area, their base at Esnaar, on the outskirts of Port Vila. During the subsequent years in which Michoutouchkine and Pilioko toured the world with their exhibitions, Esnaar was to become the headquarters of the Michoutouchkine-Pilioko Foundation, and the location of the 'Centre for the Preservation of Artistic Values in the Pacific'. In 1985, the first regional art workshop convened by the foundation and the University of the South Pacific was staged at Esnaar, bringing together contemporary artists from Papua New Guinea, the Solomons, New Caledonia, Samoa, Tonga, Fiji, and Wallis, as well as from Vanuatu. This workshop was held for four successive years at Esnaar, to the benefit of many of Vanuatu's young contemporary artists, and began to be held again in 1992 in other Pacific countries, still partly funded and coordinated by the Michoutouchkine-Pilioko Foundation. Today, Esnaar is the home and creative cradle of the two artists, enclosing within a lush tropical environment their gallery of Oceanic artifacts, studios and living areas, all decorated with artworks by them and other local and international artists, cultural artifacts from Vanuatu, and assorted miscellaneous items of interest.

It was not long after Michoutouchkine and Pilioko's arrival in the New Hebrides that another French artist, Robert Tatin, took up residence in Vila. For fourteen years, until 1976, Tatin was a mainstay of another contemporary-art scene in Port Vila, during a period in which numerous expatriate French artists (and a few anglophones) visited and resided for varying lengths of time in Vila, staging exhibitions of their work created in Vanuatu at the Vila Cultural Centre, the Michoutouchkine-Pilioko Foundation, or various hotels and private residences in the capital. Such artists as Henri Crocq, Victoria Marinoff and Allan Thornton drew and painted in Vila in the late 1960s and the 1970s, and their art, displayed in private residences, offices and public buildings throughout the capital, provides a document of this vibrant period in contemporary art in Vanuatu. The tradition of expatriate artists arriving in Vila and being inspired, and creating and exhibiting here before departing, continues today.

What was noticeable about this period, however, was the absence in the contemporary-art scene of indigenous artists. At the time, there were, of course, many ni-Vanuatu coming to terms with the idioms and media of contemporary art, in particular carving and drawing, and, to a lesser extent, painting. While carving has always been a medium for Melanesian artists, materials for painting and drawing in the contemporary style only became available to the indigenous population through the school system (albeit to a very limited degree). At this time, there was a second generation of ni-Vanuatu going through a consolidating colonial education system. With the increasing Westernisation of the New Hebrides, this generation not only had access to paper and pencils, and sometimes crayons, paint and cloth (fig. 379), but also had greater access to European conceptions and visions of creative expression. Primary-school students with particularly notable artistic talents who came into contact with sympathetic teachers were often encouraged through school and given more exposure to the notion of making contemporary art. The earliest example of this was perhaps Sero Kuautonga, a Futunese who was transferred to the regional district school on Tanna, and then to high school in Vila, largely on the basis of his artistic talents. By 1978, Kuautonga and his art teacher at the Lycée de Antoine de Bougainville, Jacqui Bourdain, were giving pottery-making classes together at the Federation des Œuvres Laiques (FOL). Like so many other art ventures in Vanuatu, however, these classes soon had to be discontinued owing to a lack of funds. A number of other ni-Vanuatu were also to gain access to further educational opportunities with assistance from their artistic talents, and by the late 1970s the stage was set for the emergence of a significant contingent of indigenous contemporary artists.

In 1979, Jacqui Bourdain left his position as an art teacher at the Lycée Antoine de Bougainville to become the teacher of the first art course at the newly created Institut National de Technologie du Vanuatu (INTV). In this course, Bourdain gave instruction in drawing, painting, sculpting and tapestry, while Tailhade, who was later to publish a book documenting traditional and sand drawings, taught carving. Bourdain's first students were the first ni-Vanuatu to receive a significant level of training in contemporary art, and included Fidel Yoringmal, John Joseph, Juliette Pita and John Fai. It was this art class that was to decorate the exterior wall of the first parliament of the new nation of Vanuatu, with the now-famous mural depicting aspects of the traditional life of the islands. Many of these students remain the most prominent names in ni-Vanuatu contemporary art today. Others have used their talents in their chosen vocations; for example, John Fai is now the art teacher at the INTV, and one of his

Fig. 379
Michael Busai.
Spirits of the forest, sky and the sea.
Fabric paint on canvas.
Approximately 120 x 70 cm.
1992.

colleagues joined the paramilitary Vanuatu Mobile Force and went on to design most of their crests and ensigns. Although there are many more very talented ni-Vanuatu who receive instruction in art at either the INTV or the other high schools at which art is taught, most never get to develop their talent beyond their period of schooling because of the combination of the fact that the required materials remain difficult to obtain, and that their art will almost invariably never receive remuneration conducive to a decent standard of living.

The first ni-Vanuatu contemporary artist to hold an individual exhibition of his work was perhaps the sculptor Emmanual Watt, in 1976. Following in his pioneering footsteps, a number of indigenous artists were to hold exhibitions of their work following Vanuatu's independence. Sylvester Bulesa first exhibited his pottery in the Vanuatu Cultural Centre in 1981, and Juliette Pita held her first individual exhibition in 1983. In 1984, both Sero Kuautonga and John Joseph were to exhibit for the first time at the Vanuatu Cultural Centre, Sero with a display of paintings, drawings and painted cloth, and John Joseph with a selection of paintings and drawings. Fidel Yoringmal held his first individual exhibition of paintings and drawings in 1985.

As ni-Vanuatu artists became increasingly prominent, however, they also became more aware of the very tenuous nature of their individual creative careers. In the time following independence in 1980, which ideas of self-reliance and strength through unity were prominent in popular discourse, a number of Vanuatu's artists began to talk – often at kava bars in the evenings – of creating an organisation of contemporary artists to help support and promote contemporary art in the country. In 1987, Emmanuel Watt (fig. 380), Sero Kuautonga, Fidel Yoringmal, Juliette Pita and Patrice Cujo, a resident expatriate artist, called a meeting to discuss the establishment of such an organisation. At this meeting, publicised by word of mouth and attended by many of the new crop of ni-Vanuatu artists – John Fai, John Joseph, Hardie Leo, Michael Busai, and Sylvester Bulesa among them – Juliette suggested that the new organisation be named 'Nawita', the term used in Bislama for octopus. This conception was embodied in the emblem of the organisation, designed by Patrice Cujo.

In 1989, the Nawita Association of Contemporary Artists was established with Emmanual Watt as president and Sero Kuautonga as vice-president. The association's constitution affirmed a non-financial membership open to expatriates and ni-Vanuatu alike, the only condition of of membership being that the association was for contemporary artists, and not for artists and artisans using traditional media and traditional principles in visual representation. The L'Atelier Art Gallery, established in 1985 by Suzanne Bastien, was where the meeting to initiate the organisation was held, and it was, with the encouragement of its proprietor, to become the association's headquarters. The first activity of the association, appropriately, was an exhibition of the work of its members, held in the exhibition space of the French embassy in 1989. Every year since there has been a Nawita exhibition at the French embassy,

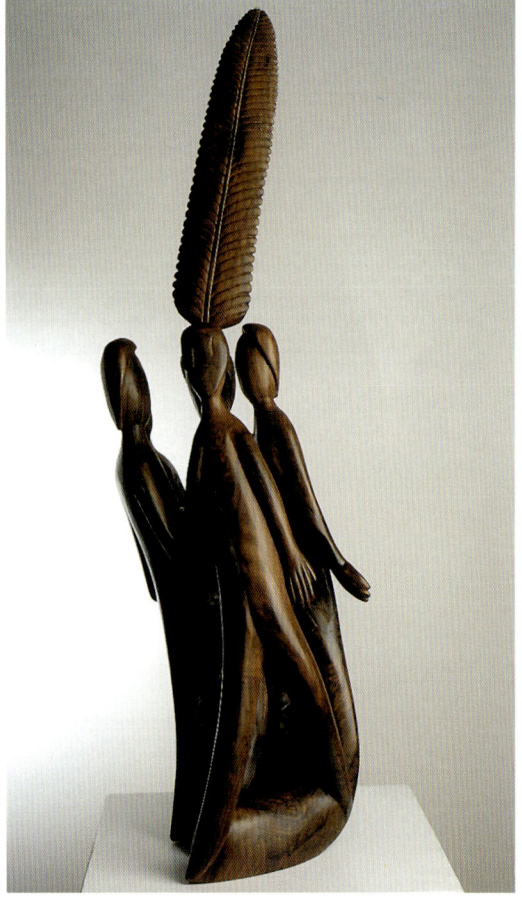

Fig. 380
Emmanual Watt.
Cultural encounter.
Wood (*Cordia subcordia*).
Approximately 150 cm tall.
1995.

and each exhibition always features work from a number of new members.

As the first organisation established specifically to provide an organised voice to represent contemporary artists in Vanuatu, Nawita retains the specific objectives of promoting established artists and encouraging potential ones. Nawita has become recognised as representing the contemporary artists, and in particular the indigenous artists, of Vanuatu. In its attributed role as the national face of contemporary art, Nawita has established links with other international artists' associations, has been invited to participate in numerous international exhibitions and artists' workshops, and selected and sent many ni-Vanuatu artists to represent Vanuatu at such events. The association has also hosted exhibitions in Port Vila by a number of expatriate artists, and also the landmark visit and exhibition by Djinu Owa, the Kanak contemporary-art association modelled on Nawita.

The Nawita Association by no means provides the only forum for contemporary artists in Vanuatu, though. An increasingly active role is being taken by the annual exhibition initiated also in 1989, simply labelled 'Art'. In a similar manner to Nawita, this forum was established to encourage new artists to publicly display their work, and to foster communication and networking between artists resident in Vila. With its aim of encouraging artistic expression in the wider community, the Art project is more crafts-based and enjoys a higher participation rate than the Nawita exhibitions. From being simply an open contemporary-art exhibition in 1989, the concept quickly progressed into the format of an open exhibition with prizes for works presented in a theme in 1990 (the theme in that year being 'Independence' to commemorate the tenth anniversary of Vanuatu's independence), and, in 1994, a theme-only exhibition coupled with a more general open exhibition later in the same year. The first Art project workshop was held in January 1994, and since then, workshops – also called 'creativity playgroups' – have been held once a month. Run by local or visiting artists, these workshops emphasise the learning of a craft and experimentation in various media. Since their inception, workshops have featured courses in weaving, quilling, card-making, and appliquéing, as well as in more conventional media.

Art 95 was the most expansive of the Art projects to date. Organised by long-time convener and founding member of the Art project Lynda Bayer, Art 95 was perhaps the most lucrative exhibition, in terms of prizes awarded, ever staged in Vanuatu, with sponsorship coming from a number of corporations, organisations and individuals in Vila. The ten categories of art being recognised was also the greatest number in the event's history, these being a theme ('Focus on Me'); collaborations in any medium; drawings, cartoons and non-painting; two-dimensional works; three-dimensional works; paintings; clay works and sculpture in any medium; wearable art; photographs and slides; fibre art; and, for the first time, video art. By the use of a theme and the creation of such categories, the Art project attempts to inspire artists' creativity, and particularly to encourage the use of a wider range of artistic media. This, in addition to the year-round workshops and the demonstrations by individual artists during the period of the exhibition, indicates the commitment of the Art project to the goals of education, the exchange of ideas, and the accumulation of skills within the contemporary-art community in Vila.

While the avenues for expression in the Vila contemporary-art community seem plentiful, the same cannot be said for artists in the outer islands of Vanuatu. Here the limitations experienced by artists in Vila – the inaccessibility of materials, the lack of financial and moral support, and the pressure of economic prerogatives – are multiplied tenfold. It is notable that, with one exception, none of the recognised contemporary ni-Vanuatu artists lives outside Vila. The exception to this is the 'Connie's Art blong Yumi' project in Luganville on Santo.

Established in the latter part of the 1980s by the artist Connie Wells, the Art blong Yumi project encompasses both a retail outlet and a workshop in which artists are trained and work to produce pieces for sale. The emphasis is on woodcarving and weaving using pandanus (the traditional medium), and on creating contemporary pieces based on traditional motifs and styles. In 1994, pieces produced by the artists of Connie's Art blong Yumi were exhibited for the first time in Port Vila to considerable critical and commercial success. This year, a branch of Connie's Art blong Yumi has been established in Port Vila, with a particular emphasis on training

Fig. 381
Eric Natuoivi.
Avtagataga.
Clay, pig tusks and wood.
Approximately 50 cm tall.
1995.

artists in the capital in contemporary styles of carving and weaving, many of which involve the modification of traditional styles. Artists working on the Art blong Yumi project are now being recognised as members of the growing contemporary-art community in Vanuatu.

There are obviously a great number of contemporary artists not included within the forums listed above. Many girls, boys, women and men are creating art in their homes and workplaces, either for leisure or with more committed or calculated intentions. A number of contemporary fabric artists, for example, can be found displaying their wares for sale in the roadside market stalls that spring up whenever a tourist ship calls into Vila. The talents of yet other artists are apparent in the colourful murals that adorn the facades of office buildings and private homes in the capital. The difficulties faced by contemporary artists everywhere that inhibit the capacity for full creative expression in individuals have found a response in Vanuatu in the formation of the Nawita Association and the Art project. Such responses will continue to develop as the contemporary-art community in Vanuatu continues to mature.

The unique cultures and environmental milieu of Vanuatu have already inspired some unique contemporary forms of visual expression in the country. There is no doubt that as the collective artistic experience matures, so will the diversity and range of this expression broaden.

Some more prominent ni-Vanuatu contemporary artists

Sylvester Bulesa

Born in 1961 in Lewawa village, central Pentecost, Sylvester is a long-term resident of Vila. He was living in Santo when his sister informed him that her European employer was looking for someone to go to Australia to learn to make pottery. He volunteered, and at the end of 1979 left to study ceramics for eighteen months at Hawkesbourne College in Melbourne. His first exhibition upon his return to Vanuatu in 1981, held in the Vanuatu Cultural Centre, was one of the first individual exhibitions by a ni-Vanuatu contemporary artist. Sylvester has subsequently exhibited another seven times, either individually or with one or two others, and in addition has participated in all of the annual Nawita Association exhibitions. Married with two children, Sylvester now works as the artist-in-residence at the Vanuatu Cultural Centre, where his latest exhibition was staged in 1995 to coincide with the fifteenth anniversary of independence. His pottery, which is practical and aesthetic, and inspired entirely from local and indigenous themes, is in high demand in Port Vila. Sylvester has run ceramics classes at the Vila branch of the University of the South Pacific, and tutors in ceramics craft at the École Colardeau.

Joseph John

Joseph John is one of only two professional ni-Vanuatu contemporary artists. Born in Makatu Village on Emae Island in 1964, Joseph went on from high school to do the four-year art course at the Institut National de Technologie du Vanuatu (INTV), specialising in painting. Joseph staged the first exhibition of his oil-on-canvas and watercolour paintings in the exhibition room of the French embassy while still attending the Institut in 1983. He has since twice held individual exhibitions in Nouméa, and was selected by the Nawita Association to represent the contemporary artists of Vanuatu at the South Pacific Arts Festival held in the Cook Islands in 1992, the Te Wakatoi exhibition and workshop in New Zealand in 1993, and the Contemporary Art of the South Pacific exhibition in Sydney in 1995. In 1994, he also exhibited his art as part of the Vanuatu Trade Expo in Nouméa. Married with two boys, Joseph enjoys the relative freedom to express himself that comes with a career as one of Vanuatu's most recognised and successful artists. As is evident in all his work, his inspirations are the environment and cultures of Vanuatu.

Eric Natuoivi

Eric was born in Matangi village on the island of Futuna in the south of Vanuatu. After graduating from Malapoa College, Eric began teaching at primary school while conducting further study towards gaining teaching qualifications. In 1986, he began teaching art to trainees at the Vanuatu Teachers College, a position he still holds. Motivated by a desire to be better able to teach art to ni-Vanuatu, Eric applied for and was awarded an Australian Development Assistance Bureau (ADAB) scholarship to study in Australia, and in 1987 attained a Graduate Diploma in Expressive and Performing Arts, followed by a Master of Education in Creative Art in 1991 from the University of New South Wales. Eric first exhibited his work as part of the graduate exhibition in that year, and he has since exhibited in Art 92, 93, 94 and 95 in Port Vila, and in the Contemporary Art of the South Pacific exhibition staged in Sydney in 1995. Eric's primary inspiration is Vanuatu's traditional culture, and this is reflected in his use of traditional themes and decorative patterns in the creation of his ceramic pieces (fig. 381). He feels strongly that a knowledge of art, traditional and contemporary, is essential for the development of a healthy self-identity in young people, and his courses at the Vanuatu Teachers College aim to impart this recognition to his students. Eric is married with five children, three boys and two girls.

Michael Busi

Michael is from the same village as Eric Natuoivi, Matangi on Futuna. Born in 1963, Michael was an artist from an early age, and became recognised as such at Malapoa College, where he studied art and contributed illustrations to a number of school texts. After a brief respite from art while he studied towards a bachelor of arts at the University of the South Pacific, Michael joined the Nawita Association after graduating in 1989 and has exhibited in all of the association's annual exhibitions since. Married with three children, Michael does his art work in his spare time away from his job as an assistant research officer at the Reserve Bank of Vanuatu. His art is inspired by the natural and cultural environments, and in particular from childhood memories of these environments on Futuna.

Ralph Regenvanu

Born in 1970, Ralph is one of a new generation of artists in the Nawita Association. An artist from an early age, Ralph painted the mural of the national coat of arms that adorns the wall of Central Primary School in Port Vila when he was in grade five, and drawings he did in the first year of Malapoa College were later painted on the front wall of the college's assembly hall. After graduating with a bachelor of arts from the Australian National University, Ralph worked as the curator of the National Museum of Vanuatu (of which he is now director) and director of the Vanuatu Cultural Centre. His first exhibition outside high school was part of the At Blong Mi exhibition staged by the Nawita Association in 1992, and in that same year he won first prize in the two-dimensional category at Art 92. In 1995, he was selected by the Nawita Association as one of the artists to represent Vanuatu at the Contemporary Art of the South Pacific exhibition in Australia. Ralph's primary inspiration is the cultures of Vanuatu, particularly the oral traditions of his home island, Uripiv, near Malakula (fig. 382). Ralph is single.

Juliette Pita

Born in 1964 on the island of Erromango, Juliette is perhaps Vanuatu's foremost woman contemporary artist. Juliette began specialising in tapestry when she attended the art course at the INTV following high school. She was to become the first woman

Fig. 382
Ralph Regenvanu.
Las kakae (The final feast).
Acrylic on cloth.
Approximately 100 x 70 cm.
1982.

graduate of this course, and her first exhibition was staged in 1983 in the exhibition room of the French embassy. Subsequently she has exhibited with Joseph John in Port Vila in 1994, with Emmanuel Watt at the Francophone 94 exhibition in Paris, and with other ni-Vanuatu artists in Sydney in 1995 as a representative of the Nawita Association. Juliette now works as a mother and part-time hand-painter of fabric with Vila Handprints. Juliette considers her main inspiration the traditional cultures of Vanuatu, but her tapestries are also created around images from daily life and the natural environments of Vanuatu.

Aloi Pilioko

Born on Wallis Island, Aloi Pilioko moved to Vanuatu and was brought into the Pacific contemporary-art community in 1959 by his subsequent long-time associate Nicolai Michoutouchkine while living in Nouméa. Originally an oil painter, Pilioko has become internationally renowned for his tapestries of cotton thread on sackcloth. He has toured his artworks individually, and with his colleague Michoutouchkine and their collection of traditional Oceanic artifacts and contemporary art. He has also left his mark on Port Vila with his distinctive raised relief murals of wide-eyed figures and local animal life on the walls of three buildings in the town (including the building that bears his name on the main street). Today he concentrates on paintings and painted cloth, sold at the downtown boutique owned by him and Nicolai Michoutouchkine. His daily routine consists of planting a plant each morning, cooking for the assembled workers and artists at the Esnaar property which is his home, and working on his art. He and Michoutouchkine remain the best-known artists in Vanuatu.

Emmanuel Watt

Born on Ambae in 1947, Emmanuel is one of only two ni-Vanuatu professional contemporary artists. In the early 1970s, Emmanuel spent six years in France, part of it studying techniques of building restoration. Upon his return to Vanuatu, he became acutely aware of the natural beauty of the country, and also what he felt was an under-appreciation of this beauty by the local people. Thus inspired, Emmanuel began in 1974 do devote all of his time to creating art out of nature's refuse – dead branches and coral, and used mother-of-pearl shells. His first exhibition, at the 1976 Vila Agricultural Show, featured his pieces moulded out of of the forms of driftwood and coral, and carved out of shell. His increasing aptitude in these media earned Emmanuel increasing recognition, and in 1989 he was elected as the first president of the Nawita Association, a position he still holds. One of Vanuatu's most critically acclaimed and commercially successful artists, Emmanuel has now exhibited more than sixty times in Vila, Nouméa, Australia and Europe.

Sero Kuautonga

One of the first ni-Vanuatu to become involved in creating contemporary art, Sero was born in 1961 in Ipau village on Futuna. His artistic talents were recognised and encouraged by his teachers while he was at the regional district school on Tanna, and this interest continued after he went on to the main French high school in Port Vila. While in high school, Sero assisted his art teacher in teaching pottery as part of the school art course. In recognition of his artistic talents, the Lands Survey Department of the pro-independence Government of National Unity asked Sero to begin working for them in 1978 in preparation for Vanuatu's independence in 1980. He worked there for more than ten years, during which time he was trained in cartography. Since 1995, Sero has held the position of curator of the National Museum of Vanuatu in the Vanuatu Cultural Centre. Regarded as one of Vanuatu's most innovative artists, Sero has worked in a variety of media and styles, and is currently particularly interested in abstract painting using experimental media. Sero's first individual exhibition was held at the Cultural Centre in Port Vila in 1983, and since then he has exhibited a number of times in Vila, and on four occasions overseas. He is vice-president of the Nawita Association of Contemporary Artists, and is single with two children. Like most other indigenous artists, his art is inspired by the ritual life and landscapes of Vanuatu.

The Demographic Past

Jean-Louis Rallu

Vanuatu has one of the poorest-known demographic histories in the world. In this archipelago, which was for a long time outside the mainstream of the world, most of the sources of information on this topic are only recent. The depopulation which took place in the 19th century are is well-attested, but its extent and the manner in which the depopulation took place are not well-known. The 'teachers' and missionaries who settled on Aneityum in the 19th century documented the spectacular fall in population numbers on that island, from 4000 in 1848 to only 680 persons in 1895. Local customs, such as infanticide, especially in the case of females, and the strangulation of widows, contributed very little to this population decline, the principal cause of which lay in new diseases, introduced by Europeans among populations without immunity because of their isolation over thousands of years. Each epidemic was catastrophic, and diseases of the respiratory system led to death upon death. Apart from the epidemics, population numbers declined as a consequence of increasing numbers of deaths and reduced birth rates, which can be put down to the higher than normal mortality rate for women, fevers, and recurring illnesses, the cause of infertility and miscarriage. Finally, after 1860, labour recruiters began to make deep inroads into the population.

In the 20th century, the end of labour recruiting, and the progressive immunisation of the population have contributed to slowing down the depopulation process, without entirely eliminating it. On the health front, progress remained very slow on the outer islands, and, in 1940, the population of Aneityum was recorded at only 186 inhabitants. With its population reduced by a factor of twenty, that island, along with Erromango, which seems to have undergone a similar evolution, is one of the worst cases of depopulation known in the Pacific.

Very fortunately, the other islands (for example, Tanna and Futuna) suffered a less dramatic fate. The population of the small island of Aniwa, rarely visited by Europeans, has remained stable, with around 200 inhabitants in 1874 and 1941.

It is often confirmed that population density in Vanuatu is inversely proportional to the size of the islands. At the end of the 19th century, the greatest densities were encountered on the small islands off north-east Malakula (250 square kilometres), and in the Shepherds (eighty-five inhabitants per square kilometre on Emau, which has an area of 7.5 square kilometres, but only sixteen on Emwae). Population density is much lower in the large islands of central Vanuatu, Santo, Malakula, Erromango, Pentecost, Maewo, Ambae, and Epi.

A genealogical study conducted in north-east Malakula shows that if the death of many adult males and the decline in the population is attributable to disease, such disease rarely attained epidemic proportions. There was also violent death. War, especially skirmishes, always requires reprisals, and the use of firearms made for a higher and higher toll. At the beginning of this century, violent death in the region represented 10 per cent of deaths for men older than twenty. As far as birth rates were concerned, these were limited by venereal diseases contracted on the plantations, by the generally poor health of the population, and also through widowhood, because this was not quickly followed by a new union in these societies where marriage was very ritualised.

The profound upheavals undergone by island societies in the 19th and 20th centuries also had considerable repercussions for population distribution. In the north of Malakula, before the arrival of Europeans, villages were situated several hundred metres at least from the shore. But once they had been ravaged by epidemics and wars, the survivors abandoned these sites and rebuilt their houses a little further into the interior, preferably near a friendly village. At the same time, the passage and settlement of Europeans, recruiters, traders and, above all, missionaries created a new world along the coastal areas, and survivors of almost-extinct villages often came and settled near the sea, and, indeed, even on nearby small islands.

What is the situation today? Since 1945 the population of Vanuatu has become reinvigorated. As with many other places in the Pacific, one occasionally encounters very high birth rates locally – more than 3 per cent a year – which go hand in hand with the creation of new centres, for the moment limited to coastal areas. But it is not beyond hope that, in the near future, new villages will see the light of day in inland areas too.

Vanuatu Today

Gilbert David

Geography
Area: 12 195 km2
The archipelago consists of eighty-three islands, of which seventy are inhabited. The islands form a kind of Y-shape, extending north-south for a distance of approximately 1000 kilometres. Relatively recent volcanoes and volcanic activity, thus the sobriquet: 'Islands of Ash and Coral'.

Average annual temperature: 24.5°C (Port Vila)
Average annual rainfall: 2332 mm/m2 (Port Vila)
Population: 164 100 (mid-1994 estimate)
Population density: 12 inhabitants per km2
Capital: Port Vila, 24 000 inhabitants
Second agglomeration: Luganville, 8000 inhabitants
Annual urban growth rate: 7.3%
Annual rural growth rate: 2.1%
Total annual growth rate: 2.8%
Life expectancy: 63.8 years
Overall fertility index: 5.6 children per woman
Birth rate: 45 births per year per 1000 inhabitants
School attendance rate: 72% between 6 and 14 years; 22% between 15 and 19 years
Languages: Bislama (Pidgin English), English, French
More than 100 Melanesian languages are spoken in Vanuatu; Bislama is the inter-community and inter-island language of communication; French and English are the languages of education.

Resources
Eighty per cent of the population lives from a subsistence economy (horticulture, fishing), from exports (copra, cocoa, cattle), tourism, forestry, and from the Finance Centre.
Copra: 28 000 tonnes exported in 1993
Cocoa: 2121 tonnes exported in 1993
Cattle: 17 516 tonnes of beef exported in 1993
GDP: US$187.4 million
GDP per head: US$1171
Currency: vatu (US$1 = 110 vatu)

Politics
Republic, parliamentary democracy. Assembly elected for a four-year term.
National Council of Chiefs: Malfatumauri
President: Jean-Marie Leye Lenelcau Manatawoi
Prime Minister: Maxime Carlot Korman
Member of the British Commonwealth and Agence de Coopération Culturelle et Technique (Agency for Cultural and Technical Cooperation).
Motto: Long God Yumi Stanap (In God we stand)

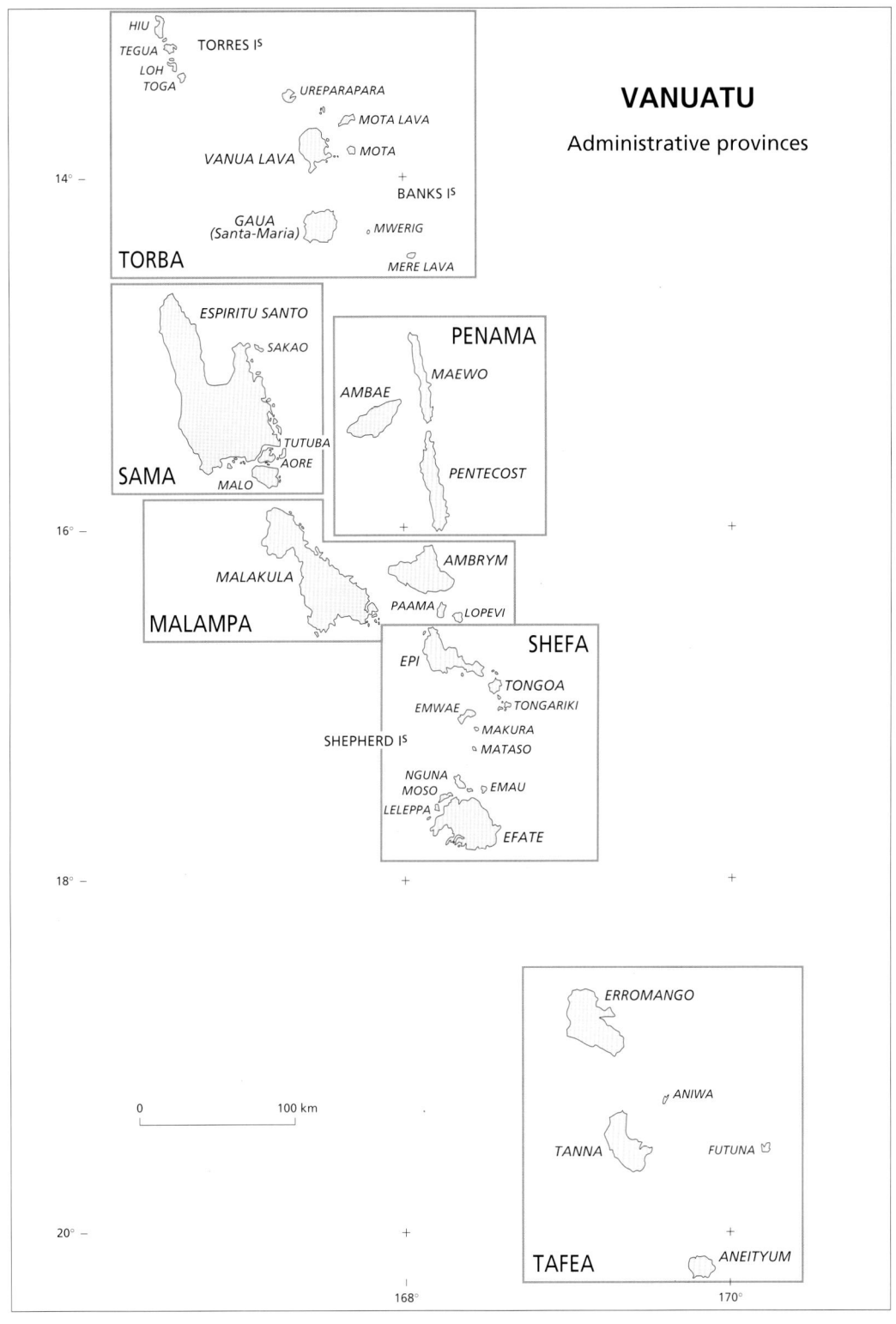

Fig. 383 VANUATU — Administrative provinces

Principal dates in Vanuatu history

- Circa 2000 BC: Arrival of the first Melanesians in the Vanuatu archipelago.
- 'Lapita' culture flourished between 1000 BC and the beginning of the Christian (or Common) Era.
- 1200 AD: Arrival of Roy Mata in the central islands.
- 1452: Eruption of Kuwae volcano (Shepherd Islands).
- 1606: The Portuguese explorer Pedro Fernández de Quirós, in the service of the king of Spain, visited the largest island of the archipelago, which he named *Austrialia del Espiritu Santo*.
- 1768: Louis Antoine de Bougainville sails through the archipelago (between Espiritu Santo and Malakula), which he named the Greater Cyclades (*Les Grandes Cyclades*).
- 1774: James Cook sailed around the archipelago and mapped it. He renamed it the New Hebrides because of its mountainous character, which reminded him of the islands of the Hebrides, off the coast of Scotland.
- 1825: Captain Peter Dillon discovered sandalwood on Erromango. The sandalwood trade lasted until 1865.
- 1839: Murder of John Williams, the first missionary to have landed on Erromango. (This murder marks the beginning of the arrival of Christianity in Vanuatu.)
- 1863-1904: Recruiting, or blackbirding, period.
- 1874: Establishment of the first European settlers in the archipelago, particularly on Efate.
- 1887: Signing of an Anglo-French agreement establishing the Joint Naval Commission, for the purpose of ensuring relative law and order in the archipelago.
- 1906: Establishment of the Anglo-French Condominium, with joint powers over the archipelago: two languages, two education systems, two police forces, one joint court, and so on.
- 1975: The beginnings of internal autonomy, with the election of the Representative Assembly (August).
- 1980: Independence attained 30 July, the New Hebrides becoming the Republic of Vanuatu; its people chose the name ni-Vanuatu for themselves.

Bibliography

Bibliography

Allen, J. 1989. When did humans first colonize Australia? *Search*. 20:149-154.

Allen, J., and C. Gosden (eds). 1991. *Report of the Lapita Homeland Project*. Canberra: Australian National University.

Allen, Michael R. 1967. *Male Cults and Secret Initiation in Melanesia*. Melbourne: Melbourne University Press.

———. 1969. 'Report on Aoba: Incidental Papers on Nduindui District Aoba Island', in *Incidental papers on Nduindui District, Aoba Island, New Hebrides, written for the British Residency in the New Hebrides*. Edited by C. Leaney. Port Vila.

———. 1972. Rank and Leadership in Ndui-Ndui, Northern New Hebrides. *Mankind*. pp. 270-282.

———. 1981. 'Rethinking Old Problems: Matriliny, Secret Societies and Political Evolution', in *Vanuatu: Politics, Economics and Ritual in Island Melanesia*. Edited by M.R. Allen, pp. 9-34. Sydney: Academic Press.

———. 1988. 'The Hidden Power of Male Ritual: The North Vanuatu Evidence', in *Myths of Matriarchy Reconsidered*. Edited by D. Gewertz, pp. 74-98. Oceania Monographs 33. Sydney: Oceania Publications.

Antoine, A., Titaÿna and R. Lugeon. 1931. *Chez les Mangeurs d'Hommes*. Paris.

Aubert de la Rüe, E. 1938. Sur la nature et l'origine probable des pierres portées en pendentifs à l'île de Tanna, *L'Anthropologie* 48:249-60.

———. 1945. *Les Nouvelles Hébrides, îles de cendre et de corail*. Montreal: Éd. de l'Arbre.

Aufray, M. 1981. Description phonologique et grammaticale de l'Anecom. PhD thesis. University of Paris III.

———. n.d. Dictionnaire Anecom-Français. MS.

Baker, John. 1929a. A New Type of Mammalian Intersexuality. *British Journal of Experimental Biology*. VI(1):56-63.

———. 1929b. *Man and Animals in the New Hebrides*. London: George Routledge & Sons.

Ballard, C. 1988. Dudumahan: a rock art site on Kai Kecil, southeast Moluccas. *Bulletin of the Indo-Pacific Prehistory Association*. 8:139-161.

———. 1992. 'Painted rock art sites in western Melanesia: locational evidence for an 'Austronesian' tradition,' in *State of the Art: regional rock art studies in Australia and Melanesia*. Edited by J. McDonald and I.P. Haskovec, pp. 9-106. Occasional Aura Publications 6. Melbourne: Australian Rock Art Research Association.

Beaglehole, J. (ed.). 1961. *The Journals of Captain Cook on his Voyages of Discovery*. Vol. II. *The Voyage of the Resolution and Adventure, 1772-1775*. Cambridge: Haklyut Society.

Beasant, J. 1984. *The Santo Rebellion: An Imperial Reckoning*. Honolulu: University of Hawai'i Press.

Bedford, R.D. 1973. *New Hebridean Mobility: A Study of Circular Migration*. Canberrra: Australian National

University.

Bellwood, P. 1978. *Man's Conquest of the Pacific: the Prehistory of Southeast Asia and Oceania*. Auckland: Collins.

———. 1985. *Prehistory of the Indo-Malaysian Archipelago*. Sydney: Academic Press.

Bensa, A., and J.C. Rivierre. 1982. *Les chemins de l'alliance*. Marseille: SELAF.

Blackwood, P. 1981. 'Rank, exchange and leadership in four Vanuatu societies', in *Vanuatu. Politics, Economics and Ritual in Island Melanesia*. Edited by M. Allen. Sydney: Academic Press.

Blust, Robert A. 1977. *The Proto-Austronesian pronouns and Austronesian subgrouping: a preliminary report*. University of Hawai'i, Working Papers in Linguistics 9(2):1-15.

———. 1978. 'Eastern Malayo-Polynesian: a subgrouping argument', in *Second International Conference on Austronesian Linguistics: Proceedings*. Edited by S.A. Wurm and Lois Carrington, pp. 181-234. Pacific Linguistics, Series C, No. 61. Canberra: Australian National University.

———. 1982. The Linguistic value of the Wallace Line. *Bijdragen tot de Taal-, Land- en Volkenkunde* 138(2-3):231-250.

Bolton, L. 1993. Dancing With Mats: Extending *Kastom* to Women in Vanuatu. PhD thesis, Manchester University.

Bolton, L., and J. Tarisesei. 1992. *Bifo yumi ting se samting nating*. Paper presented to Conference on Cultural Policy in the Pacific, Honiara, Solomon Islands, August 1992.

Bongmatur, Chief Willie. 1991. 'Report blong offis blong Malvatumauri: National Council of Chiefs', in *Museums and Cultural Centers in the Pacific*. Edited by Soroi Marepo Eoe and Pamela Swadling, p. 154. Port Moresby: Papua New Guinea National Museum.

Bonnemaison, Joël. 1972. Systèmes des grades et differences régionales en Aoba. *Cahiers ORSTOM*. IX(1):87-108.

———. 1974. Espaces et paysages agraires des Nouvelles-Hébrides. *Journal de la Société des Océanistes* 44-5:163-232, 259-281.

———. 1979. Les voyages et l'enracinement: formes de fixation et de mobilité dans les sociétés traditionelles des Nouvelles-Hébrides. *L'Espace Géographique*. 8(4):303-318.

———. 1985a. 'Territorial Control and Mobility within Ni-Vanuatu Societies', in *Circulation in Population Movement: Substance and Concepts from the Melanesian Case*. Edited by M. Chapman and R.M. Prothero, pp. 57-59. London: Routledge & Kegan Paul.

———. 1985b. 'The Tree and the Canoe: Roots and Mobility in Vanuatu Societies', in 'Mobility and Identity in the Island Pacific'. *Pacific Viewpoint*. 26(1):30-62.

———. 1986a. *La dernière île*. Paris: Arléa-ORSTOM.

———. 1986b. *Les Fondements d'une identité: territoire, histoire et société dans l'archipel de Vanuatu (Mélanésie)*. Book 1. *L'arbre et la pirogue*. Paris: ORSTOM.

———. 1986c. *Les Fondements d'une identité: territoire, histoire et société dans l'archipel de Vanuatu (Mélanésie)*. Book 2. *Tanna: Les hommes lieux*. Paris: ORSTOM.

———. 1994. *The Tree and the Canoe*. Honolulu: University of Hawai'i Press.

Bougainville, L.A. de 1772. *A Voyage Round the World*. Translated by J.R. Forster. London: J. Nourse and T. Davies.

Boulay, R. 1990. *La Maison Kanak*. Marseilles: ORSTOM.

Brachear, R. 1977. On a Rarotongan Idol from the New Hebrides. *Journal de la Société des Océanistes*. 33(54-55):87-91.

Brenchley, J.L. 1873. *Jottings during the Cruise of H.M.S. 'Curacao' among the South Sea Islands in 1865*. Vol. 6. London: Longmans Green.

Brookfield, H. 1972. *Colonialism, Development and Independence*. Cambridge: Cambridge University Press.

Bühler, A. 1946-1949. Steingeräte, steinskulpturen und felszeichnungen aus Melanesien und Polynesien. *Anthropos*. 41-44:225-606.

Cabalion, Pierre. 1981. *Affinités des cinq groupes linguistiques de l'île de Pentecôte entre eux et leurs inter-relations maritimes traditionelles*. Port Vila: ORSTOM.

Cameron, Francis. 1975. 'Slit Drums and the *Hunggwe* of Eastern Aoba.' *Australian Natural History*. 18(8):278-283.

Capitan, L. 1901. Les pierres à cupule. *Revue de l'Ecole d'anthropologie*, 10(11):114-127.

Charpentier, Jean-Michel. 1982. *Linguistic Atlas of South Malakula*. 2 vols. Paris: Selaf.

Clark, David Ross. 1983. Clusters in Vanuatu languages. Paper read to XVth Pacific Science Congress, Dunedin, NZ.

Clausen, Raymond. 1958. A Musicological Study of the Layard Collection of Recorded Malekulan Music ... B.Litt. thesis. Oxford University.

Codrington, Rev. R.H. 1885. *The Melanesian Languages*.

Oxford: Clarendon.

———. 1891. *The Melanesians: Studies in their Anthropology and Folklore*. Reprinted 1957 by HRAF Press, New Haven. Oxford: Clarendon Press.

Codrington, Rev. R.H., and Ven J. Palmer. 1896. *Mota Dictionary*. London, SPCK.

Coiffier, C. 1982. *Architecture mélanésienne*. 2 vols. Paris: École d'architecture de Paris-La-Villette.

———. 1988. *Traditional Architecture in Vanuatu*. Suva: Institute of Pacific Studies and the Vanuatu Extension Centre of the University of the South Pacific.

Crowe, Peter Russell. 1981a. After the Ethnomusicological Salvage Operation What? *Journal of the Polynesian Society*. 90(2):171-82.

———. 1981b. Polyphony in Vanuatu. *Ethnomusicology* (Pacific Issue). 25(3):419-32.

———. 1986. 'Pince son ombilic et le mien vibrera': chant muet, kava et rêves dans la musique mélanésienne. *Anuario Musical*. 39-40:217-38.

———. 1990a. Dancing Backwards? *The World of Music*. 32(1):84-98.

———. 1990b. *You you savvy sing sing?* VII. European Seminar in Ethnomusicology, Berlin. Prepublication of conference papers, pp. 93-102.

———. 1991. Tagaro seeks Mamalu: Maewo Song and Migration Traditions. *Rongorongo Studies*. I(1-2):14-21, 35-42.

———. 1992. La Naissance du Chant à Maewo (Vanuatu). *Cahiers de musiques traditionnelles*. 5:183-204

———. 1994a. Musiques mélanésiennes. Quelques publications [disques] significatives. *Cahiers de musiques traditionelles*. 7:283-292.

———. 1994b. *Vanuatu: musiques coutûmières*. Compact disc, CD 796. Geneva: VDE-Gallo.

Crowley, T. 1990. *An Illustrated Bislama-English and English-Bislama Dictionary*. Port Vila: Pacific Language Unit, Vila Branch, University of the South Pacific.

Deacon, A. Bernard. 1934a. Geometrical Drawings from Malekula and Other Islands of the New Hebrides. *Journal of the Royal Anthropological Institute*. 64:19-143, 148-175.

———. 1934b. *Malekula: A Vanishing People in the New Hebrides*. Edited by Camilla H. Wedgewood. London: George Routledge & Sons.

Docker, E.W. 1970. *The Blackbirders*. Sydney: Angus & Robertson.

Dudley, B.D. 1860. Journal of a Winter Spent on Amota, Banks Islands. MS. Hocken Library, Dunedin, NZ. Cat. PAM 186/5.

Durrad, W.J. 1940. Notes on the Torres Islands. *Oceania*. 11(2):186-201.

Eissen, J.P., M. Monzier and C. Robin. 1994. Kuwae, l'éruption volcanique oubliée. *La Recherche*. 25(270).

Elaide, M. 1952. *Images et symboles: Essais sur le symbolisme magico-religieux*. Foreword by G. Dumezil; reprint of 1982. Paris: Gallimard.

Elkington, E.W., and N. Hardy. 1907. *The Savage South Seas*. London.

Enright, N.J., and C. Gosden. 1991. 'Unstable archipelagos – south-west Pacific environment and prehistory since 30 000 B.P.', in *The Naive Lands – Prehistory and Environmental Change in Australia and the Southwest Pacific*. Edited by J. Dodson, pp. 160-198. Melbourne: Longman Cheshire.

Espirat, J.J., J. Guiart, M.S. Lagrange and M. Renaud. 1973. *Système des titres electifs ou héréditaires dans les Nouvelles-Hébrides centrales d'Efate aux îles Shepherd*. Paris: Institut d'ethnologie, musée de l'Homme.

Ferrier, J.P. 1982. 'Le territoire de la vie quotidienne et le référentiel habitant.' Colloque Géopoint 82. Avignon: Groupe Dupont.

Festetics de Tolna, R. 1903. *Chez les Cannibales, Huit Ans de Croisière*. Paris.

Foley, W.A. 1986. *The Papuan Languages of New Guinea*. Cambridge: Cambridge University Press.

Forge, A. 1979. 'The problem of meaning in art', in *Exploring the Visual Art of Oceania*. Edited by S.M. Mead, pp. 278-286. Honolulu: University of Hawai'i Press.

Forster, G. 1968. *Georg Forster's Werke: Voyage Round the World*. Vol. 1. Edited by R. Kahn. Berlin: Akademie-Verlag.

Forster, J. 1778. *Observations Made During the Voyage Round the World, on Physical Geography, Natural History and Ethnic Philosophy*. London: G. Robinson.

Fox, C.E. 1958. *Lord of the Southern Isles*. London: Mowbray & Co.

Frimigacci, D., and J. Monnin. 1980. Un inventaire des pétroglyphes de Nouvelle-Calédonie: Grande Terre et Iles. *Journal de la Société des Océanistes*. 36:17-59.

Galipaud, J.C. 1990. 'The physico-chemical analysis of ancient pottery from New Caledonia', in *Lapita Design, Form and Composition*. Edited by M. Spriggs, p. 134-142. Canberra: Australian National University.

———. (ed.). 1992. *Poterie Lapita et Peuplement*. Nouméa: ORSTOM.

Garanger, José. 1972a. *Archéologie des Nouvelles-Hébrides:*

contribution à la connaissance des îles du centre. Publication de la Société des Océanistes 30. Paris: ORSTOM.

———. 1972b. Mythes et Archéologie en Océanie. *La Recherche* 21:233-242

———. 1982. *Archaeology of the New Hebrides: Contribution to the Knowledge of the Central Islands*. Translation of 1972 French edition. Oceania Monographs 24. Sydney: Oceania Publications.

Gardissat, P. 1980. Sokomanu: Culture, coutûme, tradition. *Le Melanésian*. No. 2:8-9.

Giles, W.E. 1968. *A Cruise in a Queensland Labour Vessel to the South Seas*. Edited by Deryck Scarr. Canberra: Australian National University.

Gillot, Françoise. [Date unknown]. *Vivre avec Picasso*. Paris.

Golson, J. 1990. 'Kuk and the development of agriculture in New Guinea: retrospection and introspection', in *Pacific Production Systems – Approaches to Economic Prehistory*. Edited by D.E. Yen and J. Mummery, pp. 139-147. Canberra: Australian National University.

———. 1991. 'Bulmer Phase II: Early Agriculture in the New Guinea Highlands', in Pawley, A. (ed.) *Man and a Half: Essays in Pacific Anthropology in Ethnobiology in Honour of Ralph Bulmer*. Edited by A. Pawley, pp. 484-491. Polynesian Society Memoir 48. Auckland: Polynesian Society.

Golson, J. and D.S. Gardner. 1990. Agriculture and sociopolitical organization in New Guinea highlands prehistory. *Annual Review of Anthropology*. 19:395-417.

Gorecki, P. 1986. Human occupation and agricultural development in the Papua New Guinea highlands. *Mountain Research and Development*. 6:159-166.

———. 1992. 'A Lapita smoke screen', in *Poterie Lapita et Peuplement*. Edited by J.-C. Galipaud, pp. 27-47. Nouméa: ORSTOM.

Gorecki, P., M. Mabin and J. Campbell. 1991. Archaeology and geomorphology of the Vanimo coast, Papua New Guinea: preliminary results. *Archaeology in Oceania*. 26:119-122.

Gosden, C. and N. Robertson. 1991. 'Models for Matenkupkum: interpreting a late Pleistocene site from southern New Ireland, Papua New Guinea', in *Report of the Lapita Homeland Project*. Edited by J. Allen and C. Gosden, pp. 20-45. Canberra: Australian National University.

Gowers, S. 1976. *Some Common Trees of the New Hebrides*. Port Vila.

Green, R.C. 1973. Lapita pottery and the origins of Polynesian culture. *Australian Natural History*. 20:332-337.

———. 1979a. 'Early Lapita Art from Polynesia and Island Melanesia: Continuities in Ceramic, Barkcloth and Tattoo Decorations', in *Exploring the Visual Art of Oceania*. Edited by S.M. Mead, pp. 13-31. Honolulu: University of Hawai'i Press.

———. 1979b. 'Lapita', in *The Prehistory of Polynesia*. Edited by J.D. Jennings, pp. 27-60. Canberra: Australian National University.

———. 1991. 'Near and Remote Oceania: Disestablishing "Melanesia" in Culture History', in *Man and a Half: Essays in Pacific Anthropology in Ethnobiology in Honour of Ralph Bulmer*. Edited by A. Pawley, pp. 491-502. Polynesian Society Memoir 48. Auckland: Polynesian Society.

Groube, L.M. 1972. *Fieldwork notebooks*. Canberra: Department of Prehistory, Research School for Pacific Studies, Australian National University.

———. 1975. La recherche archéologique à Anatom. *Bulletin du Pacifique Sud*. pp. 40-43.

———. 1989. 'The taming of the rain forests: a model for Late Pleistocene forest exploitation in New Guinea', in *Foraging and farming: the evolution of plant exploitation*. Edited by DR. Harris and G.C. Hillman, pp. 292-304. London: Unwin Hyman.

Groube, L.M., J. Chappell, J. Muke and D. Price. 1986. A 40 000 year old occupation site at Huon Peninsula, Papua New Guinea. *Nature*. 324:453-455.

Groves, Colin. 1981. *Ancestors for the Pigs: Taxonomy and Phylogeny of the Genus* Sus. Technical Bulletin 3. Canberra: Department of Prehistory, Research School of Pacific Studies, Australian National University.

Guiart, Jean. 1951. Société, Rituels et Mythes du Nord Ambrym (Nouvelles-Hébrides). *Journal de la Société des Océanistes*. 7:5-103.

———. 1952. L'organisation sociale et politique du nord Malekula. *Journal de la Société des océanistes*. 8:149-230.

———. 1956a. *Grands et petits hommes de la montagne, Espiritu Santo (Nouvelles-Hébrides)*. Nouméa: ORSTOM.

———. 1956b. Notes sur les Tambours d'Ambrym. *Journal de la Société des Océanistes*. 12:334-336.

———. 1956c. *Un siècle et demi de contacts culturels à Tanna (Nouvelles-Hébrides)*. Publications de la Société des océanistes 5. Paris: ORSTOM.

———. 1956d. Unité culturelle et variations locales dans

le Centre Nord des Nouvelles-Hébrides. *Journal de la Société des Océanistes*. 12:217-225.

———. 1958. *Espiritu Santo (Nouvelles-Hébrides)*. Paris: Plon.

———. 1963a. *Océanie*. Paris: Gallimard.

———. 1963b. *Structure de la chefferie en Mélanesie du sud*. Paris: Institut d'ethnologie.

———. 1965. *Mondes et cultures: Nouvelles Hébrides*. Auvers-sur Oise: Archée.

———. 1972. 'Les Nouvelles-Hébrides', in *Ethnologie Régionale, Encyclopédie de la Pléiade*. Paris: Gallimard.

———. 1973. 'Le dossier rassemblé', in *Systèmes de titres dans les Nouvelles-Hébrides centrales, d'Efate aux îles Shepherd*. J.J. Espirat et al., pp. I-III, 47-377, 471-491. Paris: Institut d'ethnologie.

———. 1983. 'Les masques en Mélanésie orientale' in *Océanie le masque au long cours*. Rennes: Ouest-France.

———. 1990. 'Art as a Means of Communication in Pre-Literate Societies', in *Art as a Means of Communication in Pre-Literate Societies*. Edited by Eban Dan, pp. 217-243. Jerusalem: Israel Museum.

Gunn, M. 1986. Rock art on Tabar, New Ireland Province, Papua New Guinea.. *Anthropos*. 81:455-467.

Gunn, William. 1906a. Rock carvings or petroglyphs in Aneityum. *New Hebrides Magazine*. 19:16-17.

———. 1906b. Petroglyphs in Aneityum, Pitcairn Island and New Zealand compared. *New Hebrides Magazine*. 20:16-17.

———. 1909. The picture gallery of Aneityum. *New Hebrides Magazine*. 31:10-11.

———. 1914. *The Gospel in Futuna: with chapters on the islands of the New Hebrides, the people, their customs, religious beliefs, etc*. London: Hodder and Stoughton.

Gunn, William and Mrs. 1924. *Heralds of Dawn: Early Converts in the New Hebrides*. London: Hodder and Stoughton.

Haddon, Alfred C. 1894. *Decorative Arts of British New Guinea: A Study in Papuan Ethnography*. Royal Irish Academy, Cunningham Memoirs 10. Dublin: Academy House.

———. 1895. *Evolution in Art as Illustrated by the Life-Histories of Designs*. 2nd ed. published 1902. London: Scott.

———. 1934. The Geometrical Designs of Raga District, North Pentecost. *Journal of the Royal Anthropological Institute*, LXIV:143-147.

Hagen, A., and A. Pineau. 1889. Les Nouvelles-Hébrides, études ethnographiques. *Revue d'ethnographie*. 7:302-362.

Harrisson, Tom. 1937. *Savage Civilisation*. London: Gollancz.

Hauser-Schäublin, B. 1989. *Kulthäuser in Nordneuguinea*. Akademie-Verlag. Berlin.

Hayes, John. 1984. *James A. Michener: A Biography*. Indianapolis: Bobbs-Merrill.

Hébert, Bernard. 1963-1965a. Nouvelles-Hébrides: notes sur les cases traditionelles d'habitation et de réunion des îles de centre sud. Études mélanésiennes. 18-20:7-21.

———. 1963-1965b. Nouvelles-Hébrides: mégalithes sculptés de l'île Emau. *Etudes Mélanésiennes*. 18-20:56-61.

———. 1963-1965c. Nouvelles-Hébrides: contribution à l'étude archéologique de l'île d'Efaté et des îles avoisinantes. *Etudes mélanésiennes*. 18-20:71-98.

Hedrick, J.D. n.d. Archaeological Investigation of Malo Prehistory: Lapita Settlement Strategies in the Northern New Hebrides. Unpublished draft thesis. University of Pennsylvania.

Henningham, S. 1992. *France and the South Pacific: A Contemporary History*. Honolulu: University of Hawai'i Press.

Henry Matisse, A Retrospective. 1992. New York: Museum of Modern Art.

Holthouse, H. 1970. *Cannibal Cargoes*. Adelaide: Rigby.

Huffman, Kirk. 1976. The Hidden World of M'Botgot. *Australian Natural History*. 18(11):414-419.

———. 1985. An exhibition of barkcloths from Vanuatu. *COMA*. No. 16:49-50.

Humphreys, C.B. 1926. *The Southern New Hebrides: An Ethnological Record*. Cambridge: Cambridge University Press.

Imperato, P. and E. 1992. *They Married Adventure*. New Brunswick.

Inglis, John. 1882. *A Dictionary of the Aneityumese Language*. London: Williams and Norgate.

———. 1887. *In the New Hebrides. Reminiscences of Missionary Life and Works, Especially on the Island of Aneityum from 1850 till 1877*. London: T. Nelson and Sons.

Irwin, G. 1992. *The Prehistoric Exploration and Colonisation of the Pacific*. Cambridge: Cambridge University Press.

Ivens, W.C. 1931. The Place of vui and tamate in the Religion of Mota. *Journal of the Royal Anthropological Institute*. 61:157-166.

Jacquemin, Sylviane. 1991. Histoire des collections océaniennes dans les musées et établissements parisiens, XVIIIe-

XXe siècles. Mémoire de recherche de l'école du Louvre.

———. 1992. *RAO Polynésies*. Paris: Éditions Parenethèses et RMN.

Johnson, M. 1922. *Cannibal Land*. New York.

Johnson, O. 1940. *I Married Adventure*. New York.

———. 1945. *Bride in the Solomons*. London.

Jolly, Margaret. 1984. The Anatomy of Pig Love: Substance, Spirit and Gender in South Pentecost, Vanuatu. *Canberra Anthropology* (Special Volume: Pigs) 7(1-2): 78-109.

———. 1991a. 'Soaring Hawks and Grounded Persons: The Politics of Rank and Gender in North Vanuatu', in *Big Men and Great Men: Personifications of Power in Melanesia*. Edited by M. Godelier and M. Strathern, pp. 48-80. Cambridge: Cambridge University Press.

———. 1991b. 'To Save the Girls for Brighter and Better Lives': Presbyterian Missionaries and Women in the south of Vanuatu. *The Journal of Pacific History*. 26:27-48.

———. 1992a. 'Ill-natured Comparisons': Racism and Relativism in European Representations of ni-Vanuatu from Cook's Second Voyage. *History and Anthropology*. 5(3-4):331-364.

———. 1992b. Custom and the Way of the Land: Past and Present in Vanuatu and Fiji. *Oceania* 62(4):330-354.

———. n.d.a. Lascivious Ladies and Beasts of Burden: Representations of Pacific Women from Cook's Voyages. Paper prepared for David Nicholl Smith Seminar, Auckland New Zealand, August 1993.

———. n.d.b. 'Other Mothers: Maternal "Insouciance" and the Depopulation Debate in Fiji and Vanuatu 1890-1930.' in Maternities and Modernities: Colonial and Postcolonial Experiences in Asia and the Pacific. Edited by K. Ram and M. Jolly. MS.

———. n.d.c. 'The Gender of the Dying Race', in Engendering Colonialism: European Visions of Vanuatu. MS.

Kaeppler, A. 1978. *Artificial Curiosities*. Honolulu: Bishop Museum Press.

Kanegai, N. 1994. *Bure blong Ambae*. Port Vila: Vanuatu Cultural Centre.

Keller, J.D. 1988. Woven World: Neotraditional Symbols of Unity in Vanuatu. *Mankind*, 18(1):1-13.

Kelly, C. 1966. *La Austrialia del Espíritu Santo*. Vol. 1. Cambridge.

Kirch, P.V. (ed.). 1986. *Island Societies: Archaeological Approaches to Evolution and Transformation*. Cambridge: Cambridge University Press.

Kirch, P.V., and D.E. Yen. 1982. *Tikopia: Prehistory and Ecology of Polynesian Outlier*. Bernice P. Bishop Museum Bulletin 238. Honolulu: Bishop Museum Press.

Lamb, R. 1905. *Saints and Savages: The Story of Five Years in the NewHebrides*. Edinburgh and London: Blackwood and Sons.

Lambert, S. 1942. *A Doctor in Paradise*. (US edition published 1941.) London.

Lampert, R.J. 1967. Standing stones and rock art: two sites on New Hanover. *Mankind*. 6:489-492.

Langdon, R. 1967. Who was Hiu's prehistoric Michaelangelo? *Pacific Islands Monthly*. 38:91.

Lawrie, J.H. 1892. The New Hebrideans. *Scottish Geographical Magazine*. 8:302-311.

Lawrie, Rev. J. 1893. Aneityum, New Hebrides and its Customs. *Journal for the Advancement of Science*. 4.

Lawson, B. 1990. Collected Ethnographic Objects as Cultural Representations: Rev Robertson's Collection from the New Hebrides (Vanuatu). MA thesis, McGill University.

———. 1994. *Collected Curios: Missionary Tales from the South Seas*. Montreal: McGill University Libraries.

Layard, John W. 1928. Degree-taking Rites in South West Bay, Malekula. *Journal of the Royal Anthropological Institute*. 58:139-223.

———. 1942. *Stone Men of Malekula: The Small Island of Vao*. London: Chatto & Windus.

———. 1951. 'The Pilgrimage to Oba, An Atchin Sex-Initiation Rite', in *Südseestudien, Etudes sur l'Oceanie, South Seas Studies, Gedenkschrift zur Erinnerung an Felix Speiser*. pp. 331-356. Basel: Museum für Völkerkunde.

Leaney, C. 1965. A Preliminary Archaeological Survey of Malekula Island. Unpublished paper.

Lebot, V., M. Merlin and L. Lindstrom. 1992. *Kava: The Pacific Drug*. New Haven: Yale University Press.

Leggatt, T. Watt. 1903. Musical Instruments of Malekula. *Science of Man*. 6(9).

Lennier, G. 1896. Description de la collection ethnographique océanienne, Musém d'histoire naturelle et d'etHnographie du Havre, Le Havre. Imprimerie du journal *Le Havre*.

Lewis, A.B. 1932. *Ethnology of Melanesia*. Chicago.

Lindstrom, L. 1986. *Kwamera Dictionary/Nĩkukua Sai Nagkiariien Nĩninĩfe*. Pacific Linguistics Series C-95. Canberra: Department of Linguistics, Australian National University.

———. 1990. *Knowledge and Power in a South Pacific*

Society. Washington, DC: Smithsonian Institution Press.

Loy, T., R. Jones, D.E Nelson, B. Meehan, J. Vogel, J. Southon and R. Cosgrove. 1990. Accelerator radiocarbon dating of human blood proteins in pigments from Late Pleistocene art sites in Australia. *Antiquity*. 64:110-116.

Lynch, J. (ed.). 1983. *Studies in the Languages of Erromango*. Pacific Linguistics, Series C, No. 79. Canberra: Australian National University.

Lynch, J.D., and D.T. Tryon. 1985. 'Central-Eastern Oceanic: a Subgrouping Hypothesis', in *Austronesian Linguistics at the 15th Pacific Science Congress*. Edited by Andrew Pawley and Lois Carrington, pp. 31-52. Pacific Linguistics, Series C, No. 88. Canberra: Australian National University.

Mabonlala, A. 1991. Les nattes rouges: inventaire des motifs teints sur les nattes rouges de Pentecôte (Vanuatu). MS. Port Vila: ORSTOM.

MacArthur, N. 1967. *Island Population of the Pacific*. Canberra: Australian National University.

MacClancy, J. 1981. *To Kill A Bird with Two Stones: A Short History of Vanuatu*. Vanuatu Cultural Centre Publications 1. Port Vila: SOCOM.

MacDonald, D. 1913. South sea island mythology. *Journal of the Royal geographical Society of Australasia*. 30:26-44.

McLean, Mervyn E. 1995. *An Annotated Bibliography of Oceanic Music and Dance*. Revised and enlarged 2nd ed. Michigan: Harmonie Park Press.

Martin, Jean-Hubert. 1993. 'A Delayed Communication', in *Aratjara: Art of the First Australians*. Edited by Lüthi Bernard, pp. 32-36. Düsseldorf: DuMont.

MAUREL, M.C. 1984. Pour une géopolitique du territoire. *Hérodote*. 33-34:131-43.

Mescam, G. 1989. *Pentecost: An Island in Vanuatu*. Suva: University of the South Pacific.

Michener, James. 1964. *Tales of the South Pacific*. New York: Pocket Books.

———. 1992. *The World is My Home: A Memoir*. New York: Random House.

Mikloucho-Maclay, N.N. von. 1950-1954. *Sobranijé Sotchinenij*. 5 vols. Revised ed. comm. 1990. Leningrad [St Petersburg]: Akadémij Nauk SSSR.

Miller, J. Graham. 1987. *Live: A History of Church Planting in the Republic of Vanuatu*. Book 5. Port Vila and Lawson (Australia).

Miller, R.S., 1975. *Misi Gete, John Geddie, Pioneer Missionary to the New Hebrides*. Presbyterian Church of Tasmania.

Morrell, W.P. 1960. *Britain in the Pacific Islands*. Oxford: Oxford University Press.

Muller, K. 1971. Le saut du Gol dans le sud de l'île Pentecôte aux Nouvelles-Hébrides. *Journal de la Société des océanistes*. XXVII(32):219-233.

Palmer, B. and F. Clunie. 1970. *Rock Paintings and Engravings in Fiji*. Suva: Fiji Museum.

Paton, John G. 1889. *John G. Paton, Missionary to the New Hebrides. An Autobiography*. 2 vols. Edited by James Paton. London: Hodder and Stoughton.

———. 1891. *John G. Paton, Missionary to the New Hebrides. An Autobiography*. 1 vol. London: Hodder and Stoughton.

Paton, M. Whitecross. 1896. *Letters and Sketches from the New Hebrides*. London: Hodder and Stoughton.

Paton, W. 1973. *Ambrym (Lonwolwol) Dictionary*. Pacific Linguistics, Series C, No. 21. Canberra: Australian National University.

Patterson, G. 1882. *Missionary Life Among the Cannibals, being the Life of Rev. J. Geddie*. Toronto: Campbell.

Patterson, M. 1970. Ambrym Slit Gongs. *Pacific Islands Monthly*. July.

———. 1976. Kinship, Marriage and Ritual in North Ambrym. PhD thesis, Sydney University.

———. 1981. 'Slings and Arrows: Rituals of Status Acquisition in North Ambrym', in *Vanuatu: Politics, Economics and Ritual in Island Melanesia*. Edited by M.R. Allen, pp. 189-236. Sydney: Academic Press.

Paul-Levy, F., and M. Segaud. 1983. *Anthropologie de l'espace*. Paris: Centre Georges Pompidou.

Penrose, Roland. 1982. *Picasso*. Paris.

Philibert, J.-M. 1981. 'Living Under Two Flags: Selective Modernization in Erakor Village, Efate', in *Vanuatu: Politics, Economics and Ritual in Island Melanesia*. Edited by M. Allen, pp. 315-336. Sydney: Academic Press Australia.

———. 1992. 'Social Change in Vanuatu', in *Social Change in the Pacific Islands*. Edited by A.B. Robillard, pp. 98-133. New York: Kegan Paul International.

Raffestin, C. 1980. *Pour une géographie du pouvoir*. Lausanne: Libraries Techniques.

Rallu, Jean-Louis. 1991. *Les Populations océaniennes au XIXe et XXe siècles*. Paris: INED, PUF.

Rawcliffe, Right Rev. Derek, and Peter Crowe. 1980. 'Melanesia: New Hebrides.' *The New Grove, Dictionary of Music and Musicians*. 6th ed. Edited by S. Sadie, vol. 12, pp. 86-88. London: Macmillan.

Regenvanu, R. 1992. *Report No.8. Maewo: Kerepei, Betarara and Nasawa*. Interim Reports of the Vanuatu Cultural and Historic Sites Survey. Port Vila: Vanuatu Cultural and Historic Sites Survey.

Regenvanu, R. and D. Roe. 1992. *Ol damej long olgeta olfala ples we i save kamaot sipos ol i mekem rod stat long big aelan blong Vao i go long Péterpu*. Ripot Long Damej we i Save Kamaot Long Divelopmen, Namba 2. Port Vila: Rejista Blong Olgeta Olfala Ples Blong Vanuatu (Vanuatu Cultural and Historic Sites Survey; Inventaire des Sites Historiques et Culturels de Vanuatu).

Rivers, W.H.R. 1914. *The History of Melanesian Society*. 2 vols. Cambridge: Cambridge University Press.

Robertson, H.A. 1902. *Erromango. The Martyr Isle*. Edited by John Fraser. London: Hodder and Stoughton.

Rodman, M.C. 1981. 'A boundary and a bridge: women's pig killing as a border-crossing between spheres of exchange in East Aoba', in *Vanuatu. Politics, Economics and Ritual in Island Melanesia*. Edited by M. Allen. Sydney: Academic Press.

———. 1987. *Masters of Tradition: Consequences of Customary Land Tenure in Longana, Vanuatu*. Vancouver: University of British Columbia Press.

———. 1989. *Deep Water*. Boulder: Westview Press.

Rodman, W.L. 1973. Men of Influence, Men of Rank: Leadership and Graded Society on Aoba, New Hebrides. PhD thesis, University of Chicago.

Rodman, W.L. and M.C. 1985. Rethinking *Kastom*: On the Politics of Place Naming in Vanuatu. *Oceania*, 40(4):242-251.

Roe, D. 1992a. 'Rock art of north-west Guadalcanal, Solomon Islands,' in *State of the Art: regional rock art studies in Australia and Melanesia*. Edited by J. McDonald and I.P. Haskovec, pp. 128-143. Occasional Aura Publications 6. Melbourne: Australian Rock Art Research Association.

———. 1992b. *Report No. 4. Erromango: Elizabeth Bay, Potnarvin, Ipota and Ifo*. Interim Reports of the Vanuatu Cultural and Historic Sites Survey. Port Vila: Vanuatu Cultural and Historic Sites Survey.

———. In prep. Report No. 3. Malakula: Tenmaru – Tenmial. Interim Reports of the Vanuatu Cultural and Historic Sites Survey. Port Vila: Vanuatu Cultural and Historic Sites Survey.

———. n.d. Rock Art Sites of the Solomon Islands: A Site List and Annotated Bibliography. MS.

Rothwell, N. 1988. Keeping the Language Alive. *Pacific Islands Monthly*. 59(5):14-15.

Rubin, William. 1984. 'Picasso', in *Primitivism in 20th Century Art*. New York: Museum of Modern Art.

Sahlins, M. 1963. Poor Man, Rich Man, Big Man Chief: Political Types in Melanesia and Polynesia. *Comparative Studies in Society and History*. 5:285-300.

Saint-Pierre, M. and P. Wellington. 1985. *Handikrafff Blong, Artisanat de, Handicrafts of Vanuatu*. Port Vila: University of South Pacific Centre.

Schlomowitz, R. 1987. Mortality and the Pacific Labour Trade. *Journal of Pacific History*. 22(1):34-55.

Scholefield, G.H. 1919. *The Pacific. Its Past and Future*. London: John Murray.

Serres, M. 1983. *Détachement*. Paris: Flammarion.

Shineberg, D. 1967. *They Came for Sandalwood*. Melbourne: Melbourne University Press.

Shutler, M.E. 1968. Pottery making at Wusi, New Hebrides. *South Pacific Bulletin*. 18(4):15-18.

Shutler, M.E., and R. Shutler Jr. 1968. Preliminary Report of Archaeological Explorations in the Southern New Hebrides. *Asian Perspectives*. 9:157-166.

Simondon, G. 1969. *Du mode d'existence des objets techniques*. Paris: Aubier.

Skinner, H.D. 1923. Australian cultural influences in the New Hebrides: the imprint of the hand. *Journal of the Polynesian Society*. 32(2):97.

Somerville, H.B.T. 1894. Notes on some islands of the New Hebrides. *Journal of the Anthropological Institute*. 23:1-21, 363-393.

———. 1928. *The Chart Makers*. London.

Specht, J. 1979. 'Rock art in the western Pacific', in *Exploring the Visual Art of Oceania*. Edited by S.M. Mead, pp. 58-82. Honolulu: University of Hawai'i Press.

Speiser, Felix. 1913a. *Two Years with the Natives in the Western Pacific*. Translation of the 1913 German edition. London: Mills & Boon.

———. 1913b. *Urwald, Südsee, Kannibalen, Reise-Endrücke aus den Neuen Hebriden*. Leipzig: Voigtlander.

———. 1922. 'Decadence and Preservation in the New Hebrides', in W.H.R. Rivers. *Essay on the Depopulation of Melanesia*. pp. 25-61. Cambridge: University Press.

———. 1923. *Ethnographische Materialen aus den Neuen Hebriden und den Banks-Inseln*. Berlin: Kreidel.

———. 1929. L'art plastique des Nouvelles-Hébrides. *Cahiers d'art*, 4:91-94.

———. 1936. Über Kunststile in Melanesien. *Zeitschrift für Ethnologie*. 68:304-309.

———. 1966. 'Kunststile in der Südsee', in *The Many Faces of Primitive Art: A Critical Anthology*. Edited by

D. Fraser, pp. 132-160. Translation of the 1941 German edition, published in Basel. Englewood Cliffs: Prentice Hall.

———. 1991. *Ethnology of Vanuatu: An Early Twentieth Century Study*. Translation of the 1923 German edition. Bathurst: Crawford House Press.

Spriggs, M., and A. Anderson. 1993. Late colonization of East Polynesia. *Antiquity*. 67(255):200-219.

Spriggs, M., and W. Mumford. 1992. 'Southern Vanuatu rock art', in *State of the Art: regional rock art studies in Australia and Melanesia*. Edited by J. McDonald and I.P. Haskovec, pp. 128-143. Occasional Aura Publications 6. Melbourne: Australian Rock Art Research Association.

Spriggs, M., and D. Roe. 1989. *Planning for Preservation: a general evaluation of the cultural resources of Erromango, Tafea District, Republic of Vanuatu*. Hall, ACT: National Heritage Studies.

Spriggs, M., and S. Wickler, 1989. Archaeological Research on Erromango: Recent Data on Southern Melanesian Prehistory. *Bulletin of the Indo-Pacific Prehistory Association*. 9:68-91

Spriggs, Matthew. 1981. Vegetable Kingdoms, Taro Irrigation and Pacific Prehistory. PhD thesis, Australian National University, Canberra.

———. 1984. Archeology in Tafea: the Southern Vanuatu Culture History Project, Part II. *NAIKA*. No. 13:3-8.

———. 1986. 'Landscape, Land Use and Political Transformation in Southern Melanesia', in *Island Archaeological Approaches to Evolution and Transformation*. Edited by P.V. Kirch, pp. 6-19. Cambridge: Cambridge University Press.

———. 1989. The Dating of the Island Southeast Asian Neolithic: an Attempt at Chronometric Hygiene and Linguistic Correlation. *Antiquity* 63:587-613.

———. (ed.). 1990a. *Lapita Design, Form and Composition*. Canberra: Australian National University.

———. 1990b. 'Why Irrigation Matters in Pacific Prehistory', in *Pacific Production Systems*. Edited by D.E. Yen and J.M.J. Mummery, pp. 174-189. Occasional Papers in Prehistory 18. Canberra: Department of Prehistory, Research School of Pacific Studies, Australian National University.

———. 1991. 'Lapita Origins, Distribution, Contemporaries and Successors Revisited', in *Indo-Pacific Prehistory 1990*. Edited by P.S. Bellwood, volume 2, pp. 306-312. Bulletin of the Indo-Pacific Prehistory Association 11. Canberra and Jakarta: IPPA and Asosiasi Prehistorisi Indonesia.

———. 1992. 'What Happens to Lapita in Melanesia?' in *Poterie Lapita et Peuplement: Actes du Colloque Lapita. Nouméa, Nouvelle Calédonie, janvier 1992*. Edited by J.C. Galipaud, pp. 219-230. Nouméa: ORSTOM.

———. In press a. 'Landscape Catastrophe and Landscape Enhancement: Are Either or Both True in the Pacific?' in *Historical Ecology in the Pacific Islands: Prehistory Environmental and Landscape Change*. Edited by P.V. Kirch and T. Hunt. Princeton University Press.

———. In press b. 'What is Southeast Asian about Lapita?' in *Prehistoric Mongoloid Dispersals*. Edited by T. Akazawa and E.J.E. Szathmary. Oxford: Oxford University Press.

Stanley, David. 1989. *South Pacific Handbook*. 4th ed. Chio: Moon Publications.

Suas, J.B., 1921. Tamate (esprits) ou tamatologie des Lolopuepue (Aoba), Nouvelles-Hebrides. *Anthropos*. XVI-XVII:240-246.

Swadling, P., J. Chappell, G. Francis, N. Araho and B. Ivuyo. 1989. A Late Quaternary Inland Sea and Early Pottery in Papua New Guinea. *Archaeology in Oceania*. 24:106-109.

Swadling, P., and G. Hope. 1991. 'Environmental change in New Guinea since human settlement,' in *The Naive Lands – Prehistory and Environmental Change in Australia and the Southwest Pacific*. Edited by J. Dodson, pp. 13-42. Melbourne: Longman Cheshire.

Tailhade, H. 1983. *Tambours Sculptés, Dessins sur Sable, île d'Ambrym*. Port Vila.

Taki, J., and D. Tryon. 1994. The Lost Languages of Erromango. Lecture paper, World Archaeology Conference, New Delhi.

Teilhet, J. 1983. 'The role of women artists in Polynesia and Melanesia', in *Art and Artists of Oceania*. Edited by S.M. Mead and B. Kernot, pp. 45-56. Palmerston North, NZ: Dunmore Press.

Thiel, B. 1987. Early settlement of the Philippines, Eastern Indonesia, and Australia-New Guinea: a new hypothesis. *Current Anthropology* 28: 236-241.

Thomas, N. 1992. Colonial Conversions: Difference, Hierarchy and History in Early Twentieth Century Evangelical Propaganda. *Comparative Studies in Society and History*, 34(2):366-389.

———. 1995. *Oceanic Art*. London: Thames and Hudson.

———. 1996. '"On the Varieties of the Human Species": Forster's Comparative Ethnology', in *Observations*

Made During the Voyage Round the World, on Physical Geography, Natural History and Ethnic Philosophy. J.R. Forster, new ed. Honolulu: University of Hawai'i Press.

Thompson, R.C. 1971. Commerce, Christianity, and Colonialism: The Australian New Hebrides Company, 1883-1897. *Journal of Pacific History.* 6:15-38.

Tournier, M. 1979. *Entretiens, revue Silex* (numéro spécial sur les îles) 14.

Tryon, D., and R. Gély (eds). 1979. *Gazetteer of New Hebrides Place Names.* Canberra: Australian National University.

Tryon, Darrell T. 1976. *New Hebrides Languages: An Internal Classification.* Pacific Linguistics, Series C, No. 50. Canberra: Australian National University.

———. 1979. 'The language situation in the New Hebrides', in *New Guinea and Neighbouring Areas: A Sociolinguistic Laboratory.* Edited by S.A. Wurm, pp. 11-31. The Hague: Mouton.

———. 1995. 'The Austronesian languages', in *Comparative Austronesian Dictionary.* Edited by Darrell T. Tryon, Part 1:5-44. Berlin: Mouton de Gruyter.

Van Trease, Howard (ed.). 1995. *Melanesian Politics. Stael Blong Vanuatu.* Auckland and Suva: Macmillan Brown Centre for Pacific Studies, University of Canterbury, and Institute for Pacific Studies, University of the South Pacific.

Vianney, Atpatoun. 1991. 'The Vanuatu Cultural Centre', in *Museums and Cultural Centers in the Pacific.* Edited by Soroi Marepo Eoe and Pamela Swadling, pp. 155-160. Port Moresby: Papua New Guinea National Museum.

Vienne, B. 1979. Gens de Motlav: la vision du monde et la conception des rapports sociaux dans le Nord des Îles Banks (Nouvelles-Hébrides). Thesis, ORSTOM, Paris.

———. 1984. *Gens de Motlav. Idéologie et pratique sociale en Mélanésie.* Publication de la Société des océanistes 42. Paris: Musée de l'Homme.

Visitor to Vanuatu. n.d. Vanuatu Visitor's Bureau.

Waiko, John D. 1981. 'Binandere Oral Traditions: Sources and Problems', in *Oral Tradition in Melanesia.* Edited by Donald Denoon and Roderic Lacey, pp. 11-30. Port Moresby: Institute of PNG Studies.

Walter, A. 1987. *Eléments pour une étude technologique de BIBLIOGRAPHY.* Port Vila: ORSTOM.

Walter, A., C. Sam and G. Bourdy. 1994. Etude ethnobotanique d'une noix comestible: les *canarium* du Vanuatu. *Journal de la Société des Océanistes.*

Ward, Graeme K. 1979. Prehistoric Settlement and Economy in a Tropical Small Island Environment: The Banks Islands, Insular Melanesia. PhD thesis, Australian National University, Canberra.

———. 1989. 'The Mangaasi Pottery and the Mangaasi Site', in *Saying So Doesn't Make it So.* Papers in Honour of B. Foss Leach. New Zealand Archaeological Association Monograph 17. Edited by D.G. Sutton, pp. 153-167. Otago, NZ: Archaeological Association.

Webb, A.S. 1937. The People of Aoba. *Mankind.* 2(4):73-80.

Weightman, Barry. 1989. *Agriculture in Vanuatu: A Historical Review.* Cheam: British Friends of Vanuatu.

Wheatley, J. 1992. *A Guide to the Common Trees of Vanuatu.* Port Vila.

Wickler, S., and M. Spriggs. 1988. Pleistocene human occupation of the Solomon Islands, Melanesia. *Antiquity* 62:703-706.

Woodburn, M.K. 1944. *Backwash of Empire.* Melbourne: Georgian House.

Wurm, S.A. 1982. *The Papuan Languages of Oceania.* Tubingen: Gunter Narr.

Yen, D.E. 1974. Arboriculture in the subsistence of Santa Cruz, Solomon islands. *Economic Botany.* 28:247-284.

———. 1990. 'Environment, agriculture and the colonisation of the Pacific,' in *Pacific Production Systems – Approaches to Economic Prehistory.* Edited by D.E. Yen and J. Mummery, pp. 258-277. Canberra: Australian National University.

Contributors

Michel Aufray is Director of the Department of Upper Asia, South-East Asia and the Pacific at INALCO, the National Institution of Languages and Civilisations in Paris, where he lectures on Oceanic languages and cultures. He has carried out ethnolinguistic fieldwork in French Polynesia, New Caledonia and Vanuatu, where he has worked on Aneityum, Maewo and the west coast of Santo.

Lissant Bolton is Senior Collection Manager in the Division of Anthropology, Australian Museum, Sydney. Her research interests include women, cultural identity, material culture, and landscape, with particular reference to Vanuatu.

Joël Bonnemaison, a cultural geographer, was for many years an ORSTOM researcher in Vanuatu, where he began in 1968, later becoming Director of ORSTOM in Port Vila. His principal research areas have been Tongoa, Ambae, Maewo, Pentecost and Tanna. His most recent major publication, a cultural geography of Vanuatu (1996), concentrates particularly on the island of Tanna. Since 1994, Joël has been Professor of Cultural Geography at the Sorbonne (University of Paris IV).

Roger Boulay is a curator in the Oceanic section of the Musée des Arts d'Afrique et d'Océanie in Paris. He is one of the organisers of the 'Arts of Vanuatu' travelling exhibition, Port Vila 1996, Nouméa 1996, Basel 1997 and Paris 1997-98. He has carried out research in a number of the islands of Vanuatu, especially Ambrym, Malakula and Tanna.

Jean-Michel Charpentier is Chargé de Recherche, Laboratoire de Langues et Civilisations à Tradition Orale, Centre National de la Recherche Scientifique, Paris. He has conducted extensive fieldwork in Vanuatu, especially on the island of Malakula. In the 1970s, he was also curator of the Vanuatu Cultural Centre for two years.

Christian Coiffier has made a special study of traditional housing styles in Vanuatu, and is the author of a study bringing together ancient and contemporary housing styles and construction techniques. He is based in Paris.

Peter Russell Crowe, ethnologist, musician and ethnomusicologist, was born in New Zealand but lives in France. He has undertaken several years of fieldwork in Vanuatu, especially in the north-east of the country. Twenty years ago he initiated the Vanuatu Oral Tradition Program, which has become the Vanuatu Cultural Centre Fieldworkers' Program. Since 1990, Crowe has been Secretary-General of the European Seminar in Ethnomusicology.

Gilbert David, a geographer engaged as a researcher based at ORSTOM in Nouméa, has worked extensively on the socioeconomics of fisheries in Vanuatu, and on the satellite surveillance of Vanuatu coastlines. David has worked on socioeconomic geography in Vanuatu since 1986.

Marie-Joseph Dubois was a Marist missionary in New Caledonia for more than thirty years. He worked in the Belep Islands and on the Isle of Pines, but has the distinction of having lived, worked and studied ethnology and linguistics on the island of Maré, in the Loyalty Islands, east of the main island of New Caledonia.

Jean-Christophe Galipaud was Director of the Department of Archaeology at the Office Culturel Scientifique et Technique Canaque, Nouméa, from 1985 to 1990. Since 1990, he has been working with ORSTOM in Vanuatu. With David Roe, he was responsible for setting up the Vanuatu Cultural and Historic Sites Survey.

José Garanger has devoted himself to the study of Oceanic prehistory since joining the CNRS, the National Centre for Scientific Research, in 1962. He conducted two long periods of fieldwork in Polynesia and Vanuatu, his most important work being that carried out in the Efate region. In 1977 he became Professor of Prehistoric Ethnology at the University of Paris I. Among other things, José Garanger was for many years Secretary-General and then President of the Société des Océanistes at the Musée de l'Homme.

Paul Gorecki, Senior Lecturer in Anthropology and Archaeology at James Cook University, Townsville, Australia, grew up in Zaire and was educated at the Sorbonne and the University of Sydney. His major areas of research are in tropical Australia and in Papua New Guinea.

Kirk W. Huffman was educated in social anthropology, prehistoric archaeology and ethnology at the universities of Newcastle-Upon-Tyne, Oxford and Cambridge between 1966 and 1977. While a research student in ethnology at the University Museum of Archaeology and Anthropology at Cambridge, between 1972 and 1977, he worked on an ethnohistorical analysis of Malakulan art and material culture. He carried out fieldwork in Malakula in 1972, 1974 and 1976. He became temporary Assistant Curator of Anthropology at the Australian Museum, Sydney, for six months in 1976, before becoming curator of the National Museum at the Vanuatu Cultural Centre in Port Vila. He has been honorary curator at the Vanuatu Cultural Centre since 1991.

Sylviane Jacquemin works for the Musée National des Arts d'Afrique et d'Océanie. She is a commissioner of the Ra'o Polynésie exhibition, and inventory curator for Oceanic collections in the museums of France.

Margaret Jolly is a Senior Fellow and Convenor of the Gender Relations Project in the Research School of Pacific and Asian Studies, Australian National University, Canberra. She taught feminist anthropology, illness and healing, Melanesian ethnography, and Pacific colonial history at Macquarie University in Sydney for seventeen years. She has published extensively on women in the Pacific, and especially Vanuatu.

Christian Kaufmann is Curator for Oceania at the Museum für Völkerkunde und Schweizerisches Museum für Volkskunde, Basel. He conducted field research in Papua New Guinea in 1966, 1972-73, and 1983, and made extended visits to Vanuatu in 1983 and 1991. He has been involved in exhibitions and publications on anthropological subjects, as well as on the arts of Melanesia and wider Oceania. Kaufmann is a former chairman of the Swiss Ethnological Society, and from 1990 to 1993 was scientific advisor to the Musée national des Arts d'Afrique et d'Oceanie, Paris.

Lamont Lindstrom is Professor of Anthropology at the University of Tulsa, Oklahoma. His recent publications include *Cargo Cult: Strange Stories of Desire from Melanesia and Beyond*, and *Knowledge and Power in a South Pacific Society*.

Alfreda Mabonlala, from Melsisi, on the island of Pentecost, has been an ORSTOM employee since 1984. She has compiled ethnographic inventories of mats and women's dress in Vanuatu, and has published two books of traditional legends.

Mary Patterson is a Lecturer in Anthropology at Melbourne University. Her main research interests are in gender and kinship, traditional medicine, and sorcery and witchcraft, with special emphasis on Melanesia.

Philippe Peltier is Collections Curator at the Musée National des Arts d'Afrique et d'Océanie in Paris. He participated in the exhibition 'Primitivism and Modern Art' at the Museum of Modern Art in New York in

1984. He has spent more than two years working in the Sepik region in Papua New Guinea.

Jean-Marc Philibert is Professor of Anthropology, University of Western Ontario, London, Ontario. He has worked extensively on urbanisation, custom and politics in Vanuatu, with special reference to Efate, particularly the village of Erakor.

Jean-Louis Rallu, Directeur de Recherche at INED, the National Institute of Economics and Development, in Paris, previously worked on cultural change in north Malakula. Since 1977, his principal research has centred on the evolution of Oceanic populations from first European contacts to the present.

Ralph Regenvanu is Director of the Vanuatu Cultural Centre, which incorporates the National Museum, Library, Cultural and Historical Sites Register, and Film and Sound Archive. The curator of the National Museum until 1995, Ralph is the first ni-Vanuatu to have obtained qualifications in anthropology and archaeology (from the Australian National University). He is also a contemporary artist, and has exhibited in Port Vila and Australia as part of the Nawita Association of Contemporary Artists of Vanuatu.

Margaret Rodman is Professor of Anthropology, York University, Toronto. She has worked extensively in Vanuatu, especially on north-east Ambae. She has a longstanding interest in land tenure in Vanuatu.

William Rodman is Professor of Anthropology and Director of Graduate Programs in Anthropology at McMaster University, Hamilton, Ontario, Canada. He completed his PhD at the University of Chicago in 1973. Rodman has conducted research in Vanuatu since 1969, and has taken rank twice in the graded society in Longana-Malavung, east Ambae.

David Roe is Research Fellow in the Department of Archaeology at the University of Southampton, England. His research focuses on aspects of Melanesian prehistory, and, in particular, the region's rock-art traditions, trade and exchange networks, and landscape archaeology. Dr Roe first worked in the Melanesian region in 1978, when he was appointed government archaeologist in the Solomons. From 1990 to 1994, he and Dr Jean-Christophe Galipaud established and managed the Vanuatu Cultural and Historic Sites Survey.

Jacob Sam was born in the Kwamera area of south-east Tanna, and undertook film training in Melbourne for eighteen months during 1984-85. He joined the National Cultural Centre and became head of the National Film Unit in 1986. He has attended numerous cultural and filming meetings, and so on, overseas, and is head of the National Film and Sound Archives.

Matthew Spriggs was born in England, but now lives in Australia. He is Senior Fellow in Oceanic Archaeology, in the Division of Archaeology and Natural History, Research School of Pacific and Asian Studies, Australian National University. Previously, he was an Associate Professor in the Department of Anthropology, University of Hawai'i at Manoa. He completed his PhD in 1981, a study of traditional taro-irrigation techniques in Vanuatu and the rest of the Pacific.

Darrell Tryon is Senior Fellow and Convenor of the Division of Society and Environment, Research School of Pacific and Asian Studies, Australian National University, Canberra. He has researched and published extensively on the languages of the Pacific.

Bernard Vienne has had a long career as an ethnologist with ORSTOM. His association with Vanuatu goes back thirty years. Vienne's area of specialisation is the Banks and Torres groups, although in recent years he has turned his attention to the Akha people of Myanmar and northern Thailand. Most recently he has been working in an ethno-archaeological research program in Wallis and Futuna.

Annie Walter, an ORSTOM researcher, qualified in ethnology and medicine, initially carried out research on traditional medicine in Vanuatu before specialising in the study of traditional management of natural resources. She is engaged in research on fruit trees in the country. Previously, Walter also put together major documentation on the art of basket-weaving in Vanuatu.

Photographic Credits

Basel, Museum für Völkerkunde (objects Peter Horner, field photographs Felix Speiser)
figs 3, 5, 6, 19, 20, 21, 24, 27, 28, 29, 33, 36, 41, 43, 53-55, 57, 58, 62-64, 71, 91, 92a-d, 110, 112, 126, 128, 131-135, 141, 144, 145, 150, 153-166, 170-172, 174-183, 188, 191, 192, 205, 210, 212, 216, 218, 219, 222, 230, 232-235, 238, 240, 241, 244, 252-256, 259, 268, 270a-c, 271a-b, 272, 273a-b, 277-285, 287, 289-309, 327, 328, 330, 331, 347, 376.

Basel, Bernhard Gardi (postcards)
figs 362, 363.

Bordeaux, Musée d'Aquitaine
figs 2, 68.

Cambridge, University Museum of Archaeology and Anthropology
figs 1, 80, 236, 237.

Canberra, Hubert Goron (postcards)
figs 372, 375.

Canberra, Matthew Spriggs
figs 100, 101.

Chartres, Musée des Beaux-Arts
figs 224, 225, 276.

Geneva, Musée d'Ethnographie
figs 26, 30, 31, 32, 339.

Ibiza, San Antonio Abad, Kirk Huffman
figs 151, 367-369.

La Rochelle, Musée d'Histoire naturelle et d'Ethnographie
fig. 60.

Leipzig, Museum für Völkerkunde
fig. 4.

London, British Museum
fig. 351.

London, Museum of Mankind, British Museum
figs 7, 148.

London, Royal Geographical Society
figs 37, 46, 168, 215, 228, 246, 258, 361.

Massy-Palaiseau, Joël Bonnemaison, Gilles Berizzi
fig. 249.

Melbourne, Mary Patterson
figs 329, 335, 336.

Montreuil-sous-Bois, Bernard Vienne
figs 286, 310-315.

Noisy-le-Grand, José Garanger
figs 78, 79, 82-85, 87.

Nouméa, Musée territorial de Nouvelle-Calédonie
figs 48, 72, 74, 275, 370, 371.

Nouméa, David Becker
figs 13, 14, 44, 106, 107, 143, 152, 169, 217, 247, 248, 345, 348, 366.

Nouméa ORSTOM, Gilbert David
figs 190, 231.

Paris, Bibliothèque nationale de France
figs 9, 10, 11, 12, 15, 73, 167, 214, 342-344, 349, 350, 358.

Paris, Musée de l'Homme
figs 34, 35, 40, 65, 66, 140, 173, 226, 245, 267, 274a-b, 334, 340, 346, 359, 371.

Paris, Réunion des musées nationaux, agence photographique (Daniel Arnaudet and Gilles Berizzi)
figs 17, 18, 22, 23, 42, 47, 49, 50, 51, 61, 67, 69, 70, 108, 146, 184-187, 193, 195-202, 207, 220, 221, 223, 229, 239, 242, 243, 257, 264-266, 269, 325-327, 337, 338, 340.

Paris, Réunion des musées nationaux, agence photographique (Gérard Blot)
fig. 377.

Paris, Christian Coiffier
figs 250, 260-263.

Paris, Dominique Genet
fig. 86.

Paris, ORSTOM
figs 45, 56.

Port Vila, Vanuatu Cultural Centre
figs 102, 360, 364, 365.

Port Vila, Ange Bizet
figs 89, 90, 109, 136-139, 142, 317, 318, 322.

Port Vila, archives de l'ancienne Résidence de France
fig. 189.

Port Vila ORSTOM, Jean-Christophe Galipaud
fig. 105.

Port Vila, Pavel German
figs 103, 104.

Port Vila, ORSTOM, Alfreda Mabonlala (computer drawings)
figs 111, 124, 125.

Port Vila, ORSTOM, Annie Walter and G. Mescam
figs 113-123.

Port Vila, Ralph Regenvanu
figs 378-382.

Southampton, David Roe
figs 94-99.

Stuttgart, Linden-Museum
figs 147, 194.

Sydney, Australian Museum
figs 38, 39, 149.

Sydney, Lissant Bolton
figs 127, 129, 130.

Wellington, Alexander Turnbull Library
figs 332, 352-357, 374.

Zürich, Museum Rietberg
fig. 52.

All rights reserved.

Object Dimensions and Museum Registration

In the following list, objects are listed by their figure number in this book, followed by their dimensions, the museum in which they are held, and their museum registration. Figures may be unlisted because details were unavailable at the time of printing, or because they were field photographs, reproductions of paintings, figures from other publications, and so on.

2: 259 x 65 cm; MAB; 13.162 (Note: this object is deposited in MAAO.)
3: 195 x 33 x 23 cm; MVB; Vb 4450
6: 240 cm; MVB; Vb 4395
17: 110 x 35 cm; MAAO; MNAO, Saint-Germain collection 53.317
18: 120 x 22 x 16 cm; MAAO; MNAO 62.1.4
19: 60 x 32 x 33 cm; MVB; Vb 4756
20: 99 x 78 x 50 cm; MVB; Vb 4768
21: 61 x 73 x 65 cm; MVB; Vb 4209
22: 41 x 32 cm; MAAO; MNAO 31.1.29
23: 118 x 29 cm; MAAO; MNAO 31.1.12
25: 43.5 x 24 cm; MAAO; MNAO 64.2.39
26: 30 cm; MEG; 41 817
27: 26 cm; MVB; Vb 4558
28: 24 cm; MVB; Vb 4562
29: 29 cm; MVB; Vb 4560
30: 40 cm; MEG; 20931
31: 40 cm; MEG; 20932
32: 60 cm; MEG; 20933
33: 258 x 40 cm; MVB; Vb 4406
34: 300 x 34 x 30 cm; MHP; MH 38.42.8
35: 200 x 40 x 50 cm; MHP; MH 90.27.3
36: 50 x 25 x 10 cm; MVB; Vb 4745
38: 45 x 38 x 15 cm; AMS; B 4111
42: 460 x 340 cm; MAAO; MNAO 49.2.1
47: 13 x 63 x 17 cm; MAAO; MNAO 62.1.2
48: 5.2 x 58 cm; MTNC; MNC 86.6.20
49: 70 x 36.5 cm; MAAO; MNAO 70.11.2
50: 21.5 x 21 x 41.5 cm; MAAO; MNAO 31.1.8
51: 11.5 x 57.5 x 14 cm; MAAO; MNAO 66.16.3

53: 58 x 25 x 9 cm; MVB; Vb 3230
54, 055: 60 x 33 x 8 cm; MVB; Vb 3234
60: 170 x 60 cm; MHNE; H 2452
61: 27 x 23 cm; MAAO; MNAO D.62.1.6
62: 15 x 21 x 17.5 cm; MVB; Vb 4779
66: 187 x 58 x 26 cm; MNAM; AM 1989.206
67: 51 x 21 x 11 cm; MAAO; MNAO 67.2.1
68: 227 x 80 cm; MAB; 13.161
69: 74 x 34 cm; MAAO; MNAO 31.1.10
70: 79 x 35 x 33 cm; MAAO; MNAO 31.1.36
71: 90 x 40 cm; MVB; Vb 4115
72: 55 x 23 cm; MTNC; MNC 86.6.49
74: 25 x 7 x 12 cm; MTNC; MNC 86.6.11
80: 50 cm; UMAA; 1920.1020
91 (left): 4 x 4 x 0.5 cm; MVB; Vb 1743
91 (right): 7 x 6.5 x 1.5 cm; MVB; Vb 2658
92a: 4.5 x 4 x 6.5 cm; MVB; Vb 1747
92b: 6.5 x 6 x 1 cm; MVB; Vb 1715
92c: 5 x 4.5 x 0.5 cm; MVB; Vb 1744
92d: 4.5 x 4 x 1 cm; MVB; Vb 3838
110: 400 x 85 cm; MVB; Vb 4435
132: 102 x 17 cm; MVB; Vb 4234
132: 105 x 17 cm; MVB; Vb 4233
132: 95 x 12 cm; MVB; Vb 4232
134: 113 x 5.5 cm; MVB; Vb 4215
134: 130 x 4.5 cm; MVB; Vb 4216
146: 344 x 90 cm; MAAO; MNAO, Saint-Germain collection 53.313
147: 325 x 115 cm; LMS; 90 267
148: 87 x 56 cm; MML; Q.78.Oc.543
149: 188 x 80 cm; AMS; E 18 885
153: 17 x 5.5 x 1.5 cm; MVB; Vb 3222
154: 14.5 x 4.5 x 0.5 cm; MVB; Vb 3219
155: 16 x 4.5 x 1 cm; MVB; Vb 3213
156: 12 x 8 x 1.5 cm; MVB; Vb 3205
157: 31.5 x 5 x 2 cm; MVB; Vb 3151
158: 26 x 7 x 0.5 cm; MVB; Vb 3152
159: 21 x 13 x 0.5 cm; MVB; Vb 3160
160: 18 x 9 x 1 cm; MVB; Vb 3156

161: 16 x 0.6 x 7 cm; MVB; Vb 3157
162: 26.5 x 5 x 3 cm; MVB; Vb 3171
163: 14 x 3 x 2 cm; MVB; Vb 3167
164: 24 x 9 x 1.5 cm; MVB; Vb 3169
165: 20 x 5 x 1 cm; MVB; Vb 3176
166: 32 x 7 x 0.5 cm; MVB; Vb 3191
172: 55.5 cm, dia. 2.5 cm; MVB; Vb 3498
172: 64 cm, dia. 3 cm; MVB; Vb 3306
172: 75.5 cm, dia. 2.5 cm; MVB; Vb 11856
172: 78 cm, dia. 3 cm, MVB, Vb 3497
172: 83 cm, dia. 3 cm; MVB; Vb 3310
174: 52 cm, dia. 1.5 cm; MVB; Vb 3303
175: 64 cm, dia. 3 cm; MVB; Vb 3306
176: 63 cm, dia. 2 cm; MVB; Vb 3495
177: 83 cm, dia. 3 cm; MVB; Vb 3310
178: 123 cm, dia. 2 cm; MVB; Vb 3318
179: 68 cm, dia. 2.5 cm; MVB; Vb 3491
180: 78 cm, dia. 3 cm; MVB; Vb 3497
181: 75.5 cm, dia. 2.5 cm; MVB; Vb 11856
182: 55.5 cm, dia. 2.5 cm; MVB; Vb 3498
183: 186 cm; 5.5 cm; MVB; Vb 3514
184 (2nd from right): 345 x 37 cm; MAAO; MNAO 64.2.54
184 (left): 379 x 52 cm; MAAO; MNAO 64.2.32
185, 186: 80 x 13 cm; MAAO; MNAO 62.5.2
187: 352 x 32 cm; MAAO; MNAO 64.7.1
191: 10 cm; MVB; Vb 4702
193: 52 x 47 cm; MAAO; MNAO D.62.1.34
194: 53 cm; LMS; 91 810
195: 35.5 x 15.8 cm; MAAO; MNAO D.62.1.1
196: 13.5 x 3.5 cm; MAAO; MNAO 64.2.40
197: 14.5 x 4.5 cm; MAAO; MNAO 64.2.47
198: 6.5 x 9 x 4.6 cm; MAAO; MNAO 66.6.1
199: 345 x 37 cm; MAAO; MNAO 64.2.53
200: 18 x 4 x 6 cm; MVB; Vb 4198
201: 11 x 60 x 3 cm; MAAO; MNAO 83.3.1
202: 15 x 6 cm; MAAO;

MNAO 63.11.3
218: 88 x 5 x 0.5 cm; MVB; Vb 4087
219 (left): 4 cm, dia. 10 cm; MVB; Vb 1416
219 (right): 4 cm, dia. 11 cm; MVB; Vb 3873
220: 21 x 10 cm; MAAO; MNAO D.62.1.36
221: 52 x 4.5 cm; MAAO; MNAO D.62.1.35
222: 64 x 35 cm; MVB; Vb 11885
223: 77 x 17.5 cm; MAAO; MNAO D.61.1.11
224: 9.5 x 1 x 0.7 cm; MBA; 84.1.OB.307
225: 7.6 x 1.7 x 0.5 cm; MBA; 84.1.OB.306
226: 25 x 15 cm; MHP; MH 30.54.1
229: 80 x 23 x 8 cm; MVB; Vb 3024
230: 11.5 cm, dia. 9 cm; MVB; Vb 3867
230 (right): 13 cm, dia. 10 cm; MVB; Vb 3890
232: 37 x 5 x 0.7 cm; MVB; Vb 3073
233: 35 x 3.5 x 1.5 cm; MVB; Vb 3068
234: 43 x 3.5 x 0.5 cm; MVB; Vb3100
235: 58 x 2 x 0.5 cm; MVB; Vb 3099
236, 237: 49 x 2.2 cm to 69.8 x 3.5 cm; UMAA; Z11108, Z11109, Z11111, Z11119, Z11120, Z11130, Z11135, Z11138, Z11142, Z11144, Z11146, Z42645, 1920.652, 1920.655, 1920.656, 1920.658, 1920.661
238: 44 x 5.5 x 1 cm; MVB; Vb 3088
239: 29 x 4.5 cm; MAAO; MNAO 79.2.3
240: 37 x 4.5 x 1.5 cm; MVB; Vb 3089
241: 25 x 5 x 0.5 cm; MVB; Vb 3063
242: 187 x 76 cm; MAAO; MNAO 64.4.1
243: 172 x 54 x 10 cm; MAAO; MNAO 31.1.46
244: 85 x 50 (bottom), 40 (top) cm; MVB; Vb 4737
252: 65 cm, dia. 13.5 cm; MVB; Vb 4742
252: 75 cm, dia. 22 cm; MVB; Vb 4743
257 (left): 212 x 31 cm; MAAO; MNAO 64.2.6
257 (right): 240 x 32 cm; MAAO;

MNAO 64.2.8
264: 7 x 95 x 59 cm; MAAO; MNAO 68.9.4
265: 7 x 91 x 24 cm; MAAO; MNAO 31.1.57
266: 87 x 28 x 7 cm; MAAO; MNAO 78.4.3
267: 53 x 23.5 x 6.5 cm; MHP; MH 29.14.45
269: 12.5 x 67 x 31 cm; MAAO; MNAO 63.11.2
270a, b, c: 72 x 10 x 27 cm; MVB; Vb 4323
271a, b: 80 x 8.5 x 32.5 cm; MVB; Vb 4309
272: 60 x 9.5 x 50.5 cm; MVB; Vb 4332
273a, b: 41 x 47.5 x 41 cm; MVB; Vb 4327
275: 120 x 7.4 x 4 cm, MTNC, MNC 86 6 157
276: 49.2 x 0.8 x 0.8 cm; MBAC; 84.1.OB.343
277: 88 cm, dia. 3.5 cm; MVB; Vb 3117
278: 89 cm, dia. 3.5 cm; MVB; Vb 3118
279: 96 cm, dia. 4 cm; MVB; Vb 3122
280: 79 cm, dia. 4 cm; MVB; Vb 3124
281: 92 cm, dia. 4 cm; MVB; Vb 3125

285: 64 cm, dia. 6.5 cm; MVB; Vb 3110
289: 17 cm, dia. 0.7 cm; MVB; Vb 3787
290: 17 cm, dia. 0.5 cm; MVB; Vb 3783
291: 17 cm, dia. 0.6 cm; MVB; Vb 3786
292: 17.5 cm, dia. 0.7 cm; MVB; Vb 3774
293: 11 cm, dia. 0.5 cm; MVB; Vb 3778
294: 20 cm, dia. 0.6 cm; MVB; Vb 3779
295: 16 cm, dia. 0.5 cm; MVB; Vb 3773
296: 20 cm, dia. 0.8 cm; MVB; Vb 3770
297: 10 cm, dia. 0.6 cm; MVB; Vb 3771
298: 12 cm, dia. 0.6 cm; MVB; Vb 3793
299: 17 cm, dia. 0.6 cm; MVB; Vb 3782
300: 15 cm, dia. 0.6 cm; MVB; Vb 3794
301: 14.5 cm, dia. 0.8 cm; MVB; Vb 3785
302: 11 cm, dia. 0.7 cm; MVB; Vb 3784
303: 14 cm, dia. 0.8 cm; MVB; Vb 3788
304: 17 cm, dia 0.8 cm; MVB; Vb 3789

305: 12 cm, dia. 0.7 cm; MVB; Vb 3790
306: 13 cm, dia. 0.2 cm; MVB; Vb 3792
307: 22 cm, dia. 0.8 cm; MVB; Vb 3798
308: 29 cm, dia. 1 cm; MVB; Vb 3796
309: 19 cm, dia. 0.6 cm; MVB; Vb 3776
325: 215 x 40 cm; MAAO; MNAO 64.2.33
326: 243 x 41 cm; MAAO; MNAO 64.5.1
333 (2nd from right): 345 x 37 cm; MAAO; MNAO 64.2.54
333 (back): 355 x 57 cm; MAAO; MNAO 64.2.20
333 (left): 379 x 52 cm; MAAO; MNAO 64.2.32
333 (right): 430 x 60 cm; MAAO; MNAO D.62.5.5
337: 316 x 85 cm; MAAO; MNAO, Saint-Germain collection 53.314
338: 39.5 x 10 cm; MAAO; MNAO 68.9.5
339: 40 cm; MEG; 41720
340: 301 x 14 cm; MHP; MH 93.22.18
341: 118 x 7 cm; MAAO; MNAO 66.16.13
347: 110 x 31 cm; MVB; Vb 4460

371: 108 x 25 x 18 cm; MHP; MH 36.31.1
377: 135 x 63 x 92 cm; MP; MP 3634

Key to Museums
AMS; Australian Museum, Sydney
LMS: Linden-Museum, Staatliche Museum für Völkerkunde, Stuttgart
MAAO: Musée National des Arts d'Afrique et d'Océanie
MAB: Musée d'Aquitaine, Bordeaux
MBA: Musée des Beaux-Arts, Chartres
MEG: Musée d'Ethnographie, Genève
MHNE: Musée d'Histoire Naturelle et d'Ethnographie, La Rochelle
MHP: Musée de l'Homme, Paris
MML: Museum of Mankind, British Museum, London
MNAM: Musée National d'Art Moderne, Paris
MP: Musée Picasso, Paris
MTNC: Musée Territorial de Nouvelle-Calédonie, Nouméa
MVB: Museum für Völkerkunde Basel
UMAA: University Museum of Archaeology and Anthropology, Cambridge

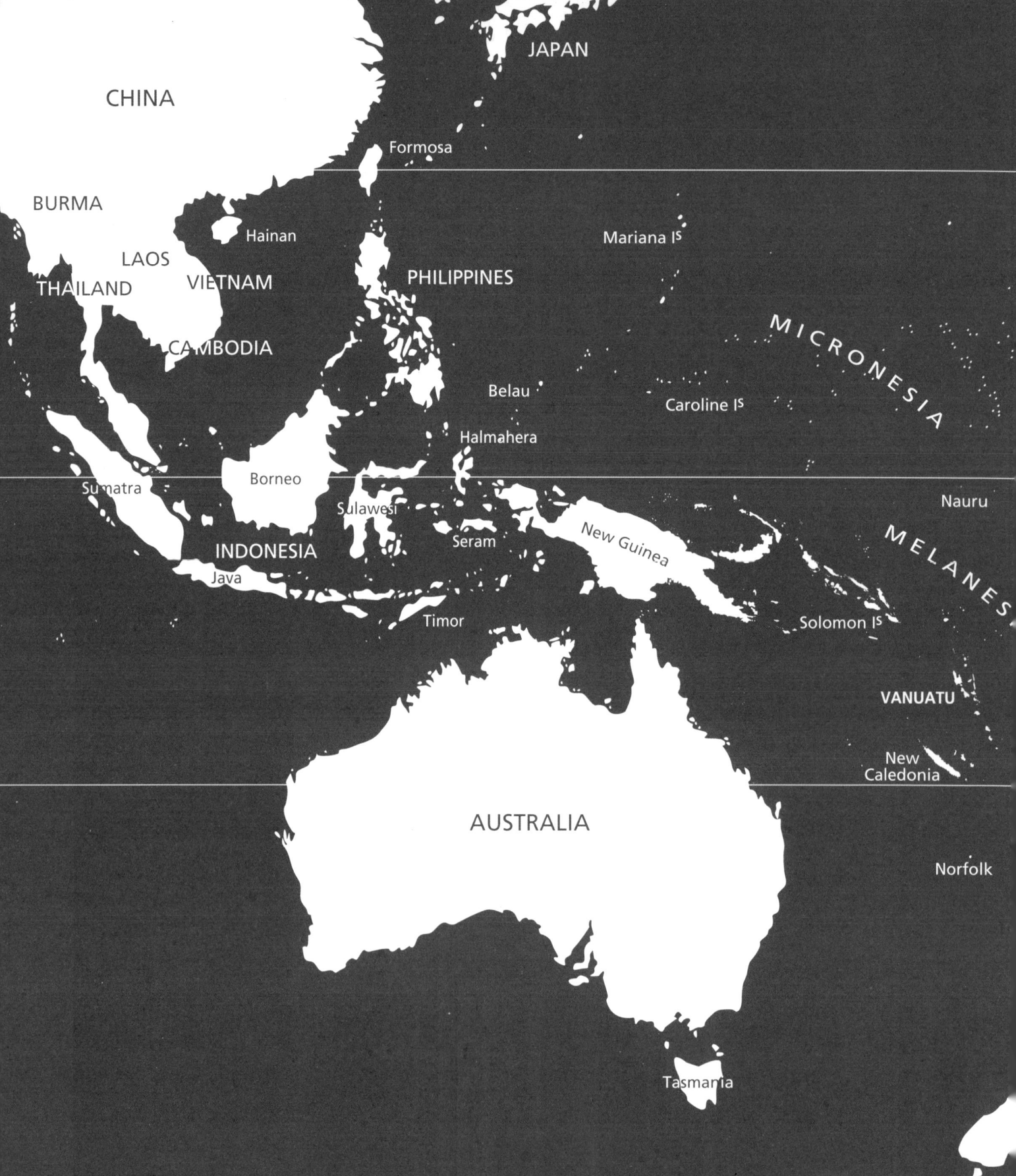